Observation Skills
for Effective Teaching

SIXTH EDITION

Observation Skills for Effective Teaching

Gary D. Borich

The University of Texas at Austin

Boston   Columbus   Indianapolis   New York   San Francisco   Upper Saddle River
Amsterdam   Cape Town   Dubai   London   Madrid   Milan   Munich   Paris   Montreal   Toronto
Delhi   Mexico City   Sao Paulo   Sydney   Hong Kong   Seoul   Singapore   Taipei   Tokyo

Editor in Chief: Paul A. Smith
Acquisitions Editor: Kelly Villella Canton
Editorial Assistant: Annalea Manalili
Director of Marketing: Quinn Perkson
Senior Marketing Manager: Darcy Betts
Marketing Assistant: Robin Holtsberry
Production Editor: Cynthia Parsons
Cover Designer: Elena Sidorova
Text Designer: Omegatype Typography, Inc.
Photo Researcher: Annie Pickert
Full-Service Project Management: Omegatype Typography, Inc.
Composition: Omegatype Typography, Inc.
Printer/Binder: Bind-Rite

Credits and acknowledgments borrowed from other sources and reproduced, with permission, in this textbook appear on appropriate page within text.

Photo Credits: Krista Greco/Merrill, pp. 21, 22; Hope Madden/Merrill, pp. 8, 9; David Mager/Pearson Learning Photo Studio, pp. 152, 153; Anthony Magnacca/Merrill, pp. 71, 72, 113, 114, 132, 133, 193, 194; Barbara Schwartz/Merrill, pp. 52, 53; Patrick White/Merrill, pp. 1, 2, 36, 37, 93, 94, 172, 173.

Library of Congress Cataloging-in-Publication Data

Borich, Gary D.
   Observation skills for effective teaching / Gary D. Borich. — 6th ed.
         p.   cm.
   Includes bibliographical references and index.
   ISBN-13: 978-0-13-703972-2 (pbk.)
   ISBN-10: 0-13-703972-7 (pbk.)
   1. Observation (Educational method)   2. Effective teaching.   I. Title.
   LB1027.28.B67   2011
   371.102—dc22

                                           2009047292

10 9 8 7 6 5 4 3 2 1   BRG   14 13 12 11 10

www.pearsonhighered.com

ISBN-10: 0-13-703972-7
ISBN-13: 978-0-13-703972-2

About the Author

Gary Borich grew up on the south side of Chicago, where he attended Mendel High School and later taught in the public school system of Niles, Illinois. He received his doctoral degree from Indiana University, where he was director of evaluation at the Institute for Child Study. Dr. Borich is a professor of educational psychology and a Cissy McDaniel Parker Endowed Fellow in the College of Education at the University of Texas at Austin and a past member of the Board of Examiners of the National Council for the Accreditation of Teacher Education. Dr. Borich's other books include *Effective Teaching Methods* (7th ed.), *Educational Assessment for the Elementary and Middle School Classroom* (2nd ed.; with M. Tombari), *Clearly Outstanding: Making Each Day Count in Your Classroom, Becoming a Teacher: An Inquiring Dialogue for the Beginning Teacher, Educational Psychology: A Contemporary Approach* (2nd ed.; with M. Tombari), *Educational Testing and Measurement* (9th ed.; with T. Kubiszyn), *The Appraisal of Teaching: Concepts and Process,* and *Teacher Behavior and Pupil Self Concept.* Dr. Borich lives in Austin, Texas, with his wife, Kathy, and children, Brandy and Damon.

Brief Contents

Contents

3 Making Classroom Visits   21

4 Seeing beyond Personal Experiences and Expectations: Learning to Observe Systematically   36

5 Considering the Learning Climate   52

10   Examining Engagement in the Learning Process   152

11   Measuring Student Success   172

12 Looking for Higher Thought Processes and Performance Outcomes   193

Preface

Knowing is using what we observe.

Some put it into practice and let it

change their lives. Others don't.

That's the difference between

a novice and an expert.

People in all walks of life want to know how they can acquire the skills and competencies to become professionals. All of us want to become experts or *professionals,* but we know that it requires more than simply a desire to be good at what we do. This book focuses on one of the principal means by which you can become a professional—by observing others and incorporating what you see and hear into your own teaching.

To become competent at teaching, you must know what to look for, and you must have a framework or structure by which what is observed can be made meaningful for becoming effective in your classroom. Other skills are needed, too. You must be psychologically ready and physically prepared to observe, have tools for categorizing and recording what you see, and have knowledge of teaching content and methods. And, most important of all, you must be able to "see" the patterns and sequences that effective teachers use which make all of the parts work as a whole.

Where do effective teachers learn to see all of the parts working as a whole? How do they bring their natural abilities, knowledge of content and teaching methods, and professional goals together into a harmonious pattern of behavior to become a professional? It isn't from texts, university classes, and practice teaching alone, and the hectic pace of classrooms makes it difficult for many teachers to reflect on their own patterns of behavior. Only through observing more experienced teachers can all of these ingredients be brought together into meaningful patterns of effective teaching to be modeled in your own classroom.

As you will see in the very first chapter, the purpose of observation is to improve yourself. Plans for self-improvement are realistic when they are based on your own unique strengths and on the school context in which they are to occur. The importance of this latter point is not always recognized: A teaching activity that is effective in one school or classroom may not be effective in another. No amount of student teaching experience or formal instruction can prepare you to teach in every classroom context. Although student teaching and classroom instruction can point you in the right direction to maximize your growth as a teacher, the realities of a specific classroom and the students within it can only be determined by *what* and *how much* you learn as a teacher. This is the unique function of classroom observation: to understand teaching within specific classrooms of learners and to develop a program of self-improvement based on that understanding. In short, the dimensions of effective teaching ultimately must be defined by the qualities and characteristics of those who must be taught. This is why classroom observation is so important: It reveals the patterns of practice by which experienced teachers refine and match the dimensions of effective teaching most appropriate to a specific population of learners.

To accomplish this goal, this book presents effective teaching practices that can be observed during three stages of your career—preteaching, student teaching, and induction-year (first-year) teaching. At each of these stages this text provides competencies for preparing you to observe, for learning how to observe, and for knowing what to observe in order to improve your own teaching. This text has also been organized efficiently to accomplish these goals.

NEW TO THIS EDITION

Some revisions from the last edition were again updated and/or revised for this edition.

- In keeping with the practical nature of this book, we have continued to use perforated pages to make the more than 50 revised and updated observation instruments and records easily accessible, increasing its value as a handbook and practical tool that can be carried into the classroom. In this edition, you will also find these observation instruments better formatted for reproducing and using in the classroom, assembled in one easy-to-access place (Appendix B) in the book.

- This edition continues to be closely aligned with the National Board for Professional Teaching Standards (NBPTS) and the Interstate New Teacher Assessment and Support Consortium (INTASC) principles and standards, so that you learn the important role that effective, research-based teaching practices play in the larger regional and national certification process. New and updated activities at the end of each chapter reinforce this important alignment with national standards as they prompt you to learn and practice observing specific effective teaching practices.

- This edition also includes expanded coverage of the important role of instructional media and technology and its importance to effective teaching behaviors. Each end-of-chapter section titled "For More Information" includes websites keyed to each of the effective teaching behaviors.

- Readers of previous editions will also find updated and integrated into each chapter the most recent findings on teaching culturally, linguistically, and academically diverse learners. In addition to updated sections on diversity within each chapter, discussions and citations have been added to emphasize the importance of differentiated instruction and what to observe in today's heterogeneous classrooms.

- Added discussion and references on the social dynamics of the classroom, including reference to the work of Robert Pianta, appear in Chapter 2.

- The Glossary—an "at a glance" summary of some of the most important professional terms and concepts you will use in your professional life—has been expanded for this edition.

These changes, along with the most recent references and presentation of new classroom research, continue to make this edition an up-to-date, user-friendly, and practical resource for the beginning teacher.

ORGANIZATION OF THIS TEXT

Chapter 1 focuses on the close and necessary relationship between attributes for becoming a professional and for becoming an effective teacher. It explores the general characteristics that make a teacher a professional and the specific competencies that you will need to earn that title.

Chapters 2 and 3 focus on the psychological preparation and attitudes important to observing the complex patterns of events that occur in classrooms. These chapters explain why observation is important (Chapter 2) and how to transform the casual process of *looking* into the systematic process of *observing,* from which your teaching can grow (Chapter 3).

Chapter 4 is devoted to the technical competence that must precede systematic observation, describing the tools that observers use to record life in classrooms and to organize their observations in useful ways. You will learn how to develop and use simple tools of observation and how to modify them to fit a particular school context and your own observation goals.

Chapters 5 through 12 present the framework or lenses through which life in classrooms can be organized and made meaningful. Observation skills are presented according to eight lenses found by researchers to be related to desirable cognitive, social, and emotional outcomes in learners. These eight interrelated ways of understanding effective teaching, each containing patterns for observation, are learning climate, classroom management, lesson clarity, instructional variety, teacher's task orientation, student engagement in the learning process, student success, and higher thought processes and performance outcomes. Each chapter in this section combines a study of observation skills with the patterns of effective teaching practice identified in the research literature. The methodological concepts and dialogues they contain are designed to help the beginning teacher see and practice research-based patterns of effective teaching. This is the unique focus of *Observation Skills for Effective Teaching,* Sixth Edition.

USES OF THIS TEXT

This book can be used in several ways. First, it can serve as a companion volume to *Effective Teaching Methods: Research-Based Practice,* Seventh Edition (Borich, 2010), in which some of these same pedagogical concepts are presented in a methods text format. In *Observation Skills for Effective Teaching,* Sixth Edition, students learn how to observe and practice many of the behaviors and patterns of practice presented in *Effective Teaching Methods.*

Second, this text can be used for a preteaching or observation course taken prior to, or in conjunction with, a methods course. Thus, it can serve as an advance organizer for more specific content and pedagogically oriented courses that follow.

Third, this text may be used as a resource during student teaching and your first years of teaching to provide a direction and foundation for a program of self-improvement, training, and mentoring. It provides many practical tools for use by a mentor and mentee for teacher self-development and renewal through the early years of teaching. In each of these applications, the major goal of this text is to sensitize the beginning teacher, through observation, to research-based patterns of effective teaching and to begin the process of incorporating these patterns of effective teaching into your own classroom teaching.

SPECIAL FEATURES

- Beginning chapters (on why observe, preparing to observe, and how to observe) that familiarize the beginning teacher with the psychological, technical, and cognitive demands of observing in classrooms.
- Integration of the most recent, up-to-date research-based practices for establishing a positive and cohesive learning climate, focusing on classroom management, looking for lesson clarity, verifying instructional variety, observing teacher task orientation, examining student engagement in the learning process, measuring student success, and looking for higher thought processes and performance outcomes, with discussions of why these lenses for observation are important and how they can be integrated into your own teaching to form effective patterns of teaching practice.
- Classroom examples of more effective and less effective teaching practices and what they look like through the eyes of an observer. Through the use of realistic classroom dialogues in a variety of subject-matter areas, grades, and levels of schooling and integrative discussions that follow and reflect on these dialogues, you will see effective teaching practices alongside less effective practices. These Time to Reflect sections interpret and place in perspective the most relevant features of each practice dialogue from the observer's point of view.
- More than 50 full-page, easy-to-copy pull-out instruments, scales, and recording formats for observing and implementing major patterns of effective teaching.
- Discussions within each chapter that sensitize the reader to the cultural, linguistic, and academic diversity that exists in almost every classroom, and how it is important to your observation of effective teaching.
- Activities at the end of each chapter that engage the beginning teacher in the observation process and the development of research-based patterns of effective teaching aligned with national professional standards.

ACKNOWLEDGMENTS

Many individuals have contributed to the preparation of this book, not the least of whom are the many professionals whose studies of classroom life have contributed to the patterns of effective teaching described here. The work of these professionals representing a variety of methodological perspectives has made possible the synthesis of research-based effective teaching practices provided here. Although I accept responsibility for my translations of this research into practice, the credit for any strengths the reader may see in this approach must be shared with the many who have contributed to the research on which this book is based.

I would also like to thank those teachers who have shared their insights about the teaching process with me over the years. Among these have been teachers in the Austin, Texas, Independent School District, especially Travis Heights Elementary and William B. Travis High School. Their teachers have provided many opportunities for observing the effective teaching methods described in this text and developing and field testing the instruments provided here for observing in classrooms.

I would also like to thank the National Council for the Accreditation of Teacher Education for providing me the opportunity, as a member of the Board of Examiners, to visit and observe many teacher training programs across the country.

For their helpful reviews of the manuscript, I extend my gratitude to Elizabeth Beavers, The University of Southern Mississippi; and Heather Brace, Sonoma State University.

Gary D. Borich
Austin, Texas

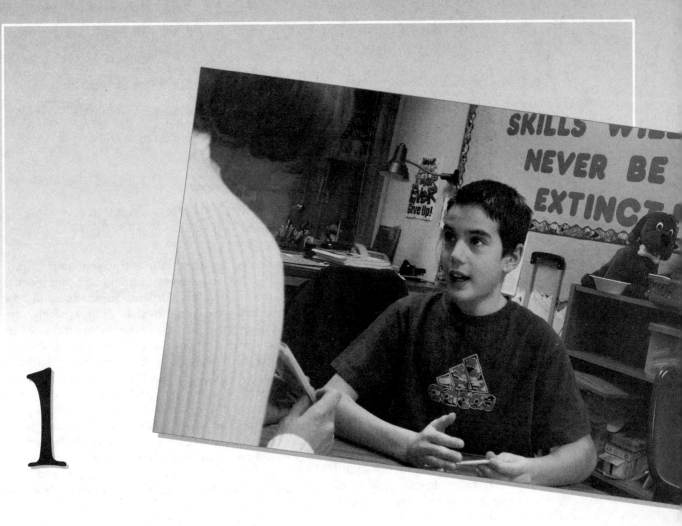

1

Why Observe?

Auguries of Innocence

To see a world in a grain of sand

And a heaven in a wildflower:

Hold infinity in the palm of your hand,

And eternity in an hour.

William Blake

William Blake, "Auguries of Innocence," 1863.

What we see is often determined by what we want to see—or are prepared to see. Have you ever noticed that when you look closely at something, you discover details never seen before? When your observation is focused, even the slightest variations take shape. With this chapter we begin our journey of learning to observe—to notice grains of sand in the span of a single lesson, and to see eternity in an hour.

Playing in the park, 3-year-old Jake looks up to see his mother approaching. He runs down the sidewalk to greet her. In his haste, he trips on an uneven stone and lands, unceremoniously, at his mother's feet.

For a moment, Jake looks stunned—about to cry. His mother wonders if he is hurt as he glances up at her face with a questioning look.

Laughing, Jake's mother scoops him into her arms. "Hi, honey!" she chuckles. "What fun to have you so excited to see me!"

The imminent clouds on Jake's face clear, and the toddler smiles.

How often have you observed a similar event—noting that split second when a child seems to decide how to respond to a given situation? Like Jake, each of us experiences many interactions with the world every day. As we try to make sense of these events, we create a personal framework or set of expectations about the nature of the world and our appropriate responses to events within it. This set of expectations influences what we see in a particular setting, as well as what we choose to ignore.

Many psychologists believe that professionals create frames for understanding within their chosen fields, just as individuals construct frames for interpreting the events of daily life. Experts know what to look for and rapidly learn from what they see, thereby rising to the top of their profession long before others who do not have a structure for sorting out the least relevant from the most relevant details. Sternberg (2007) believes that intelligent behavior may be marked more by the structure or frame one brings to a problem or task than by what one knows about the problem or task beforehand. Thus, developing a **professional frame*** from which to evaluate and act objectively on events is a critical skill for becoming an expert.

* Summary and extended definitions of key concepts in bold can be found in the Glossary at the end of the text.

STANDARDS FOR THE TEACHING PROFESSION

From observing the actions and interactions of professionals, less experienced individuals gain a sense of what is valued in a particular discipline and how professionals working in that field typically respond to events. But, although observation seems as simple and commonplace as dressing, eating, or driving a car, it is important to remember that, like Jake, each of us interprets the world and responds to it according to our personal frame (Fosnot, 2005; Walqui, 2000a). Without some outside direction, it is possible that our classroom observations may serve only to validate much of what we already "expect" to see—leading us to overemphasize some things and overlook others. As a result, observations need to be focused if they are to be helpful in our professional life.

National and State Standards

The focused observation techniques described in this book come from years of research on effective teaching and from current national and state standards for the teaching profession representing how students and teachers best learn.

For decades, U.S. teaching reflected a direct instruction model, by which teachers were expected to present or "transmit" knowledge to students—who were expected to receive, store, and return information on request (Szymanski & Haas, 2007; Williams, 2003). Many researchers and educators have challenged this view, suggesting that learners do not simply "receive" knowledge; rather, they actively construct knowledge through interacting with the social, cultural, and linguistic context in which an experience occurs (Chaille, 2007; Gallego & Cole, 2001). Effective teachers function as able facilitators, coaches, and guides for students' knowledge-building processes.

Reflecting this more interactive view of teaching, the **National Board for Professional Teaching**

Standards (NBPTS) was formed in 1987 with three major goals:

1. To establish high and rigorous standards for what accomplished teachers should know and be able to do
2. To develop and operate a national, voluntary system to assess and certify teachers who meet these standards
3. To advance related education reforms for the purpose of improving student learning in U.S. schools

Governed by a board of 63 directors, the majority of whom are classroom teachers, the NBPTS (2001) has listed five propositions essential to effective teaching:

1. Teachers are committed to students and their learning.
2. Teachers know the subjects they teach and how to teach those subjects to students.
3. Teachers are responsible for managing and mentoring student learning.
4. Teachers think systematically about their practice and learn from experience.
5. Teachers are members of learning communities.

Standards for Beginning Teachers

During the same year (1987), the **Interstate New Teacher Assessment and Support Consortium (INTASC)** was formed to create "board-compatible" standards that could be reviewed by professional organizations and state agencies as a basis for licensing beginning teachers. The INTASC standards (Miller, 1992) are written as 10 principles, which are then further explained in terms of teacher knowledge, dispositions, and performance. In other words, they describe what a beginning teacher should know and be able to do. The 10 INTASC principles, listed below, can be accessed along with example lesson plans and a description of the mission and accomplishments of the INTASC consortium at http://filebox.vt.edu/users/cmarshal/intasc_standards.htm and www.ccsso.org/projects/Interstate_New_Teacher_Assessment_and_Support_Consortium/#resource.

- *Principle 1*. The teacher understands the central concepts, tools of inquiry, and structures of the discipline(s) he or she teaches and can create learning experiences that make these aspects of subject matter meaningful for students.
- *Principle 2*. The teacher understands how children learn and develop, and can provide learning opportunities that support their intellectual, social, and personal development.

- *Principle 3*. The teacher understands how students differ in their approaches to learning and creates instructional opportunities that are adapted to diverse learners.
- *Principle 4*. The teacher understands and uses a variety of instructional strategies to encourage students' development of critical thinking, problem solving, and performance skills.
- *Principle 5*. The teacher uses an understanding of individual and group motivation and behavior to create a learning environment that encourages positive social interaction, active engagement in learning, and self-motivation.
- *Principle 6*. The teacher uses knowledge of effective verbal, nonverbal, and media communication techniques to foster active inquiry, collaboration, and supportive interaction in the classroom.
- *Principle 7*. The teacher plans instruction based on knowledge of subject matter, students, the community, and curriculum goals.
- *Principle 8*. The teacher understands and uses formal and informal assessment strategies to evaluate and ensure the continuous intellectual, social, and physical development of the learner.
- *Principle 9*. The teacher is a reflective practitioner who continually evaluates the effects of his or her choices and actions on others (students, parents, and other professionals in the learning community) and who actively seeks out opportunities to grow professionally.
- *Principle 10*. The teacher fosters relationships with school colleagues, parents, and agencies in the larger community to support students' learning and well-being.

Frames of Understanding

Because you are sure to work with the INTASC standards at some time during your professional development program (and with the NBPTS standards later in your career), this text will discuss research-based strategies, methods, and practices used by effective teachers that can help you achieve these standards. The information included in this text will help you expand your professional knowledge structure to include insights about teaching within eight interrelated conceptual frameworks that follow the INTASC and NBPTS standards. In this text you will learn about and acquire the professional frames necessary for observing

1. The learning climate (NBPTS 3; INTASC 3, 5)
2. Classroom management (NBPTS 3; INTASC 2, 4, 6)
3. Lesson clarity (NBPTS 2, 3; INTASC 1, 2, 3, 7)

4. Instructional variety (NBPTS 2, 3, 4; INTASC 1, 2, 3, 4)
5. Teacher's task orientation and content presentation (NBPTS 1, 2, 4; INTASC 7, 9)
6. Students' engagement in the learning process (NBPTS 1, 2, 3; INTASC 1, 2, 3, 4, 5, 6, 7, 9, 10)
7. Student success (NBPTS 1, 3, 4, 5; INTASC 8, 9, 10)
8. Students' higher thought processes and performance outcomes (NBPTS 2, 3, 4; INTASC 1, 4, 5, 6, 7, 8)

This book devotes a chapter to each of these dimensions of effective teaching. In Appendix B you will find teaching methods and observation instruments to help you better understand, observe, and eventually implement these key aspects of effective teaching.

GOALS OF REFLECTIVE TEACHING

Much of this text focuses on ways in which you can observe other teachers to learn about the teaching profession. This book also addresses ways to apply these observation techniques and insights to your own teaching. Therefore, while you are observing others to learn about their approaches to teaching, you will also be learning to observe yourself—and to be observed by others. These observations will provide important insights about your growth and development as a teacher.

The ability to consciously consider your personal growth is called **reflective teaching.** There are many goals you will want to work toward in order to reflect on your own behavior. But some of the most important for focused observations are to achieve empathy, establish cooperative relationships, become realistic, establish direction, attain confidence, express enthusiasm, become flexible, and become self-reliant. As you observe professionals working to achieve each of these goals, you will want to reflect on your own development—and then set some goals for yourself. Because a cycle of observation, reflection, and goal setting is so important to becoming a productive and successful professional, let's consider these goals for focused observation in more detail.

Goal I: To Achieve Empathy

Effective teachers exhibit *empathy*—a willingness to see events from different and nonjudgmental points of view and to appreciate others' interpretations or reasons for acting the way they do. An empathic approach can help you understand student behavior from the student's point of view, which often provides insights for effective ways of dealing with problems or challenges. Your ability to empathize during classroom observations will serve you well both as an observer and as a teacher. For example, when you observe a teacher implementing an unusual classroom rule, you may be tempted to pass judgment on the teacher's effectiveness or on the rule's appropriateness—from your point of view. Although your own experiences are an important source of information in evaluating what you observe, you will also benefit from trying to understand events from the teacher's vantage point. You may ask yourself, "Is what I am seeing working within the context of this classroom? Why or why not?" As you consider these questions, you may discover that a seemingly inappropriate strategy in one context may be appropriate in another. And as a result, your observations will extend beyond your personal and textbook knowledge of teaching to include an awareness of the variety of social and emotional contexts that can influence a teacher's decisions. Enhancing your ability to empathize will help you approach your own teaching with more flexibility—and with the instructional alternatives you need to be an effective teacher.

Goal 2: To Establish Cooperative Relationships

Early on, effective teachers identify people who can help them in their teaching. They understand that, in the hectic and stressful environment of the classroom, people need people to offer ideas, support, and collegiality. As you become involved in student teaching and then the beginning years of teaching, you will find a need to develop cooperative relationships with your colleagues. Experienced teachers have a wealth of information about the students, curriculum, textbooks, and media with which you will be working. As you observe in different classrooms, you can and should take the opportunity to discover how professionals create and maintain cooperative relationships and how you can become an active participant in these relationships. These experienced teachers can answer many questions you will have now—and later.

In addition to answering questions about lesson formats, grouping of students, and instructional methods, your colleagues can be an important source of emotional support. During student teaching and your beginning years of teaching, you will often want to express concerns and problems in the privacy of a nonevaluative context. If you have established a network of professional colleagues, you will have a safe place to share unanticipated problems and to brainstorm solutions. Teaching can be a lonely profession at times—facing a full day of classes filled with surprises and challenges can occasionally dishearten even the most enthusiastic or experienced teacher. Recognizing the need to turn to others for emotional support and creating a network for collegial sharing can help you to meet unanticipated challenges and to renew your dedication and vigor.

Goal 3: To Become Realistic

Most beginning teachers understandably have an idealistic view of schools and teaching. Although idealism motivates us to renew and extend our efforts, it also creates pitfalls when we are unreasonable in our expectations of students or ourselves. For example, beginning teachers who believe that schools *should be* a certain way may spend a great deal of time and effort trying to change a particular setting—failing to see and accept the strengths of the context they are working with. From your classroom observations, you will learn that schools and classrooms vary widely and that each context offers both advantages and challenges. As you observe and reflect on different classrooms, you will become more realistic in evaluating both what is desirable and what is possible.

In addition to seeing life in different classrooms, it is important to place your own successes and failures in learning to teach in proper perspective. In the classroom, just as in life, it can be tempting to attribute successes to factors outside ourselves (e.g., the students are bright, the lesson topic was interesting) and to attribute failures to personal failings (e.g., the students would have passed the test if I had covered more content, the class wouldn't have misbehaved if I had been more prepared). It's important to realize that events involving misbehaving students, running out of time for a lesson, or other disappointments might not always result from our personal inadequacies or lack of effort. There are times when some events are beyond the control of *any* teacher. As you observe, you will become increasingly aware of just how frequently these types of events occur in classrooms, regardless of almost any effort on the part of the teacher to prevent or alter their occurrence. Indeed, observation reveals the important role of serendipity in classrooms—that many unplanned outcomes happen in spite of, not because of, the efforts of teachers.

Serendipity is sometimes difficult for a beginning teacher to accept. We tend to derive a feeling of success or failure from those events for which we feel we *should* be responsible. Yet a class of very bright, easy-to-manage learners, preselected for advanced placement, might produce outcomes astonishingly different from those of another class learning the same subject. Knowing which outcomes are under your control and, as a consequence, accurately judging the influence of your own actions is one of the most important goals a teacher can attain. An ineffective teacher might work countless hours to change student behavior that cannot be changed in the course of a lesson or a unit—or a semester. This teacher might never see the desired results and might feel an unrealistic sense of failure. Effective teachers, on the other hand, work to improve behavior that can be attributed to the strategies, materials, and methods they select. They learn where to look for improvement daily and can thus attribute to themselves a realistic sense of success. By observing which behaviors are changeable in classrooms, you can learn to more accurately attribute success and failure to particular actions of the teachers you observe and, later, to yourself.

Goal 4: To Establish Direction

Another purpose of classroom observation is to establish the professional goals toward which you will want to work during your student teaching and first years of teaching. By observing others, you will identify characteristics and practices you will want to emulate in your own teaching. Recording these characteristics and practices during observation can form the basis of short- and long-term goals of self-improvement. One of the advantages of focused observation is the opportunity to identify particular patterns and sequences of teacher behavior and to evaluate their effectiveness in a variety of settings. Over time, you should be able to identify teaching strategies specific to particular purposes and contexts that you value and to integrate them into your own teaching.

Goal 5: To Attain Confidence

Most of us in the course of learning to become teachers make judgments about what we consider effective teaching. In the course of teaching, we then make decisions that follow from these judgments. Many of these decisions about what and how to teach represent gut feelings, the exact source of which might not be known to us. Some writers have referred to this way of knowing as **tacit knowledge** (Gill, 2000; Polanyi, 1958). Tacit knowledge represents what we know by experience, but rarely, if ever, articulate. Just like the toddler Jake, each of us compiles vast amounts of tacit knowledge through everyday experiences (Krogh, Ichijo, & Nonaka, 2000). These thoughts and feelings often guide our actions, sometimes unconsciously, as effectively as the knowledge we gain from formal instruction. Tacitly acquired knowledge often helps us distinguish right from wrong, appropriate from inappropriate, and effective from ineffective.

Even though tacit knowledge can guide us in many ways throughout our lives, many beginning teachers reject this acquired knowledge in favor of less familiar and less appropriate responses. Some are afraid to trust their instincts, which can seem too subjective to be trusted. Unfortunately, many problems encountered by beginning teachers stem, in part, from a lack of confidence in their ability to act spontaneously in a given situation. This can prove unfortunate because sometimes spontaneous judgments and instincts may serve the decision-making process better than a less relevant mechanical or academic response. It is important for beginning teachers to learn to trust their initial responses to a classroom problem or decision—especially when those decisions are also informed by academic knowledge. This trust can be developed by considering *what we feel* as we observe particular classroom events and then by reflecting on whether our intuitions are borne out. Effective teachers learn to contrast school-based knowledge with their personal intuitions and to compare the results. Through observation, beginning teachers learn to test their judgments and to trust their instincts.

Goal 6: To Express Enthusiasm

Effective teachers demonstrate an enthusiasm for the subject matter they teach and for the teaching profession. The ability to express enthusiasm stems from a belief that what we do matters. Having an image of a future self who is growing provides us with the motivation to work hard and attain the goals we select.

Interestingly, the ability to express enthusiasm can also be accompanied by fear. Even though we desire to learn and to grow, we sometimes fear that releasing our imaginative potential and trying to realize our goals may leave us open to failure. Indeed, some people *want* to improve but are afraid to leave the safe confines of the familiar (Borich, 1993). As a result, we might want to be enthusiastic about our teaching, but fear the ramifications of letting ourselves go to seek that goal.

We enhance our enthusiasm and learn to calm our fears by seeing others attain goals, perform activities, and produce results that we ourselves would like to accomplish. As you observe successful teachers, you will find yourself saying, "I want to be like that." From this, you will set goals such as, "I want to *try* that." And, as you try various techniques, you will discover that you *can* accomplish what you desire, and your enthusiasm grows. Focused observation of successful and enthusiastic teachers can help you dare to express the enthusiasm within you.

Goal 7: To Become Flexible

As we have seen, a part of setting and achieving any goal is being willing to take risks. Effective teachers most often achieve their goals in the context of trial and error. This means that to develop as a professional, you must try new things and risk occasional failure. We seldom succeed in attaining a goal, successfully performing an activity, or achieving the desired results the first time we try something. The key to our improvement is to persevere long enough for success to occur. This is why enthusiasm and the energy it releases are so important for self-improvement. Enthusiasm provides us with the stamina to practice desired behaviors in the face of less-than-perfect results until success arrives. Because some struggle is inevitable in becoming an effective teacher, it is important to develop a flexible attitude. For example, you might try a strategy or technique exactly as you observed it in a particular classroom and not achieve the same result. This is the time to consider aspects of your behavior that could be changed or altered in some way. Your observation of teachers in different classroom settings will provide the opportunity to see procedures and techniques in one classroom that have been revised or modified to work in another classroom, from which you will gain the skill to choose flexibly and modify what you see.

Goal 8: To Become Self-Reliant

Perhaps the most important goal of focused classroom observation is becoming self-reliant. As you observe across many educational contexts, you will be building a professional frame from which to interpret events and make decisions. The greater the detail and scope of your observations, the greater your sense of personal confidence, enthusiasm, and flexibility will be in achieving your goals. Focused observation in classrooms will reveal that teaching is a complex profession for which no amount of formal training can provide all the preparation needed. It will also underscore the fact that effective teachers exist because of the challenges of teaching and that, with careful reflection and effort, you can be one of them.

A BEGINNING THOUGHT

This book will address many of the facets of becoming a skilled observer. But mastering the contents of this text is no guarantee that classroom observation alone will improve your teaching. A carpenter, plumber, physician, or lawyer might know the mechanics of a given trade and still not be expert at providing the service required. Something more is needed to achieve expertise—something beyond factual, observational, or academic learning. That *something* is a desire and openness for growth. No one becomes effective or achieves the status of a professional without the desire to continually adapt to the ongoing stream of challenges and problems in his or her particular work. Schools are no different from executive boardrooms, hospital emergency rooms, or 10th-inning baseball games: They all require split-second decisions—new and spontaneous reactions that sometimes defy even the best-laid plans. As you seek to become a professional, you will need a willingness to open yourself to new ways of responding to your world—beyond the set of expectations you have developed over the years. Learning to teach is a process of expanding one's personal frame to include new insights and accepting the fact that frame building is a lifelong process. Effective executives, surgeons, and athletes, as well as teachers, bring to their work the personal attributes of empathy, cooperativeness, realism, goal orientation, confidence, enthusiasm, flexibility, and self-reliance that make success happen. Each of these attributes will help you grow and develop through the focused observations described in the chapters ahead.

For More Information

During the past decade, there have been a number of national and state standards efforts, such as those by the National Council of Teachers of Mathematics (NCTM), the International Reading Association (IRA), and others, that have sought to define knowledge and performance for students or teachers in particular subject areas. Mid-continent Research for Education and Learning (McREL) has created a large database that synthesizes many of these efforts. You may enjoy visiting their website at www.mcrel.org to learn more about these ideas.

Key Terms

Interstate New Teacher Assessment and Support Consortium (INTASC), 3
National Board for Professional Teaching Standards (NBPTS), 2

professional frame, 2
reflective teaching, 4
tacit knowledge, 5

Activities

1. Using an example from your own observation experience, explain what is meant by a "professional frame." What is an advantage of observing with a "frame"?
2. The National Board for Professional Teaching Standards (NBPTS) and the Interstate New Teacher Assessment and Support Consortium (INTASC) have been created with different, albeit related, missions. Describe their missions with example teacher behaviors and identify how each is likely to affect your professional life.
3. While you are observing in a classroom, identify a student or teacher behavior that provides an example of each of the eight professional frames of observation (learning climate, classroom management, lesson clarity, instructional variety, teacher's task orientation, student engagement in the learning process, student success, and higher thought processes and performance outcomes).
4. Choose three of the eight personal goals for observation presented in this chapter and explain why you believe these goals are important for your development as a teacher.

2

Lenses for Observing

Could a greater miracle take place than for us
to look through each other's eyes for an instant?

Henry David Thoreau

Henry David Thoreau, *Walden,* 1854.

What we see is often determined by our own view of life, a view that is often personal, sometimes unstructured, and occasionally biased. In this chapter we offer a more objective framework for observing, representing different professional frames—or lenses—for viewing life in classrooms. It is a framework developed from classroom research that is shared by many who teach and observe in classrooms. In this chapter you will begin to see classrooms through the eyes of others—a view less personal than your own.

As you prepare to observe in classrooms, it is important to consider what sort of "lens" you will observe through. As noted in Chapter 1, all of us develop our own views of the world or ways of looking at life based on the experiences we have, the emotions we feel, and the ways we choose to interpret them. What are the characteristics of your world view? How might they affect the way you "see" particular teachers or classrooms? Let's try a little experiment to find out. Read the following sentence (from a study by Sanford & Garrod, 1981, p. 114), and create a mental picture from the words.

John was on his way to school.

What picture formed in your mind as you read the sentence? How old is John? What does he look like? What time of day is it? What is the weather like? Remember what you pictured and read on.

He was terribly worried about the math lesson.

Now what is the picture you see? Has it changed? Does being worried about a math lesson "fit" the picture you have already developed in your mind about what John is like? Keep reading.

He thought he might not be able to control the class again today.

Has anything in your mental picture changed? What? Why? Now keep reading.

It was not a normal part of a janitor's duties.

What do you see now in your mental picture? How old is John? What does he look like? Were you surprised at the information in the last sentence? Why?

Just as you formed mental images and expectations while reading about John, you have probably formed a number of mental images and expectations about schools and classrooms. To explore a few of these images, take a minute and make a list with the headings shown in Figure 2.1.

Now, take a minute to create a second list with the headings in Figure 2.2.

What do you notice about the two lists you have created? Can you think of any specific experiences that might have influenced each of your lists?

WHAT REAL CLASSROOMS ARE LIKE

As you make formal and informal observations on your way to becoming a teacher, it is important to realize that you are about to enter a complex and

---

FIGURE 2.1 Positive Images of Schools and Classrooms

An Effective Classroom (how it looks, smells, feels, etc.)	**An Effective Teacher** (classroom management, instructional methods, presentation style, etc.)	**An Effective Lesson** (subject, duration, type of activities, etc.)

FIGURE 2.2   Negative Images of Schools and Classrooms

An Ineffective Classroom (how it looks, smells, feels, etc.)	An Ineffective Teacher (classroom management, instructional methods, presentation style, etc.)	An Ineffective Lesson (subject, duration, type of activities, etc.)

demanding profession—a profession that requires not only intelligence, physical stamina, and motivation, but also an acute sense of sight and sound. Your ability to perceive what is happening in a classroom will be critical to your success as a teacher. Because the teaching profession is complex, it is important for you to consider how your preconceived ideas about teaching and students may influence what you see and hear—and how you interpret that information. No doubt you have already formed, from your years as a student, a set of beliefs about good and poor teaching, teachers, students, and lessons. Although these opinions and beliefs comprise an important part of your view of education, they can also act as "blinders" and even limit your teaching goals for particular students or settings. In order to look beyond personal experience to obtain a more complete view of classrooms, let's consider four characteristics of classrooms that will affect what you see: rapid pace, immediacy, interruptions, and social dynamics.

Rapid Pace of Classrooms

One of the first things you will notice from observing in classrooms is that events move rapidly. In fact, some authors (Clark & Peterson, 1986; Jackson, 1968) have estimated that there are up to 1,000 teacher–student interchanges in most classrooms in a single day. These interchanges include asking questions, soliciting information, clarifying answers, probing for details, reciting facts, and responding to student requests. In other words, events do not move slowly in classrooms; they are constantly changing at a rapid rate from teacher question to student response, and from student question back to teacher response—creating a momentum of classroom activity that puts the teacher on the front lines practically every minute of the day. The teacher's ability to move the class along at a brisk pace

and keep transitions between major instructional events short and orderly, while establishing milestones toward which all students work, contributes momentum and a sense of accomplishment to the classroom.

Being able to see how the rapidly changing events in a classroom can be used to establish momentum is an important observation skill. But even more important will be your ability to understand why a teacher responds in a particular manner to a particular event. For example, you might at first judge a teacher's response to a given student as unnecessarily abrupt but then realize that, to maintain the momentum of the classroom, the teacher might have considered it more important to move the group forward and come back to the student at a later time. Your sense of how rapidly events move in classrooms will be an important observation skill.

Immediacy of Classrooms

Closely related to the rapid pace of life in classrooms is the immediacy of the interactions that occur within them, demanding quick responses to rapidly occurring events. For example, teachers often do not have time to think about how they will respond to a student question, but must rather have an answer—some answer—ready for almost any question or situation that may occur. A lengthy delay while pondering what to say might create an awkward void in the flow of classroom events that can, and often does, result in a loss of momentum and problems in classroom management (Emmer & Evertson, 2009). But even more important, the momentum of the classroom must be maintained with responses and interactions that satisfy student needs and instructional goals. Few reactions or teacher responses can be put off until tomorrow, until the end of the period, or even for a minute. Most queries, questions, and solicitations need immediate responses if they are to be effective in satisfying student needs. This makes practically every exchange a test of the teacher's responsiveness. It also tests the teacher's skill at keeping the flow going in ways that respond to, rather than put off, student needs for information, clarification, or further discussion.

Interruptions in Classrooms

A third characteristic of classroom life that you will notice is the number of times the natural flow of the classroom is interrupted. Think back to some of your experiences as a student. How often were classroom routines broken by an unexpected announcement from the office or someone at the door? A source of frustration for most teachers, such events can so alter the momentum within a classroom that both student achievement and classroom discipline are negatively affected. Perhaps in no other profession are individuals interrupted so frequently in the course of delivering or providing a message than in teaching. Even unsolicited salespeople generally are allowed to complete their message—and who ever heard of a surgeon being disturbed during an operation by a messenger at the door? Messengers, public address bulletins, students straggling in late for class, unexpected student needs, getting parent signatures, and making announcements are only some of the many disruptions that invade the instructional routine of daily classroom life. As even your earliest classroom observations will reveal, teachers do a lot more than teach and sometimes are interrupted more than they teach.

Researchers have noted that the amount of uninterrupted time a student spends actively engaged in the learning process (e.g., contributing to a discussion, answering a question, or completing an assignment in a workbook) is an important condition for learning. This time is even more valuable when it is spent on learning tasks that afford students the opportunity to achieve moderate to high levels of success. However, interruptions can make it difficult for students to become actively engaged in a learning task. Results of research studies have shown that, even though 50 minutes might have been assigned to a subject, students may be actively engaged in learning only about half that time because of clerical interruptions and distractions (Good & Brophy, 2007; Slavin, 1991). An even smaller portion of that time may be devoted to tasks in which your students are achieving at a moderate to high level of success. Being able to see the many types of interruptions that occur in classrooms and how effective and ineffective teachers manage these interruptions is another important skill for observation and for teaching.

Social Dynamics of Classrooms

Social dynamics is a fourth classroom characteristic that effective teachers must consciously consider. Let's not forget—teaching is a group process. Even in one-on-one encounters, students are aware of other members of the group and thus rarely perceive themselves as individuals in the classroom. As a result, teachers confront many important instructional and management decisions related to group dynamics (Johnson & Johnson, 2005; Pianta, 1999, 2005; Schmuck & Schmuck, 2001). One of the more interesting of these is a phenomenon Larson and Irvine call **reciprocal distancing** (1999, p. 394), in which teachers and students (both consciously and unconsciously) use language to include or exclude various individuals from the group. For example, in an exchange between a white teacher and her African American students about Martin Luther King, Jr., students used the pronoun *we* to clearly position themselves as members of a group that excluded the teacher.

[An African American boy takes a picture of Martin Luther King, Jr., out of his desk to color.]

Teacher: Let's not look at that now! That's for after lunch.
Student: I like him. I just want to look at him.
Teacher: Well, that's nice. Put him away. We'll do Martin Luther King after lunch.

[An African American boy across the room calls out, "We call him Dr. King."]

Teacher: He's not a real doctor like you go to for a cold or sore throat … (Larson & Irvine, 1999, p. 395)

To capitalize on the positive aspects of group membership and to encourage a sense of inclusion rather than distancing, many teachers implement discussion sessions, student teams, small groups, and the sharing of instructional materials to create opportunities for positive social interaction among their students. These various forms of cooperative learning provide alternatives to the traditional lecture format that can heighten motivation and the excitement of learning (Burbules & Bruce, 2001; Johnson & Johnson, 2005; Jolliffe, 2007). But learning in groups can also create opportunities for social distraction—which may dampen the learning process. Friends and enemies are often found in the same class, and excitement and expectations that often start outside class are easily carried into the classroom. There is, in other words, ample opportunity for groups in school to behave as groups do outside of school, with all the same characteristics—jealousies, competition, playfulness, laughter, and argument. Although common outside the classroom, these characteristics can create social distraction and off-task behavior within the classroom.

Few professions require their members to work in such a confined space with so many individuals for so long a time during the day as does teaching. Add to this scene the fact that some individuals do not want to be there, and you have the perfect social setting for learners to become distracted by one another. The teacher's ability to plan and carry out activities that promote cooperative interaction and discourage social distraction can make the difference between an effective and an ineffective classroom. Observing the social dynamics of classrooms will help you discover what types of activities minimize social distraction and maximize cooperative interaction among students. It will also help you understand how and why teachers can sometimes be unaware of how their own behavior contributes to or detracts from establishing a cooperative and cohesive learning environment that includes rather than distances learners (Pianta, 2005).

BECOMING AWARE OF CLASSROOM BEHAVIOR: LENSES FOR SELF-IMPROVEMENT

Given the rapid pace and immediacy of classrooms, with their complex social dynamics and frequent interruptions, it is easy to see why teachers are busy people. Few other occupations can boast of having a thousand or more interactions with clients or customers in a single day, yet teachers customarily do this not just for one day, but for practically every day of the school year. Add to this the fact that the teacher's job is to facilitate the learning of subject matter content and to determine that what is taught is learned, and we have a particularly demanding job. The effect of this ambitious undertaking is that most of a teacher's attention is focused on the subject matter and the students rather than on self-reflection. Within the busy schedule of a school day, teachers do not have many opportunities to reflect on the relative merits of the strategies and methods they use. To pause for contemplation during instruction could disrupt the pace of classroom events and almost surely would result in a loss of momentum; to reflect on events after class or at the end of the school day would require the ability to accurately remember events that might have occurred hours earlier. As a result, teachers frequently can be observed performing unintentional behaviors of which they are unaware, such as dominating discussions and allowing too little response time for students to think

through an answer (Rowe, 1986, 1987), staying with or encouraging answers from high-ability students more than low-ability students (Good & Brophy, 2007; Rist, 1970), calling on members of one gender more than the other (Gage & Berliner, 1998; Good & Brophy, 2007), giving preferential treatment to high-achieving students and more frequently criticizing the wrong answers of low-achieving students (Good & Brophy, 2007), and responding to students from various cultures and linguistic backgrounds differently than to those of the teacher's background (Delpit & Dowdy, 2008; Lustig & Koester, 2006; Moran & Hakuta, 2001; Neuliep, 2008). These behaviors have been observed even among experienced teachers, suggesting that at least some teachers may be so involved in conveying their subject matter content that they are unconscious of many of their own patterns of interaction.

A second reason teachers may be unaware of their own teaching behavior is that they are not always given specific signs defining "good" teaching. Broad indices of effectiveness, such as the number of students completing homework, high grades on classroom quizzes, accumulated points for work completed, and improvement from year to year on standardized tests, are often used to gauge progress within a classroom. Although these are convenient end products of individual student progress, their disadvantage for determining a teacher's effectiveness is that many factors other than the instruction being provided can contribute to them—student motivation, aptitude, past achievement, learning readiness, and support and nurturance at home, to name only a few. Also, because end products often result from many different instructional activities over an extended period of time, they rarely point explicitly to what should be changed to improve the quality of the outcome, and therefore provide little corrective value for changing teacher behavior.

Without clear signs of what to look for to evaluate their teaching, and without the time to consider and think about classroom events, many teachers fail to adequately reflect on their teaching behavior. The focused observation activities and accompanying observation tools provided in this book are designed to help you develop professional "lenses" for observing others, as well as reflecting on your own development as a teacher. As you learn to observe through these lenses, you will be working toward four major goals: (1) to become aware of your own teaching behavior, (2) to discover alternative instructional practices and new solutions to instructional problems, (3) to share your personal teaching strengths, and (4) to focus your reflections on important areas of teacher growth and effectiveness. Let's look more closely at each of these goals.

To Become Aware of Your Own Behavior

Although teachers make many decisions each day about the instructional process (how to capture student attention, how they will structure a lesson, whom they will call on, how misbehavior will be handled, what seatwork to assign, etc.), they sometimes make these decisions unconsciously in the course of meeting the rapid demands of the classroom. They might become bound by routine, failing to recognize how easily decisions can be altered. Instead of being pulled along unconsciously by the stream of rapidly paced events in the classroom, teachers can and should be active decision makers who influence the quality and nature of events in the classroom. They should actively question their own assumptions and seek input from parents and others on a regular basis (Compton-Lilly, 2000; Delgado-Gaitan, 2006).

As you observe in classrooms, you will become aware that the stream of events is not the same in every classroom and that sometimes teachers make decisions simply out of habit. If your observations lead to questions such as "Should I be doing that?" "Could that work in my classroom?" or "Would I have done that?", your observations are beginning to make you more aware of your own teaching. That awareness can help you discover some of your own unconscious decisions and unchecked assumptions. Even after you complete your university preparation, taking the opportunity to observe others will help remind you of your own behaviors and how they might appear to others.

Learning to observe and listen carefully will be your vehicle to becoming a reflective teacher. Just as a medical student observes a procedure many times before attempting it alone, you too will observe master teachers as part of your professional development. As you reflect on the actions and intentions of professionals, you will learn more about yourself. Some of this learning will be exciting as you discover your personal strengths and talents for teaching. Other aspects of this learning will be challenging as you identify areas in which you want to improve. One of the advantages of focused observation is that you can accomplish much of the reflection necessary for professional growth in the privacy and security of your own mind. As you observe others, take the opportunity to reflect on what you see; it will tell you as much about yourself as it will about those you are observing.

To Discover Alternative Instructional Practices and New Solutions to Instructional Problems

Another purpose for observing is to seek information and example behavior related to a specific area of interest. Although each of us has experienced a number of instructional practices as a student, there are many we did not experience—or that we experienced in a limited context. As you enter the teaching profession, it is natural to wonder about new instructional practices, methods, and strategies, and whether new and different educational ideas will help you become a more effective teacher. As you read textbooks, observe other teachers, and practice teach, you'll develop questions about the "how-to's" of teaching. Whether the basis of your curiosity stems from wondering about your own experiences as a student, from wanting to see some textbook procedure come alive in the classroom, or from having experienced a seemingly intractable problem in your own teaching, observation of other classrooms is often a practical solution for discovering and applying new ideas.

Developing a professional curiosity can help you refine the focus of your observations. For example, as you watch a teacher lead a class discussion, you may wonder how you can successfully blend fact and concept questions in the midst of the same discussion. Or you may encounter a problem with misbehavior in your own classroom and want to learn more about the rules used by other teachers for keeping students from calling out without being acknowledged. Focused observations can be among the most rewarding because they occur in response to an immediate need that has some sense of urgency for your thinking—and later, for your teaching. When you focus your observations on specific questions, your observations can result in a special sense of satisfaction when you discover new approaches worth trying. They can also be a source of comfort when you encounter a problem that seems to have no easy solution, and discover, through your observations, that others struggle with similar challenges, and that the source of the problem might lie outside yourself.

To Share Your Personal Teaching Strengths

Aside from helping you find solutions to instructional problems, focused observation helps put your personal teaching strengths in perspective. Teachers do not always see that a decision they have made, either consciously or unconsciously, could solve an instructional problem of another teacher. This might be because many teachers rarely observe others and do not have sufficient opportunities to describe to others the positive achievements in their own classrooms. As you observe, you will discover areas where *your* knowledge and experience provide insights that can help other teachers address a particular challenge. Taking the opportunity to share insights about successes and challenges builds a healthy sense of competence and shared professionalism. This benefit alone is why so many career-ladder and professional development programs require peer observation.

To Focus Your Reflections on Important Areas of Teacher Effectiveness

Handbooks and reviews of classroom research, such as those by Banks and Banks (2001); Borich (2008, 2010); Brophy (2002, 1989); Marzano, Pickering, and Pollock (2004); Richardson (2001); Rosenshine (1971); Wittrock (1986); and Zemelman, Daniels, and Hyde (2005), summarize the results of research in classrooms. In these and related texts the processes used by teachers to instruct students (e.g., questioning strategies, methods of organizing content, teaching methods) are related to student outcomes (e.g., engagement in the learning process and performance on classroom and standardized tests). This research has identified effective teaching behaviors related to eight areas of instruction: (1) the learning climate, (2) classroom management, (3) lesson clarity, (4) instructional variety, (5) teacher task orientation, (6) student engagement in the learning process, (7) student success, and (8) student higher thought processes and performance outcomes. Because so much effort, experience, and time have been devoted to researching these areas, let's look at them more closely.

The easiest and most efficient way to learn about these effective teaching practices and to understand their applications in the classroom is to observe them. Rather than simply waiting for interesting events to occur, the observer begins by looking for evidence of specific effective teaching practices already identified by the researchers. Let's look at some areas of effective practice that can help guide your classroom observations.

EIGHT LENSES FOR CLASSROOM OBSERVATION

Because classrooms are complex, observers often choose a particular professional frame—or lens—to gain insight regarding a particular aspect of classroom life. Over time, observations are completed using different lenses, resulting in a more comprehensive and detailed understanding of teaching and learning. Although the lenses we will use are not the only ones that could guide observation in classrooms, each has been researched and shown to influence the performance of learners. Other lenses for viewing classroom behavior are also available, and new lenses will undoubtedly emerge from classroom research in the fu-

ture. For our purposes, the following lenses will serve as an introduction to acquiring classroom observation skills and beginning to teach effectively. Each will be discussed and illustrated in later chapters.

Lens 1: Consider the Learning Climate

The **learning climate** of a classroom refers to its physical and emotional environment. Some of the most important observable features of the learning environment are (a) the warmth, concerns, and expectations conveyed to students by the teacher, (b) the organization of the physical aspects of the classroom, and (c) the competitiveness, cooperation, or independence encouraged by the structure of activity within the classroom that can promote or preclude cohesion and interaction among students.

As you observe the learning climate of a classroom, you will want to note how students feel about themselves, about one another, and about their classroom, and which activities and materials promote the feelings most conducive to learning.

Lens 2: Focus on Classroom Management

Classroom management involves how teachers organize the classroom and anticipate and respond to student behavior to provide an environment for efficient learning. Some observable features of classroom management include arranging the physical aspects of the classroom to match instructional goals, preestablishing and communicating classroom rules, developing and communicating instructional routines, establishing a system of incentives and consequences, and using techniques for low-profile classroom management.

Because many beginning teachers find effective classroom management challenging, you'll want to pay close attention to how effective teachers orchestrate and facilitate learning with their classroom management skills.

Lens 3: Look for Lesson Clarity

Lesson clarity refers to a teacher's ability to speak clearly and directly and to organize and structure content at the students' current level of understanding. Some observable approaches to lesson clarity include informing learners of expected skills and understandings before a lesson; providing advance organizers that place the lesson content in the perspective of past and future learning; using examples, illustrations, demonstrations, and instructional media that can expand and clarify lesson content; and reviewing and summarizing during and at the close of a lesson.

Lens 4: Verify Variety

As you can recall from your own experiences as a student, **instructional variety** involves the teacher's use of different modes of learning (visual, oral, and tactile) to arouse and maintain student interest and attention. Effective teachers select an appropriate mix of instructional approaches to support particular learning objectives. Some observable features of instructional variety include attention-gaining devices; variation in eye contact, voice, and gestures; alternate learning modes (seeing, listening, and doing); using appropriate rewards and reinforcement to sustain student interest and engagement; and providing alternative opportunities for assessment.

Lens 5: Observe Task Orientation

Task orientation involves effective teaching practices that help the teacher maintain an instructional focus, such as methods of managing classroom activities efficiently, ways of handling misbehavior with minimal disruption to the class, reducing instructional time devoted to clerical duties, and maximizing time devoted to content coverage. Methods of task orientation can be observed in lesson plans that reflect the text and follow state standards, rules and procedures that anticipate and thereby reduce misbehavior, and established milestones (e.g., tests, reviews, and assignments) for maintaining instructional momentum.

Lens 6: Examine Engagement

Students learn best when they become actively engaged in the learning process. Teachers promote **student engagement** by providing exercises, problem sets, and activities that allow students to think about, act on, and practice what they learn. Some observable ways that teachers facilitate student engagement are activities for guided practice, frequent feedback and correctives, individualized and self-directed learning activities, the systematic use of meaningful verbal praise, and checking and monitoring of classroom assignments and seatwork.

Lens 7: Measure Student Success

Students' learning is enhanced when they complete work at moderate to high levels of success. Some observable ways that teaching promotes **student success** are unit and lesson organization that reflects prior learning, immediate feedback and corrections, gradual transitions to new content, and a classroom pace and momentum that build toward major milestones (e.g., reviews, projects, practice exercises, and tests).

Lens 8: Look for Higher Thought Processes and Performance Outcomes

Higher thought processes are critical thinking, reasoning, and problem-solving behaviors that alone cannot be measured by tests of cognitive achievement. Some observable features of teaching for higher thought processes include using collaborative and group activities, demonstrating for students mental models and strategies for learning, arranging for student projects and demonstrations, engaging students in oral performance, providing opportunities for independent practice and problem solving, and using performance assessments and student portfolios.

CHALLENGES TO OBSERVING IN CLASSROOMS

So far we have discussed four purposes for observing in classrooms.

1. Becoming aware of your own behavior to help make decisions that consciously control and alter the stream of events in your classroom
2. Discovering alternative instructional practices and new solutions to instructional problems
3. Sharing your personal teaching strengths to help colleagues determine areas of improvement
4. Focusing your attention on important dimensions of teaching effectiveness and best practices

Before undertaking an actual observation, let's take one more step in preparing to observe by considering how easily biases and personal experiences can influence your observations. Let's peek in on three imaginary teachers who have been instructed by the school counselor to write down their impressions of Peter after observing him during their first day of class. As each teacher "speaks" about Peter, make some mental notes of your impressions about Peter and about the teacher.

Teacher A: Peter arrived late to my classroom and took a seat in the last row without even acknowledging that he was late. Most of the class brought the required supplies—paper, pencil, and ruler—but Peter had none of these. I have had students like this before—lazy and irresponsible—and it's like pulling teeth to teach them anything. I don't know for sure, but I'm willing to bet I'm going to have trouble with him this year.

Teacher B: Well, you've asked me to comment on Peter, but I don't have much to say so early in the school year. In fact I wouldn't have even noticed Peter if he hadn't walked in late, probably due to all the commotion and noise in the halls this morning. At any rate, Peter seems like a quiet, maybe even shy, boy. He seemed embarrassed to even say he was late and went directly to a seat in the last row. I predict Peter won't have much to say during my class this year.

Teacher C: When you asked that I give you my impressions of Peter, I looked up his achievement scores and grades from last year. After meeting him for the first time today, everything made sense. Peter is going to be a very high achiever in my class. He's the type that gets right down to work. For example, when he came into the class, he went to the corner of the classroom to get away from the commotion caused by students arriving late. Peter seems like a sensitive, high-achieving student who probably will have to be given extra work to keep him challenged this year.

What did you notice about the three reports? Could these different perceptions of the same student emerge on the same day? Researchers such as Good and Brophy (2007), Tauber (1998), and Rist (1970) have noted such instances among teachers, attributing differences in observation to **selective perception,** which involves seeing what we want to see or allowing our perceptions to be unduly influenced by factors outside the immediate context of the observation. Selective perception can be either positive or negative in its influence on students. As Tauber (1998) notes, "Teachers, more often than not, get from students what they expect from them!" Notice how each of the three observers gives different interpretations of Peter's behavior, reaching conclusions that will probably influence how they relate to the student for the rest of the school year.

Teacher A seems convinced that Peter will be a troublemaker and, therefore, will need close watching if he is to learn. Teacher A assumes that Peter has a poor disciplinary record—often coming late to class, failing to follow school rules, and, if given the chance, seizing any opportunity to become a troublemaker.

Teacher B's description suggests that Peter will need no special attention, that he will blend into the woodwork of the classroom. In fact, Teacher B predicts, based on only a single class period, that Peter will be easy to teach.

Teacher C believes that Peter is a high achiever. Teacher C's observations, after checking the records, focus on Peter's academic skills and she seems convinced that Peter will require supplemental learning materials to keep him challenged.

Each of these observations of Peter could eventually prove to be accurate—or just as easily could prove to be false. The point is that each of the observers observed and commented on only a small part of Peter's behavior—that which each assumed was the most important, without knowing the reason why Peter's behavior was of concern to the counselor in the first place. In other words, they unconsciously selected what they saw and maybe what they thought the counselor wanted to hear.

Each of the three teachers made not only some selective observations, but also some interpretations to go along with them. In their written accounts, facts about Peter's behavior were blended with interpretations about what these facts might mean. From similar observations, Teacher A observed a troublemaker, Teacher B saw a quiet and shy student, and Teacher C noted a high achiever with academic talent and a responsiveness to school. In each instance, these teachers not only recorded the facts as they saw them, but interpreted them according to their own opinions, formed by, for example, their past experiences with similar students, their own values about the appropriateness or inappropriateness of the behaviors observed, and what they thought the counselor to whom they were reporting wanted to hear. Each of these teachers unknowingly set up different expectations for Peter, which might lead them to each treat Peter in distinctive ways for the rest of the school year. These initial impressions might encourage them to selectively perceive Peter's future behavior in ways that reinforce their initial impressions.

There will be more to say about how to recognize and control selective perception. For now, let's identify some of the sources of influence outside the immediate context of an observation that can create selective perception—and which you will want to consider as you complete your classroom observations.

SOURCES OF INFLUENCE ON OBSERVATIONS FROM OUTSIDE OURSELVES

One of the most significant sources of selective perception comes from the school and classroom environment in which you will be observing. A variety of student, teacher, school, and classroom characteristics can affect your perceptions and observations.

Student Ability and Achievement

One of the most persuasive influences on your observations will come from the known or presumed abilities of the students you will be observing. Although student abilities are often a legitimate focus of observation and an obvious influence on what goes on in a classroom, they can bias an observation if their influence is not recognized and limited to a specific area of observation. So-called "high-IQ" or high-achieving classrooms, which might be denoted by tracked classes or advanced subject matter, can establish expectations that force seemingly neutral or irrelevant data to confirm that everything is going well in these classrooms. Conversely, when low-ability or remedial classes are observed, expectations might focus your attention on student inattention, poor quality of work, lack of student participation, or teacher difficulty in controlling the class, to the exclusion of the many positive events that may be happening in the classroom. Although these factors might be part of the legitimate focus of the observation, they should not influence you to selectively perceive or overemphasize these characteristics simply because they are expected. Especially when observing predesignated categories of students (e.g., "gifted," English language learners, "at risk," or mainstreamed learners), regardless of whether such categories are established informally by the teacher or formally by the school, it is important to recognize that many such categories represent stereotypes.

One example of this stereotyping is presented by the underrepresentation of minority and female students in math and science professions (National Science Foundation, 2000). Also, more minority than Anglo students tend to be assigned to low-ability classes (Murphy, 1996; National Science Foundation, 2000), especially in large urban school districts, in which teachers may be less likely to emphasize the skills needed for advanced math and science concepts. In reality, minority and female students represent a much wider range of student behavior and skill than an observer might assume or expect.

Classroom Characteristics

A second source of potential bias in your observations will be the immediate physical context in which the instruction takes place. This includes the general attractiveness of the classroom (e.g., neat and clean, bulletin boards filled with interesting displays, desks and chairs in order), as well as some less tangible aspects of the classroom, such as its apparent warmth and nurturing atmosphere. Although these can be important areas of observation, they can preclude your ability to perceive other important areas of classroom behavior if they are allowed to dominate your attention. In other words, observations preceding instruction, and especially those pertaining to the physical context in which instruction takes place, should not lead you to presuppose anything about the learning process. Physical characteristics of the classroom will naturally yield both positive and negative expectations, but these impressions should not be allowed to color your observations, unless they are the specific focus of your observation.

Participatory and Cooperative Student Behavior

A third possible bias in what an observer sees is the responsiveness of the students to the instruction and the teacher. These behaviors often represent a cooperativeness or willingness on the part of the students to become active participants in the classroom and are particularly influential because they are often the most obvious to observers. For example, the willingness of students to comply with a teacher's instructional requests and obedience to classroom rules can quickly establish a tone of effective or ineffective instruction long before any other event takes place. But student cooperative or participatory behavior can result from many factors outside the control of the teacher, and effective instruction can, and often does, go on in spite of such behaviors. Every teacher is fearful of students acting up just when an administrator or observer is present, especially when such an observation is scheduled for a particularly difficult class. A trained observer, however, while noting the responsiveness, participation, and obedience of the class, should not necessarily presume that such behavior is the result of effective or ineffective classroom management or poorly chosen instructional practices. Observations specifically targeted in these and related areas must reveal the extent to which the teaching practices observed are the result of, or the cause of, these student behaviors. The cooperative and participatory behavior of the students should not influence the observation of other important classroom events that may be occurring simultaneously.

Experience and Education of the Teacher

Most observers generally know the number of years a teacher has been teaching, if only by age. Some observers also know whether or not a particular teacher has received an advanced degree or has attended special seminars or workshops. Such factors, or just knowing the teacher is well regarded by some other colleague, can shape what an observer sees or fails to see in a classroom if their influence is not recognized at the outset of an observation. Called *halo effects,* these influences can easily intimidate an observer and affect what is perceived as relevant to the observation. They might also bias the degree of emphasis placed on certain instructional events. For example, better classroom management skills are usually expected from an experienced teacher. But the truth is that years of experience, advanced degrees, and special commendations do not always result in more effective classroom management skills or better teaching. This is not to lessen the value of experience and advanced training, but rather to suggest that they are not the only way of becoming an effective teacher. For some, they might not even be the best or quickest way. They might represent important avenues for becoming an effective teacher, but they do not guarantee effectiveness. The point is that observers often unconsciously allow perceptions of events within the classroom to be influenced by the presumed stature a teacher has attained outside of it. Such presumptions can lead you to notice only that which fits your expectations.

School, Grade, and Subject Matter

Another influence leading to selective perception comes from a knowledge of the school, grade, or subject matter to be observed. Poor and rich neighborhoods are a fact of life that have spawned their own expectations. Similarly, certain expectations surround various instructional levels or grades, as well as certain subject matter areas. Observers in schools in poor or high-crime neighborhoods, for example, often approach their task fearing the worst. Observers who visit schools with better reputations often come with an optimistic attitude. One often hears reference to students in the elementary grades as "sweet," in junior high as "difficult," and in the 12th grade as "mature." Vocational and technical subjects, remedial or basic track classes, and college preparatory or advanced placement courses have their own stereotypes. But these stereotypes can restrict what you see according to what the stereotype implies. If stereotypes could predict life in classrooms, they would have long ago become accepted facts rather than the inaccurate caricatures of classroom life that they often turn out to be. Effective teaching does not occur any more often, on the average, in advanced college-bound classes with high-IQ students taught by experienced teachers with master's degrees than in any other setting, contrary to many expectations and stereotypes. This is one of the best reasons for not allowing school, grade, and subject to influence what is, or can be, observed.

Individual and Cultural Diversity

Another outside influence on observation is the individual and cultural diversity found in every classroom. Although the physical school setting has remained largely unchanged over the past 75 years, the major participants—the students—have not. Today's typical classroom contains a more diverse group of learners than at any other time in our history. This diversity reflects not only the motivational and cognitive abilities that children bring to school, but also the culture that accompanies them (Gerald & Hussar, 2003; Minami & Ovando, 2001; Sable & Hoffman, 2008). It is no longer accurate to say that we are a nation and an education system *with* minorities; rather, we are a nation and an education system *of* minorities. At the beginning of this decade, nonwhite students made up over 40% of all students in America (Llagas, 2003; Mercado, 2001). Nonwhite students currently make up the majority of learners in our 27 largest school districts.

Add to this medley of cultures in our schools an increasingly diverse assortment of family patterns and lifestyles (Sable & Hoffman, 2008), and the result of this cultural, familial, and socioeconomic diversity is an ever-increasing range of individual differences in the classroom. This diversity will be equaled by the diversity in how teachers deal with it (Lustig & Koester, 2006). For example, the research of Neuliep (2008); Olneck (2001); Cheng, Chen, Tsubo, Sekandari, and Alfafara-Killacky (1997); Cheng (1996); Griggs and Dunn (1995); Bowers and Flinders (1991); and Tharp and Gallimore (1989) present convincing arguments that different cultures react differently to the nonverbal and verbal behavioral management techniques of proximity control, eye contact, warnings, and classroom arrangement. Furthermore, these authors cite numerous examples of how teachers from one culture interpret behaviors of children differently than do teachers from another culture (Banks & Banks, 2001, 2006; Cheng, 1998).

As we observe in classrooms, there is a need to be aware of potential biases related to diversity (Banks & Banks, 2001, 2006; Santos & Reese, 1999). For example, gender-, racial-, and ethnic-specific clothing, dialect, and mannerisms can lead us to expect and look for one type of behavior more than another, or to place stereotypic interpretations on classroom behavior to which gender, race, and ethnicity actually have no relationship. For now, it is important to know that some of the patterns of effective teaching techniques you will observe are culturally sensitive. The astute observer will consider instructional and management techniques not only in relation to classroom context, but also in relation to the cultural history of the learner or learners with whom they are being used.

Sometimes teachers' own limited experiences can exclude them from discovering important insights that would make their teaching more effective with students from other cultures. Lustig and Koester (2006) suggest a number of ways teachers can develop **intercultural competence,** the ability to interact smoothly and effectively with members of various cultures. Among these they include reaching out to others from different cultures to ask for input and insight. There will be more about the issue of individual and cultural diversity as it applies to the observation and recording of specific teaching and student behavior throughout this text. As you consider these ideas, your careful observations and reflection will help you expand your own intercultural competence.

SOURCES OF INFLUENCE ON OBSERVATIONS FROM WITHIN OURSELVES

In addition to the influences of external factors, several factors within yourself can determine what you choose to perceive.

Your Own Experiences in School

We often compare present experiences with past ones, and our experience with school is no exception. As noted in Chapter 1, much of what we see and hear in classrooms can be related to what we saw and heard in school when we were growing up. This creates a strong tendency on our part to make comparisons between what is being observed and what classrooms were like when we were in school. Sometimes there is a tendency to hold up the past as a standard against which present classrooms should be measured. Aspects of a classroom that are unlike those in our own school experience may be placed in a negative light, or instructional activities that worked well in our own past experiences can inadvertently become the standard for today's classrooms. For example, a tightly managed lecture format from our own school days might lead us to see a classroom with a high degree of student talk as a poorly managed classroom (Cazden, 1988). Whenever we allow our previous school experiences to form the basis of what we see, our observations again are being influenced by selective perception. Although we cannot ignore our past experiences, it is important to continually examine how they might influence our current perceptions.

Recent Influences and Training

Aside from past experiences in school, our perceptions and judgments are often influenced by our most recent experiences and training. Workshops on new teaching techniques, books on innovative instructional methods, education problems covered in the mass media, and university coursework can all influence what we see. These experiences and events can provide a useful additional focus to our observations, or they can serve as a distracting influence. We tend to be enthusiastic about our most recent experiences, perhaps because they are more memorable. A halo effect is formed by our excitement about something new and different, which, sometimes, can exaggerate its true effects. At first we use or see the new approach at every turn and expect others to do so as well. At this stage, even inconsequential events can sometimes be mistaken for evidence that the approach is or is not being used. In time, however, the newness of the idea wears off, and it is placed in the context of other ideas. Our perspective broadens, changing our initial absolute acceptance of a new or innovative approach to an acceptance that is more conditional. In other words, influential events, ideas, or experiences occurring in the life of the observer at the approximate time of an observation can unconsciously direct an observer to overemphasize the importance of what is being observed in another context. This is another instance when the focus of an observation can be clouded by selective perception.

Who Might Be Watching; Who May Find Out

It is no secret that we often modify our behavior because of who might be listening or who may see the data from the observations that are made. This is one of the reasons observations of teachers by school administrators as part of yearly appraisals and career-ladder enhancements are often discredited by teachers and sometimes, privately, by administrators. Teachers give them what they want, changing their typical behavior—even rehearsing desirable behaviors—for the sake of an observation and then reverting to the original behavior immediately afterward, as almost any of us might in an evaluative situation.

Observers change their behavior as well. Teachers believed to be less effective by an administration observer might be given somewhat inflated ratings to minimize a potentially argumentative confrontation; conversely, teachers perceived to be more competent by an observer might be given somewhat deflated ratings to keep the teacher working toward higher levels of performance and to minimize the disappointment of others who may think their performance is equally effective. For these reasons, peer observations often are more conducive to the professional development of teachers than administrator observation. Many of the political factors apparent in administrator observation are minimized when teachers observe other teachers. That is why the purpose of your observation—your own reflection, self-improvement, and professional development—must always be clear to those you are observing.

CHOOSING A USEFUL LENS: THE NEED TO STRUCTURE OBSERVATIONS

Wise observers separate the informal process of looking from the systematic process of observing. The difference between just looking at an event and carefully observing it is in the structure an observer brings to the observation. This structure provides a framework to sort the myriad events of the classroom into manageable and comprehensible categories that have professional relevance for the practice of teaching. Without this structure, an observer is left to cast about for relevant events and runs the risk of not knowing whether an event that may appear "minor" is of major importance or an event that may appear "major" is of minor importance. In short, without an appropriate lens for observing, we would be in the same position as Teachers A, B, and C, who attempted to record their observations of Peter without knowing what aspects of Peter's behavior were of concern to the counselor. The lack of a professional frame—or lens—leaves our observations open to se-lective perception, contradictory explanations, and false expectations. All of these can confuse or distort our observations, rendering them of limited value.

The eight patterns of effective teaching practice described in this chapter will become the lenses through which we will learn to observe life in classrooms. In Chapter 3, we will see how these patterns of practice occur simultaneously and in rapid succession in a quickly paced classroom. Chapter 4 will present some of the recording methods that can be used to observe each of our patterns. And Chapters 5 through 12 will focus on the individual and interactive effects of each of these patterns of classroom life that provide the foundation for effective teaching practice.

For More Information

Martin Haberman, a professor in the School of Education at the University of Wisconsin–Milwaukee, has developed an interview protocol intended to help principals identify teachers who will be effective in urban schools. The protocol is designed to elicit prospective teachers' attitudes and behaviors and compare them with the attributes of "star" teachers gleaned from interviews Haberman and his colleagues have conducted. In the interviews, principals examine seven dimensions of teaching and rate prospective teachers as "average," "high," or "star." Haberman's seven dimensions of effective teaching can be found in the January/February 2004 issue of the *Harvard Education Letter.*

Key Terms

classroom management, 14
higher thought processes, 15
instructional variety, 15
intercultural competence, 18
learning climate, 14
lesson clarity, 14

reciprocal distancing, 11
selective perception, 16
student engagement, 15
student success, 15
task orientation, 15

Activities

1. Provide classroom examples from your own school or observation experience that illustrate the (1) rapid pace, (2) immediacy, (3) interruptions, and (4) social dynamics that are likely to characterize the classrooms in which you will teach.
2. Prepare a brief dialogue between teacher and student representing a classroom interchange featuring "reciprocal distancing."
3. Identify four personal goals for improving your teaching skills as a result of the classroom observations you will complete this semester.

4. Identify the eight lenses for observation you will be using during this course and provide an example of classroom behavior related to each lens.
5. From your own observation experience, provide an example of selective perception that distorted the truth of what you observed.

3

Making Classroom Visits

David says
that since he
made his bed this morning,
there's a
train track

in his blankets.
Before,
when I looked,
I only saw
that it was wrinkled.

Eleanor Schick

Like the poem's author, each of us sees what we expect to see most of the time. Interestingly, when someone points out another view, or when we look at a situation with a different perspective, we often gain new insights. This is also true of classroom observation—and it is an important notion. In this chapter we'll consider various perspectives we may want to take in observing classrooms and why those perspectives may be useful to us.

Although you'll often want to observe classrooms with very specific questions or goals in mind, your first few observations should be more general so that you can get a feel for a particular grade level or classroom. The eight lenses discussed in the previous chapter can be used to get an overall picture of a classroom. To see how all eight lenses can work together to inform your observation and suggest specific questions for further study, let's visit a fictional classroom taught by Ms. Koker.

A CLASSROOM DIALOGUE

The scene is a seventh-grade social studies classroom. Ms. Koker is beginning a unit on forms of government. It is early in the school year, so the class is still new to her. The first several weeks of school were a bit rough for Ms. Koker because she was somewhat unprepared for the aggressive talking-out behavior of some of the students and because of the new textbook, which devotes less time to some of her favorite topics. Things have calmed down a bit now that Ms. Koker has established some classroom rules and has decided to organize her lessons more tightly with questions and recitation. Ms. Koker's goals for this lesson are to introduce three types of government and then begin to develop the concept of democracy. Aside from a tendency to be loud and talkative, this class is composed of mostly average-performing students, with a few high-performing students and a few who regularly challenge her authority.

Ms. Koker: Today we begin a unit on various forms of government. In the next few days, we will study the concepts of monarchy, oligarchy, and democracy, and how governments are formed using each of these three concepts. In fact, we will cover these three forms of government so thoroughly that at the end of the week, each of you will know how to create a government of your own—but, please, don't start any revolutions with what you learn! [Class laughs.] Let's start by defining what a monarchy is. Does anybody know? [At this point, some class members turn to their neighbors to ask if they know the answer.]

Ms. Koker: Please, no talking. Bobby, do you know what a monarchy is?
Bobby: No.
Ms. Koker: Christina, do you have any idea?
Christina: No, I'm afraid I don't, Ms. Koker.
Ms. Koker: Tim, you're not in your seat, so I'll have to ask you. Do you know what a monarchy is?
Tim: Yep, it's a butterfly. [Class bursts out in laughter.]
Ms. Koker: That's an extra assignment for you tonight. Write your name on the board as a reminder. [Ms. Koker and class wait.] Okay, I'll tell you. A monarchy is a government that is ruled or governed by a single person. It's a form of government in which a single person, a king or queen for example, is the supreme head of a state for his or her entire lifetime. Now, what other names besides King or Queen do we have for individuals who serve as head of a country for a lifetime? Let's go from left to right across the first row.
Mary: I'm not sure what you mean, Ms. Koker.
Ms. Koker: Next. Felipe?
Felipe: You mean, what do we call someone who is just like a king, but called something else?
Ms. Koker: You're on the right track. Next. Anna?
Anna: Well, I would call a king an emperor.
Tim: [Talking out] Yeah, like in "The Emperor's New Clothes!" [Class laughs.]
Ms. Koker: Okay, that's the second time you've spoken out of turn, Tim. You will answer two extra homework questions tonight if you don't want me to write up a detention slip. Now, go up and write your name on the board again, so I won't forget to give you the assignment. [By now, talking has grown louder and a few students have left their seats waiting for Tim to return from the board.] Let's see now, where were we?
Student: [From somewhere in back of room] We were talking about emperors.
Ms. Koker: Yes, emperors, like kings, usually indicate a monarchy—or rule by a single person over a long time. Other names for heads of state that indicate a monarchy are *czar*, which was a title once used in Russia; *kaiser*, which was a term used in the early German empire; and *sultan*, which is a word still used today in the Middle East. These individuals, like kings and emperors throughout history, have often had absolute power over the people and lands they ruled. Traditionally, these rulers gained their power from the family they were

born into, and not from any accomplishments of their own. In some cases today, a type of monarchy exists alongside some other form of government. Can anyone think of a country like our own but that has a king or a queen? Let's go across the second row this time. Rashaun?

Rashaun: England. They have a queen and royal weddings and that kind of stuff that we don't have in this country.

Ms. Koker: Good, Rashaun. Some present-day monarchs, like the Queen of England, still exist. However, in England the queen possesses only minor authority and exists for mostly symbolic purposes, or as a way of showing the country's historical roots. Although kings and queens did at one time have absolute authority over England, today they serve mostly ceremonial functions. That was a good answer, Rashaun. Now, before we move to another form of government, called an *oligarchy,* does everyone understand what a monarchy is? [No one responds.]

Ms. Koker: Okay, I guess we can go on. Let's see, where did we leave off in the second row? [Tricia meekly raises her hand.] Can you tell us what an oligarchy is, Tricia?

Tricia: I don't know.

Ms. Koker: Next. Raul?

Raul: Don't know.

Ms. Koker: Well, I guess I'll have to tell you—but it's in the chapter, which you should have read. An oligarchy is a form of government in which absolute power or authority is given to a few persons, instead of a single ruler as in a monarchy. These individuals usually come to power not through heredity or being born into the right families, but through some political struggle or compromise. Oligarchies, which were common in ancient times, are hard to find today, but some governments almost like an oligarchy still exist. Can anyone think of one? Jeff, Kathy, you're the last two in the second row. Any ideas?

Jeff: I'm not sure, but is it like a mother and father in a family?

Ms. Koker: What do you mean?

Jeff: Well, my parents have a kind of agreement—not written or anything like that—in which my mother is responsible for taking care of the house and my brothers and sisters, and my father is responsible for his job and doing repairs. That's a kind of sharing of responsibility, isn't it?

Ms. Koker: Yes, maybe. But it's not what we're talking about here. Kathy?

Kathy: I can't think of any examples.

Ms. Koker: Well, you probably never heard of the Peloponnesian Wars, but shortly after one of these, in about 400 B.C., ancient Greece was ruled for a brief time by a group of persons called the Thirty Tyrants. This might have been the very first oligarchy. Also, we've been hearing a lot lately about Iraq. In that country the new constitution ensures that some powers and authority are to be divided among individuals representing each of the country's major population centers, occupied by the Kurds, the Sunnis, and the Shiites.

Now, let's compare the two forms of government we've been discussing—monarchy and oligarchy—with our own form of government. Let's begin by reminding ourselves of what our form of government is called. Let's pick up with the first person in the third row. Quann?

Quann: I'm not ready.

Ms. Koker: Everyone should be ready when I call on them.

Quann: Well, I didn't get to read this yet. [Class begins to snicker at Quann getting in trouble.]

Ms. Koker: Okay, I'm going to make a rule that everyone must read the assignment before we begin a topic. That means that the reading for the entire week must be done by class on Monday. [Loud moans are heard.]

Tim: [Speaking without acknowledgment] But that means we'd have homework over the weekend, and no other teacher makes us do that.

Ms. Koker: [Ignoring Tim's comment] We still have one more form of government to discuss. Joan is next. [Class becomes noisy and restless at the thought of weekend homework.]

Joan: We live in a democracy.

Ms. Koker: What else can you tell us about a democracy?

Joan: Well … [Just as she is about to begin, the public address system clicks on.]

Principal: [On P.A.] I'm sorry to interrupt, but two lunchtime jobs are still available for any students who want to be paid for working in the cafeteria during the second half of their lunch. We need some workers for today, so, teachers, if anyone is interested, please write them a hall permit and send them to the office immediately. Thank you. [Roberto and Tim raise their hands, indicating their interest in the job. The teacher ignores Tim and writes a pass to the office for Roberto.]

Ms. Koker: Okay, we were discussing democracy. Time is short, so take out paper and pen and write down everything I say. Another rule we will start, since you're not doing the reading, is to take notes. The word *democracy* comes from the Greek word *demos,* which means "the people," and the Greek word *kratein,* spelled K-R-A-T-E-I-N, which means "to rule."

Brittany: [Calling out] How is that first word spelled?

Ms. Koker: [Responds by spelling the word.] D-E-M-O-S. So, who's next to be called on? [Rhonda raises her hand.] Okay. Rhonda, putting these two words together, what does the word *democracy* mean?

Rhonda: It means that the people rule.

Ms. Koker: Good. And who are the people in a democracy? Sam?

Sam: I guess it's all of us—everyone that lives in a certain place.

Ms. Koker: Okay, a democracy differs from a monarchy and an oligarchy by who is given the authority to rule. As we have seen, in a monarchy, a single person, usually chosen through heredity, is given absolute authority, and in the case of an oligarchy, persons or groups representing different portions of all the people in the land are given the authority to rule. In a democracy, authority to rule rests in the hands of all the people. But how could such a system work when everyone has authority over everyone else? Next person. Diana?

Diana: We—all the people—elect persons to represent us. I guess that's what our senators and representatives do.

Ms. Koker: So when we say that all the people have the authority to rule in a democracy, we really mean . . . Next. That's you, Phil.

Phil: We elect persons—like Diana said—representatives and senators, and we give them the authority to rule.

Ms. Koker: Yes. So in a democracy like ours, the people have authority, but indirectly, through the election of individuals that represent their interests. In our form of democracy, called "representative democracy," a legislature composed of senators and representatives is elected by the people. Does anyone know of any other kind of democracy? Mark, you're next.

Mark: Nope.

Ms. Koker: Did you take notes on the chapter?

Mark: I was going to do that tonight.

Ms. Koker: I will begin checking notes at the end of every class. Since some of you haven't read the assignment, we'll use the remaining time to read Chapter 7.

TIME TO REFLECT

Although this dialogue might not have been fair to Ms. Koker's everyday teaching, classroom exchanges such as this occur at almost all levels of schooling. They are, to be sure, uneven, rough, and sometimes even crude attempts to convey information in the midst of all sorts of competing forces—misbehaving and unprepared students, interruptions, quickly sketched lesson plans, and insufficient instructional time, to name only a few. The flow of events in a classroom, as shown in the dialogue, is not always a neatly packaged, smooth unit of instruction. Instead, teachers and students often struggle, sometimes with themselves and sometimes with each other, to complete the day's lesson. Although Ms. Koker's classroom might have had some problems, these problems are not uncommon for any teacher at one time or another.

Think back for a moment on the dialogue you have just read. In your opinion, was it an example of effective teaching or ineffective teaching, or did it contain some examples of each? What are your impressions of Ms. Koker as a person and as a teacher? What about her knowledge and use of instructional methods? Did she do the right things most of the time, even though not all the students conveniently cooperated, or did some of her decisions make it less

likely that the goals of the lesson would be achieved? Do you believe the goals for this lesson, as stated before the dialogue, were met? If not, whose fault was it—Ms. Koker's, for not motivating the students; the students', for not reading the assignment; Tim's, for misbehaving; or the principal's, for creating a distraction at a crucial time?

Of course, all of these factors and more were instrumental in the way events in this classroom unfolded. But if we were to attempt to fully understand this classroom, each question we asked ourselves would point us in equally narrow, and perhaps even biased, directions. A broader set of lenses than individual questions or idiosyncratic concerns that happen to gain our attention would be necessary to view classroom events. As you consider the interactions in Ms. Koker's classroom, take a moment now to complete the General Observation Form (Instrument 3.1a) in Appendix B.

In what areas did you notice positive interactions? In what areas did you feel concern? Did completing the form help you "see" Ms. Koker and her students more accurately or comprehensively?

The eight areas of effective teaching considered in the form can help us achieve the breadth of vision we need to understand the events in Ms. Koker's classroom. Let's use each of these "professional frames" as a lens to achieve a more focused observation of life in Ms. Koker's classroom as it unfolded during this lesson. After viewing the events through each of these lenses, we will bring all our data together to form some general impressions of the strengths and weaknesses of Ms. Koker's presentation. As you read the following discussion, add any notes to your General Observation Form that may help you remember key points about each of the eight lenses.

OBSERVING THE LEARNING CLIMATE

Recall from Chapter 2 that the learning climate of a classroom involves the social and emotional environment in which learning takes place. Using these aspects of the learning environment as our lens, let's look back at the dialogue to see how the learning climate might have influenced the achievement of Ms. Koker's goals for the lesson.

In many ways, the learning climate in Ms. Koker's classroom appears tense. On one hand, Ms. Koker seems genuinely committed to having students contribute their ideas to the development of the concepts she is teaching. On the other hand, few students seem to feel free or relaxed enough to share anything but the most obvious answers. As a result, very little genuine discussion takes place.

The manner in which Ms. Koker responds to students might have even increased tension in the classroom. Rarely is an answer followed by another question to the same student. In the case of an inaccurate answer or no answer, the teacher quickly moves to the next student instead of staying with the student to correct a partially wrong answer or drawing out a partially correct response that another student might build on. Even when opportunities present themselves to stay with and further develop a student's response, such as when Jeff equates the sharing of responsibilities among members of an oligarchy with the sharing of responsibilities between his mother and father, the teacher responds with a curt "But it's not what we're talking about here." These responses by Ms. Koker enhance the competitive nature of the classroom by treating each individual student response as either all right or all wrong, thereby missing the opportunity to connect the discussion to the students' own experiences.

Another aspect of the learning climate results from Ms. Koker's desire to keep firm control over the events evolving in her classroom. She decides on a carefully controlled row-by-row recitation of answers instead of an open discussion. Perhaps in an effort to enhance classroom management, she restricts any interaction that is not a direct response to her questions. Consequently, she restricts the very type of response that her discussion-oriented agenda seems to call for. Without realizing it, Ms. Koker sets up a learning climate of opposing forces. The students resist being drawn into the discussion to avoid saying anything unacceptable; the teacher asks for student participation but responds with mostly unrewarding answers. Had the atmosphere of the classroom been less rigid, this class might have been more conducive to the cooperative interchanges being sought by the teacher. We will return to the learning climate and how to observe it in a later chapter. For now, however, let's get a feel for some of the other lenses through which life in Ms. Koker's classroom can be observed.

OBSERVING CLASSROOM MANAGEMENT

What do you notice about Ms. Koker's classroom management style? Does it appear to be more of a reaction to student behavior than a well-organized system of rules and procedures thought out in advance? At several points in the lesson, Ms. Koker seems to make up rules on the spot. Although sometimes necessary, this practice is risky. It can convey to students a sense of arbitrariness about the rule itself, making it seem less credible and therefore less likely to be obeyed. Apparently, Ms. Koker failed to convey some basic rules earlier in the school year (e.g., about when to complete assigned reading and to take notes). Without a well-organized system of rules and class procedures, Ms. Koker may continue to react defensively, at first tolerating a wide range of behavior and later using valuable class time pulling back to respond to unforeseen behaviors.

You might also notice that Ms. Koker's classroom exhibits some problems with conduct. Talking out, for which presumably a rule exists, seems to be a persistent problem. This comes as no surprise because Ms. Koker's response to talking out, even in this short episode, is inconsistent. Notice that Ms. Koker is adamant at first about not speaking out. After reminding the class at the beginning of the lesson, "Please, no talking," and reprimanding Tim for talking out, she accepts without reprimand a call-out, "We were talking about emperors," from an anonymous student after she asks the indirect question "Let's see now, where were we?" This question, the result of losing her focus after dealing with Tim's misbehavior, results in the very behavior she wishes to avoid. The conflict occurs when she switches unexpectedly to a nondirective style ("Let's see now, where were we?") more suited to an informal discussion session than to the row-by-row recitation format she has pursued from the beginning of the lesson.

Did you also notice the amount of class time used by Ms. Koker in responding to Tim's misbehavior? Although Tim's misbehavior might have been unpredictable, Ms. Koker's response to it might have created an even bigger problem. First, she responds by assigning extra homework, thereby equating homework with punishment. Second, during the time it takes for Tim to leave his seat, go to the board to write his name, and return, the rest of the class waits without direction. The momentum, or pace, which previously kept the class moving forward and focused on the lesson, is lost. These momentary lapses, whether due to interruptions from misbehaving students, public address announcements, or visitors at the door, require special classroom management procedures to keep students engaged in the learning process. Ms. Koker's costly use of instructional time for discipline might have been avoided had she done a better job of establishing and consistently reinforcing an organized system of classroom rules and procedures from the start of the school year.

OBSERVING LESSON CLARITY

Lesson clarity involves communicating clearly and directly and presenting content at the students' current level of understanding. Clarity involves not only the visual and oral clarity of a teacher's delivery, but also the proper organization and structuring of the material to be taught. For example, to organize and structure the material to be taught, the teacher must know how much knowledge the students already have about the day's lesson. Notice that Ms. Koker begins the lesson by saying, "Let's start by defining what a monarchy is. Does anybody know?" The responses she receives, however, are not too encouraging. The first two students called on say "No," after which Ms. Koker says, "I guess I'll have to tell you then." This beginning involves two aspects of clarity: checking for relevant prior knowledge and summarizing or reviewing when it is discovered that the students do not have the knowledge necessary to begin the day's lesson. Had Ms. Koker not discovered early in the lesson that students had little or no knowledge of the day's topic, she might have gone on to more advanced concepts, never realizing her students did not have a basis for understanding the material she was presenting. As it was, most of the lesson seemed to cover the basics of what the students should have already learned from reading the text. Phrases such as "Okay, I'll tell you" and "It's in the chapter" are clues that this class might never have encountered this information before, leading Ms. Koker to make explicit a rule that, in the future, all assigned reading for a topic must be completed before the lesson in which it is discussed.

Some other aspects of clarity involve informing the students of the skills or understanding expected at the end of the lesson and organizing the content for future lessons. Recall that, to some extent, Ms. Koker's opening remark reflects both these aspects of clarity. The students are informed of the three forms of government to be covered and are told that they are expected to know how to form the three types of government at the end of the unit. Both of these ingredients of the day's lesson help to organize Ms. Koker's lesson in advance and make it more understandable.

OBSERVING INSTRUCTIONAL VARIETY

Another lens through which to observe Ms. Koker's classroom is instructional variety, which includes the varied use of rewards, reinforcements, and types of questions asked (e.g., recall vs. application), as well as the teacher's use of instructional media to enhance student attention and engagement with the lesson. It also involves the flexibility of the teacher to change strategies or shift directions when needed. Variety can be enhanced by a teacher's animation (through variation in eye contact, voice, and gestures), as well as through the use of different instructional strategies and media within the same lesson. We do not see Ms. Koker teaching, but from what we read, there seems to be little variety in her classroom. She persists with her questioning technique, even though she seems to have little success with it, until finally, out of necessity, she assumes a more direct lecture approach by the end of the lesson. Also, notice that her questions call only for basic facts and definitions: "What is a monarchy?" and "Can you tell us what an oligarchy is?" instead of "What are its advantages and disadvantages?" "How is it formed?" or "What value should we place on the three forms of government for governing ourselves?" Focusing only on the factual recall of information might have failed to engage some students in the learning process who might have been able to speak to the application, analysis, and even synthesis of this knowledge.

Instructional variety is also achieved by choosing specific activity structures to convey lesson content. The term **activity structure** refers both to how the students are organized for learning and to how the lesson is organized. Both categories of structure appear in Ms. Koker's classroom. For example, we note that Ms. Koker chooses to organize her instruction around student recitation in an almost drill-and-practice format. The choice of a recitation format leads Ms. Koker to call on students one by one in a predesignated order, as might be done if students were giving their answers orally to questions from a workbook. The results are factual responses that avoid any risk on the part of the students, rather than the type of responses that could result in more complex or integrated learning. We noted previously the possible mismatch between such a format and what appears to be the discussion-oriented goal of her lesson. At that time, we suspected that this structure was selected more as a way to manage classroom talk than as an effective vehicle for achieving the goals of the lesson.

Perhaps because of her concern about classroom management, Ms. Koker relies on questions and lecture to transmit the content of the lesson and devotes little time to applying the concepts learned, checking for the accuracy of understanding, or summarizing and reviewing. All of these activities may not be equally appropriate for this lesson, and all need not be present for effective instruction; however, the conflict between Ms. Koker's activity structure and the goals of the lesson suggests the need for more instructional variety than has been offered. For instance, Ms. Koker might use group discussion and questions having several right answers to elicit critical thinking, reasoning, and problem solving, especially with regard to the applicability of her lesson to current events.

OBSERVING THE TEACHER'S TASK ORIENTATION

A teacher's task orientation is the percentage of time allocated to a lesson in which the teacher is actually teaching material related to the topic. In the dialogue, attention to the misbehavior of individual students, time spent introducing new rules about conduct and academic work, and interruption from the school administrator all take their toll on the time that could have been devoted to instruction. As a result of these interruptions, the time Ms. Koker actually spends teaching the content is limited. When teachers inefficiently handle misbehavior or spend large amounts of class time doing clerical chores (e.g., passing out papers, stapling and collating, reprimanding misbehaving students) that might be done more efficiently in other ways or at other times, a teacher's task orientation might be only a small percentage of the total amount of time allocated to the lesson. Although we have no way of knowing the exact amount of time during which Ms. Koker's instruction was interrupted by noninstructional demands, a simple count of the total number of lines of dialogue minus the number of lines containing dialogue *unrelated* to the goals of the lesson reveals that about 34% of Ms. Koker's teaching was off-task. If this continued throughout the school day, more than 18 minutes of every hour would be devoted to noninstructional events.

Although we see only a brief view of Ms. Koker's classroom, she makes some important decisions about classroom rules, the use of reinforcement, and the handling of misbehavior that affect the amount of time devoted to instruction during the lesson.

OBSERVING STUDENTS' ENGAGEMENT IN THE LEARNING PROCESS

A sixth lens through which to observe a lesson is student engagement in the learning process. Like the task orientation of a teacher, this behavior is often measured as a percentage of time. Student engagement in the learning process pertains to the percentage of time during which the teacher is presenting instructionally relevant content (is task oriented) that students are acting on, thinking about, or otherwise using. In contrast to a teacher's task orientation, a student's engagement in the learning process may be much more difficult to determine. A student may look attentive or appear to be working through the workbook, but her thoughts may be miles away. During the time Ms. Koker is teaching, we can be sure that at least some of her students are not engaged in the learning process.

By relying on individual recitation, Ms. Koker does little to actively involve students in the lesson. Aside from her questions and a few attempts to reward a correct answer with praise, Ms. Koker seems to encourage only a passive or mechanical involvement in the lesson. Absent from Ms. Koker's lesson is a broad range of questions that might excite the imagination of students and encourage them to keep trying after a wrong answer or no answer.

Perhaps most relevant to the apparent disengagement of some of the students is Ms. Koker's drill-and-practice style, which requires students to respond in order across rows. This ordered-turns approach is often recommended for content in which many discrete pieces of knowledge with clearly defined right and wrong answers are being recalled. But Ms. Koker's content seems concept-oriented. Yet after a time, students in certain parts of the room can be fairly sure that they will not be called on for a while, providing even more opportunity for these students to disengage from the learning process. This, together with Ms. Koker's sometimes critical responses to a wrong answer or no answer, may provide a reason for those who have already responded to turn their attention elsewhere. If Ms. Koker is seeking more complicated and time-consuming responses, it may be better for her to call on students who volunteer or who can provide answers around which she can build lesson content. And, toward the end of the lesson, Ms. Koker can also use any of a number of cooperative group activities to encourage greater student participation.

Finally, did you notice the unevenness of the praise given to students during this dialogue? Ms. Koker does not do much to encourage participation in the learning process or to reinforce effective performance, and so she fails to offer much motivation or a reason for students to work harder. The word *good* to acknowledge a correct answer is used only twice during the entire lesson and, when used, is not accompanied by any specifics to make the praise meaningful to the learner. A *meaningful* system of praise and feedback is essential to encourage student engagement in the learning process.

OBSERVING STUDENT SUCCESS

What signs of student success do you see in Ms. Koker's classroom? Student success pertains to the percentage of correct responses given to classroom questions, class exercises, and workbook assignments. When an expository or didactic approach (which seems to fit Ms. Koker's recitation format) to learning is used, the percentage of student success after the first time through the material should be about 60 to 80% to encourage further response and engagement in the learning process. When the success rate is, on the average, less than 60%, it might indicate that the lesson content is too difficult or that exercises and questions are at an inappropriate level for the material being taught. Ultimately, homework and further assignments should work toward creating an average success rate of 90% or higher. Failure to actively involve students in the lesson and present instruction that most students can respond to correctly are indications that the level of the lesson might not be properly matched to the students' current level of understanding.

As with student engagement, there are certain teacher activities that encourage a moderate to high success rate. These include providing correctives immediately following a wrong or partially right answer, dividing lesson content into small segments at the learners' current level of understanding, planning transitions to new content in small easy-to-grasp steps, and continually relating the parts of the lesson to larger objectives and goals (e.g., "We're heading toward an understanding of democracy").

It also seems that Ms. Koker's questions function more as a test to see how much the students already know than as a way to build on their existing knowledge. Instead of using her questions to fine-tune and lift student responses to higher levels, Ms. Koker's questions cover broad, undigested areas of content. Some retrenchment—or returning to simpler concepts or divisions of content—might be called for. Seatwork assigned prior to the day's lesson is one way to check student success rate. If a low success rate is confirmed, Ms. Koker could provide more practice opportunities or cooperative learning activities to actively engage students in the learning process before embarking on the next lesson.

OBSERVING HIGHER THOUGHT PROCESSES AND PERFORMANCE OUTCOMES

The final lens through which to observe Ms. Koker's classroom takes the previous lens, student success, to a higher level. For this lens our focus turns from the recitation of correct responses to higher thought processes, which arise out of teaching and learning activities that promote critical thinking, decision making, and problem solving. These processes cannot be measured by tests of cognitive achievement alone. The higher thought processes required for analyzing, synthesizing, and decision making in adult contexts are stimulated by interacting with peers and adults and by increasing awareness of one's own learning.

By requiring oral responses, Ms. Koker encourages students to exhibit higher thought processes. But then she fails to follow up on her students' responses and lift them to a higher level. Recall that most of her responses are short and noncorrective, often moving to another student if the response was right or failing to probe more deeply with another question if the response was incorrect. Ms. Koker saw each answer as either correct or incorrect—not as an opportunity to make a wrong answer right or a good answer better. This left her students responding at the lowest level of behavioral complexity, even though her lesson seemed, at times, aimed at acquiring concepts that allowed for patterns of decision making and judgments to emerge.

In other words, Ms. Koker's presentation lacked a plan for helping her students meaningfully learn the content. For example, alerting her students at the start of the lesson to look for some of the features that could be used to distinguish a monarchy from an oligarchy from a democracy might have encouraged her students to analyze the differences between various forms of government, their purposes in history, and their advantages or disadvantages in today's world. Although not every lesson need achieve these types of higher thought processes, teachers can and should capitalize on potential opportunities when they are present.

Even when student collaboration is not a stated lesson objective, students collaborating with one another or building on the responses of others spontaneously create classroom interaction that engages more students and improves student understanding of the concepts being presented. Ms. Koker could have shaped responses in small steps or allowed the thoughts and judgments of individual students to inform the group, so that larger concepts, patterns of thinking, and judgments could have accumulated gradually and cooperatively. With the use of student responses and collaborative learning activities to encourage problem-solving and judgment skills, routine recitation at the beginning of the class might have turned into higher thought processes by the end of the class. In later chapters, you will learn about strategies that can be used to achieve and observe higher thought processes in your classroom.

PREPARING TO OBSERVE IN REAL CLASSROOMS

If you think our description of this classroom seems a bit unfair, you're probably right. A lot happens to Ms. Koker in less time than it generally takes to teach a single lesson. Although our picture is compressed for illustrative purposes, teachers at all levels of experience and training face and must manage similar events. Real teachers in real classrooms are never immune from these and similar problems, despite the extent of their training or years of experience.

As we prepare to leave Ms. Koker's class, it is important to note the interrelationship among all eight lenses through which we viewed these classroom events. Seldom is the behavior observed under one lens independent of that observed under others. This reflects the interactive nature of life in classrooms. In other words, if we were to observe Ms. Koker's classroom with only one or even a few of our lenses, an incomplete and possibly distorted observation would result. This is especially obvious when we consider how the learning climate established by Ms. Koker, her classroom management techniques, and the presentation of content all worked to influence student behavior. Remember, too, that Ms. Koker's behavior, classroom management style, and presentation were influenced by her students' behavior. Therefore, it would be futile to separate these interactive aspects of a classroom in real life. Although future chapters will cover each of the lenses individually to reveal their unique features, our final goal as experienced observers is to understand the overall patterns and rhythms of classrooms using all of our lenses.

Using these eight lenses as a guide, your visits to classrooms will be even more productive if you plan what will be needed before your classroom visit, during your observation, and after you leave.

Activities before the Observation

Except for an occasional school administrator, most teachers are not accustomed to being observed. As a result, the teachers you observe might feel some anxiety and even wonder if their professional competence will be questioned or judged. During an observation, these concerns can interfere with a teacher's performance and make it less representative of typical behavior. This is why establishing a congenial relationship with the teacher is an important first step to observing in classrooms. This section first looks at some of the ways you can create and maintain a positive relationship with the teachers you will be observing and then introduces some of the tools needed to make this relationship enduring and productive.

One of the first tasks you will face in this process is selecting whom to observe. If you are observing prior to practice teaching, the classrooms will most likely be chosen for you, and cooperation will be ensured through prior agreement. During your practice teaching, however, some observation outside your cooperating teacher's classroom may be expected of you, which you will need to arrange on your own. It is here that you will need to make some important decisions concerning whom to observe and how to introduce yourself and the observation task.

Whom to Observe

As you become familiar with your school, many subjects of observation will appear as a result of your informal day-to-day interactions with teachers and students. Your initial observations should be of those who are teaching in your areas of certification, and preferably those teaching the subjects you will be assigned to teach. Naturally, therefore, your first subject of attention should be your cooperating/supervising teacher. This will create a convenient opportunity to rehearse the skills you will need later in less familiar settings.

Your next priority for observation should be a teacher who teaches grades or subjects similar to those of your cooperating teacher, who can help introduce you to others teaching at the same grade level or content area. Over time, your observations can include other teachers in the school who may not be teaching grades or subjects you are likely to teach in the immediate future but which you may be interested in at some subsequent time.

Finally, observations should be made in classrooms where your experience within the school, communication with other teachers, and attention to student comments indicate something of special importance is happening. These observations might afford you the opportunity to view particularly dynamic personalities, innovative teaching methods, or instruction devoted exclusively to a particular type of student (e.g., gifted, English language learners, or at-risk students). Because these targets of observation might come to your attention informally, they may be far removed from the grade level or subject matter you will be teaching. These excursions into unfamiliar subjects and grades are well worth the effort because of the new ideas, creativity, and excitement they will return to you.

Introducing Yourself

During your first days in a school, introduce yourself to as many teachers as possible. Few teachers will simply turn down a request to observe, but some might provide excuses why it would not be advisable that day or that week, until they know something about you. As odd as it might seem, even some of the best and most experienced teachers are sometimes defensive and shy about being observed. Without extra effort on your part, some of the teachers from whom you might benefit the most might not, at first, comply with your request. This is all the more reason that a pleasant introduction should precede a request to observe. Blurting out "I'd like to observe you during fourth period today" before a teacher has even had the opportunity to get to know you is likely to create some defensiveness. The purpose of a prior introduction is to reduce any defensiveness and dispel the fear of the unknown. Identifying yourself by name, the institution at which you are studying, and the cooperating teacher with whom you are working may be a sufficient introduction. But, if time permits, mentioning your career goals ("I would like to teach such and such in such and such type of school") and how the subject or grade you are requesting to observe relates to those goals ("You are teaching the type of students I am likely to face on my first job") will enhance your chances of obtaining permission. Your request to observe, therefore, should follow a friendly exchange in which the teacher from whom you are requesting permission learns your name, institution, cooperating teacher, immediate career goals, and how your career goals relate to the teaching you will be observing. Once permission is obtained, the important information described in the following sections should be exchanged with the teacher prior to your observation.

Identifying Your Goals for the Observation

It is important to convey to the teacher your goals for the observation. This need be only a sentence or two that communicates your reason for being there (other than that the observation is being required of you). Your reason can be general ("I would like to observe students at this age" or "learn about classroom management techniques") or specific ("I would like to get

familiar with the texts and instructional material being used at this grade level"). Relaying your observation goals tends to reduce the anxiety a teacher might otherwise experience because of a belief that your observation may include a personal value judgment on professional competence.

Finding Out the Day's Lesson

Next, you will need to determine the teacher's goal for the lesson and how this goal fits into some broader sequence of instruction. Without knowing the purpose of the day's lesson, what you see can easily be taken out of context. Goals can be misunderstood, procedures misread, and reasons behind activities confused unless you find out where a given lesson is coming from. Knowing lesson and unit goals will help you avoid wasting precious observation time trying to figure out the purpose of the day's lesson.

Finding Out about the Students

Before your observation, you will want to know about the ability level of the students. This might seem obvious in some cases (e.g., when the course you will be observing is a tracked or pregrouped class devoted entirely to the needs of certain types of learners). Yet every group has unique characteristics, no matter how it may be described. Ask if any students in the class are being mainstreamed, are English language learners, or have special learning needs that may influence what you see. Although your observation may confirm or challenge these labels, your knowledge of how the teacher views this class might be as important for making sense of what you see as the observation data itself. Knowing how a teacher perceives the class might provide valuable insights as to why she engaged in one activity over another, or why she used some materials rather than others.

How to Be Introduced

You will also need to consider how you wish to be introduced. Often, the teacher you are observing will have a preference for introducing you. At other times, however, you will be asked how you wish to be introduced. Typically, such introductions are short, stating your name, affiliation, and a few other details. Limiting the introduction to only a few brief facts will diminish attention to you during your observation. If the class experiences frequent visitors like yourself, the teacher may even choose not to introduce you. However, if the class is unaccustomed to having visitors, an introduction is desirable because the students' attention during much of the class may be devoted to figuring out just who you are and why you have come to their class.

Where to Sit

Prior to your observation, you'll need to determine where to sit. Although the existing arrangement of desks and chairs in the classroom might limit some options, it is preferable for you to be seated outside the center of action. Front-row seats or seats in which the majority of students are facing you usually deter effective observation by making your every move noticeable. Consequently, your placement in the classroom, preferably toward the back and out of the center of attention, can be an important aid to your observation. When, out of kindness or respect, a teacher places you in the center of attention, you should politely request a change if an alternative seating arrangement is available.

In summary, prior to an observation you should

1. Decide whom to observe.
2. Introduce yourself.
3. Identify your goals for the observation.
4. Determine placement of the lesson in the curriculum.
5. Find out about the students to be taught.
6. Arrange for your introduction to the class.
7. Establish a place to sit.

Steps 1 through 5 are best completed during a conference prior to the lesson you will be observing. Because these steps might require more than a few moments on your part or the teacher's, it is best if they are not completed in the few hectic minutes before class, when the teacher might be trying to prepare for the next class or make the transition to the next subject. On the other hand, steps 6 and 7 often are completed immediately before the observation begins.

Activities during the Observation

Activities at the start of the lesson are designed to help you feel comfortable in the role of observer and avoid some of the problems that typically confront someone attempting to record events in a fast-paced classroom. Simple preparations at this stage can have a large impact on the quality of your observation.

Unless you feel comfortable physically, you will not feel comfortable psychologically. This means that your body comfort often takes precedence over, and can even control, your thoughts and actions. Your comfort and ability to feel natural in the classroom therefore might be of paramount importance to being able to accurately perceive events around you. As we will see in subsequent chapters, some types of observations require that classroom events be coded and recorded rapidly and systematically. To do this

you must be seated in a way that allows you to see all the events occurring in a classroom. Sit at a desk or in a chair with a back, so that your notes and records will not have to be taken from an awkward or artificial position. If a desk is not used, you'll need a practical writing surface that can be supported effortlessly, such as a clipboard. These choices will help you avoid fatigue, writing cramps, and frustration at not being able to record your observations quickly and legibly. Although your choice of a seat will be determined by the type of furniture in the classroom, avoid the use of stools, chairs of awkward height, or tables covered with equipment or materials, and don't try to write against a wall or on the top of a file cabinet or bookcase. Some of these suggestions might seem unimportant before you observe; however, you'll discover that the task of observing and recording classroom events is demanding enough that, even when you are seated comfortably, you may tire before the end of a single class period.

Once you're seated comfortably, wait until things calm down to begin your observation. You'll probably be the center of attention for the first few moments, regardless of your out-of-the-way placement in the classroom and low-key introduction. Depending on the number of other recent visitors to this classroom, an initial period of turbulence set off by your presence may last from a few seconds to several minutes. Before useful observation can begin, you will want to wait out any disturbance your presence might have caused in the natural flow of events. To help reestablish a normal routine, wait calmly with a pleasant expression and with your eyes focused on the teacher.

As classroom activities unfold, a source of distraction to your observations may come from the students seated around you, asking questions about you, about your purpose for being there, or even about their schoolwork. Usually, a polite but firm refusal to be drawn in will help students turn their focus away from you. You might find it helpful to avoid direct eye contact, especially with those students seated closest to you. Scan the room broadly, focusing most of the time on the teacher and, when necessary, on individual students seated at more distant points.

Activities after the Observation

At the conclusion of your observation, give a brief word of thanks to the teacher. Teachers rarely have more than a few moments of free time between classes or periods, and even less when changing from one subject to another at the elementary level, so a quick comment such as "Thanks, I enjoyed the class" is always welcome. Just as your introduction before class served to break the ice and turn possible anxiety about your presence into a more constructive feeling, so can your goodbye dispel any remaining anxiety or apprehension. The intent of both these communications, before and after, is to dispel any belief that value judgments are being made about the professional competence of the teacher.

Because this moment is very important in setting the stage for future observations, try to relate an upbeat or memorable event that occurred during the observation. For example, you could mention how the observation session was helpful to you: "Seeing how you used the overhead projector was helpful to me because I'm required to use visuals in my next presentation" or "The approach you used to handle Jason's off-task behavior seemed really effective." Although it is important not to exaggerate the importance of seeing a particular event, nearly all observers see interesting, if not effective, techniques during a single period of instruction. Make a mental note to look for such an event before your observation begins and write it down when it occurs so you can relate it to the teacher when you offer thanks for being allowed to observe.

Finally, immediately following your observation you will need to find a quiet place to review and enhance the notes and records you made. As we will see in subsequent chapters, these notes and records can take many forms; however, they seldom will be in final, usable form immediately following an observation, because of omissions, vague references, incompleteness, and illegibility. Classroom events occur far too rapidly for notes to perfectly represent the events that took place, although a laptop computer can help. Therefore, some filling in is usually necessary while the events of the classroom are still fresh in your mind. Even an hour's delay can make an important difference in filling in the subject of a vague reference, remembering an antecedent event that makes a later event more logical, or correcting illegible handwriting, which may be the key to deciphering important words later. Because the observation will still be fresh in your mind, this period of reflection can also be a time of insight and understanding. You will want to make more notes—or notes about your notes—reminding you of and highlighting events you may want to bring up later in discussions with the teacher you observed, your cooperating teacher, your college or university supervisor, or in a methods class you might be taking.

Now that we have covered some of the basics of what to do before, during, and after an observation, you're ready to work through the following activities to apply your understanding. In the next chapter we will look at some ways of recording your observations, and, in the chapters ahead, we will consider each of the eight lenses in greater detail.

For More Information

A helpful guide to getting ready for your first classroom observation has been prepared by Marianne Pennekamp and edited by Tom Allen. Their guide includes important steps to follow, some professional behavior you will need to be mindful of, and some additional elements to look for during your observation. Their guide can be accessed at www.humboldt.edu/~tha1/observ.html.

Key Term

activity structure, 26

Activities

1. Using Instrument 3.2, identify the subjects and grade levels you would like to observe. Assign numbers to the boxes to indicate the order in which you would like to observe these classrooms. For each entry, identify one purpose for observation in that area. Express your purpose in a form suitable for communicating to the teacher being observed, such as "I would like to see your class of fourth graders in reading to observe student interaction (or interruptions, learning styles, etc.)."

2. Seating arrangements of two different classrooms appear in Figures 3.1 and 3.2. Place an X on two seats in each classroom to indicate suitable observation positions. Now refer to the classroom dia-

FIGURE 3.1   Classroom 1 Seating Arrangement

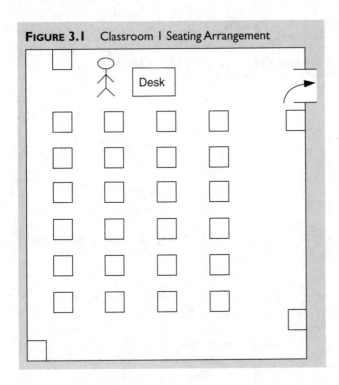

gram in Figure 3.3. Assume you can move a seat to a point from which to observe. Indicate where you would place it with an *X*.

3. Look over the dialogue from Ms. Koker's classroom for other observable signs of effective or ineffective teaching. Make a list of the signs you notice. Compare your list with a classmate's and revise yours to include any additions or omissions suggested by your classmate. Using the signs you and your classmate listed, in what ways could Ms. Koker improve her teaching?

4. With a classmate, arrange to observe a classroom for approximately one class period. During this time, use the second copy of the General Observation Form (Instrument 3.1b) to focus on the eight patterns of effective teaching. Immediately following the observation, compare your ratings, discuss your differences, and try to create a common rating on which you both can agree. What are your overall conclusions pertaining to each of the eight lenses?

5. To gain a sense of the number and content of teacher–student exchanges that occur in a classroom, arrange to observe in a classroom where there is likely to be some teacher–student interaction (questions and answers, discussion, or oral checking and feedback). Divide the time devoted to your observation into three equal parts (e.g., approximately three 15-minute segments). This activity may be completed in pairs.

FIGURE 3.2   Classroom 2 Seating Arrangement

a. During the first 15 minutes, count the number of teacher-to-student and student-to-teacher interchanges that occur and record the occurrence of each with a tally in the appropriate box in Figure 3.4. For example, a teacher question addressed to a student would count as one tally, and a student response back to the teacher would count as another.

b. During the next 15-minute segment of your observation, continue observing teacher–student

FIGURE 3.3   Classroom to Be Observed

FIGURE 3.4 Number of Classroom Interactions between Teacher and Students

Teacher Exchange Directed to Student	Student Exchange Directed to Teacher

interaction, but this time record the number of student-to-teacher and teacher-to-student exchanges that pertain to (a) lesson content, (b) procedural matters (directions and clerical tasks), and (c) discipline or classroom management (restating rules, giving warnings, or assigning punishment). Use the boxes in Figure 3.5 to tally the number of teacher–student exchanges in each of these areas during this part of your observation.

c. During the last 15 minutes of your observation, continue observing teacher–student interactions. This time, record your tallies according to whether the exchange is brief (lasting approximately 5 seconds or less) or extended (lasting more than 5 seconds), using the boxes in Figure 3.6. Include the complete exchange as a single tally—record the teacher-to-student statement and the student response to the teacher (if applicable) as a single unit.

d. After the observation, state three general conclusions, supported by the data you have collected

in each of the three boxes, about the climate, focus, and pace of the classroom.

6. Reflecting on the classroom you have just observed, write down on the back of the General Observation Form any interruptions you can recall that might have occurred either for administrative or clerical reasons or as a result of student misbehavior. How typical do you feel these interruptions are of this and other classrooms throughout the school year?

7. In the classroom you have just observed, identify one significant event, behavior, or episode that you noticed but the teacher did not. Suggest some reasons why, in this instance, the teacher might have been unaware. If the teacher had noticed this event, behavior, or episode, would it have changed in any way the manner in which this lesson was presented?

8. Think about whether your impression of this classroom was generally positive or negative. Now consider the following sources of selective percep-

FIGURE 3.5 Classroom Interactions in Three Areas

Exchanges Involving Lesson Content	Exchanges Involving Procedural Matters	Exchanges Involving Discipline or Classroom Management

Figure 3.6   Duration of Classroom Interactions

Brief Exchange (5 seconds or less)	Extended Exchange (more than 5 seconds)

tion both from outside ourselves and from within ourselves:

- Student ability and achievements
- Classroom characteristics (physical context)
- Participation and cooperativeness of students
- Experience and education of the teacher
- School, grade, and subject matter
- Individual and cultural diversity
- Your own level of experience with similar classrooms
- Recent educational influences and training
- Who might be watching (e.g., your supervisor, the students)
- Who may find out (e.g., the teacher)

Place a check mark beside any of the statements that you believe might have influenced your ratings on the General Observation Form you completed for Activity 4.

9. If you are interested in teaching elementary grades, reading instruction will be an important part of your developing expertise. Copy the Reading Lesson Observation Framework from the article listed here and use it to observe a reading lesson. What did you notice about the framework? What important insights about this classroom did the "Observation Framework" provide?

Henk, W. A., Moore, J. C., Marinak, B. A., & Tomasetti, B. W. (2000). A Reading Lesson Observation Framework for elementary teachers, principals, and literacy supervisors. *Reading Teacher, 53*(5), 358–369.

4

Seeing beyond Personal Experiences and Expectations: Learning to Observe Systematically

There is no such thing in anyone's life as an unimportant day.

Alexander Woollcott

One assumption of an experienced observer is that nothing observed is unimportant. What the experienced observer is saying is that "everything is related to everything else" and that there are few, if any, coincidences in life—or in classrooms. This chapter will provide tools and techniques that can help you make sense out of the myriad relationships that occur in classrooms—relationships between students and teacher, among students, between students and text, and between teacher and media, as well as the more subtle relationships and patterns that occur over days, weeks, and months in a classroom. When you use the tools and techniques of this chapter to observe systematically, you will soon realize that nothing is as important to life in classrooms as that which, at first glance, appears unimportant.

In Chapter 2, we learned that structure—or focus—is a key element that distinguishes *observing* from *looking*. We also discussed the fact that our personal observations are colored by our experiences and expectations. Learning to observe in a focused or systematic way can help us balance what we expect to see with what actually occurs in a classroom, resulting in a more complete understanding of teaching. This chapter will present several methods for observing systematically and recording what is seen.

WHY OBSERVE SYSTEMATICALLY?

Like the humans in the cartoon (Figure 4.1), we often go through life seeing what we expect to see, failing to question our assumptions and our conclusions—even though they may be erroneous. If we approach learning to teach in the same manner, we will likely miss many learning opportunities. But how does a person learn to *observe* rather than merely *watch* or *look at* classroom events? Systematic observation, defining a specific purpose for observing and choosing a method for recording the observations, is one way to enhance observation skills. In Chapter 2, eight professional frames—or lenses—for observation were introduced. Some specific purposes for observing in these areas were also described, such as the extent to which

1. A teacher's classroom conveys a balance between warmth and control (learning climate).
2. A system of rules and procedures operates to minimize interruptions and time spent on noninstructional tasks (classroom management).
3. The instruction presented is at, or slightly above, the students' current level of understanding (lesson clarity).
4. The teacher conveys enthusiasm and animation through variation in eye contact, voice, and body movement and selects appropriate experiences to engage students in a wide variety of learning activities (instructional variety).
5. The teacher exhibits a systematic cycle of instruction, review, testing, and feedback (task orientation).
6. The teacher monitors work in progress and checks for student understanding (student engagement in the learning process).
7. Feedback is given immediately following student responses to firm up, extend, or correct responses (student success).
8. Models or strategies for learning are provided that promote critical thinking, reasoning, and problem solving (higher thought processes and performance outcomes).

Although a classroom observer could gain much insight into classroom processes and events by asking teachers and students about their thoughts and feelings, opportunities for such interviews will probably be rare, given the busy nature of most classrooms. Furthermore, interviews do not always accurately reflect a person's interpretation of the world because interviews can be influenced by many other factors, including the participant's view of why the interview is taking place. For example, a student or teacher might answer your interview questions based on a perception of how you want them answered rather than on an honest personal opinion. As a result, we must find additional ways to gain insights about teaching that

FIGURE 4.1

Larson, G. (1984). *The Far Side Gallery*. Kansas City, MO: FarWorks, Inc., p. 26.

may complement or support what might be reported in an interview.

One alternative involves the use of classroom visits. Much useful information can be gained during these visits by noting observable behaviors and the contexts in which they occur. Table 4.1 identifies some observable signs that might be used to record behavior through each of our eight lenses. These signs can be recorded independently of the subjective perceptions of the classroom participants. This allows you, as the observer, to determine what to observe as well as what importance to assign to particular events. Making a record of what you observe *while you observe* will also help you remember events

you might otherwise forget after the visit *and* notice patterns you didn't see while in the classroom.

METHODS FOR OBSERVING AND RECORDING

Because systematic observation involves observing and then recording behavioral signs in a form that can be retrieved and studied at a later time, it usually involves a recording form, or instrument. The instruments used for recording classroom behavior can range from relatively unstructured (taking notes)

TABLE 4.1   Observable Signs Pertaining to the Eight Question Areas

				Question Areas			
Learning Climate	Classroom Management	Lesson Clarity	Instructional Variety	Task Orientation	Student Engagement in the Learning Process	Student Success	Performance Outcomes and Higher Thought Processes
Degree to which students can express their feelings and opinions	Use of preestablished classroom rules	Frequency of examples, illustrations, and demonstrations	Use of attention-gaining devices	Orderliness of transitions	Use of exercises and activities to elicit student responses	Number of correct or partially correct answers	Use of teaming, pairing, or other cooperative activities that encourage student problem solving
Frequency with which student responses are used and extended	Use of instructional routines	Percentage of students who can follow directions given	Changes in voice inflection, body movement, and eye contact	Teacher's preorganization of administrative tasks	Monitoring and checking during seatwork	Number of right answers acknowledged or reinforced	Display of student products and projects
Amount of interaction and sharing among learners	System of incentives and consequences	Use of review and summary	Use of a mix of learning modalities (visual, oral)	Cycles of review, testing, and feedback	Use of remedial or programmed materials for lower-performing learners	Number of delayed corrections vs. immediate corrections	Opportunities for independent practice and application

to highly structured (involving explicit procedures for when and how long to observe specific behaviors). This chapter will discuss and illustrate three general methods that are useful for recording behavior in classrooms—narrative (open-ended) reports, rating scales, and classroom coding systems. These methods are arranged in order from least structured to most structured and include examples for actual use in classroom observation. Although classroom observers may not need to construct instruments or recording formats of their own, the need often arises to revise existing instruments to better fit local conditions and specific observation needs. Accordingly, it is important that classroom observers be aware of the formats available for recording their observations and the advantages and disadvantages of each.

Method 1: Narrative Reports

Narrative reports represent the least structured of our three general categories. Narrative reports do not specify the exact behavioral signs to be observed, but instead simply describe events, in written form, as they occur. Little guidance is given to the observer about what to include or exclude from the observation. Therefore, narrative reports are sometimes referred to as **open-ended reports,** meaning that

considerable flexibility is given to the observer. You may find it helpful to think of narrative reports as note-taking activities. Although there are many ways to take notes, four methods will be particularly helpful for you as you observe in classrooms—anecdotal reports, ethnographic records, thematic notes, and visual maps, each of which has advantages and disadvantages.

Anecdotal Reports

An **anecdotal report** describes a critical or unusual classroom incident, which might be related to an event of larger consequence. It takes the form of a written paragraph that describes what, how, when, and to whom the critical incident happened. Because of the special significance of separating fact from interpretation, anecdotal reports are divided into two distinct parts: (a) facts and (b) an interpretation of the facts. Example 4.1 illustrates the form of an anecdotal report.

Notice how Seana divided fact from interpretation in her report. In the first part, she writes a matter-of-fact description of what happened. In the second, she speculates about John's self-concept and even offers a judgment about the effect of this teacher's behavior on potential volunteers. Example 4.2 shows how the first part of this anecdotal report might have been

Example 4.1

Teacher: Robins

Class: Fifth grade

Subject: English

Date: January 17

Place: Oakleaf Elementary

Purpose: To observe student participation and engagement

Observer: Seana Hawkins

Incident: As class started, the teacher asked if anyone would like to read the story they had written for last night's assignment. John raised his hand. The teacher gave him permission, and he came to the front of the room. John began to read the story in a very low voice; when he had been reading for about 30 seconds, the teacher asked him to read louder, saying "Speak up, or you'll never be any good at public speaking." At this point, John stopped reading, returned to his seat, and remained silent for the rest of the class.

Interpretation: John appears to enjoy writing and sharing his creations with others. It seems, however, that he is very sensitive and gets upset easily when he receives the slightest criticism, indicating he might not have confidence in himself or in his abilities as a public speaker. The teacher's comment to John in front of the class might have reduced his confidence even further, and may discourage him and others from volunteering in the future.

Example 4.2

Teacher: Robins

Class: Fifth grade

Subject: English

Date: January 17

Place: Oakleaf Elementary

Purpose: To observe student participation and engagement

Observer: Katy Williams

Incident: As class started, the teacher asked if anyone would like to read the story they had written for last night's assignment. John shyly raised his hand. The teacher gave him permission, and he nervously came to the front of the room. John reluctantly began to read the story in a very low voice, probably because he was having second thoughts about volunteering. After what surely seemed a long time for John, the teacher asked him to speak up, scaring him with the possibility that he will never be a good public speaker. At this point, John broke down from nervousness and returned to his seat, crushed by the insensitive remark of the teacher.

written had both parts been blended together by a less skilled reporter.

Notice how Katy blends fact and speculation in her description. How did she know, for example, that John raised his hand *shyly,* came to the front of the room *nervously,* began to read *reluctantly, broke down from nervousness,* or returned to his seat *crushed?* All this might have been true, but no description in the narrative pointed to the factual character of these expressions. As you can see, separating fact from interpretation can require additional observations in other contexts before your interpretations can be verified as relevant facts or instead need to be discarded as isolated incidents that do not reflect John's (or his teacher's) typical behavior.

Anecdotal reports are most useful when they occur over time. For example, an observer who makes an initial interpretation can return to the classroom at a later date (perhaps several times) to clarify that interpretation. The focus of later observations is to expand on the interpretation's usefulness and validity. Later anecdotal reports should help clarify ambiguities, identify misinterpretations in past reports, and update and enhance factual descriptions with more recent data. Most important, when anecdotal reports focus on the same target behaviors over time (e.g., John's subsequent performances in front of the class), they can reveal patterns and regularities that might reveal the true cause of the original critical incident. For example, maybe it was the personal nature of the topic and not the teacher's behavior that was the primary cause of John's behavior in the first observation. Patterns and regularities observed over time can then be used to form a single, coherent interpretation that identifies what should be changed in the classroom or environment for improvement to occur.

Advantages

1. Anecdotal records allow behavior to be observed as it occurs in the natural setting of the classroom.
2. Data can be gathered unobtrusively, without involving those who are being observed.
3. The observer is not restricted in what to look for and can therefore feel free to record seemingly minor or unexpected behaviors that may be of significance later.
4. The observer needs little or no special training.

Disadvantages

1. The time required in maintaining and interpreting anecdotal reports can be extensive when many reports are accumulated over time.
2. The objectivity of the "facts" in a record might be overly influenced by the past behavior of the persons being observed or the beliefs of the observer about the appropriateness of what is observed.
3. Incidents recorded might be taken out of context or interpreted incorrectly because of an inadequate sampling of behavior, especially when records are not cumulative.
4. Narrative descriptions can be difficult to analyze and interpret when the behavior being observed is complex or has many different causes (school, home life, peers).

Ethnographic Records

Another method of observing and recording in a narrative form is an **ethnographic record,** which reports events sequentially, as they occur, without selecting a specific focus or incident. Ethnographic records differ from anecdotal reports in that the observer records a continuous stream of events, usually for the duration of an entire class period and occasionally longer, and records all the behavior, not just selected incidents. As with anecdotal reports, it is important that the observer record only what is observed and avoid judgments or interpretations, unless they are clearly divided from the factual portion of the record. An ethnographic record is illustrated in Example 4.3.

Notice how this ethnographic record captures the flow and sequence of events, which the anecdotal report could not. Also note how it captures almost everything, whether or not it appears to be relevant to the instructional goals of the classroom. During the class or immediately afterward, the observer can write comments in the margins that bring particularly noteworthy events into focus (e.g., effective use of rewards, student restlessness and inattention, or revealing expressions on students' faces). The numbers running down the left margin can help reference each comment for later discussion and analysis.

Unless a lesson is taped and then transcribed, it is almost impossible for an observer to record every word or action that occurs. Therefore, the objective in creating an ethnographic record is to capture, with the aid of a laptop computer, the essence of what occurs and not every detail. In this example, the observer did an effective job of recording the flow of activity in a factual, nonjudgmental manner. Later, she could highlight certain aspects of the record in bold or add interpretative comments in the margins. These could be points for discussion with a supervisor, topics to be discussed in a college or university methods class, or ideas for subsequent observations.

Advantages

1. An ethnographic record provides a comprehensive picture of the continuous flow of events from the beginning to the end of a period of observation.
2. It places events in perspective by indicating possible cause-and-effect sequences that occur in a classroom.
3. Like the anecdotal report, it requires little training or special skill.

Disadvantages

1. It can be fatiguing to record for periods longer than about 45 minutes to an hour.

Example 4.3

Teacher: Mrs. Tyler and a teacher aide

Date: November 12

Subject: Second-grade class, open classroom with teacher and aide. I will be simultaneously observing 18 children in two reading groups, 9 in each group.

Observer: Keiffer Sunden

8:30

1. The children have just been let into the
2. classroom, taking their coats off and
3. wandering around the room. Several boys
4. are in the corner, and some girls
5. are sitting on the floor playing with a puzzle.
6. The teacher is walking back and forth in the
7. back of the classroom, attending to some of
8. the children. Then, teacher and teacher aide
9. go to desk to talk to one another.

8:35

10. Mrs. Tyler leaves room. Teacher
11. aide stays seated behind her desk.

8:40

12. Mrs. Tyler comes back into
13. room. She walks to the desk at
14. far left-hand side of the classroom,
15. where there is a round table, and sits on
16. the edge. She says, "Blue Group, get your
17. folders and go up to the front. Green Group,
18. come here." Noise level drops and
19. children begin to follow orders. She
20. says, "Anybody lose a quarter?" No one
21. responds, and she repeats the question.
22. She says, "I know someone found—
23. someone lost a quarter because it was
24. found in the coat room. Look in your
25. pockets and see." No one says anything.
26. She now stands up and pulls a pile of
27. workbooks from across the table over to her.

28. They are the reading workbooks.
29. She opens the one on the top.
30. "Ah, Daniel!" she says loudly. "Your
31. work yesterday was not too bad but you
32. need some help. Evidently there are still
33. some words you don't understand." She
34. thumbs through the rest of his lesson. Danny
35. is standing at the outside of the circle around her,
36. not listening to what she is saying. Mrs. Tyler
37. now stands and gives instructions to the Green
38. Group. She tells them to go through pages
39. 8–13, reading the two stories between those
40. pages and to go over the work in the workbooks
41. that she is about to give back. She tells them
42. that they may sit anyplace but not together, and
43. then says, "And I don't want any funny business."
44. She opens the next workbook, which is Nicole's.
45. She tells Nicole she is having the same problem
46. that Danny is having, without specifying further.
47. Nicole looks up at her without any expression.
48. She then turns to a third book and says, "Michelle,
49. you're having the same problem." She says,
50. "*Snatch* means to grab. *Beach,* what
51. does it mean?" Michelle doesn't answer.
52. She has her finger in her mouth and
53. looks anxious. The teacher closes
54. the workbook and gives it to Michelle.
55. Michelle takes it and walks away with Nicole.

8:50

56. Teacher then opens the next workbook.

2. Some events might be missed because of the intense concentration required to continually record almost everything that occurs.
3. It can be inefficient and incomplete when different but equally important activities are occurring simultaneously: three or four small groups working at the same time; low-, average-, and high-performing groups pursuing their own activities; or Mike, Sue, and Betty all acting out at the same time.
4. Compiling an account of events during even a single class period can produce a voluminous document that can be time-consuming to read and digest.

These limitations aside, there are few methods that capture the real-life drama of the classroom as well as the ethnographic record.

Thematic Notes

Thematic notes are facts recorded in traditional outline form, according to predesignated categories of observation. Much like the detective at the scene of a crime who jots down facts about suspects, motives, times, and places in a notebook, you can use thematic notes to jot down relevant data. Thematic notes can be recorded using Roman numerals—I, II, III, and so on—representing the major areas to be observed (such as classroom climate, classroom management, instructional variety) and letters of the alphabet—A, B, C, and so on—representing the factual information observed under each of the more general areas. To prepare thematic notes, first determine the precise themes or areas on which to focus the observation and then jot down key facts corresponding to these areas as the action unfolds. Example 4.4 shows what an observer might have written if he had chosen to create a set of thematic notes based on the events observed during Mrs. Tyler's class.

Advantages

1. Thematic notes preorganize and focus the observer's attention, thereby increasing the depth and accuracy of what is observed.
2. If the themes are chosen thoughtfully, they can relate the events observed to previously established and theoretically sound dimensions of effective teaching.

3. They are briefer, more concise, and less time-consuming than most other types of narrative records.
4. They can provide the content outline for a more formal record or report if one is needed later.

Disadvantages

1. Thematic notes provide only general statements that may be too sketchy for recalling the factual events on which they are based.
2. They do not reveal order or sequence; for example, data recorded under Roman numeral I might not be antecedent to data recorded under Roman numeral II.
3. They focus attention only in predesignated areas, precluding the observation of other important classroom events that may arise spontaneously.

Visual Maps

Visual maps use pictures instead of words to serve much the same purpose as narratives. Visual maps

---

Example 4.4

   I. Learning climate
     A. This is an open classroom with two team teachers.
     B. Teacher speaks in firm voice, encouraging control and obedience. Teacher makes it clear to kids she doesn't want any "funny business."
     C. Teacher exchanges with kids are mostly businesslike.
     D. Atmosphere competitive (workbooks being checked) and independent (individuals reading stories and going over their workbooks).

   II. Task orientation
     A. Some students off-task during first 10 minutes of class.
     B. Teacher devotes some class time to noninstructional tasks; e.g., "Who lost a quarter?"
     C. Teacher moves from student to student informing them of the correctness of their answers in workbook.

   III. Classroom management
     A. Students enter classroom and begin work independently without specific routine (see IIA).
     B. Some feedback for good work; e.g., "Your work was not too bad," but no praise.
     C. Teacher rotates around room monitoring workbook exercises in progress.
     D. Blue Group without supervision or direction (in front of room) while teacher checks work of Green Group.

   IV. Student engagement
     A. Some students off-task first 10 minutes of class (see IIA).
     B. Students left waiting some of the time; e.g., Blue Group waits in front of room while teacher deals with Green Group.
     C. Teacher chooses not to engage students in extensive recitation or probe about workbook content. Exchanges are brief.

portray the spatial relationships among physical objects—learning centers, reference libraries, groups at work—that may be important as supplements to fully understanding anecdotal reports, ethnographic records, or thematic notes. For events that are clearly related to the spatial layout of a classroom, you'll want to construct a visual map to help you (and others) better understand your narrative record. Often, a visual map can help you explain how a particular instructional activity was implemented or cooperative activities were organized.

For example, in the ethnographic record presented in Example 4.3, it was difficult to know exactly where the Blue and Green reading groups were in the classroom, other than that the Blue Group was told to get their folders and go to the front. Did something physically divide the groups to help foster (or perhaps detract from) their respective assignments? If the observer had provided a visual map with his ethnographic record, we might have better understood the fact that two groups were being taught at the same time and that Mrs. Tyler was dealing with only one, the Green Group, while leaving the Blue Group somewhere in front of the class awaiting instruction. A visual map corresponding to this record might take the form shown in Figure 4.2.

We learn a number of important details from this picture. For example, neither the Blue nor the Green

Group has enough chairs to be seated as a group. Danny is standing, apparently because there is no seat, and the teacher's aide is far removed from the Blue Group, leaving this group almost entirely on its own. Our understanding of the events in this classroom is also increased by seeing that *front*, as it is used by Mrs. Tyler in her instructions to the Blue Group, represents a portion of the classroom unattended by either the teacher or the teacher aide. These might be significant details for gaining a complete picture of this classroom and for properly interpreting the events occurring within it.

Method 2: Rating Scales

Narrative reports allow the observer a great deal of flexibility in choosing which behaviors will be observed. On the other hand, rating scales are more structured and offer you the opportunity to record not only what behaviors you observe, but also the degree of the behavior observed. In order to use a rating scale, you identify in advance the behaviors you want to observe. **Rating scales** can be used individually or in conjunction with other observation tools such as narrative reports or thematic notes. Two popular rating scale formats are checklists and summated ratings.

Checklists

The simplest type of rating scale, a **checklist**, consists of a list of the behaviors to be observed alongside a yes/no or present/absent response scale. Your job as an observer is simply to note the presence or absence of a particular behavior during an observation and mark it on the scale. Simple checklists of this sort are most useful when you are observing behaviors that are difficult to evaluate in degree, but that can be confidently identified as either present or absent.

Checklists can be scored by assigning weights of $+1$ and -1 to the behaviors rated, depending on whether the behaviors are positively or negatively stated. After the weights are summed and averaged across items, a decision can be made as to whether the average score indicates a positive or negative outcome, as seen in Figure 4.3. Notice that this method of coding responses automatically places the concept being observed (e.g., group participation) on a -1 to $+1$ continuum, with 0 as the neutral point. The average of the seven items on this scale would be $4 + (-3) = 1, 1/7 = 0.14$, indicating a slightly positive outcome, with 0 as the neutral point.

There are times, however, when you might not have the opportunity to observe all the behaviors on a checklist. For example, if you observed a class only

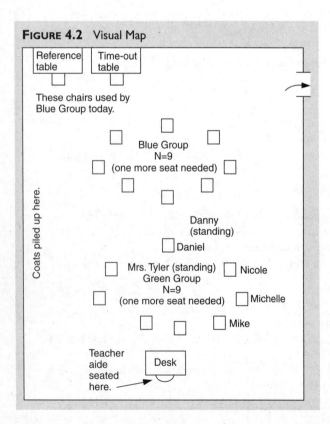

FIGURE 4.2   Visual Map

FIGURE 4.3 Checklist for Determining an Individual Student's Group Participation

Shares information	(Yes)	No
	(+ 1)	(− 1)
Contributes ideas	(Yes)	No
	(+ 1)	(− 1)
Listens to others	Yes	(No)
	(+ 1)	(− 1)
Follows instructions	(Yes)	No
	(+ 1)	(− 1)
Shows initiative in solving group problems	(Yes)	No
	(+ 1)	(− 1)
Accepts and carries out group-determined tasks	Yes	(No)
	(+ 1)	(− 1)
Gives consideration to the viewpoints of others	Yes	(No)
	(+ 1)	(− 1)

while a student was discussing her own ideas, there would be no opportunity to determine whether that pupil "Listens to others." Thus, a checklist should indicate whether the observer had the opportunity to observe the behavior, as well as the presence or absence of that behavior, as shown by the checklist format in Figure 4.4, in which summation and averaging of codes would be done only for the behaviors that were actually observed. Thus, the average for this set of items would be 3 + (−1) = 2, 2/4 = 0.50, indicating a fairly positive outcome.

Summated Ratings

Summated ratings differ from checklists in that more than two degrees of discrimination are possible. Summated rating scales help you focus more closely on the degree of behavior because they typically allow descriptions of behavior at either extreme and at selected intermediate points. Summated rating scales require an observer to discern not only whether a behavior is present or absent, but to what degree

the behavior is present or absent. As you observe a behavior, you compare what you observe with the scale and choose the degree that best matches your observation. When items represent a common underlying theme, scores across individual scales are summed and averaged, hence the name **summated ratings.** Although summated rating scales require more knowledge on the observer's part, they also provide more specific information regarding the focus of the observation. The most common summated rating scales offer five or seven degrees of discrimination.

5-Point Scales. 5-point rating scales are customarily referred to as Likert scales. In the Likert scale, five intervals, or degrees of differentiation, are used to distinguish levels of proficiency. Because you may need to construct a summated rating scale to reflect your particular observation interests and questions, Figure 4.5 includes a number of examples of how this can be done.

FIGURE 4.4 Checklist and Codes for the Presence or Absence of a Behavior

No Opportunity to Observe	Observed		Code Given
☐	☐	Shares information	−1
☐	☑	Contributes ideas	+1
☑	☐	Listens to others	none
☐	☑	Follows instructions	+1
☐	☑	Shows initiative in solving group problems	+1
☑	☐	Accepts and carries out group-determined tasks	none
☑	☐	Gives consideration to the viewpoints of others	none

FIGURE 4.5   5-Point Scales

Example 1: Item from a summated rating of teacher clarity

Teacher informs learners of skills or understanding expected at end of lesson.

_____ Always

_____ Frequently

_____ Occasionally

_____ Seldom

_____ Never

Example 2: Item from a summated rating for lesson preparation

Quality and accuracy of ideas

1	2	3	4	5
Very limited investigation; little or no material related to the facts.		Some investigation; attention to the facts is apparent.		Extensive investigation; extensive representation of the facts.

Example 3: Item from a summated rating for student cooperation and participation

Does the student give consideration to the viewpoint of others?

_____	_____	_____	_____	_____
Never	Infrequently	Sometimes	Frequently	Always

Example 4: Item from a summated rating of a teacher's oral delivery

Teacher's enunciation of technical vocabulary

1	2	3	4	5
Very poor	Poor	Adequate	Good	Very good

To complete a Likert scale, check or circle the appropriate alternative. The scale is then scored by assigning weights to each response item: 5 indicates the most positive; 1 indicates the least positive. Scale items measuring a common underlying concept are then summed and averaged. As noted in the examples, scales can be positioned vertically or horizontally, whichever is most convenient. Although verbal descriptions are used on each end and the middle of the scale, they need not be placed at each interval. Generally, the longer the observation period before a rating is made, the more accurate the rating will be. However, observations that extend over days and are only rated at the end might be subject to losses in memory, which could make the rating less trustworthy.

7-Point Scales. These scales are similar to 5-point scales, except that fewer verbal descriptors are used. One of the most popular 7-point scales is the semantic differential, which uses polar, or opposite, adjectives for each end of the scale. By checking one of the seven choices on the scale, the observer indicates the degree to which he feels a particular adjective is rep-

resentative of the events observed. You completed a semantic differential when you filled out Instrument 3.1, the General Observation Form. The following is another example of a 7-point scale.

This Lesson Is

Clear	_ _ _ _ _ _ _	Unclear
Unorderly	_ _ _ _ _ _ _	Orderly
Organized	_ _ _ _ _ _ _	Disorganized
Unfocused	_ _ _ _ _ _ _	Focused

Notice that all the adjective pairs focus on a single topic, "This Lesson," thereby creating a homogeneous set of items whose ratings can be averaged. Also, it is customary to alter the lineup of the pairs in a more-or-less random order so that all positively or all negatively worded adjectives do not appear on the same side of the page. This helps keep the rater vigilant. As you read the various descriptors, you'll notice the differences and, it is hoped, avoid generalizing a highly positive or negative rating for one item to the item immediately following it.

Depending on your interpretation and use, the middle blank can serve two different purposes. In cases where too little information is available, you can mark the middle blank to indicate no preference for either descriptor. Or in the event that you see both positive and negative trends occurring equally in the same lesson, you can mark the middle blank to suggest that both ends of the continuum have been evenly exhibited. If the scale does not include instructions about how the middle blank is to be interpreted, it is a good idea for you to decide *before* the observation what it means when you mark the middle blank.

To score a semantic differential scale, numerical weights are assigned, depending on whether the positive statement is on the left (the extreme positive blank is assigned a 7) or whether the negative statement is on the left (the extreme negative blank is assigned a 1). All the remaining blanks are coded in descending order if the statement on the left is positive and in ascending order if the statement on the left is negative. The weights for the blanks checked are then averaged. Because 7.0 is the highest attainable average, a score of greater than 3.5 indicates a positive overall rating.

When more than five levels of a behavior can be reliably distinguished by a relatively untrained observer, 7-point scales are preferred over 5-point scales. When this is not the case, or when each interval on the continuum that underlies the behavior must be explicitly identified, a 5-point scale is a better choice.

Advantages

1. Summated rating scales direct observation toward specific aspects of behavior and thereby structure what is to be observed.
2. They provide a common frame of reference for comparing all teachers, classrooms, or students with the same set of items.
3. They are easy to construct and can be quickly tailored to a specific observation target.

Disadvantages

1. Summated rating scales can be easily influenced by the observer's general impression of the person or classroom being rated.
2. Because of their general nature, they allow for only relative judgments (more/less) and not absolute judgments (present/absent).
3. They tend to force ratings toward the middle of the scale when the continuum is large or when endpoints represent extreme or highly undesirable responses.
4. They might require the observer to distinguish finer details of a behavior than can be reliably detected in a relatively short observation period (this especially applies to 7-point scales).

Although narrative records and rating scales can provide a wealth of information, sometimes even more specific detail is needed. In such cases, observers, often in the context of a research study, turn to classroom coding systems, the most structured observation instruments. You might not frequently use classroom coding systems, but you should know something about them because they have been used extensively in the research that underpins the eight lenses for effective teaching to be studied in the chapters ahead.

Method 3: Classroom Coding Systems

Observation systems that help you record the *frequency* with which various teacher and student behaviors occur are called **classroom coding systems.** They are sometimes referred to as low-inference observation systems because they require fewer judgments or inferences on the part of the observer than summated ratings. Unlike the general concepts measured by rating scales, coding systems count specific and distinct units of behavior, such as "Teacher asks question" or "Teacher uses example," that can be recorded during relatively brief intervals of time. Two frequently used methods for coding patterns of behavior are counting and sign systems.

Counting Systems

One type of observation coding system is called a **counting system.** With a counting system, the observer counts the number of time intervals in which various teacher or student behaviors occur. A time interval (such as every 5 seconds) represents a frame for the observation that is established before the observation begins. Every time the interval or frame elapses, a tally is made to indicate which behavior on the instrument occurred during that interval. Needless to say, the behaviors must be specific enough to be easily recognized during the time interval chosen, and the number of behaviors must be small enough that the observer can remember them and code them as they occur.

Figure 4.6 shows 10 behaviors from a popular counting system developed by Flanders (1970). The observer using this system records behavior every 3 seconds or whenever behavior changes. On the next page is a brief classroom dialogue and how it would be coded using the behaviors and codes specified in Figure 4.6.

FIGURE 4.6   Summary of Categories in Flanders Interaction Analysis System

Teacher Indirect Influence

1. *Accepts feeling*. Accepts and clarifies the tone of the students in a nonthreatening manner. Feelings may be positive or negative. Predicting or recalling feelings is included.
2. *Praises or encourages*. Praises or encourages student action or behavior. Jokes release tension, but not at the expense of another individual; nods head or develops ideas suggested by student. As more teacher ideas brought into play, shift to category 5.
3. *Accepts or uses ideas of students*. Clarifies, builds, or develops ideas suggested by a student. As more teacher ideas brought into play, shift to category 5.
4. *Asks questions*. Asks a question about content or procedure with the intent that a student answer.

Teacher Direct Influence

5. *Lecturing*. Gives facts or opinions about content or procedures; expresses own ideas, asks rhetorical questions.
6. *Giving directions*. Directions, commands, or orders with which a student is expected to comply.
7. *Criticizing or justifying authority*. Statements intended to change student behavior from nonacceptable to acceptable pattern; bawling someone out; stating why the teacher is doing something; extreme self-reference.

Students Talk

8. *Student talk–response*. Talk by students in response to teacher. Teacher initiates the contact or solicits student statement.
9. *Student talk–initiation*. Talk by students that they initiate. If "calling on" student is only to indicate who may talk next, observer must decide whether student wanted to talk. If yes, use this category.
10. *Silence or confusion*. Pauses, short periods of silence, and periods of confusion in which communication cannot be understood by the observer.

Speaker	Dialogue	Code
Ms. Chin:	What system of grids identifies the location of any object on the globe?	4, 4
Bobby:	Latitude and longitude.	9
Ms. Chin:	Good, I can see you've been studying. What does longitude mean?	2, 4
Bobby:	It's the grid on the globe that . . . goes up and down.	8
Ms. Chin:	What do you mean, "up and down"?	4
Bobby:	They extend north and south at equal intervals.	8
Ms. Chin:	Okay. Now tell me, where do they begin?	4
Bobby:	Well, I think they begin wherever it's midnight and end where it's almost midnight again.	8
Ms. Chin:	Let's think about that for a minute. Wouldn't that mean the point of origin would always be changing, according to where it happened to be midnight?	4
Bobby:	Yes, so the grids must start at some fixed point.	8
Ms. Chin:	Anybody know where they begin?	4
Sue:	Our book says the first is one marked "0" and starts at a place called Greenwich, England.	9
Ms. Chin:	How can a grid that runs continuously north and south around the globe start anyplace, Sue?	4
Sue:	I meant to say that it runs through Greenwich, England.	8
Ms. Chin:	Good. Now let's return to Bobby's point about time. Now that we have a fixed line of longitude, marked "0," how might we use it to establish time?	4
Bobby:	Now I remember. Midnight at the "0" longitude—or in Greenwich, England—is called "0" hours. Starting from there, there are timelines drawn around the world, so that when it's midnight at the first timeline, it will be 1 o'clock at Greenwich, England, and when it's midnight at the next timeline, it will be 2 o'clock back at Greenwich, England, and so on.	9, 9, 9
Ms. Chin:	So what does that mean?	4
Bobby:	Each line equals one hour . . . so . . . so there must be 24 of them!	8
Ms. Chin:	So it should be no surprise that time determined in reference to the "0" grid of longitude is called Greenwich Mean Time or Universal Time Coordinated (UTC).	5, 5

Notice that the first statement is coded "4, 4," indicating that this was a question that lasted for two 3-second intervals. The second statement is coded "9" to indicate that Bobby volunteered or initiated a response to the teacher's question. In subsequent statements, Bobby's responses are coded "8" to indicate that the teacher's question is directed specifically to Bobby and only Bobby was expected to answer. Notice also the "2, 4" code for the third statement. Here the teacher praises Bobby's response and then goes on to probe with a follow-up question, which extends into the second 3-second interval. Later, Sue joins the discussion by initiating a response to a teacher question. This is coded "9" because she was not specifically asked to respond. Shortly afterward, a second question is directed specifically to her—that is coded "8." Next, Bobby volunteers some information as a result of a question that takes three 3-second intervals to answer. Finally, the dialogue ends with the teacher giving some facts about the content, coded "5," which extends into a second 3-second interval. When the codes are entered into a specially prepared matrix, the sequence or patterns in which various behaviors occur can also be recorded. More information on how to record interaction sequences and patterns with the **Flanders Classroom Interaction Analysis System** can be found in Hopkins (2002).

To be practical, counting systems such as the one by Flanders must be simple enough to provide an accurate assessment of classroom behavior with relatively little practice. Many different behaviors can be chosen to replace those in the Flanders instrument to focus on specific behaviors that may be of interest. After a practice session observing for about 30 minutes, two observers should be able to agree to within about 75% on the number of tallies they record for a given behavior. Appendix A describes a simple procedure for determining observer agreement for a counting system.

Advantages

1. Counting systems provide for a large sampling of behavior.
2. They allow for sequences or patterns of behavior to be recorded.
3. The data derived from them are adaptable to statistical indices, such as ratios and percents.

Disadvantages

1. Behaviors must be limited to those that can be divided into specific, discrete units that occur frequently.
2. Coding can be stressful and intense, especially when time intervals are short or the behaviors to be coded cannot be quickly and unambiguously recognized in the interval chosen.
3. Some training to acquire a common understanding of the behaviors to be counted and a thorough definition of each behavior is required to achieve satisfactory agreement between observers.

Sign Systems

Another procedure for observing patterns of classroom interaction, a **sign system** requires an observer to record an event only once, regardless of how often it occurs within a specified time period. Sign systems differ from counting systems in that (a) the interval of observation tends to be considerably longer, about 2 to 15 minutes, and (b) the presence of more than one behavior can be recorded during the interval. Each behavior that occurs is given a sign, for example, a check mark, indicating its presence or absence within a particular block of time. A sign system using the same behaviors observed with the Flanders Interaction Analysis System appears in Figure 4.7.

FIGURE 4.7 Sign System

1	2	3	4	5	6	7	8	9	10	Behaviors
										Teacher accepts feelings.
✓				✓						Teacher praises or encourages.
						✓				Teacher accepts or uses ideas of students.
					✓	✓				Teacher asks questions.
✓	✓							✓		Teacher lectures.
					✓					Teacher gives directions.
✓		✓								Teacher criticizes or justifies authority.
			✓					✓		Student talk—response.
		✓								Student talk—initiation.
						✓				Silence or confusion.

(5-Minute Periods)

A useful sign system created by Soar and Soar (1983) for studying the classroom management behavior of teachers has been adapted in Instrument 4.1. Notice that 27 different teacher behaviors pertaining to classroom control are observed. The presence or absence of these behaviors over a 30-minute period indicate the verbal (items 1–17) and physical (items 18–27) behaviors used by the teacher to maintain classroom control. Also, within each of these two categories, items are listed in order from least to most obtrusive (for example, "Acknowledges, agrees, complies" to "Scolds, punishes"; "Nods, smiles, facial feedback" to "Ignores, abandons"). Use of these categories in a sign system over several class periods can provide a detailed description of the classroom management style being used.

Advantages

1. A larger set of behaviors can be observed with sign systems than with a counting system because of the longer time interval.

2. Because behavior is coded within a longer time interval, the data tend to be more dependable than with a counting system.
3. Unlike counting systems, sign systems require little or no training.

Disadvantages

1. Sign systems do not indicate the frequency with which a behavior occurs within an interval.
2. The tallies recorded cannot be used to establish the sequence of behavior because the size of the interval might allow intervening events to go unrecorded.

Now that you have gained familiarity with some techniques for observing, we will turn our attention to using these techniques as you observe in the classroom. In the following chapters, you will combine your recently acquired knowledge of the instruments of observation with the eight lenses to study and record patterns of effective teaching.

For More Information

Early research by Soar and Soar (1983) and by Glasgow, McNary, and Hicks (2006) reveals the importance of a teacher's warmth and control on both the behavior and achievement of learners. Specifically, this research has shown the delicate balance between warmth and control that best fosters the teacher's instructional as well as affective goals.

It has been said that good teachers are both warm and demanding. Being warm means caring and pro-

viding emotional support for students. Being demanding means expecting something from your students, in terms of both academic work and behavior.

The following document provides a further look inside this fascinating aspect of a teacher's (and parent's) warmth and effectiveness: www.parentmagic.com/uploads/ParentMagic%20News%20Special%20Edition%20For%20Teachers1.pdf.

Key Terms

anecdotal report, 39
checklist, 44
classroom coding systems, 47
counting system, 47
ethnographic record, 41
Flanders Classroom Interaction Analysis System, 49

open-ended reports, 39
rating scale, 44
sign system, 49
summated ratings, 45
thematic notes, 42
visual maps, 43

Activities*

1. Recall a memorable critical incident you were involved in during your elementary or secondary school years. Write a brief factual paragraph concerning exactly what happened to you and a second paragraph giving your interpretation of the incident. Have a classmate read your two paragraphs and make a judgment about your success in separating fact from interpretation.

*Some of these activities may be grouped into a common activity, divided among classmates, and completed from a single observation.

2. The following examples provide some useful themes for making thematic notes in different classrooms by answering the question "What kinds of events would I want to look for in this classroom?": (1) a 10th-grade algebra class reviewing for a test in a question-and-answer period (e.g., Do the questions and answers stay on topics related to the test?); (2) a social studies class of lower-performing seventh graders involved in a group discussion (e.g., Do all the students choose to participate?); and (3) a class of second graders completing seatwork while the teacher monitors and checks their homework (e.g., Does the teacher get to check the work of each pupil?). Identify other events in these three classrooms that reflect special areas of interest that you might have and that are consistent with the content and grade level of the classroom.

3. Construct a checklist for recording five observable signs that you feel would reflect the learning climate of a classroom. Using a recent class you have attended and the five observable signs you have chosen, in your judgment, was the climate of this classroom generally favorable or unfavorable?

4. Construct a five-item Likert instrument suitable for observing instructional variety. Check Chapter 3 for a definition of this lens. Vary the format for your items according to the examples provided in this chapter, but remember to keep all the items focused on instructional variety. To provide practice in scoring your scale, assign responses to each of the five items using a recent class you have attended. Based on the average of the five items, was the instructional variety in this classroom favorable or unfavorable?

5. Using a 7-point scale, write a set of five different bipolar adjectives that could be used to observe a teacher's task orientation. Arrange these on the page exactly as you would want them used by an observer, being sure to write the theme or concept to which your adjectives refer at the top of the page. At the top write some instructions informing an inexperienced observer how to interpret the middle blank.

6. Assume that two observers have used a counting system to observe teacher questioning for 45 minutes. During this time, one observer records 45 instances of questioning, and the second observer records 25 instances of questioning. What is the estimated percentage of agreement between observers, using the formula in Appendix A? Would you consider the percentage of agreement for the observation of this behavior adequate or inadequate? If it is inadequate, suggest some modifications that might increase the percentage of observer agreement for this behavior.

5

Considering the Learning Climate

Being Nobody

Have you ever felt like nobody?

Just a tiny speck of air.

When everyone's around you,

And you are just not there.

      Karen Crawford (Age 9)

A critical aspect of the classroom relates to how it "feels." Imagine spending several hours every day in a place where you "felt like nobody." How would such feelings affect your learning? Your self-concept? Your belief in your ability? How do teachers create a learning climate that encourages risk taking and nurtures and supports the development of each individual's abilities? These are crucial questions for the observer to consider.

In this chapter, we begin the process of observing by focusing on the learning climate in a classroom. As you will see, learning climate is a multifaceted concept that can be influenced by many different sources (Cambourne, 2000; Gallego & Cole, 2001; Hensley, Powell, Lamke, & Hartman, 2007). We will study three of these sources—teacher concerns, teacher warmth and control, and social environment—as examples of some of the characteristics of the classroom that can influence and create a positive environment for learning. Let's begin our study by observing in the classrooms of two student teachers who have taken the same university courses and have done well throughout their teacher preparation program. We'll visit first in Stephanie's class and then drop in on Jan.

As we enter her classroom, Stephanie greets us with a quick smile, encourages us to make ourselves comfortable on the beanbags and other chairs around the room, and then kneels to talk with Erika. Erika's drooping shoulders straighten as she searches Stephanie's eyes. Suddenly she reaches toward Stephanie's shoulder, touches it lightly, and smiles. Abruptly, she turns to join her 6-year-old peers at their table.

Stephanie shares Erika's concern with us: "She's worried that Ms. Martinez will send her out of the room for forgetting her poem. Poor thing. She's so afraid to talk to anyone. I try to show her I want to hear what she says."

A few minutes later, Stephanie joins a reading group on the rug. Seven first and second graders read aloud with her, often interrupting the flow to share personal connections to the story or to ask questions about the text. Expertly, Stephanie weaves their comments into the plot, and then gently resumes the reading. William is a handful—rocking back and forth and tugging at Jennifer's jacket. Stephanie doesn't miss a beat as she hugs him to her side; she never breaks eye contact with José, who spontaneously volunteers what he thinks will happen next in the story.

"Do you think so too, William?" Stephanie asks. Calmed by her touch, William stares down at the pages before him. "I know William has something wonderful to tell us," Stephanie confides to the others. William looks at her, his eyes widening in surprise. "You think . . ." Stephanie prompts. She nods at William, serenely.

"I . . . I . . . I just think Grandma is mean," William offers tentatively.

Stephanie laughs delightedly, hugging William with her right arm—and everyone else in the group with her sparkling eyes. "You know what, William? I've been thinking that very same thing!"

As we leave, we wave goodbye to Stephanie, silently mouthing our thanks. She winks, and we head down the hall to Jan's room. Our short discussion centers on how hard it is to believe that Stephanie has been student teaching for only 2 weeks. When we enter Jan's classroom, we find a row of chairs placed across the back of the room. Jan is already conducting class, so we quietly file in and take our places along the wall.

Jan presides at the overhead projector, red pen in hand. "Maria?" she intones. "Prewriting." "Kathleen?" "Drafting." One by one each child reports his or her progress within the five-stage writing process. Jan prints each response carefully on a "State of the Class" transparency.

"All right. Time for writing conferences. First student?" Jan scans her clipboard. "Ah yes, Nick. Mario, to the waiting chair. Everyone else to your work." Seated in rows spaced at equal intervals throughout the room, students rummage through their desks for writing materials. Silently, Nick and Mario approach a small table at the back of the room as Jan settles into a chair at its head. Clutching a dog-eared paper, Nick sits beside Jan while Mario slips into the "waiting chair" a few feet away. Turning the pages on her clipboard, Jan queries in a businesslike voice: "Name?"

We wonder if we've heard correctly. Surely Jan knows Nick's name. "Nick Mariani," Nick answers softly. We strain to hear his voice.

Jan writes Nick's name on a checklist on the clip-board. The form includes spaces for each phase of the writing process.

"Now, let's see. Have you completed a group response sheet?" Nick nods. Jan makes a notation.

"An editing checklist?" Another nod. Another notation.

"Very well then. You may read your piece aloud to me. Wait! What is that word?" Jan points at the offending letters on Nick's paper. "C-o-o-k-y? Is that how you spell cookie? Perhaps you'd better look this over again before we conference."

Eyes downcast, Nick slides from the chair and slinks toward his desk. At Jan's insistent nod, Mario replaces Nick in the seat.

We watch the diminutive fourth grader slouch into his chair and lay his head on his desk. As we move our eyes toward the floor, we wonder what Nick's story was about.

As you imagine having observed both teachers, what are you thinking about the learning climate in their classrooms? Jan and Stephanie have much in common. Both are 21 years old and were raised in middle-class families. They were assigned to the same university cohort and achieved excellent grades in their teacher education courses. For 5 months, they observed their cooperating teachers and completed practice teaching in the same elementary school. How, then, do we account for the differences between Jan and Stephanie in the classroom? How is it that Stephanie readily connects with her learners—draws them out and draws us in? And how is it that Jan manages to proceduralize all her interactions with her learners to the point that her intended child-centered focus is obscured?

Perhaps Jan and Stephanie simply differ in personality or in their approaches to children and classroom tasks. Or perhaps they are merely exhibiting different levels of concern associated with the challenges of beginning teaching (Borich, 2010; Fuller, 1969). As we consider some dimensions of creating a classroom learning climate, perhaps we can also gain insight into the differences we have observed between Jan and Stephanie.

DIMENSIONS OF LEARNING CLIMATE

As you can tell from the climate in these two classrooms, the learning environment is an important lens through which to view life in classrooms because of its effects on how teachers teach and how students learn. We can imagine how students in Stephanie's classroom might respond to the spontaneity and risk taking required for learning compared to the students in Jan's room. Not surprisingly, researchers have proposed and studied a model of classroom behavior that identifies the climate of the classroom as a cause of many subsequent events that occur within it (Fraser & Walberg, 1991). Fraser and Walberg's model, illustrated in Figure 5.1, places learning climate in an important moderating role for determining classroom behavior.

We see from Figure 5.1 that one influence on classroom behavior comes from institutional roles and expectations. Roles are partly defined by institutions, such as schools, that bestow on individuals certain obligations, responsibilities, and privileges. Groups such as students and teachers interpret and assume these roles, which come with certain expectations that guide their behavior. For example, common role expectations for students are that they come to class, get good grades, conform to the rules of the classroom, and get along with others. For teachers, role expectations include planning lessons that follow the curriculum, managing the classroom, and raising each student's level of achievement during the school year.

A second influence on classroom behavior comes from the individual personalities and dispositions of the students and teachers within a classroom (Sutton & Wheatley, 2003). Primary elements of this dimension are the cultural influences and past experiences

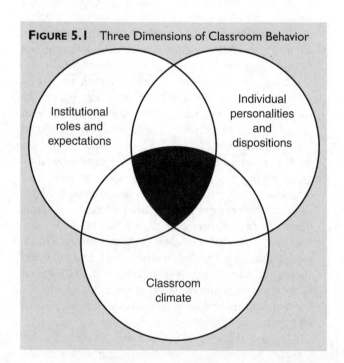

FIGURE 5.1   Three Dimensions of Classroom Behavior

Institutional roles and expectations

Individual personalities and dispositions

Classroom climate

of individuals that create dispositions, or tendencies to act in a certain way. Cultural beliefs and practices vary from home to home and from student to student and exert a large influence on what students value and believe to be appropriate (Banks & Banks, 2006; Dilworth & Brown, 2001; Irvine & York, 2001). The diversity of students' personalities and dispositions can be surprising, as has been noted in recent research on "resiliency" (Benard, 2004; Henderson & Milstein, 2002). "Resilient" children are those who seem to defy the odds—becoming productive and happy individuals in spite of backgrounds that would suggest otherwise. Several long-term studies suggest that resilient children are more numerous than might be expected. Werner and Smith (1992) noted that between 50 and 70% of children born into extremely high-risk environments "grow up to be not only successful by societal indicators but 'confident, competent, and caring' persons" (Benard, 2004; Manson, 2005). Many researchers believe that through a positive and inclusive learning climate resiliency can be fostered in *all* youth (Benard, 2004). Walqui provides an important link between learning climate and cultural diversity by noting that in effective classrooms, teachers and students together construct a climate that "values the strengths of all participants and respects their interests, abilities, languages, and dialects" (2000b, p. 2).

For the teacher, therefore, learning climate may be one of the most important influences on classroom behavior. Unlike institutional roles and expectations and individual personalities and dispositions, which are often beyond a teacher's control, many aspects of the learning climate can be established and maintained by the teacher's efforts to include all the different personalities and dispositions likely to be met in the classroom. Indeed, a positive learning climate can include and moderate the dispositions and expectations of an entire class, which in turn can influence the behavior of individuals (Hargreaves, 2000), by an atmosphere, or climate, that encourages some classroom behaviors and discourages others, without the aid of formally stated rules or procedures. This is why the learning climate within a classroom is so important: If properly established, the learning climate can promote among all students high expectations to perform and a commitment to learn (Bamburg, 1994; Cambourne, 2000; Gallego & Cole, 2001).

We will study three different but related approaches to observing the learning climate. One of these will lead us to explore the concerns of the teacher, which can be influential in determining a climate for learning. Research has suggested that whether a teacher is primarily concerned with *self* ("Can I get through the day?"), the teaching *task* ("How can I cover the content?"), or her *impact* on students ("Are my students learning?") makes a difference in establishing an effective learning climate. Next, we will look at the dimensions of teacher warmth and control. Although these are often expressed as a single dimension, we will learn some advantageous ways of observing these elements as two separate but compatible dimensions. Finally, we will explore the interpersonal or social relationships among students, and between students and teacher, that can establish either more or less effective contexts for achieving instructional goals within a classroom.

Teacher Concerns

Before we discuss the influence of a teacher's concerns in establishing an effective learning environment, let's visit Mr. Jenkins's seventh-grade social studies class. Mr. Jenkins, a first-year teacher, is being observed during the first month of school. As you read the ethnographic record (Chapter 4) shown in Example 5.1, think of the kinds of the concerns or worries (self, task, or impact) that Mr. Jenkins seems to have. You may want to make some notes in the margin as you read as reminders of what you notice.

What do you notice about Mr. Jenkins and his class? What seems to be the source of greatest concern for this teacher? If you are a typical beginning teacher, your thoughts and concerns, like those of Mr. Jenkins, will at first focus most predominantly on your own well-being (self), and then on your teaching (task), and eventually on your students' mastery of content (impact). According to Fuller (1969), a progression from concern about oneself (Will the students like me? Can I control the class?), to concern about the task at hand (Are there sufficient instructional materials? Is there time to cover all the content?), to concern about student understanding (Are my pupils learning? Can they apply what they've learned?) commonly occurs among new teachers—and among student teachers. Fuller speculates that concerns for self, task, and impact are the natural stages that most teachers pass through, representing a developmental growth pattern extending over months, and even years, of a teacher's career. Although some teachers might pass through these stages more quickly than others and at different levels of intensity, Fuller (1969) suggests that almost all teachers can be expected to move from one to another, with the most effective and experienced teachers expressing student-centered concerns at a high level of commitment.

Fuller (1969) developed her theory, known as the **concerns theory,** from a careful analysis of recorded

---

Example 5.1

Name of Teacher: Mr. Jenkins

Subject of Observation: A seventh-grade social studies class

1. Ss (students) have just completed filing in for
2. class. T (teacher) begins class promptly at bell,
3. saying that some parents have called about
4. last week's especially long assignment.
5. T tells Ss not to complain to their parents
6. and that in the future, long assignments will
7. be given extra credit. T picks up with
8. Chapter 6 on who is allowed to vote. Asks
9. the minimum voting age. Class blurts out
10. several different answers in unison. One S
11. says, "When you can drink you can vote."
12. T retorts that only one S is allowed to speak
13. at a time in his class, then calls on Sue. Sue
14. responds that the voting age has nothing to
15. do with the legal age for drinking. Some in
16. the class show disagreement by shaking their
17. heads. T then points out that individual
18. states control the legal age to buy alcoholic
19. beverages, but the federal government
20. sets the voting age. T asks if everyone understands
21. that. Most of the class nods. T reminds
22. class of a school rule against speaking out,
23. and that the principal listens in on the
24. P.A. system. Two Ss start bickering over the
25. answer, and T tells one to change desks with
26. another S seated in the back of the room.
27. Class quiets down, and T reads from text the
28. constitutional amendment governing the
29. voting age. T explains that there
30. never seems to be enough time for class discussion,
31. so that's why he has to read from the textbook.
32. Next, T asks for a show of hands indicating
33. how many Ss really know the procedure for
34. registering to vote. About half the class
35. raises their hands. T says that a pamphlet
36. describing how to register will be placed at the
37. learning center for those who need it
38. to complete their last assignment. T
39. indicates that the text doesn't contain enough
40. information to complete the assignment, but
41. that reference texts from his
42. personal library will be placed at the learning
43. center. Ss are reminded once again that anyone
44. who dislikes the way he is doing things in the
45. class should see him before complaining to
46. their parents. T indicates the class must move
47. on to keep up with Ms. Bennett's class, who
48. will be taking the test at the same time.
49. T continues by asking, "Where do people vote?"
50. One S responds by asking if they can discuss
51. why in some states you're old enough to vote,
52. but not old enough to buy alcohol. T responds
53. that discussions like that will take place only
54. when the class has proved it can behave
55. in a responsible manner and show respect.
56. Someone shouts out, "That's not fair," and T
57. indicates that he will assign punishment
58. for those who speak out. Reminds class of the
59. rule on speaking out mentioned the first
60. class day. T picks up with a presentation of
61. the material in Chapter 6 on places to vote.

---

transcripts of interviews with student teachers. Over an extended period of time, these records were used to identify and classify problems that student teachers experienced and the concerns they expressed about these problems. When grouped into developmental and sequential stages, these expressed concerns showed that student teachers with the least experience were most concerned about self and self-survival; student teachers with more experience and in-service teachers were more concerned about student achievement and learning.

Stated in its simplest terms, the concerns theory describes the learning process for a prospective teacher as a natural flow from concerns for self (teacher) to task (teaching) to impact (pupil). The physical, mental, and emotional state of the prospective teacher plays an important role in the shift of focus from self to task to impact. Lack of adequate knowledge or emotional support during the critical preteaching and student teaching experience can result in a slower, more labored shift of focus from self to task. This, in turn, can result in a failure on the part of the teacher to reach a concern for his impact on students that can influence the learning climate of a classroom.

There are several other implications of Fuller's concerns theory (1969). Some teachers might return to an earlier stage of concern (e.g., from a concern for pupils back to a concern for task) as a result of suddenly having to teach a new grade or subject. Or a teacher might move from a concern for task back to a concern for self as a result of having to teach in a new and unfamiliar school. Therefore, teacher concerns

---

FIGURE 5.2   Areas of Concern

Self Concerns

I'm worried about whether the students really like me or not.

I'm under pressure a lot of the time.

I worry about doing well when a supervisor (or visitor) is present.

Task (Instructional) Concerns

I lack the freedom to initiate innovative instructional ideas.

I'm concerned about the availability and quality of instructional materials.

I worry about adequately presenting all the material.

Impact (Student Needs) Concerns

I'm concerned about increasing students' feelings of accomplishment.

It's important to me to recognize the social and emotional needs of students.

I'm concerned about challenging unmotivated students.

---

might not always be determined developmentally; they can be context dependent as well. However, the time spent in a stage the second time is expected to be shorter than the first. Further, the three stages of concern need not be exclusive of one another. A teacher could have several concerns in one area, yet still have concerns of less intensity in one or both of the other stages.

Think back to the descriptions of Jan and Stephanie at the beginning of this chapter. Knowing what you now know about the concerns theory, how might you account for at least some of the differences in the learning climates of these two classrooms? It may help you to consider a list of concerns typically expressed by teachers (and the stages they reflect) and imagine whether Stephanie or Jan would agree with the expressions. Do you see any connections between the predominant areas of concern shown in Figure 5.2 and the classroom learning climates established by Jan and Stephanie?

A Teacher Concerns Instrument

You learned in Chapter 4 that it is often easier to "see" a classroom behavior, such as teacher concerns, when it is in the form of a measuring instrument. Researchers have created an instrument that allows us to measure teacher concerns (Borich, 1993, 2010;

Fuller, 1969; Rogan, Borich, & Taylor, 1992). Instrument 5.1, found in Appendix B, applies a 5-point rating scale to a series of statements based on Fuller's concerns theory. To acquaint yourself with the concerns theory, turn to Instrument 5.1, read each of the items you see there, and ask: When I think about teaching, how concerned am I about this? Use the scale to indicate your level of concern, placing your responses in the boxes to the left. After you complete the scale, you'll learn how to score your responses.

The items representing the dimensions of self, task, and impact are the following:

Self	Task	Impact
2	1	5
4	3	15
8	6	17
9	7	19
13	10	22
14	11	23
18	12	29
20	16	34
24	21	36
26	25	37
28	27	38
30	31	39
32	33	41
35	40	43
44	42	45

To determine your level of concern, total the number of responses in each of the three categories of concern—self, task, and impact. The higher your score in a category (out of a maximum 75 per category), the more you are identified with that stage of concern. An average rating for each of the three areas can be computed by summing responses to items in each category and dividing by the number of items completed.

The concerns instrument indicates a teacher's level of concern for each of 45 items. Imagine how helpful it would be to our understanding of their teaching if we could ask Jan, Stephanie, and Mr. Jenkins to complete the concerns instrument you just completed. We might gain important insights into why each teacher acted as he or she did. When you observe a classroom, you might wonder how the teacher's concerns may be influencing the learning climate. In most instances, asking the teacher you will be observing to complete the concerns instrument can tell you that teacher's predominant stage of concern. The instrument can be completed in about 10 minutes, and teachers often consent to do so out of personal interest and curiosity about their concerns.

Knowing about your own concerns can be helpful for your professional development as well. You can complete the concerns instrument at the beginning of and again at the end of your student teaching or field observation experience, noting any changes in the three areas of concern over time. The sum of the scores for each of the three areas of concern (maximum = 75) can be recorded in the following format, shown here with example data.

Stage	Beginning	End	Change
Self	60	45	−15
Task	45	60	+15
Impact	15	30	+15

This example profile indicates a shift of concern from self to task and from self to impact. This is typical of student teachers who spend about a semester in a field experience. Smaller shifts following this same pattern are not uncommon after a semester of in-school observation without practice teaching. Larger shifts, particularly from task to impact, are frequently noted for beginning in-service teachers during their first 2 to 3 years of teaching.

Observing Teacher Concerns in the Classroom

Now, let's look more closely at what we might see in a classroom that could indicate a teacher's concern for self, task, and impact and how these concerns can influence the learning climate. For this observation we will return to the ethnographic record of Mr. Jenkins's class. Recall from Chapter 4 that an ethnographic record reports events sequentially as they occur, often with the aid of a laptop computer. At first, the observer records everything that occurs without selecting a specific focus or incident.

As you reread the record of Mr. Jenkins's classroom, your goal will be to identify those lines of the record that indicate a concern for self, task, or impact. Before beginning, go back and label each item on the concerns instrument with an *S*, *T*, or *I* to remind you of the stage of concern to which each item belongs. Read each set of items (2, 4, 8, etc.; 1, 3, 6, etc.; 5, 15, 17, etc.) as a unit to get a feel for the kind of behaviors that reflect each of the three levels of concern (self, task, impact). Then reread the ethnographic record, placing an *S*, *T*, or *I* in the margin when you see any sign of these three areas of concern. You may want to reread the record with a partner to check and discuss the accuracy of the signs of concerns you noted in the margin and adding others.

Although you may have found others, the following are some of the lines on this ethnographic record an observer might have indicated as references to concerns for self, task, and impact. Let's examine them to see if any single stage of concern emerges.

Self	Task	Impact
3–7	29–32	20–21
22–23	35–43	32–34
43–46		
46–48		
52–55		
57–60		

Notice that, according to this observer's judgment, all three stages are represented, but more entries appear under self concerns than for the other two stages. To substantiate this teacher's predominant stage of concern, the observer might point to three themes in the dialogue related to self: the teacher's need to (a) control the class, (b) be liked by the class, and (c) be the final and perhaps only authority. These themes are not uncommon among beginning teachers, who on one hand might be unsure of their ability to manage the class and on the other want to be liked and respected as an authority. These behaviors often originate with a concern for self, which can unintentionally promote a learning climate in which the teacher vacillates between being overly permissive to gain the cooperation of students and overly restrictive to maintain control of the class. There is, therefore, a mixture of climates. Both cooperation and control are being sought, but in different ways. The result can be confusing, with students attempting to follow in whatever direction (cooperation or control) the pendulum may be swinging at any given moment.

Although our record is too brief to indicate the typical climate that may prevail in this classroom, it does portray a number of contradictions that might spell trouble for this teacher at a later time. Some of the opposing forces that might have been set in motion by this teacher's self concerns include

Leniency versus rigor

Cooperation versus obedience

Choral responses versus individual responses

Teacher facts versus student opinion

As we consider Mr. Jenkins's class, it appears that the students received little, if any, information about where the teacher stood on these issues. How lenient would the teacher be on difficult assignments? When was disobedience to classroom rules to be taken seriously? When would choral responses to questions be permitted? These are some of the questions left unanswered because this teacher is juggling a need to be liked and respected with a need to be in control. Every teacher has these needs, but it is important that a concern for self be balanced with concerns for task and impact if an optimal learning climate is to be established.

Let's look at another record indicating a different emphasis. Let's imagine that an observer has com-pleted the ethnographic record shown in Example 5.2 of Ms. Chau's presentation of the same lesson. Again, try to identify and code any lines you believe reflect a concern for self, task, and impact by placing an *S*, *T*, or *I* beside them.

The following are some of the lines from this eth-nographic record that an observer might have in-dicated as containing some reference to a concern for self, task, and impact. Although you might have found others, let's examine these to see if any single stage of concern emerges.

Example 5.2

Name of Teacher: Ms. Chau

Subject of Observation: A seventh-grade social studies class

1. Ss have just completed filing in for class.
2. T begins class promptly at the bell. T tells
3. class that today they will discuss who
4. can vote and how votes are cast in a national
5. election. T says this will serve as a
6. review of Chapter 6 and provide a chance
7. to catch up for anyone having trouble with
8. Chapter 6. T acknowledges that last week's
9. homework assignment was difficult, but not to
10. complain to their parents. To help any Ss
11. still having difficulty, a reference library
12. helpful in completing the assignment
13. has been set up at the learning center. T offers to
14. read and make comments on anyone's draft
15. before they turn it in. Calls on Bobby to tell the
16. class what the minimum voting age is for an
17. election. Bobby says he thinks it's 21 because
18. that's the legal age to buy alcohol. T asks
19. if all the laws that govern the behavior of
20. citizens within a state are the same across
21. states. Bobby doesn't say anything. T says,
22. "What about the speed limit?" Bobby then
23. remembers that his family had to
24. drive at different speeds, depending on what
25. state they were in. T then says, "That applies to
26. the legal drinking age, also." Points out a
27. number of examples not in text illustrating
28. the independence of states to establish their
29. own laws; for example, laws pertaining to
30. safety, banking, and purchase of alcohol.
31. T asks another student "When would it be
32. important that the behavior of citizens be the
33. same across all states?" Calls on Betty, whose
34. hand is raised. Betty answers, "When the
35. behavior being governed pertains to the nation
36. as a whole." T responds, "Such as election of
37. the president of the United States." T then asks
38. what the minimum voting age is for a national
39. election. Two Ss start bickering over the correct
40. answer. T then asks one of these students to read
41. a page in the text covering the constitutional
42. amendment pertaining to the minimum voting
43. age. When S finishes, T asks the second student
44. to summarize the two most important points
45. read by the first student. S says that
46. state and federal laws can be different, but
47. laws pertaining to the nation are always the
48. same across states, and that the minimum voting
49. age has been set at 18 for everyone. T praises
50. both students, then moves on to how one
51. registers to vote. T gives students a handout that
52. paraphrases a pamphlet called "How to Vote,"
53. which has been placed at the learning center.
54. T says the handout should make completing last
55. week's homework assignment easier. Goes
56. over six points on handout, and then checks for
57. understanding by asking Ss to recall one
58. point on the handout from memory until all
59. six are covered. T indicates that last
60. week's homework assignment should help
61. in reviewing these six points before the
62. exam next week. T then starts
63. discussion on where to vote in a national
64. election. S interrupts by asking if they
65. can discuss why in some states you're old
66. enough to vote but not old enough to buy
67. alcohol. T acknowledges the question by
68. adding, "Or old enough to go to war but not
69. yet old enough to vote." T says, "Let's cover
70. the section in the text on 'places to vote,'
71. which will be on the test, and then
72. have a class discussion by dividing
73. class into those who see this as a contradiction
74. and those who do not." T picks up with
75. a presentation of material in Chapter 6 on
76. places to vote.

Self	Task	Impact
8–10	10–13	5–8
	26–30	13–15
	43–45	49–51
	51–55	56–59
	59–62	67–68
	69–71	72–74

Contrary to the previous record, this one has more indications of task and impact concerns. Notice the change from a focus on self to a focus on instructional materials, student expression, and student understanding in these two records. The first indication of this change comes when Ms. Chau acknowledges the difficulty of last week's homework assignment. Instead of avoiding the issue by giving extra credit as Mr. Jenkins did, Ms. Chau provides added references to help in the assignment. This shows a concern for task and impact by encouraging more thoroughly completed assignments.

Another indication of concern for task and impact is Ms. Chau's strategy of staying with a student longer after a wrong or partially wrong response. For example, the teacher follows up a question to Bobby by asking if all the laws that govern behavior of citizens within a state are the same across states. Bobby doesn't respond, so Ms. Chau follows up again with "What about the speed limit?" This elicits a satisfactory response. These follow-up questions refine the quality of responses, engage the student in the learning process, and encourage the student to think about, work with, or otherwise act on the content presented. This indicates an increasingly student-centered focus.

Notice also how the potential discipline problem involving two students bickering over the voting age question is turned into a constructive activity. By having the first student read from the text and the second summarize what was read, these simple assignments keep the students task oriented, quickly directing them back on task without disrupting the flow of the discussion.

Other events in this record indicate a concern for task and impact. Ms. Chau focuses on the quality of the instructional materials by drawing students' attention to the relationship between the previous week's homework assignment and the upcoming exam. She responds to additional student needs by making possible a future discussion on the contradictions between the voting age and the minimum age for other social behavior.

These two ethnographic records, although brief, are intended to illustrate the subtle but important differences in learning climate and instruction that can be created by a teacher's concerns for self, task, and impact. Every teacher will have concerns in all three areas, but the balance among the three can significantly affect learning climate. In Ms. Chau's class, there is more concern shown toward students by the teacher, leading to a greater degree of spontaneity and responsiveness on the part of the students. Also, some aspects of the classroom (the learning center, handout, and reading from text) are directed at fulfilling student, rather than teacher, needs, leading to a greater degree of cooperation between student and teacher. The point of these two records, however, is not to suggest the superiority of one teaching style over another, but rather to show how the balance of your concerns can, over time, affect the learning climate of your classroom. By not being aware of a preponderance of self concerns to the exclusion of task and impact concerns, you might run the risk of unintentionally creating a learning climate that may be contrary to the goals of your lesson. Let's continue our exploration of learning climate by next considering how characteristics of warmth and control can influence classroom behavior, as well as the learning climate.

Warmth and Control

Another aspect of the learning climate of a classroom pertains to teacher warmth and control. For many years the dimensions of warmth and control were studied as opposite ends of a continuum. Some teachers falsely believed that before the first day of class they had to choose either to be warm or in control because, in their minds, to be both would be a contradiction. For example, a teacher who was accepting of student ideas and allowed spontaneity of expression was "warm"; a teacher who was always content focused and limited student expression to technically correct answers was "cold."

Early research that used the Flanders (1970) Classroom Interaction Analysis System (Chapter 4) to describe the degree to which a teacher was indirect (e.g., used questions and answers and group discussion as the primary instructional strategy) or direct (e.g., used lecture, drill, and recitation as the primary instructional strategy) equated warmth with indirectness and control with directness, thereby placing warmth and control at opposite poles of a continuum. But as Soar and Soar (1983) and Gootman (2008) have found, teacher warmth and control are two related but separate dimensions. As shown in Figure 5.3, different degrees of warmth and control may occur simultaneously and behavior on one dimension does not necessarily preclude behavior on the other. In other words, a teacher doesn't have to give up con-

FIGURE 5.3 Teacher Warmth and Control on Two Separate Axes

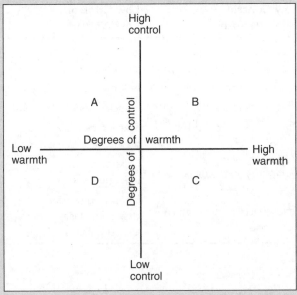

Source: Soar & Soar, 1983.

trol to be warm or give up warmth to be in control. In fact, in her work with African American and Hispanic parents, Compton-Lilly (2000) found that parents and teachers who exercised control by keeping close tabs on children and their behavior were viewed as more caring than those who did not. Pianta (1999) discusses complementary findings with regard to the enhancing relationships between children and teachers. As we consider variations in teacher warmth and control, four major combinations emerge to describe the learning climate.

The first combination is represented by Quadrant A, in which the teacher is characterized as *cold and controlling.* A teacher who falls in the upper left corner of this quadrant might humiliate and criticize students to control all aspects of their behavior. Actions placed in the lower right corner of this quadrant represent a teacher who provides little praise or reward. This quadrant generally represents a learning climate that is businesslike and almost always task oriented, with few teacher–student interchanges that are not initiated by the teacher. It also might be a classroom in which motivation for high-level work is inspired more by a fear of punishment, embarrassment, or, in extreme cases, humiliation than by the expectation of praise, reward, or reinforcement.

The second type of learning climate is represented by Quadrant B, in which the teacher is *warm but controlling.* If warmth were seen as a contradiction of control, as in some early definitions of learning climate,

this quadrant could not occur in practice. However, high degrees of both warmth and control can operate simultaneously. A teacher who falls in the upper right corner of this quadrant associates almost every desirable student behavior with some expectation of reward. The result may well be an almost suffocating climate in which students have little if any room to pursue a behavior or activity on their own. Only those behaviors that have been previously identified by the teacher are eligible for a reward—all others are presumably less worthy. As Soar and Soar (1983) have noted, this may create a learning climate in which students have little "wiggle room" to pursue any independent behavior because of the tightly managed praise-and-reward system established by the teacher. A less extreme and more desirable portion of this quadrant (toward the lower left) would represent a classroom that balances rewards and consequences, therefore promoting a climate of both warmth and control. This quadrant differs from Quadrant A primarily in that motivation for good behavior comes from a well-defined and consistently applied system of praise and rewards. In Quadrant A, good behavior results from a well-defined and consistently applied system of rules or punishment.

The third learning climate is characterized by Quadrant C, in which the teacher is *warm and permissive.* A teacher who falls at the lower right corner of this quadrant praises and rewards students frequently, while providing students almost complete freedom in choosing the limits of their own behavior, which sometimes can result in chaos or confusion. A less extreme example of this quadrant would be a classroom in which praise and rewards are apparent, but student spontaneity (e.g., calling out) and risk-taking behavior are limited to certain times (e.g., group discussion and problem solving but not recitation) or certain types of content (e.g., concept development and problem solving but not knowledge acquisition). During these times, the teacher acts more as a moderator or participant, guiding and directing, but not controlling, classroom behavior. This quadrant represents a learning climate in which students have considerable freedom in how and when to speak and in which the teacher's warm and nurturing attitude toward students is for the most part conveyed nonverbally through a mutually agreed-on set of classroom rules.

The fourth learning climate, Quadrant D, represents a classroom that is *cold and permissive.* A teacher who falls at the lower left corner of this quadrant spends most of the time scolding and criticizing students but has few classroom rules to control or limit the behavior being criticized. Such an extreme

TABLE 5.1 Four Types of Classroom Climate

A High Control Low Warmth	B High Control High Warmth	C Low Control High Warmth	D Low Control Low Warmth
High task orientation	Clearly identified and frequent use of rewards for desirable behavior	Frequent use of praise and reinforcement	Frequent scolding and criticism
Frequent use of punishment or humiliation	Unsolicited student responses discouraged	Informal classroom rules	Few classroom rules
Lack of praise, reward, or reinforcement	High task orientation	Students have say in establishing limits on their own behavior	Students frequently call out
Mostly teacher-initiated interchanges	Mostly teacher-initiated interchanges	Student spontaneity and risk-taking behavior allowed	Teacher talk focuses on minimizing misbehavior
High amount of time devoted to teacher talk	High amount of time devoted to teacher talk	Teacher acts as moderator or participant	Classroom lacks task orientation
			Frequent delays for classroom management and reprimands

climate might prevail in a classroom taught by an unprepared substitute teacher, where some students might take advantage of the teacher's unfamiliarity with classroom rules to act out, thereby eliciting reprimands and criticisms from the teacher. Because the classroom rules normally in place are unknown to the substitute, there are no rules to fall back on to prevent misbehavior from recurring. The substitute's role is to keep order, not to create or discover the rules, so much of his behavior is an attempt to "hold the line" by criticizing, reprimanding, and punishing, if need be, to keep the class under control. Overall, this quadrant is characterized by a lack of task orientation and teacher control over the subject matter content and by frequent scolding, criticizing, and reprimanding.

Table 5.1 summarizes the most characteristic aspects of learning climate in these four types of classrooms. A number of unique features can be identified for the dimensions of control and warmth. For control, student spontaneity, risk-taking behavior, and self-initiated responses (low control) versus teacher talk, task orientation, and authority (high control) are key ingredients. For the dimension of warmth, praise and rewards, use of student ideas, and responsiveness to student requests (high warmth) versus amount of criticism and scolding, frequency of reference to formal rules and procedures, and use of punishment (low warmth) are key ingredients.

Dimensions of Warmth and Control

Instruments 5.2 and 5.3 record the dimensions of warmth and control using 7-point rating scales. Each scale item is completed according to how frequently or infrequently the behavior (item) occurs, indicated by the words *High* and *Low,* and scored according to the numbers shown under each blank. The average rating from each scale can be placed on the axes of Instrument 5.4 to determine the quadrant that best represents the climate of the classroom being observed. The two averages, one for control and the other for warmth, are entered as a dot in the proper quadrant. For example, an average rating of 6.6 on warmth and 6.0 on control corresponds to Quadrant B, indicated by the dot on Instrument 5.4. Such a classroom would be characterized as having a high degree of warmth and a considerable degree of control. Verbal descriptions corresponding to the average rating computed for each scale can be used to describe different quadrants. Some example descriptions are shown in Table 5.2.

The nearest whole number can be used to determine the best verbal description. For example, a classroom rated 2.1 on the scale pertaining to warmth and 3.3 on the scale pertaining to control could be described as having "a slight amount of warmth, with a small amount of control." A classroom rated 6.3 and 1.8 on warmth and control, respectively, could be described as having a "considerable amount of warmth, with a slight amount of control."

Behavioral Signs of Warmth and Control

A related approach to observing the dimensions of warmth and control is to look for the presence or absence of specific behavioral signs that indicate these two dimensions. Chapter 4 discussed using a time

TABLE 5.2 Verbal Descriptions

Average Scale Rating	Warmth Dimension	Control Dimension
1	No warmth	No control
2	Slight amount of warmth	Slight amount of control
3	Small amount of warmth	Small amount of control
4	Neutral/50–50	Neutral/50–50
5	Fair amount of warmth	Fair amount of control
6	Considerable amount of warmth	Considerable amount of control
7	High degree of warmth	High degree of control

interval counting system to record totals of specific, discrete behaviors that could be judged present or absent during a time interval. As an alternative to a counting system, which records the presence of a behavior each time it occurs, a sign system, which records a behavior only once no matter how many times it occurs during the designated interval, can also be used to record behaviors.

Instrument 5.5 represents a sign system for observing the learning climate using 28 discrete behaviors that correspond to various dimensions of warmth and control. Equally divided between warm and cold, 14 behaviors measure the degree of warmth displayed in a classroom; 14 additional behaviors, equally divided between high and low, measure the degree of control in a classroom. Items for the control dimension were taken from the Teacher Practices Observation Record (Brown, 1968). Items for the warmth dimension were written by the author to parallel, in number and type, the items measuring control (Borich, 1993). The result is a 28-item sign observation system in four parts suitable for measuring the learning climate in terms of both warmth and control.

Notice that the behaviors relevant to these two dimensions are recorded in four 15-minute blocks, requiring an hour of observation. This time period is intended to cover a lesson and can be adjusted by dividing the time allotted to a lesson into four equal parts. One of the advantages of recording learning climate over several time intervals is the opportunity to note changes from the beginning to the end of a lesson. In this example, four complete records of the learning climate will have been obtained at the end

of a single observation period. As you observe how learning climates vary among teachers, you might find it helpful to complete a sign system instrument like this one. Reading the descriptors and looking for different behaviors can help you look past your own assumptions and expectations to see a classroom's learning climate in greater detail.

Social Environment

A third approach to observing the learning climate is to measure the social environment that prevails within a classroom. Unlike the observation of teacher concerns and practices related to warmth and control, this approach focuses on the classroom as a unique social system, including the interpersonal relationships among students; relationships between students and the teacher; and students' perceptions of the social dimensions of a classroom, such as its activities, organization, and level of cooperation.

The concept and rationale for studying a classroom as a social system are based on the early work of Parsons and Shills (1951). Parsons (1959) describes two functions of school: socialization and allocation. *Socialization* involves helping a learner translate personal wishes about herself into more realistic adult views and perspectives typical of the world outside the classroom. *Allocation* is the process by which learners are prepared and selected for roles and responsibilities outside the classroom, such as more advanced training and occupations. Parsons (1959) believes that these two functions of schooling could be either stimulated or dampened by the social environment prevailing in classrooms.

One of the earliest research studies based on the work of Parsons was conducted by Walberg and Anderson (1968). Walberg (1966) developed a questionnaire that tapped 18 dimensions of a classroom's social environment to measure the class as a social system. He then gave the questionnaire to students who were enrolled in a new physics curriculum called Harvard Physics in 57 classrooms across the United States. The intent of the study was to have the students describe the quality of their class as a social system based on the 18 dimensions and then determine the degree of relationship between the dimensions and various measures of student achievement, attitude, and creativity. The results of this early study suggested that there is a significant relationship between the social environment in which learning takes place and important school outcomes related to adult roles and responsibilities, such as creativity and achievement.

Dimensions of Social Environment

Subsequent research has updated and expanded Parsons's (1959) social climate concept. Fraser and Walberg (1991) focus on 15 dimensions that describe the classroom as a social system, discussed in the following paragraphs with brief descriptions based on work by Fraser, Anderson, and Walberg (1982). Also included are results of studies by various authors on how these dimensions might apply to students from culturally diverse backgrounds. As you read the descriptions, decide how much you agree with these authors and point to specific instances from your own school years that would affirm or refute their recommendations.

Cohesiveness

When a group of individuals interact for a period of time, a feeling of intimacy or togetherness develops. Too much cohesiveness in a classroom might separate members of the group from nonmembers and may also reduce the motivation and willingness of some students to become engaged in the learning process. Too little cohesiveness might discourage students from an allegiance to group norms and encourage them to focus exclusively on their own personal interests and desires. Delpit (1995) and Delpit and Dowdy (2008) argue that students of color can be unintentionally excluded and a less cohesive classroom can result when teachers frequently use language patterns that establish and maintain social control, such as describing desirable behavior in terms of "demands" instead of "requests." They note that students of underrepresented populations may be uncomfortable with such language, and teachers need to use alternative expressions in talking and writing to the minority culture in order for them to more fully feel a part of the classroom.

Diversity

The extent to which the class provides for different student backgrounds, interests, and activities is important to learning. Too much diversity in a classroom can make teaching difficult because students might share little in terms of language, culture, and related expectations. On the other hand, too little diversity might encourage teachers to believe students are more alike than they are and therefore overlook individual needs. For example, a teacher might plan a single lesson for a class of English language learners, assuming they are more alike than different. However, the lesson might overlook a number of important differences among students, including linguistic distance between the native language and English, students' varying levels of proficiency in their native language(s), students' past experiences with English, and the depth of each student's desire to learn English (Cheng, 1998; Delpit, Boyd, Brock, & Rozendal, 2003; Walqui, 2000a).

Formality

The extent to which behavior within a class is guided by formal rules can influence the flexibility necessary for both teacher and students to achieve stated goals. A classroom with an extensive or inflexible system of rules and procedures might be less productive than a classroom with fewer rules that are changed periodically to accommodate changing goals and conditions, as long as students who have experienced highly structured home and school environments are provided the time and support that may be needed to feel comfortable in a less structured classroom (Dunn, Griggs, & Price, 1993; Dunn & Kontos, 1997; Walqui, 2000b).

Speed

Student commitment to the goals of the class is best achieved when students feel they are learning at the same rate as other students. A pace that is too fast will discourage commitment to group goals on the part of lower-performing learners; a pace that is too slow will discourage commitment from higher-performing learners (Schwartz, 2000; Walqui, 2000a). Generally a moderate to brisk pace and smooth transitions between activities are associated with effective teaching as well as good classroom management (Emmer & Evertson, 2009).

Environment

The classroom's physical environment, including its temperature, lighting, amount of space, and type and arrangement of seating, can influence the structure of the group and the relationships among its members (Gallego & Cole, 2001; Griggs & Dunn, 1996). Generally, the more the classroom reflects the world outside, the more opportunity there is to learn. Further, the placement and storage of instructional materials can send a strong message to students. Students who find it difficult to obtain necessary instructional materials (e.g., textbooks, paper, craft materials) are less likely to enjoy and complete assignments and may feel they have little control over their own learning. Placement of furniture also sends a message to students: Rows of rigidly spaced desks suggest a very different learning climate than that suggested by small groups of desks turned toward one another.

Friction

The extent to which certain students are responsible for class tension and hostility among members of the class indicates the amount of classroom friction. The greater the friction, the more time spent on classroom management and the less task oriented the classroom will be. School size might also be a factor contributing to increased friction; small schools tend to have fewer serious behavior problems than larger schools. This finding has led, in part, to the "school-within-a-school" concept, whereby some educators are experimenting with subdividing larger groups into smaller subgroups based on grade levels, special needs, or interests. Curwin, Mendler, and Mendler (2008) also note that today's schools need to help students learn to recognize and resolve conflict in positive ways.

Goal Direction

Clearly stated goals and their acceptance by the group orient the class and communicate expected roles for class members. Students in highly goal-directed classes reach instructional goals more quickly than students in classes where the goals are unspecified. Students who are encouraged to set their own learning goals and are supported in their efforts are also likely to make greater progress, especially in the case of English language learners (Walqui, 2000a).

Favoritism

The extent to which some students and the teacher behave in ways that benefit some class members at the expense of others can weaken the self-concepts of those who are not favored and disengage them from a commitment to class goals. In one study, less-favored African American high school students who exhibited behavioral challenges in the classroom revealed in interviews that they wanted their teachers to discover what their lives were like outside of school and also wanted an opportunity to take part in the school's reward systems (Kea, 1996).

Cliquishness

Cliques within a class can lead to hostility among class members and engender alternate norms, which may lead to less than optimal group productivity. A high degree of cliquishness can make some students become distracted or off-task, especially during group work, when students might be more loyal to the clique than to the teacher. For example, Merten (1997) notes that competition and conflict among cliques of girls can result in harrassment, negatively affecting how Latina adolescents feel about school and their ability to learn. Some researchers are also concerned about the underrepresentation of minority students in science and mathematics courses and are seeking interventions that might help such students feel more willing to enter into what might be perceived as traditionally white, male academic "cliques" (Clark, 1999).

Satisfaction

Whether or not students gain a sense of accomplishment from completing the events and activities that are assigned affects their learning. Low satisfaction, or sense of accomplishment, leads to greater frustration and less interest in the class, eventually reducing a student's desire to achieve. What contributes to this sense of satisfaction might differ according to students' developmental levels, however. Several researchers have noted that for very young children (e.g., preschool through grade 1), more creative, child-initiated environments produce less anxiety and greater confidence than does involvement in highly academic programs, particularly for children from low-income or culturally and linguistically diverse groups (Dunn & Kontos, 1997).

Disorganization

Class disorganization is believed to be related to reduced instructional time and therefore reduced opportunity to learn. Extreme disorganization can result in classroom management problems and large increases in the time needed to achieve instructional goals. A survey of more than 1,300 high school students underlined this point; when asked what they think of and want from their schools, teen responses reflected a yearning for order, a yearning for moral authority, and a yearning for structure. Indeed, students complained about lax instructors and unenforced rules, stating they would work harder if more were expected of them (Public Agenda, 1997).

Difficulty

Generally, students who perceive the content as easy tend to perform more poorly on measures of achievement than those who do not. A degree of perceived difficulty that is too high, however, will make some students give up and disengage from the learning task. According to Gagné and Deci (2005), humans are intrinsically motivated by three needs—to feel competent, to exercise autonomy (choice), and to develop a sense of relatedness (belonging). Unless they are able to see ways to grow and improve, students who fail in academic tasks are more likely to avoid similar tasks in the future. Teachers who teach from students' strengths rather than their deficiencies set up a positive attitude that encourages students to work harder.

Apathy

Students who fail to see the purpose or personal relevance of class activities perform more poorly than those who do see the connections between classwork and their lives. Disenchanted students fail to behave according to the accepted group norms, thereby increasing the rate of misbehavior and time spent on classroom management. Many researchers and theorists have suggested that motivation (the opposite of apathy) comprises a number of factors. Helping learners take ownership of their learning and allowing them some voice in class activities as well as their evaluation are often suggested as important parts of increasing motivation (and thus decreasing apathy). This appears to hold true across cultural and linguistic lines, as well as across academic disciplines (Ngeow, 1998).

Democracy

Measures indicating where a class perceives itself on an authoritarian–democratic continuum show that optimal learning may occur under both extremes, depending on the degree of warmth perceived by students. An authoritarian climate in which the teacher is warm and nurturing might be as productive for learning as a democratic climate in which students have greater control over the learning environment. Curwin, Mendler, and Mendler (2008) note that the existence of a warm democratic atmosphere is a key component in classrooms (and homes) that successfully nurture nonviolence in society.

Competitiveness

The effect of competitiveness has been shown to differ widely both within and across classrooms. Too little or too much competitiveness is believed to be detrimental to learning, with repetitive cycles of competition and cooperation being optimal. Competitiveness is also valued differently among students from various cultures. For example, students from a culture that values group norms and sharing might be uncomfortable in an individualistic, competitive classroom (Schmuck & Schmuck, 2001). Recent studies of effective literacy instruction have noted that teachers who regularly assess students' strengths and needs are able to create flexible short-term instructional groups to aid students in gaining facility with a particular concept (Cantrell, 1998/1999; Taylor, Pearson, Clark, & Walpole, 1999). Groupings change on a frequent basis, thus encouraging students to work with various peers over time and discouraging the overly competitive "us versus them" feelings that can arise when students function within a single ability-level group for an extended period of time (such as a semester or school year).

Observing the Social Environment of the Classroom

Instrument 5.6 represents a learning climate scale based on the work of Fraser and Walberg (1991). The observer responds to 45 items, 3 for each of the 15 learning climate dimensions just described, using a strongly agree, agree, disagree, or strongly disagree response format. For items about which there is insufficient information, a "no information" response alternative, which is not scored, has been provided.

The social environment scale should be completed at the end of a series of observations or when the observer has gained sufficient familiarity with the class being rated. There are three blocks of 15 items (items 1–15, 16–30, 31–45), with each block containing one item from each of the 15 dimensions. To acquaint yourself with the social environment scale, read the items in Instrument 5.6, try to associate them with a classroom with which you are familiar, and complete the scale as a practice exercise.

After completing the ratings, the three items for each dimension can be averaged. For example, Items 1, 16, and 31 are averaged for the cohesiveness dimension; Items 2, 17, and 32 for the diversity dimension; Items 3, 18, and 33 for the formality dimension; and so on, until averages for all 15 dimensions have been computed. Although three items for each dimension would not be sufficient to provide dependable scores for research purposes, the averages obtained can help the observer become aware of the various facets of a classroom's social environment. The instrument can be used to record changes over time (beginning of school year, end of first grading period, etc.), across units of content whose presentation can be expected to stimulate or create different social environments (whole class, small groups), and across different classes (social studies, math, etc.) to see how the learning climate can change over these contexts.

Finally, note that some of the items are worded negatively. The numbers under these items have been reversed so that a larger number always represents a more positive degree of the dimension being measured. For several of the dimensions being measured, however, a higher score might not necessarily be more desirable for improving classroom achievement, attitude, creativity, or other school behavior. Research has not demonstrated that one end of the scale is necessarily more desirable than the other for the five dimensions of diversity, speed, difficulty, democracy, or competitiveness. A judgment about the degree of their desirability in a given classroom would depend on one's personal beliefs, the types of students being taught, the goals of the instruction, and the presence of other related circumstances that might make a judgment possible (e.g., the speed of the presentation is so fast that it creates friction among students, or the content is so difficult that it makes students apathetic and dissatisfied).

CULTURAL DIVERSITY AND THE LEARNING CLIMATE

One of the first things you will notice when observing in classrooms is the variety of learning climates both within and across schools. The variety you will observe—in degrees of teacher warmth and control; in the self, task, and impact concerns of teachers; and in the social interactions of learners—can be influenced by the predominant cultures and ethnicities within a school and classroom. The following list describes what you can expect to observe in today's heterogeneous classrooms.

- Interactions among students and between students and teachers influenced by cultural expectations. Cooperative learning, peer tutoring, and collaborative problem solving might establish an effective learning climate for some students; discussion, review, testing, and feedback might be equally effective for others.
- The learning climate in a classroom influenced by members of a subculture, minority, or ethnic group, increasing opportunities for cohesiveness, informality, and cooperativeness.
- The noise level, use of classroom space, turn taking, and negotiation varying among classrooms to create different, but equally productive, learning climates when properly managed and matched to cultural expectations.

Lockwood and Secada (1999) summarized the findings of the national Hispanic Dropout Project (HDP) and cited specific school programs that support the education of not only Hispanic students, but all students. They found that students should (1) have an adult mentor; (2) attend school in a safe and inviting place where they are allowed to assume positions of leadership and responsibility; (3) be enrolled in small classes with a lower student–teacher ratio or school-within-a-school format; (4) have access to high-quality, relevant, and interesting curriculum; (5) have access to differentiated instruction based on

materials that are successful with groups of students like themselves; (6) be involved in instructional conversations and cooperative learning activities rather than lecture; and (7) attend schools where their parents and extended families are invited into a partnership of equals for achieving the education of their students.

Your role as a classroom observer, therefore, is to consider learning climate in the context of the norms and expectations of the school in which you are observing. Cultural and ethnic information you should become aware of prior to and during your observation includes

- Ethnic, racial, and gender composition of the class and school
- Predominant family conditions for the majority of students (e.g., single-parent vs. two-parent households)
- Sense of ethnic identity among teachers and students
- Levels of student self-concept and motivation
- Individual differences related to economic and social class

It is also a good idea to examine your own background from a cultural, ethnic, and economic point of view. Your experiences and expectations will play an important role not only in what you notice about the culture, ethnicity, and economic status of others, but also in how you value what you see. Observing in a classroom without prior examination of your personal beliefs will be less productive than if you have taken some time to consider your own background and culture and how these may affect what you see and interpret during your observation. It might not be possible or necessary for an observer to entirely leave his or her world view behind. However, periodic examination of our own cultural background helps us become aware of the powerful interaction between our own views and how we observe and interpret the behavior of others.

In the following chapters, we will explore other equally important lenses for classroom observation. These lenses—classroom management, lesson clarity, instructional variety, task orientation, student engagement in the learning process, student success, and higher thought processes—are always observed in the context of a particular learning climate and are therefore inseparable from it. As we turn to our next lens, classroom management, keep in mind the significant impact of the dimensions of learning climate on both student and teacher.

For More Information

Jane Bluestein, author of *Creating Emotionally Safe Schools* (2001), created a checklist for determining whether a classroom is emotionally safe. A shortened version of the checklist appears in *Scholastic Instructor,* September 2000, pp. 36–37. Read through the four areas listed. How do they connect to the information in this chapter?

Key Term

concerns theory, 55

Activities*

1. In your own words, list one original concern that you have in each area of self, task, and impact. Using the following format and examples as a guide, list one observable sign of teacher behavior corresponding to each of your three concern statements.

    Self

    Concern: whether the students really like me
    Sign: planning lessons that incorporate the interests of the students

    Task

    Concern: covering required material
    Sign: completing lesson plans keyed to the curriculum guide

    Impact

    Concern: challenging unmotivated, less able learners

    Sign: directing less complex questions to unengaged learners

2. If you have not already done so, complete the teacher concerns instrument on page 217. Calculate your average score for each of the three stages: self, task, and impact. Plan to complete the survey a second time at the end of this semester. For which of your three concerns identified in Activity 1 do you predict you will change the most?

3. Read Figure 5.4 with a classmate and agree on the stage of concern with which each sign most closely corresponds. If a consensus cannot be reached, state (a) your reasons for the disagreement and (b) what other signs, if observed, would tend to support the stage of concern you have chosen.

4. In Figure 5.5 identify the areas of subject matter content, teaching methods, and learning climate

*Some of these activities may be grouped into a common activity, divided among classmates, and completed from a single observation.

FIGURE 5.4   Behavioral Signs That Indicate Teacher's Stage of Concern

Sign	Stage of Concern	Other Signs Needed (If Any)
1. Dressing smartly		
2. Revising the objectives to fit the class		
3. Testing slow learners for learning disabilities		
4. Reviewing and summarizing before a big test		
5. Telling students their parents can call you at home		
6. Complaining about the time devoted to collecting money for school pictures		
7. Spending Saturday night writing the week's lesson plans		
8. Telling your students that if they act up, you won't be afraid to call their parents		
9. Placing troublemakers in the front of the room		
10. Creating a list of extra credit readings for those who have already completed their term papers		

FIGURE 5.5 Self Concern, Task Concern, and Impact Concern: Examples

Teacher A (Self Concern)	Teacher B (Task Concern)	Teacher C (Impact Concern)
1. _____	_____	_____
2. _____	_____	_____
3. _____	_____	_____
4. _____	_____	_____
5. _____	_____	_____

that you expect teachers would be most concerned with during the first few days of the school year.

5. Teachers A, B, C, and D have the following score profiles on the teacher concerns instrument:

	Self	Task	Impact
Teacher A	Low	Medium	High
Teacher B	High	Medium	Low
Teacher C	Low	High	High
Teacher D	High	Low	High

One teacher has been teaching for 4 months; one has taught the same subject in the same school for 8 years; another has taught in the same school for 11 years but recently has been reassigned a subject never taught before; and the fourth teacher has taught in the same school for 6 years but recently was unexpectedly declared "surplus" and reassigned to a different grade in an unfamiliar school. Which teacher would most likely have which teaching assignment? Why would each be likely to have the concerns they do?

6. Using up to four different observable signs of teacher or student behavior, describe a classroom that reflects each of the climates listed in Figure 5.6.

7. Using the scales identified in Instruments 5.2 and 5.3, an observer assigned the following ratings to each item after a 1-hour observation. For the six items measuring control, the observer's ratings were 6, 6, 7, 7, 6, 5. For the six items measuring warmth, the ratings were 2, 1, 4, 4, 3, 3. On the axes in Figure 5.7, place a dot representing the climate of this classroom. What verbal descriptions would you use to communicate the meaning of your numerical ratings?

8. For what five dimensions on the social environment scale might either a low or a high numerical rating represent an undesirable learning environment? For one of these five, describe how two classrooms with climates at opposite ends of the scale might be equally detrimental to learning.

9. The following mean scores correspond to 10 dimensions of the social environment scale. Interpret their meaning in terms of the degree to which a positive classroom climate is present.

Dimension	Mean Score
1. Cohesiveness	3.5
2. Formality	3.8
3. Environment	2.1
4. Friction	1.2
5. Goal Direction	3.0
6. Favoritism	1.5
7. Cliqueness	4.0
8. Satisfaction	3.3
9. Disorganization	2.5
10. Apathy	3.0

Overall, how would you rate the social environment in this classroom with respect to its potential effect on student achievement, attitude, and creativity?

10. In 1995, the National Middle School Association (www.nmsa.org) published a position paper entitled "This We Believe: Developmentally Responsive Middle Level Schools," which included the following essential elements of an effective middle school. As you read these elements, identify which of them you believe could be most influenced by classroom

FIGURE 5.6 Classroom Climates and Behavior

High Control/ Low Warmth	High Control/ High Warmth	Low Control/ High Warmth	Low Control/ Low Warmth
1. _____	_____	_____	_____
2. _____	_____	_____	_____
3. _____	_____	_____	_____
4. _____	_____	_____	_____

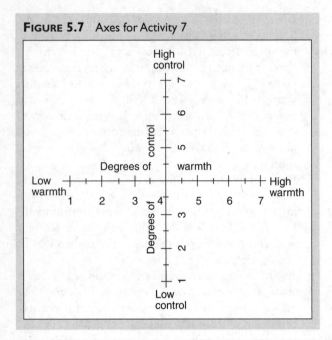

FIGURE 5.7 Axes for Activity 7

climate. Why or why not? Should these elements only occur at the middle school?

Developmentally Responsive Middle Level Schools Need

Curriculum that is challenging, integrative, and exploratory

Varied teaching and learning approaches

Assessment and evaluation that promote learning

Flexible organizational structures

Programs and policies that foster health, wellness, and safety

Comprehensive guidance and support services

6

Focusing on Classroom Management

Rules

Do not jump on ancient uncles.

Do not yell at average mice.

Do not wear a broom to breakfast.

Do not ask a snake's advice.

Do not bathe in chocolate pudding.

Do not talk to bearded bears.

Do not smoke cigars on sofas.

Do not dance on velvet chairs.

Do not take a whale to visit Russell's mother's cousin's yacht.

And whatever else you do do,

It is better you

Do not.

Karla Kuskin

Rules, rules, and more rules! Is that what you think of when you hear the words "classroom management"? Although effective rules are an important part of successful classroom management, by the time you finish reading this chapter you should attribute more to successful classroom management than just making and obeying rules.

In this chapter, we continue to explore the process of observing by considering dimensions of classroom management, including many different skills, such as the way the teacher arranges the classroom, establishes classroom rules, responds to misbehavior, monitors student activity, selects rewards and reinforcement, and uses daily routines to maintain an efficient and productive learning environment. This chapter will introduce some of the most important aspects of managing your classroom.

If you ask a number of teachers how to handle a particular classroom management issue, you're likely to receive several different and perhaps even contradictory responses. Depending on their own experiences and personal views, teachers approach this topic from a number of different philosophies. For our purposes, these approaches to dealing with classroom behavior can be grouped into three general traditions.

1. *The humanistic tradition.* This approach emphasizes the critical role of communication and shared problem solving between teacher and students (Bluestein, 2004; Curwin, Mendler, & Mendler, 2008; Ginott, Ginott, & Goddard, 2003; Glasser, 1998a,b,c).
2. *Applied behavior analysis.* This approach applies behavioral principles, such as behavior modification, to the classroom (Alberto & Troutman, 2006; Canter, 2001; Landrum & Kauffman, 2006).
3. *The classroom management tradition.* This approach, which is the most recent, emphasizes skills involved in organizing and managing the classroom (Doyle, 1986; Emmer & Evertson, 2009; Emmer & Gerwels, 2006; Evertson & Emmer, 2009; Good & Brophy, 2007).

Our discussion in this chapter will emphasize the classroom management tradition. Although it shares some characteristics with the other two traditions, this text will highlight this approach because its principles are derived from research in classrooms and because it emphasizes the critical role of prevention in managing the classroom.

Successful teachers recognize that research can often provide helpful insights for teaching. For example, a year-long observational study of third-grade teachers yielded several insights about effective classroom management (Emmer, Evertson, & Anderson, 1980). Emmer, Evertson, and Anderson recruited 27 third-grade teachers in eight elementary schools into a year-long observation study. During the first 3 weeks of school, observers gathered several types of information on each of the teachers, including room arrangement, classroom rules, consequences of misbehavior, response to inappropriate behavior, consistency of teacher responses, monitoring, and reward systems. In addition, observers counted the number of students who were on-task or off-task at 15-minute intervals to determine the extent to which students were attending to the teacher. From these data the researchers classified the teachers into two groups, consisting of more effective managers and less effective managers, for more in-depth observation the rest of the year.

Those teachers who were categorized as more effective classroom managers had significantly higher student engagement rates (more students actively engaged in the goals of the lesson) and significantly lower student off-task behavior (fewer reprimands and warnings) throughout the school year. The more effective managers established themselves as instructional leaders early in the school year. They worked on rules and procedures until students learned them. Instructional content was important for these teachers, but they also stressed group cohesiveness and socialization, achieving a common set of classroom norms. By the end of the first 3 weeks, these classes were ready for the rest of the year.

In contrast to the more effective managers, the less effective managers did not have procedures well worked out in advance. This was most evident among the first-year teachers being observed. For example, the researchers described one new teacher who had no procedures for using the bathroom, pencil sharpener, or water fountain, and as a result the children seemed to come and go, complicating the teacher's instructional tasks.

The poorer managers, like the better managers, had rules, but there was a difference in the way the rules were presented and followed up. In some cases, the rules were vague: "Be in the right place at the right time." In other cases, they were introduced casually without discussion, leaving it unclear to most children when and where a rule applied.

The poorer managers were also ineffective monitors of their classes, caused, in part, by the lack of efficient routines for pupil activities. In other cases teachers would remove themselves from the active surveillance of the whole class to work at length with a single child. A major result of the combination of vague and untaught rules and poor procedures for monitoring and establishing routines was that students were frequently left without sufficient guidance to direct their own activities.

One further characteristic of the less effective managers was that consequences of inappropriate behavior either were not explained or were not delivered in a timely manner. For example, sometimes teachers issued general criticisms that failed to identify a specific offender or a particular event. Some of these teachers would frequently threaten or warn children but not follow through, even after several warnings. This tended to allow children to push the teacher to the limits, causing more problems. Others issued vague disciplinary messages ("You're being too noisy") that were not adequately focused to capture the attention of any one child or subgroup of children to whom they were directed. It was easy to see how deficiencies in rules, establishment of routines, monitoring, and praise and reward structure negatively affected the overall management and organization of the classroom. Most of the time these deficiencies became windows of opportunity that prompted a wider range of pupil misconduct, off-task behavior, and disengagement from the goals of the classroom. After only a few weeks had elapsed in the less effective managers' classrooms, undesirable patterns of behavior and low teacher credibility that persisted throughout the school year tended to become established.

One of this study's major findings is that effective classroom management during the first few weeks of school reaped teacher and student dividends throughout the school year. This finding has been extended and reinforced by Burke (1997) in a summary of studies that investigated the effects of classroom management procedures with students who had the same teacher for three consecutive years. These studies found that students responded more favorably to positive approaches to classroom management in their second and third years because of their knowledge and comfort with the teachers' classroom management procedures established in the first year.

From these and related studies of classroom management (Bluestein, 2004; Brophy, 1983; Emmer & Evertson, 2009; Evertson & Emmer, 2009), we learn that effective classroom managers possess three broad classes of effective teaching behaviors.

1. They devote extensive time prior to and during the first few weeks of school to planning and organizing their classroom to minimize disruption and enhance work engagement.
2. They approach the teaching of rules and routines as methodically as they approach teaching their subject area. They provide their students with clear instructions about acceptable behavior and monitor student compliance with these instructions carefully during the first few weeks of school.
3. They inform students about the consequences of breaking the rules and enforce these consequences consistently.

Effective classroom managers not only structure the environment to minimize disruptive behavior in the first few weeks of school but also present instruction in a format designed to stimulate student interest, establish clear expectations for learning, provide skilled explanations, summarize key ideas, encourage practice, and engage in continuous review. We will study the relationship of these behaviors to classroom management in the chapters ahead. First, however, let's take a closer look at some of the dimensions for observation of classroom management.

DIMENSIONS OF CLASSROOM MANAGEMENT

Table 6.1 summarizes five behaviors related to effective classroom management.

1. Arranging the classroom to meet instructional goals
2. Preestablishing and sharing classroom rules
3. Developing and communicating instructional routines
4. Instituting a system of incentives and consequences to respond to behavior
5. Using low-profile classroom management

TABLE 6.1 Indicators for Classroom Management

More Effective Classroom Management	Less Effective Classroom Management
1. Arranges the classroom to meet instructional goals (e.g., uses appropriate classroom organization to promote lesson goals)	Fails to establish a classroom arrangement that matches the instructional goal
2. Preestablishes classroom rules (e.g., for speaking out, getting out of seat, group work, make-up work, in-class assignments, and rule violations)	Fails to inform students orally and visually of expected behavior
3. Develops instructional routines (e.g., for beginning of class, group activities, assignments, instructional activities)	Fails to develop procedures that guide students through most frequently repeated tasks
4. Establishes a system of incentives and consequences to respond to appropriate and inappropriate behavior	Fails to develop an adequate system of reward, reinforcement, and consequences to promote appropriate behavior
5. Uses low-profile classroom management to maintain instructional momentum	Responds to misbehavior in ways that disrupt the flow of the lesson and increase loss of instructional time

PRACTICE OBSERVING CLASSROOM MANAGEMENT: A DIALOGUE

The following dialogue illustrates several dimensions of classroom management. First, review the behaviors in Table 6.1 and then read the dialogue using the checklist in Instrument 6.1 to look for signs of classroom management.

Brownwood is a K–8 comprehensive school with a total student body of 850. The school is brand new; in fact, it is in the process of being completed. Workmen move in and out of classrooms daily, painting and adding finishing touches to the carpentry work. Classroom equipment is sparse. Many rooms have an insufficient number of desks. The desks that are available are old and in need of repair; most were originally produced for use in elementary schools. In some of the classrooms, folding chairs are used in place of desks.

The total effect is one of incongruity. The outside of the school building is modern and attractive. It is shaped like a giant doughnut, with classrooms circled around an atrium. Inside, the halls are spacious and carpeted. The brightly painted rooms, which open to the halls, all appear attractive—until the observer notices the desks and chairs. The central office is a large, spacious room that houses the principal and her secretary. In one corner, large boxes, a key plaque, and filing cabinets line the wall to the right of the counter, which partially shields the principal's desk.

On this morning, several teachers are milling around in the office. Some are talking quietly; a few stand before the bulletin board examining an announcement of coming school events.

Mrs. Towers, a confident and secure-looking woman, stands before the mailbox collecting a sheaf of envelopes and folded papers. She sees Mrs. Gates approaching, and her face lights up in a friendly smile. She moves forward a step.*

Mrs. Towers: Hi, Mrs. Gates. I've been meaning to chat with you ever since the principal introduced you at the faculty meeting last week. I'm Beth Towers. I teach eighth-grade science. [She extends her hand.] Welcome to Brownwood.

Mrs. Gates: [Smiling] Oh, thank you for the welcome. I need it!

Mrs. Towers: How are things going?

Mrs. Gates: Well [ruefully], not so good, really. I'm still a little . . . [she hesitates a moment, then continues] a little disoriented, I guess. Somehow, everything seems so unreal.

Mrs. Towers: [Smiling] Yes, I can imagine. Changing teaching assignments to a completely different school in midyear must be pretty frustrating.

Mrs. Gates: Oh, it is! [She looks around.] There I was last week, in the school where I'd taught for years, where I knew all the children—and their parents, too . . . [Her voice trails off.] Everything seemed to run so smoothly there. But, here—[She looks around again, this time with a frown on her face.] It's all so confused! [With an embarrassed expression on her face she continues.] Oh, I don't mean to imply that this is a bad place to be . . . it's just . . . different. I'm sure I'll feel right at home soon. [She concludes with bravado.]

*Based on an excerpt from *Problem Situations in Teaching* by Gordon Greenwood, Thomas Good, et al. (Harper & Row, 1971).

Mrs. Towers: [With warmth] Yes, I'm sure you will. [She touches Mrs. Gates's arm.] Say, why don't you stop by my room some afternoon before you go home. We'll go to the lounge, have a soda, and talk. I'd like that.

Mrs. Gates: [Smiling] Yes, I'd like that, too! Thank you.

The first bell rings. Mrs. Gates collects her keys from the board and starts to go. In her haste she drops a book, which Mrs. Towers retrieves for her.

Mrs. Towers: [Glancing at the title] *The Lives of 10 Great Classical Composers.* Are you going to use this with your music class?

Mrs. Gates: Oh, yes. It's so inspirational. My students at Edgewater loved it. They loved reading aloud in small groups about the lives of great composers. We'd arrange our desks in circles, so students could talk to one another without interrupting the other groups. I've arranged my classroom the same way for today's lesson.

Mrs. Towers: [Hesitantly] Do you think the children will appreciate classical composers without having been introduced to classical music?

Mrs. Gates: [Breezily] Sure—they'll love them! You'll see. I've done this at least six or seven times before, and it's always been successful.

Mrs. Gates smiles confidently, gathers her materials, and goes out of the office. She leaves Mrs. Towers standing alone with a slight frown of consternation on her face. Mrs. Towers then shrugs to herself, shakes her head, and turns to go to her classroom.

Mrs. Gates walks down the hall to the music room. Her first class consists of 37 students from the seventh and eighth grades. The ages range from 11 to 14. When Mrs. Gates examined the cumulative record of five of the students, she found such teacher comments as "unruly," "difficult," and "inattentive."

Mrs. Gates enters a small classroom that serves as the music room. The chairs and desks are arranged in haphazard circles around the teacher's desk. Mrs. Gates places her materials on the desk and puts a book on each desk as the last bell rings and the children noisily push and shove their way into the room. Desks are moved about, chairs are pulled across the floor, and books are dropped on the floor. Several students put their other books on top of their music books or put their music books inside their desks.

Mrs. Gates: [In a firm voice] All right, class, go to your groups. [The talking and the jostling behavior continue. She focuses her attention to one child.] Rosalyn!

Rosalyn has been standing in the doorway talking to several boys in the hall. She turns her head momentarily in Mrs. Gates's direction, ignores the admonition to sit down, and then calmly resumes her discussion. Mrs. Gates appears nonplussed by Rosalyn's behavior and turns to Carlos in the back of the room.

Mrs. Gates: Carlos, please sit down. [Carlos is seated on the windowsill.]

Carlos: [Mockingly] But I am sitting down!

Mrs. Gates: [With some frustration] Carlos, you know what I mean. [Firmly] In a chair, this minute! [Then, to the rest of the class] Go to your seats!

The noise and the movement in the room continue as the teacher attempts to direct students to their assigned seats. Rosalyn finishes her conversation with the boys in the hallway and slowly takes a seat.

Mrs. Gates: Adam, please take your seat.

Adam picks up a chair, puts it noisily into the corner.

Mrs. Gates: Jeanne, will you take your seat?

Jeanne: I don't know where I sit. [Several students laugh.]

John: Sit next to me.

Mrs. Gates walks over to Jeanne's seat and puts her hand on the desk. Jeanne works her way over to the desk, drops her books on it, and slides into the seat, smiling. The noise in the room continues. Mrs. Gates goes to her desk.

Mrs. Gates: Whoever continues to talk will be assigned to detention! [Two students come in late. Mrs. Gates turns to them.] I've warned both of you to be on time. Report to the principal's office. [The two students leave the room, talking as they go.] Turn to page 13.

Students: We've read that before. We've done that part.

Mrs. Gates: I'm sorry. Turn to page 14.

Students: Do we have to read again today? Why can't we do something else? [The noise level begins to build up again.]

Mrs. Gates: Let's get started. [Her voice is strident and the students become quiet; then, in a softer voice, she continues.] This is a beautiful story about Beethoven's early life as a young musical prodigy. He began composing when he was even younger than you. Now, I want you to take turns reading this story orally. Jodi, will you begin reading first?

As the children take turns reading, they frequently falter and attempt to pronounce words, often with difficulty. Most of the students appear diffident about the assignment, and some start shuffling papers on their desks. Carlos begins tapping his pencil on his desk in a distinct rhythm. Rosalyn, across the room, looks up, winks at Carlos, and begins to accompany him. The beat is contagious, and Tina and Joan begin to bob their heads. Mrs. Gates turns first to reprimand Tina and then Joan. The noise fades, but starts up again as soon as another student begins to read. This continues until the bell rings. The students walk in noisy clusters out of the room; a few smile sheepishly, but most talk and laugh loudly as they enter the hallway.

■ TIME TO REFLECT

What did you notice about Mrs. Gates's classroom? What advice would you give her to help her manage her classroom better? Did you see any signs of our five dimensions of classroom management—or lack of them? Let's consider her lesson in light of the five behaviors for effective classroom management on our checklist (Instrument 6.1).

Arranging the Classroom to Meet Instructional Goals

The way a classroom is arranged—furniture aligned, partitions placed, walls and bulletin boards decorated, and the environment "softened"—may have as much to do with achieving your instructional and behavioral goals as the rules and routines that you put in place. Psychologists use the term "behavioral setting" to refer to how particular environments elicit specific behaviors, regardless of who is in them. A classroom is an example of a behavioral setting. There are numerous choices to be made about how to arrange a behavioral setting, and each choice encourages certain student behaviors and discourages others. The

first step in designing a behavioral setting is to identify what students are to do when they are in it.

Take a moment to think back to one of your favorite classes. What do you remember? How did the classroom arrangement contribute to the fond memories you have of events in that room? How might the arrangement have been improved? Did your teacher alter the behavioral setting of this classroom often? How did those alterations affect instructional outcomes?

Because behavioral and instructional goals for students will vary from day to day and from month to month as learner needs are identified, behavioral settings should be flexible. Although it may not be possible to create exactly the environment you desire for every instructional activity, often a simple alteration or adaptation will help match the behavioral setting to your behavioral goals.

The physical arrangement of a classroom is important because it communicates the kinds of behaviors expected of learners. For example, the arrangement shown in Figure 6.1 would be more appropriate for acquiring knowledge, rules, and concepts than for developing relationships and learning to cooperate. This traditional arrangement is better suited for a presentation and teacher-led discussion format than

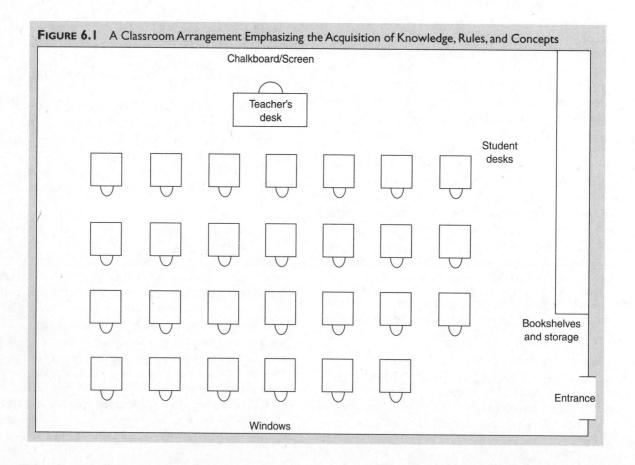

FIGURE 6.1 A Classroom Arrangement Emphasizing the Acquisition of Knowledge, Rules, and Concepts

Chalkboard/Screen

Teacher's desk

Student desks

Bookshelves and storage

Entrance

Windows

it is for more interactive formats. At the beginning of the school year such an arrangement might make it easier to minimize distractions, monitor students, and hold their attention. As students become familiar with classroom rules and routines and as instructional goals require more student-to-student and student-to-teacher interaction and group problem solving, your classroom may change to the more collaborative style, as shown in Figure 6.2.

With this arrangement, more expression of student opinion, increased student talk, and greater spontaneity in student responses can be expected. As the internal features of the classroom evolve from formal to less formal, so will the learning climate. Because a less formal arrangement suggests that interpersonal communication and sharing are being encouraged, increased interpersonal communication and sharing will undoubtedly occur, whether desired or not. Different classroom arrangements can occur simultaneously, as shown in Figure 6.3, when both individualistic and collaborative activities are frequent

instructional goals. Regardless of the arrangement chosen, the social climate created by the classroom's physical arrangement should always match the learning climate intended by the teacher's instructional goals.

It is also important not to assume the traditional or conventional classroom arrangement is always best. For example, the traditional arrangement calls for the teacher to stand in front of the classroom presenting and calling on students seated in neatly ordered rows. This arrangement of space encourages certain patterns of student involvement: in this case, speaking turns allocated in sequential order, one-to-one involvement with the teacher based on a first-come, first-served basis, and individual seatwork in which the book is a primary source of learning. But some students, because of culture or ethnicity, may be less responsive to classroom arrangements that limit the teacher to calling out to individual students who then must respond under the spotlight of the entire class (Lustig & Koester, 2006). Thus, classroom

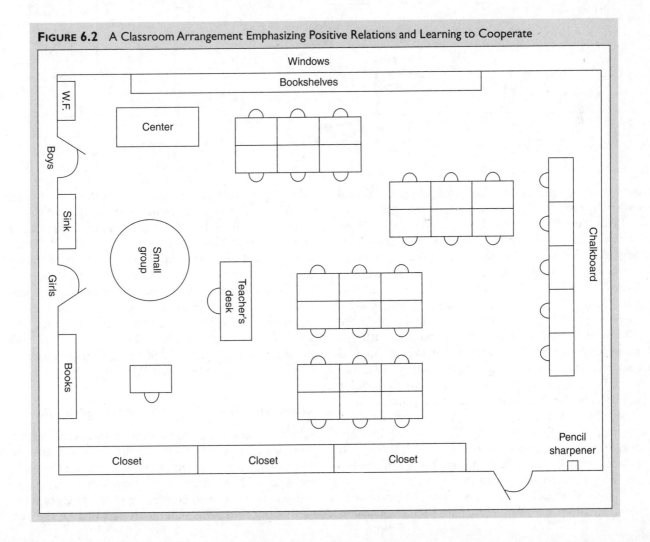

FIGURE 6.2   A Classroom Arrangement Emphasizing Positive Relations and Learning to Cooperate

FIGURE 6.3 A Compromise Classroom Arrangement Allowing Independent, Group, and Cooperative Learning

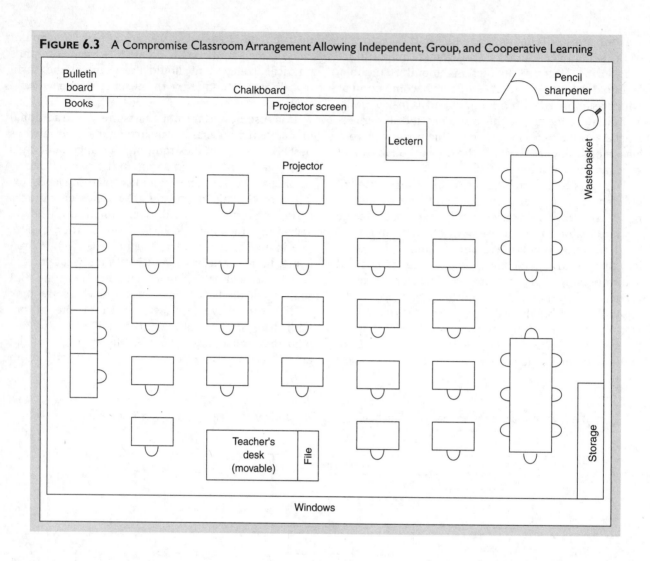

arrangement also should be responsive to cultural expectations as well as your instructional goals.

With these ideas in mind, let's consider the behavioral setting in Mrs. Gates's classroom. Mrs. Gates began her lesson with the assumption that what worked in the past at another school would work at Brownwood. However, it soon became apparent that Brownwood isn't the same as her previous assignment. The students and the instructional context are different. Brownwood students might have little or no familiarity with what Mrs. Gates is teaching and may be less ready for independent reading and group work than her previous classes. Mrs. Gates's students might lack the prerequisites necessary for them to study the topic at the level of appreciation she is expecting. More than anything, Mrs. Gates's assumption that her students were ready to read, listen, and discuss collaboratively might have been responsible for the disorderly classroom that ensued.

Notice also that Mrs. Gates's assignment to read aloud and to sit in groups might have been inconsistent with her instructional goals. Little of the day's lesson actually required group work, and small groups scattered throughout the classroom made management of her group of learners even more difficult. Thus, the physical organization of the classroom actually discouraged, rather than promoted, the purpose of the lesson, which was to acquire an appreciation and understanding of classical music through oral reading. Oral reading is a valuable aid to teaching, but small groups might not have been an effective way in which to begin the lesson. What alternative might you have chosen if you were Mrs. Gates?

Observing the Classroom Arrangement

A behavioral setting can promote certain types of student behavior, with or without the aid of the teacher. Therefore, the social and physical context of the classroom should be arranged to promote and encourage those behaviors most conducive to the goals of a lesson. Many times this will mean deciding on the best classroom arrangement to promote a competitive, individualistic, cooperative, or combination work environment. Instrument 6.2 provides a format for drawing the arrangement of a classroom with respect to the placement of desks, tables, chairs, and media, as well as students and teacher, to reflect its social and organizational climate. When you observe in a classroom, consider the items in the left margin and then sketch the classroom organization. You can summarize the overall social and organizational message of the classroom by checking the appropriate boxes at the bottom of the instrument. Multiple check marks can be used to indicate a combination classroom arrangement. It's a good idea to sometimes make a sketch of a classroom you observe, with specific notes on how you believe the behavioral setting supported or challenged the teacher's instructional goals. How might you have arranged Mrs. Gates's class?

Preestablishing and Communicating Classroom Rules

The second behavior for effective classroom management is establishing classroom rules (Evertson & Emmer, 2009; Forton, 2003; Wells, 2005). Just as there is no one behavioral setting or classroom arrangement that's best for all students and every teacher, there is no single set of rules that's best for directing student behavior. Rules make a statement about the type of climate desired in a behavioral setting. They are a message system whereby the teacher's beliefs and philosophy about academic and conduct-related behavior are communicated to students. If an orderly, businesslike, task-oriented climate is desired, rules such as "Speak (or leave your seat) only when recognized" are appropriate. But such a rule might be inappropriate for a classroom (e.g., Figure 6.2) where students are expected to discuss, obtain resources in different parts of the room, problem solve, and cooperate with one another. Let's discuss some general guidelines for establishing rules.

First, rules should be consistent with the learning climate (Curwin, Mendler, & Mendler, 2008). To understand this relationship, remember the quadrants of classroom warmth and control in the previous chapter (Figure 5.3). Does the teacher want the learning climate for a specific instructional task or activity to emphasize control (Quadrant A), warmth (Quadrant C), or some of both (Quadrant B)? Rules should reflect the degree of warmth and control desired for a particular set of goals, and the classroom's physical arrangement should be chosen to promote it.

Second, rules should be enforceable. A rule that says "No talking or getting out of your seat" might be impossible to enforce when the teacher's personal philosophy or a particular instructional activity encourages independent thinking, problem solving, and group work. Nothing will be more damaging to management of the classroom than unfairness and inconsistency in applying consequences for violations of rules to which the teacher is not fully committed or that do not match a classroom's instructional goals.

Third, only rules that are necessary should be established. There are four reasons to have rules; if a rule cannot be matched to one of the following purposes, it probably is not necessary.

1. Enhancing work engagement and minimizing disruption
2. Promoting safety and security
3. Preventing disturbance to others or to other classroom activities
4. Promoting standards of courtesy and interpersonal relations

Rules should be stated at a level general enough to include a range of specific behaviors. The rule "Respect other people's property and person" covers a variety of problems, such as stealing, borrowing without permission, and throwing objects. Similarly, the rule "Follow teacher requests immediately" might put an end to a variety of off-task, disruptive behaviors that no list of rules could anticipate or comprehensively cover. However, a rule may be stated so generally that the specific problems to which it pertains remain unclear to learners. For example, a rule that simply states, "Show respect" or "Obey the teacher" might be vague enough to be ignored by most learners and consequently may become unenforceable.

Teachers often ask how many classroom rules are appropriate. If you follow the suggestions just given, you'll probably create six to eight classroom rules. Once you've determined what your classroom rules should cover, it's important to consider how to phrase those rules.

One of the most widely recommended techniques for writing rules is "State rules positively" (Bluestein, 2004; Jones & Jones, 2007). Although in general it is better to state what you want to happen rather than what you don't want to happen ("Take notes" vs. "Don't daydream"), it is sometimes necessary to state rules negatively. If all you want to communicate is not to shout, it is clearer if the rule simply states "No shouting" instead of "Be polite and respectful." The former is to the point; the latter may be interpreted so broadly that most learners will miss the point.

Not all rules are equally important, and some may have to be added as special circumstances require. But rules about responding and speaking out, getting out of one's seat, communicating during group work, making up work, missing due dates, completing in-class assignments early, and violating rules are often among the most troublesome for the beginning teacher. You'll want to consider the following issues in each rule area.

Rule Area	Issues
Responding, speaking out	Must hands be raised? Are other forms of acknowledgment acceptable (e.g., head nod)? What will happen if a student speaks when others are speaking? What will you do about shouting or using a loud voice?
Getting out of seat	When is out-of-seat movement permissible? When can a student come to the teacher's desk? When can reference books or learning centers be visited? What will be done if a student visits another?
Communicating during group work	Can a student leave an assigned seat? How loudly should a student speak? Who determines who can talk next? Will there be a group leader?
Make-up work	Will make-up work be allowed? Will there be penalties for not completing it? Will it be graded? Whose responsibility is it to know work is missing?
Missing due dates	What happens when repeated violations occur? Where can a student learn the due dates if absent? What penalties are there for copying another person's assignment? Will make-up work be required when a due date is missed?
Early completion of class assignments	Can work for other classes or subjects be done? Can a newspaper, book, or magazine be read? Can the next exercise or assignment be worked on? Can students rest their heads on their desks?
Rule violations	Will names be written on the board? Will warnings be given? Will you have after-class detention? When will a disciplinary referral be made?

Establishing rules for dealing with many possible problem areas will help you feel more secure in your

teaching. However, unless the rules are clearly communicated and consistently applied, they will not be effective (Emmer & Evertson, 2009; Evertson & Emmer, 2009). Also, the choice and expression of rules must be consistent with the culture and ethnicity of the students in order to avoid conflicts with parental values; home life conditions; and culturally determined participation patterns that can influence assignment completion, speaking out, and interpersonal communication (Bowers & Flinders, 1991).

Some researchers suggest that rules are especially effective when students are involved in their formulation (Curwin, Mendler, & Mendler, 2008). As you read the dialogue, did you sense that shared classroom norms had been established in the classroom? What led you to believe otherwise? Let's consider how Mrs. Gates might have better applied rules and consequences in her classroom.

On a number of occasions the mention of a rule might have stopped, or at least lessened, the seriousness of a misbehavior in Mrs. Gates's classroom. One such event occurred with Rosalyn standing at the door talking to several boys after the start of class. A rule that requires everyone to be in their seats at the bell would have helped prevent this problem, and a verbal reference to it by Mrs. Gates would have immediately communicated the seriousness of Rosalyn's behavior.

To be effective, rules must include logical and consistent consequences. For example, Carlos, who fails to sit down after being requested to, not only appears to be unaware of any rule that requires students to be in their seats at the start of class, but also fails to associate his disobedience with any sort of consequence. Mrs. Gates's problems escalate as other students speak out freely, continue to move around the room, and finally instigate antagonizing behavior toward one another. Although not all of Mrs. Gates's problems could have been solved with rules, three rules would have been especially helpful at the start of class.

- Students must be quiet and in their seats at the start of the bell.
- Students must raise their hands and be acknowledged before speaking.
- Students must ask permission before leaving their assigned seats.

These rules would have allowed Mrs. Gates to cite an individual's name and the rule at the first sign of misbehavior, with the understanding that a rule violation automatically incurs a predetermined consequence. They also would have helped her avoid relying on her personal frustration or disapproval as the only way in which to communicate a rule. As you visit classrooms, you'll want to look for evidence of rules and the ways teachers communicate them to students. You will want to pay particular attention not only to the words a teacher uses, but also to the way in which those words are delivered—and note the apparent effectiveness of the communication.

Observing Classroom Rules

As we have seen, rules help make a classroom an efficient and productive learning environment. Although many rules might be needed for an efficient and productive classroom, only six to eight rules are used frequently enough to warrant visual or oral presentation the first day or two of the school year. Many other rules are best left until a particular event that makes the rule meaningful and memorable occurs (e.g., when a visitor first comes to the door or when laboratory equipment is used for the first time). You can use Instrument 6.3 to record classroom rules that correspond to seven areas pertaining to academic work and to conduct. Add to the list at least one rule that you think is particularly important. Did you ever hear or see this rule formally communicated? Do you feel it is broad enough to cover a number of behaviors, and yet not overly vague? What other rules might you want to add to this list and to include in your own classroom?

Developing and Communicating Instructional Routines

The third dimension of classroom management involves **instructional routines.** As we have discussed in previous chapters, classrooms are busy places. Students and materials must be checked in and out; activities must be begun and ended; learners must be moved through the lessons; and assignments must be given, completed, and evaluated. Groups are formed, disbanded, and rearranged. In the midst of these activities, students need, forget to bring, and borrow things. They get thirsty, hungry, tired, or sick and have to use the bathroom. Handling all this complexity requires a systematic routine. A **classroom routine** is a set of rules organized around a particular time (the beginning of day), a concept (group work), or a place (library, learning center, or playground) that helps guide learners through the day. Well-taught routines can keep learners engaged in learning and the teacher in control.

The amount of time learners spend thinking about, acting on, or working with a learning task (e.g., responding to a question, completing an exercise in a workbook, writing a paragraph or essay, reading the text) is referred to as **engaged learning time** (Savage, 1999; Woolfolk, 2007). This is different from the time spent teaching a particular lesson or activity. Although a teacher may allocate 35 minutes for a particular activity, students might spend only 15 minutes of that time actively engaged in completing the learning task. What happens to the other 20 minutes? Most likely they are used passing out materials, making announcements, giving directions, dealing with student requests to leave the room or to borrow materials, cleaning up, and handling discipline problems. In the studies of effective classroom managers cited previously, the teachers who most successfully engaged students in learning were those who communicated routines to their students during the first few weeks of school (Emmer & Evertson, 2009; Emmer, Evertson, & Anderson, 1980). This research also found a significant relationship between engaged learning time and achievement, suggesting that students achieve more in classes with well-established routines. Let's look at some example routines and how they are established.

Figure 6.4 lists some situations for which routines are commonly established. Each routine has a corresponding set of procedures or informal rules pertaining to specific areas of concern. For example, a beginning-of-class routine includes expectations for what students should be doing while roll is being taken (sit still without talking, check over homework or last assignment, or read silently from text). It must also include how a student should enter the room after the bell has rung (come to the teacher, go directly to his seat, or see a counselor) and how handouts, tests, and assignments are to be turned in or dispensed (e.g., first person in each row collects enough papers for row members from stacks conveniently placed in front and back of room and passes them to the other students). The procedures established for each routine will depend on the classroom's learning climate and the teacher's instructional style. They are the procedures most comfortable for the teacher and learners, given the instructional goals and climate of the classroom.

Teaching a routine takes time and energy. But routines established during the first weeks of school will save time later and give students a sense of organization and order. Routines enhance the speed and efficiency with which things get done, especially time-consuming noninstructional activities. Therefore, they allow the teacher more time to teach and learners more time to become engaged in the

FIGURE 6.4 Examples of Classroom Routines and Some Topics They May Address

Beginning Class Routine

A. Roll call, absentees
B. Tardies
C. Distributing materials

Work Requirement Routine

A. Heading of papers
B. Use of pen or pencil
C. Writing on back of paper
D. Neatness, legibility
E. Incomplete work

Instructional Activity Routine

A. Student attention
B. Obtaining help
C. Student talk
D. Activities to do when work is completed
E. Student movement
F. Bringing materials

Group Activity Routine

A. Expected behavior in group
B. Expected behavior of students out of group
C. Sharing of resources
D. Individual responsibilities
E. Choosing a group leader

Ending Class Routine

A. Putting away supplies, equipment
B. Cleaning up
C. Dismissing class

Interruption Routine

A. Talk among students
B. Turning in work

C. Handing back assignments
D. Getting back assignments
E. Out-of-seat policies

Use of Room/School Area Routine

A. Shared materials
B. Teacher's desk
C. Water fountain, bathroom, pencil sharpener
D. Student desks
E. Learning centers, stations
F. Playground
G. Lunchroom

Assignment Routine

A. Returning in-class assignments
B. Homework assignments
C. Turning in assignments

Checking Assignments in Class Routine

A. Students exchanging papers
B. Making and grading assignments
C. Turning in assignments

Grading Routine

A. Recording grades
B. Grading criteria
C. Contracting with students for grades

Academic Feedback Routine

A. Rewards and incentives
B. Posting student work
C. Communicating with parents
D. Students' record of grades
E. Written comments on assignments

learning process. Routines should be taught with as much planning and thoroughness as learning objectives and should be followed up with monitoring (Jones & Jones, 2007).

As we consider Mrs. Gates's experience at Brownwood, we can't help but wonder if having some established classroom routines would have helped. Certainly a beginning-of-class routine that included procedures for taking roll (absentees, tardies) would have brought some immediate structure and order to the start of class by requiring students to be in their assigned seats to avoid being counted absent or late. Other routines for oral reading and subsequent class discussion might also have been helpful. For example, Mrs. Gates might have benefited from us-

ing a classroom routine for oral reading, such as the following set of procedures:

1. Look at the board to find the pages to be read.
2. Scan the pages to be read to get the main idea.
3. Write down one question to ask about the reading.
4. Be ready to discuss your question with the class at the end of oral reading.

If these instructions were written on the board at the time the students entered the classroom, the signal "Let's go to our reading routine" is all that might have been needed to establish task orientation at the very start of class. A routine for class noise might also have helped to change the pace and return the class to a quieter state, such as the following simple routine:

1. Stop activity.
2. Return to seat.
3. Open book to page noted on the board.
4. Begin reading silently.

Mrs. Gates could have benefited from such a "Stop" or "Time Out" routine as her problems began to escalate. As you noticed, however, few if any routines were evident in Mrs. Gates's classroom.

Observing Instructional Routines

A routine is an expected sequence of events that is repeated during a day (or week) to accomplish a given task in the quickest and most efficient manner possible. As noted in Figure 6.4, there are many possible routines for handling specific classroom events such as beginning of class (roll call, absentees, tardies), managing group activities (talking, sharing resources, individual responsibilities, choosing a leader), and handling assignments (completing and handing in work). Regardless of the task, however, each routine communicates a set of procedures that must be completed and, when applicable, the order in which they should be followed (e.g., raise hand before speaking and then wait to be acknowledged, or stand by the door when late, be acknowledged, and then go to seat). Established routines help ensure an orderly class day and provide the structure that maintains classroom momentum without the need to repeat verbal messages over and over. The key to avoiding this repetition is to teach routines as a single activity and not as a set of related but different activities. This means that you will need to demonstrate before the class each routine you wish your students to follow from beginning to end, not simply communicate it as a set of verbal instructions. In this manner students come to recognize routines as a unit, with a beginning, middle, and end, and can reproduce them as a single activity.

Although you may not have the opportunity to observe a teacher setting up a routine at the beginning of a school year, you can gain a sense of how routines work and what makes them effective through careful observation. Instrument 6.4 provides four different situations for you to consider as you observe routines. Record your observation for each situation and then add one of your own. Indicate how well the students appear to have learned each routine by circling 1 if you think the routine was not learned or only minimally learned, 2 if some but not all of the students knew the routine, and 3 if the routine was

learned with efficiency and precision by most of the class.

Establishing a System of Incentives and Consequences

The fourth behavior for promoting effective classroom management involves establishing a system of incentives and consequences. Motivating learners to behave appropriately requires knowing the difference between consequences and punishment (Reeve, 2006, 2008). In a school setting, it often is natural to set an aversive tone—to say why students *should not do* something and punish them when they do, rather than to say why they *should do* something and reward them when they do. Recall how frequently you have heard

If you don't study, you'll flunk the course.

If you don't do the homework, I'll take points off.

Do it right the first time, or you'll have to do it over.

If you don't get it today, you'll have to get it on your own.

If it's too difficult, you shouldn't be in this class.

In any environment where a few individuals hold most of the power (e.g., schools), it might be natural to reinforce the existing structure with penalties. However, when the *only* incentive for good conduct involves avoiding punishment, learners associate school with punishment and their motivation to learn decreases. Learners generally respond far better to rewards for acceptable behavior than to punishment for unacceptable behavior. Unless special circumstances prevail, rewards are more effective than punishment in encouraging individuals to behave appropriately.

Television advertisers learned this lesson the hard way when they discovered that the rewards of having fresh, clean teeth persuaded more people to change brands of toothpaste than the negative consequences of tooth decay. When negative consequences (penalties) provoke high levels of anxiety and fear of the consequences, they no longer function to motivate behavior. The implications of advertising research should not be lost on educators: It is more effective to inform learners of the positive consequences of appropriate behavior than to enumerate the negative consequences of misbehavior.

Although both rewards and penalties are necessary, the emphasis on rewards (the positive consequences of the right behavior) should always outweigh the emphasis on penalties (the negative consequences of the wrong behavior). Compare this list with the previous one; it has been rephrased to emphasize reward and not punishment.

> Remember to study. It will make the lessons a lot easier.
>
> If you do the homework, the tests will be easier.
>
> Save time. Follow the directions.
>
> Listen carefully; it will be easier to understand my explanations.
>
> Notice where this assignment is difficult. That will indicate what you should study.

Table 6.2 contrasts phrases that emphasize reward rather than punishment for five strategies that promote appropriate behavior. Notice how a small change in wording can make the difference between a punishment and a reward.

Other types of incentives can also increase the probability of a desirable response. Some of the most frequently used include

- Verbal or written praise
- Smile, head nod
- Special privileges (e.g., visit to the learning center or library)

TABLE 6.2   Five Strategies for Promoting Appropriate Behavior

Strategy	Appropriate	Avoid
Using praise and encouragement	You've got it.	That's a dumb answer.
	Good work.	You're being lazy again.
	Good try.	I can see you never study.
	That was quick.	You can never pay attention, can you?
Providing explanations	The reason this is so important is …	Today you will have to learn this, or else …
	We are doing this assignment because …	Complete this exercise; otherwise, there'll be trouble.
	This will be difficult, but it fits in with …	This is a long assignment, but you'll just have to do it.
	Experience has shown that without these facts the next unit will be very difficult.	We must cover this material, so let's get going.
Offering to help	Should you need help, I'll be here.	You should be able to do this on your own.
	I'll be walking around, so catch me if you have a problem.	Please don't ask a dumb question.
	Don't be afraid to ask a question if you're having trouble.	Raise your hand only if you're stuck on a difficult problem.
Accepting diversity	That's not the answer I expected, but I can see your point.	That's not the kind of answer we can accept around here.
	That's not how I see it, but I can understand how others might see it differently.	I've never heard that expression before—so let's not start something new.
	This is not something I'm familiar with.	Please use ideas that fit in with what I say in class.
	Where did you get that idea?	Don't ever use foreign words in this class.
	That is not a word I've heard before.	
	Tell us what it means.	
Providing specific rewards	All homework completed means 5 extra points.	5 points off for missing homework.
	If you get a C or better on all the tests, I'll drop the lowest grade.	If you have less than a C average on all your tests, you'll have to take an extra test.
	Those who complete all the exercises on time can go to the learning center.	If you don't complete the exercise on time, there can be no use of the learning center.
	If you have a C average, you get to choose any topic for your term paper.	If you don't have a C average, you must choose your term paper topic from a restricted list of difficult topics.

- Time out of regular work to pursue a special project (e.g., read)
- Permission to choose a topic or assignment
- Getting to work in a group; being allowed to select group members
- Extra points toward grade
- "Smiley face" stickers on assignments
- Note to parents on top of a test or paper
- Special recognitions and certificates (e.g., "most improved," "good conduct award," "neatest," "hardest worker")

Not all of these incentives may be equally reinforcing, however. Some learners might be uncomfortable with verbal praise (Cheng, 1998); others will have no desire to visit the library or learning center. Some students like to be called on; others might be too shy and dislike the personal attention. An incentive that works for one student may be completely irrelevant to another. Finding the right incentive for each student often requires trial and error; if one type of reward does not seem to increase a desirable behavior, try another. Knowing the interests, needs, and aspirations of learners helps in finding the right mix of rewards. Students can be asked for a menu of rewards (e.g., readings, music, magazines) that reflect their specific interests, and you can then select the most feasible and desirable from their list.

Unfortunately, incentives for desirable behavior are not always effective. However, there are many ways to deal with misbehavior when incentives fail. On one end of the continuum, you might choose to ignore an infraction if it is brief and not likely to recur (e.g., when a student jumps out of and back into his seat to stretch after a long assignment). At the other extreme, you may need to summon outside help (an administrator, a school counselor, or a colleague down the hall) to help resolve a problem. Fortunately, there are many alternatives for handling misbehavior that fall between these two extremes, as shown by the following list, set in approximate order of increasing severity.

- Looking at the student sternly
- Walking toward the student (called **proximity control**)
- Calling on the student to provide the next response
- Asking the student to stop
- Assigning the student to another seat
- Discussing the problem with the student
- Assigning the student to detention or "time out"
- Calling the student's parent(s)

More important than the variety these alternatives offer is the goal of matching the correct response to the type of misbehavior that has occurred. Although all rule violations should receive a consistent response, the severity of the consequence can and should vary according to not only the nature of the violation and the frequency with which it has occurred, but also the context in which it occurred. If your response is too mild when a student has violated a major rule many times before, nothing is likely to change. If your response is too severe when a student commits a minor violation for the first time, you will be perceived as unfair. It helps to be flexible as you seek to resolve discipline problems; take into account both the context in which the violation occured and the type of misbehavior that has occurred when you determine your response. For example, studies have shown that students from Hispanic, Asian, and Middle Eastern cultures will respond more positively to a quiet, private correction, as opposed to a public display such as writing their name on the board (Adeed & Smith in Banks, 1997; Cheng, 1998; Lockwood & Secada, 1999; Saito, 1999; Walqui, 2000a).

General Guidelines for Dealing with Mild, Moderate, and Severe Misbehavior

- Talking out, acting out, getting out of one's seat, disrupting others, and similar misbehaviors might deserve a mild response at first. But if they occur repeatedly, a moderate response may be appropriate. In unusual cases, such as continual talking that disrupts the class, a strong response may be warranted.
- Misbehaviors such as cutting class, abusive conduct toward others, fighting, and failure to complete an assignment might deserve a moderate response at first. But if these behaviors become frequent, a strong response may be warranted.
- Misbehaviors such as cheating, plagiarism, stealing, and vandalism usually warrant a stronger response. These include major incidents of vandalism, theft, incorrigible conduct, and substance abuse in the classroom, which should be brought to the immediate attention of a school administrator.

As we consider Mrs. Gates's classroom, we can see the important role of the teacher in assigning certain consequences to rules. In other words, a rule without clearly communicated consequences is an ineffective rule. Consequences can range from a simple warning (a mild response) to withholding privileges (a moderate response) to detention or a visit to the office (a strong response). Whatever alternatives are chosen, they should be made known to students in advance. Mrs. Gates apparently had few alternative consequences in mind, except for detention and a trip to the principal's office. These strong responses might have been unnecessary if a mild or moderate response had been invoked at an earlier time.

Finally, we note that few if any incentives were used by Mrs. Gates to promote positive behavior. Instead, most of her attempts to control the class were negatively worded reactions that served only to increase the emotional temperature of the classroom and create an adversarial relationship between Mrs. Gates and her students.

As you observe in classrooms, you'll want to be particularly alert to incentives and positive comments and record them for your own use. Remember, it is far more effective to focus on offering positive comments and incentives to *prevent* student misbehavior than it is to wait until student misbehavior escalates and then express personal disapproval and frustration. Take every opportunity to observe how teachers redirect student behavior and consider how you might apply their approaches to your own teaching.

Observing Incentives and Consequences

Incentives and consequences are tools for encouraging appropriate behavior and discouraging inappropriate behavior. Together, they represent a strategy for maintaining a productive learning environment in the midst of what is often a day filled with rapid decision making ("Gosh, they've finished; what do I do now?"), immediacy ("Angela, stop talking back"), administrative disruption ("Who's that at the door?"), and social distraction ("Mark, you can't sit next to Sue"). These and many other features of busy classrooms make a system of incentives and consequences an indispensable tool for managing a classroom.

The manner in which a system of incentives and consequences is applied is important. As we saw earlier, rules and consequences should be stated positively wherever possible. Research has shown that we are more apt to change our behavior to gain something positive we do not already possess than to protect what we already have (hence, two-for-one sales, cash rebates, and coupons for new products and services). Negative consequences work best when they are used to motivate one to behave appropriately, not to inflict pain or discomfort. This subtle but important difference can be achieved by positive consequences that are thoughtfully worded (instead of "If you don't study, you'll flunk the exam," "Let's not forget to do the studying, so that we all get a high grade").

The most effective and practical incentives for encouraging appropriate behavior are orally delivered phrases that

- Convey praise and encouragement
- Provide explanations

- Offer to help
- Acknowledge diversity
- Identify a specific reinforcement or reward

To help you focus on positive and helpful verbal phrases, Instrument 6.5 provides a format for recording a teacher's oral incentives either to a student or to the class in these five areas. Try to find one example of each during a class observation and record the teacher's words as you hear them. Afterward, notice whether each statement was positively worded ("I'm here if you need my help") or negatively worded ("If you don't think for yourself, I can't help you"). How would you reword a negatively phrased comment? Which phrasing do you think would encourage *you* to do your best work?

Using Low-Profile Classroom Management

The fifth behavior for promoting effective classroom management is the use of low-profile techniques. As we have seen, a behavioral setting suited to the goals of instruction, a carefully crafted set of rules and routines, and a system of incentives and consequences are important dimensions of classroom management. Some students, however, might choose not to follow rules and routines or respond to rewards and consequences because of a disinterest in school, a lack of skills needed to profit from the lesson, a desire to escape from the routine of the classroom, or for other personal reasons. Some of these disruptions will be minor, lasting for only a short time and resolving themselves. But others will persist. In the face of their persistence, it is important to respond in ways that promote a positive learning climate.

Rinne (1984) uses the expression **low-profile classroom management** to refer to strategies used by effective teachers to stop misbehavior without disrupting the flow of a lesson. These techniques are effective for **surface behaviors** (Levin & Nolan, 2006), which include the overwhelming majority of disruptive classroom actions, such as laughing, talking out of turn, passing notes, daydreaming, not following directions, combing hair, doodling, humming, and tapping. They are called surface behaviors because they are the normal developmental behaviors of children confined to a small space with large numbers of other children. They are not indicative of some underlying emotional disorder or personality problem, but they can disrupt the flow of a lesson and the work engagement of others if left unchecked. In a synthesis of 57 research articles concerned with classroom time and student achievement, Cotton (1996) found that approximately one-half of all classroom time is taken up by noninstructional activities, with surface behaviors representing a significant portion of that time.

Figure 6.5 depicts several components of low-profile classroom management as a set of techniques for dealing with surface misbehavior that require *anticipation* by the teacher to prevent problems before they occur, *deflection* to redirect disruptive behavior that is about to occur, and *reaction* to unobtrusively stop disruptions immediately after they occur. Let's take a closer look at each of these components.

Anticipation

Alert teachers have their antennae up to sense changes in student motivation, attentiveness, arousal level, or excitability. They are aware that at certain times of the year (before and after holidays), week (just before a major social event), or day (right after an assembly, a trip to the playground, or a physical education class), the readiness of the class for doing work will differ from the norm. Skilled classroom managers are alert not only to changes in the group's motivation or attention level, but also to changes in specific individuals as soon as they enter class.

At these times, anticipation involves scanning back and forth with active eyes to quickly size up the seriousness of a potential problem and head it off before it becomes a bigger problem. For example, a teacher might decide to pick up the pace of the class to counter perceived lethargy in the class after a 3-day weekend or to remove magazines or other objects that may distract the attention of individuals or the group before a long holiday. Some teachers maintain a reserve of activities that are likely to boost student interest during times when it is difficult to stay focused on normal day-to-day activities. Others boost interest by being more positive or eager in the face of waning student enthusiasm—for example, raising and lowering voice pitch or moving to different parts of the room more frequently. At other times it might be necessary to quickly change seating arrangements to minimize antagonism when arguments occur between students. Anticipation involves knowing not only what to look for, but where and when to look. It also involves having a technique ready, no matter how small, for changing the environment quickly and unobtrusively to prevent problems from occurring or escalating. The time you invest in observing what to look for, and where and when to look for it, will be well spent in developing a valuable skill—one that will enhance your ability to anticipate problems in your own classroom.

Deflection

As we have noted, good classroom managers sense when disruption is about to occur. They are attuned to verbal and nonverbal cues, called *antecedents* or *precursors,* that have preceded disruptive behavior in the past. Such cues might involve a student who abruptly closes a textbook, sits and does nothing, squirms, asks to be excused, ignores a request, sighs in frustration, or makes a facial expression of annoyance or anger. Although not disruptive by themselves, these behaviors may signal that more disruptive behavior is about to follow.

Some teachers who are aware of the significance of these antecedents deflect many problems by simply moving nearer to the student who may be about to misbehave, thus preventing a more disruptive episode. Other teachers might make eye contact with the learner, combined with certain facial expressions such as raised eyebrows or a slight tilt of the head, to communicate a warning. Both these techniques are effective nonverbal signals to deflect a potential problem.

But verbal signals are also effective. Verbal deflection techniques include prompting (the teacher reminds the class of the rule or says, "We are all supposed to be doing math now"), name dropping (the target student's name is inserted into the teacher's explanation or presentation; for example, "Now if

FIGURE 6.5 Characteristics of Lower- and Higher-Profile Management

Lower Profile ←		Higher Profile →
Anticipation	**Deflection**	**Reaction**
Scanning	Proximity control	Warning
Pick up the pace	Eye contact	Loss of privileges
Remove temptation	Prompting	Time out
Boost interest	Name dropping	Restitution
Change seating arrangements	Peer recognition	Removal

Angela were living in Boston at the time of the Boston Tea Party, she might have . . .”), and peer recognition (the teacher notices a student engaged in appropriate behavior and acknowledges this to the class). As the potential for the problem to escalate increases, the effective manager shifts from nonverbal to verbal techniques to keep pace with the seriousness of the misbehavior that is about to occur.

Reaction

Anticipation and deflection can efficiently and unobtrusively prevent behaviors that disrupt the flow of a lesson. These techniques allow students the opportunity to correct themselves, fostering the development of self-control. However, the classroom is a busy place, and there might be many demands on a teacher that make problem behavior difficult to anticipate or to deflect.

When disruptive behavior occurs that cannot be anticipated or deflected, the teacher's primary goal should be to end the disruptive episode as quickly as possible. An effective reaction requires a class rule that corresponds with the behavior in question and specifies the consequences for violating the rule. Charles and Senter (2007) and Glasser (1998b) point out that an effective consequence for breaking a rule can be temporary removal from the classroom—provided the classroom is a place where that student wants to be—or loss of a privilege, such as recess, time at a learning center, or other activity the learner would miss.

When Disruptive Behavior Occurs

A suggested anticipation–deflection–reaction sequence might include the following responses:

1. As soon as a student disrupts, acknowledge a nearby classmate who is performing the expected behavior: “Chris, I appreciate how hard you are working on the spelling words.” Then wait 15 seconds for the disruptive student to change her behavior.
2. If the disruption continues, say, “Clara, this is a warning. Complete the spelling assignment and leave Carrie alone.” Wait 15 seconds.
3. If the student doesn't follow the request after this warning, say, “Clara, you were given a warning. You must now leave the room for 5 minutes (or you must stay inside during lunch, or you cannot go to the resource center today). I'll talk to you about this later.”

The low-profile techniques of anticipation, deflection, and reaction, when used skillfully, promote lesson flow. When these techniques do not work for a particular student or group of students, it might oc-

casionally be a signal that other needs of the student are not being met and a school counselor or school psychologist should be consulted. We will look at other patterns of low-profile classroom management in the chapters ahead.

If we consider the application of low-profile management in Mrs. Gates's lesson, it appears that Mrs. Gates failed to anticipate, deflect, and react appropriately to surface behaviors in her classroom. In fact, almost all of Mrs. Gates's problems stemmed from minor infractions of unspoken rules that could have been handled easily with low-profile management. Scanning, picking up the pace, boosting interest through intriguing questions or instructional variety, removing temptation, and changing seating arrangements might have diminished, if not eliminated, the minor forms of misbehavior Mrs. Gates was experiencing—had they been used early enough. If these techniques were not effective, Mrs. Gates could have employed physical movement (walking near a misbehaving student), eye contact, prompting, name dropping, and peer recognition to avoid escalating problems. And finally, warnings or loss of privilege could have been invoked, if necessary. Mrs. Gates's only response, regardless of offense, seems to have been detention or a visit to the office—two of the strongest reactions possible. When these are used immediately, there are few other stronger responses available. Being quick to use strong responses can make a teacher look ineffective in the eyes of students and may send a message that the teacher is not in control. This is why low-profile classroom management is important: It provides the opportunity for the teacher to help correct misbehavior with a mild response and prevent the behavior from escalating.

Observing Low-Profile Classroom Management

Remember that the purpose of low-profile management is to respond to surface behaviors (i.e., small incidents of misbehavior, such as laughing, talking, passing notes, daydreaming, not following directions) without losing the rhythm and momentum of your instruction. Dealing with a single student's behavior at length can encourage reactions from other students and promote acting-out behavior that halts the forward movement of a lesson, sometimes irretrievably. Recall that low-profile management comprises three separate behaviors—anticipation, deflection, and reaction—any one or a combination of which might be used to deal with misbehavior quickly and unobtrusively. To focus an observation on low-profile classroom management, use Instrument 6.6. Place a check mark in a box each time you observe an example of any of the types of anticipation, deflection, and reaction listed. Add examples of your own as you see them.

As you observe teachers and consider how to apply these concepts to your own teaching, it is important to remember that the largest part of effective classroom management involves anticipation. Wise teachers anticipate the types of problems that are most likely to occur in a given class or during a particular lesson and then plan, in advance, how they will respond when problems do occur. For example, imagine the first week of school during your first teaching assignment. How would you answer the following questions?

- Will students do more listening or talking?
- Should they be calm and quiet or excited and talkative?
- Is conversation to be encouraged or discouraged?
- Will an atmosphere of independence and self-study, or one of cooperation and group problem solving, prevail?
- How will you arrange the physical space in your classroom to encourage the kinds of behavior you hope to see?
- What rules and routines will you have?

As you observe experienced teachers, keep these questions in mind—and each of them will be answered.

Our reactions to Mrs. Gates's lesson are summarized in Figure 6.6. Although we saw only a small example of Mrs. Gates's teaching under the challenge of a new school and curriculum, we gave Mrs. Gates poor marks for her classroom management during this lesson. Comments on the checklist indicate some of the most noticeable problem areas that may be observed on a subsequent visit. For example, with some passage of time the observer might want to see if Mrs. Gates uses low-profile classroom management techniques, refers to classroom rules, and has incentives to help make her rules effective.

CULTURAL DIVERSITY AND CLASSROOM MANAGEMENT

One of the most difficult problems of effective classroom management is deciding on a response that is culturally appropriate and well matched to the type of misbehavior (Peretz, Eilam, & Yankelevich, 2006). The effectiveness of some responses to misbehavior

FIGURE 6.6   Checklist for Observing Mrs. Gates's Classroom

Behavior	Observed	Not Observed	No Opportunity to Observe
1. Arranges classroom to match instructional goals		✓ Collaborative seating did not match oral reading goal	
2. Has preestablished classroom rules in place		✓ Failed to cite rules or have rules posted	
3. Exhibits use of instructional routines for most frequently performed activities		✓ Did not have routine for most frequent activities (e.g., beginning of class)	
4. Institutes incentives and consequences to promote appropriate behavior and discourage inappropriate behavior		✓ Used mostly negative phrases and consequences to encourage desirable behavior	
5. Uses low-profile classroom management to maintain instructional momentum		✓ Did not use anticipation, deflection, or reaction techniques	

may differ significantly, depending on a student's culture and ethnicity (Lustig & Koester, 2006). Cheng, Chen, Tsubo, Sekandari, and Alfafara-Killacky (1997); Cheng (1996); and Griggs and Dunn (1995) point out that we send messages through our body language; indeed, the body can be read as a "fluid text." For members of some cultural or ethnic groups, a stern look at a student might be interpreted as a more severe response than asking the student to stop a particular behavior—especially depending on how the same action is used at home. Calling on a student who is misbehaving might not only send a message to stop misbehaving, but also serve as a punishment for students who don't want to be spotlighted during large-group instruction. Thus, research suggests that a teacher's response to misbehavior should match the student's cultural and ethnic background as well as the offense.

Tharp and Gallimore (1989), Dillon (1989), and Bowers and Flinders (1991) have provided convincing arguments that different cultures react differently to nonverbal and verbal classroom management techniques, including proximity control, eye contact, warnings, and classroom arrangement. Furthermore, these authors cite numerous examples of how teachers of different cultures interpret disruptive behaviors and children differently.

For example, facial expressions during a reprimand have been found to communicate different messages concerning the importance of the reprimand. Others have pointed out that some actions of teachers may diminish participation among minority students or build resentment because the actions are culturally incongruent. One suggestion is that teachers examine their own value and belief systems to become more aware of how different these systems might be from their students' and use the social organization of the classroom to bridge cultural gaps by

- Establishing an open, risk-free learning environment where students can feel good about themselves
- Planning and structuring lessons that meet the interests and needs of students
- Implementing lessons that allow all students to be active and successful learners through activities and responsibilities that are congruent with the learner's culture

One of the most encouraging advances in the understanding of classroom management is the emerging field of **culturally responsive teaching** (Edwards & Kuhlman, 2007; Gay, 2000; Irvine, Armento, Causey, Jones, Frasher, & Weinburgh, 2001). Research supporting culturally responsive teaching

has yet to provide explicit prescriptions for teaching culturally different learners, but it can help us better understand students in multicultural classrooms.

The traditional method of conducting classroom research is to study large groups of teachers, classify their teaching methods, give learners achievement tests, and try to find relationships between achievement test scores and particular teaching practices. Dillon (1989), however, used a different approach. She studied one teacher, Mr. Appleby, and his class for a year using a research method called *microethnography*. Her study provided valuable insights into what a teacher can do to create a classroom where culturally different learners experience academic and personal success.

Dillon concludes that Appleby's effectiveness as a classroom teacher was due to his ability to assume the role of "translator and intercultural broker" between the middle-class culture of the school and the lower-class African American culture of his students. As a cultural broker and translator, Appleby was thoroughly knowledgeable about the backgrounds of his learners, and as a result he was able to bridge the differences between school and community or home cultures. He had acquired a high degree of what Lustig and Koester (2006) call intercultural competence. With this cultural knowledge, Appleby created a classroom with three significant attributes:

1. He created a social organization where teacher and learners knew one another, trusted one another, and felt free to express their opinions and feelings.
2. He taught lessons built around the prior knowledge and experiences of his learners. Having an understanding of his learners' backgrounds, he was familiar with their knowledge, skills, and attitudes toward the content. This understanding allowed him to represent the subject matter in ways that encouraged his students to link it with what they already knew and felt.
3. He used instructional methods that allowed learners to actively participate in lessons, to use the language and sociolinguistic patterns of their culture, and to use the language and social interaction patterns both he and his learners were familiar with.

Antón-Oldenburg (2000), Miller (2000), and Lustig and Koester (2006) conclude that what teachers need to know in order to teach successfully in multicultural classrooms has more to do with knowing the values, socialization practices, interests, and concerns of their learners than with knowing about presumed learning style preferences and cognitive styles and the do's and don'ts of teaching learners with these traits. Researchers believe that the cultural knowledge teachers such as Appleby have about their learners allows them to represent subject matter content in ways that are meaningful to students while developing lessons that gain their active participation and creating social organizations in the classroom within which learners feel free to be themselves. These will be important considerations during your observations of classroom management.

In the following chapters, we will turn our attention to several other equally important lenses through which to observe classrooms. However, lesson clarity, instructional variety, task orientation, student engagement in the learning process, student success, and higher thought processes are always observed in the context of the dimensions of classroom management. As we turn now to our next lens, lesson clarity, keep in mind the significant impact of the dimensions of classroom management studied in this chapter.

For More Information

Classroom management challenges regularly surface as a major concern for teachers. For practical tips and ideas for handling misbehaviors as well as common teacher mistakes that might perpetuate problems, you may want to visit the following website: www.theteachersguide .com/ClassManagement.htm.

Key Terms

classroom routines, 81
culturally responsive teaching, 90
engaged learning time, 81
instructional routines, 81

low-profile classroom management, 86
proximity control, 85
surface behaviors, 86

Activities*

1. Use the checklist in Instrument 6.1 to observe a lesson for signs of classroom management. At the end of your observation, add a brief description to each box, highlighting at least one specific reason why you placed each of your check marks as you did.
2. Following the examples of 5-point scales in Chapter 4, convert the indicators of classroom management listed in Table 6.1 into a Likert (5-point) scale. Consider whether you want each of your scales positioned horizontally or vertically and which words (for example, *a lot, much, some, a little, none*) will correspond to each number on the scale. Show your scale to a classmate who also has constructed a 5-point scale. Together, create a single revised version incorporating the best wording of each.
3. Using the format provided in Instrument 6.2, draw the arrangement of a classroom you have recently observed. Indicate whether the arrangement of this classroom is best suited for group projects, independent work, lecture or discussion, or some combination of these. Draw how this classroom could be most easily changed to better match the instructional goal of the lesson.

4. Using the format provided in Instrument 6.3, create one rule of your own for each of the seven rule areas. Indicate the order in which your rules would be listed on a handout to your students and which rules you believe might be culturally sensitive.
5. Using the format provided in Instrument 6.4, indicate the steps or procedures you would use to teach routines for the beginning of class, handing in assignments, transitions, and the violation of rules. Indicate how you would communicate each routine to the class at the beginning of the school year.
6. For the following behaviors, identify a response that you believe would match the severity of the problem.

   Talking back
   Sleeping in class
   Leaving seat
   Provoking or arguing
   Taking another's property
   Defacing books or materials

7. Use the format provided in Instrument 6.6 to observe low-profile classroom management. Check

*Some of these activities may be grouped into a common activity, divided among classmates, and completed from a single observation.

each observed occurrence of anticipation, non-verbal deflection, verbal deflection, and reaction techniques. Write down any other responses that you believe represent low-profile classroom management. Which were used the most often? Which were used least often? And which not at all?

8. Work with a classmate to create a number of positive phrases, other than general statements such as "Good," "Right," and "Keep working," that you could use to provide a greater incentive to a student who is behaving appropriately.

7

Looking for Lesson Clarity

Beside the Line of Elephants

I think they had no pattern

When they cut out the elephant's skin;

Some places it needs letting out,

And others, taking in.

Author unknown

Just as an accomplished seamstress creates a garment well fitted to the intended wearer, so too do wise teachers develop lesson objectives and plans that fit instructional goals, resulting in seamless instruction tailored to particular learners. In this chapter, we'll focus on seven dimensions of lesson clarity that will enable you to observe and create optimal learning environments.

Imagine a scene from an old spy movie. The mission leader says to the others, "Is that clear?" The others nod solemnly, synchronize their watches, and prepare to enter the dangerous world of espionage and intrigue.

What does it mean to be "clear"? How important is clarity when it comes to instructional design and delivery? In the old movies the value of clarity was crucial: Agents who misunderstood secret codes or other important information risked their lives. Although it's unlikely that our students will encounter life-and-death situations as a result of lesson clarity, our choices as instructors will certainly influence the rate at which students learn in our classrooms. In this chapter, we will consider ways of looking for lesson clarity.

For a lesson to be clear, its focus should be readily apparent. Learning activities should be understandable and easy to connect to one another, and to the overall lesson focus. As you observe lessons for clarity, some aspects will probably stand out immediately. For example, does the teacher explain concepts in a logical, step-by-step order that students are able to follow? Is the teacher's oral delivery audible, intelligible, and free of any distracting mannerisms? Are the points the teacher is making at the students' current level of understanding? Do students know how particular learning activities relate to the overall lesson objective?

Classroom research indicates that teachers vary considerably in clarity. Not all teachers are able to communicate clearly and directly to their students without wandering, speaking over students' heads, or using speech patterns that confuse listeners. Teachers who fail to achieve lesson clarity often exhibit one (or more) of the following language patterns (Blythe, 1997; Land, 1987; Newton, 2007):

1. They rely on vague, ambiguous, or indefinite language (e.g., "might probably be," "tends to suggest," "could possibly happen").
2. They use overly complicated sentences (e.g., "There are many important reasons for the start of World War II, but some are more important than others, so let's start with those that are thought to be important but really aren't").
3. They give directions that are frequently followed by student requests for clarification (e.g., "Which learning center do we go to first?" or "What did you want us to do again?").

Clarity is a complex behavior because it extends beyond a teacher's oral presentation to many other behaviors, such as how a teacher organizes the lesson, uses media and illustrations, and delivers the content to learners (e.g., using examples, discussion, question and answer, recitation, or cooperative group work). Generally, teaching with a high degree of clarity helps students focus on specific learning objectives, allowing them to answer questions correctly the first time through a lesson. Students experience a higher degree of success and spend more time actively engaged in instruction.

DIMENSIONS OF LESSON CLARITY

Take a moment and recall a lesson that was clear and specific. What did the teacher do to create this lesson? List some of your ideas on a sheet of paper.

Table 7.1 summarizes seven teaching behaviors that contribute to lesson clarity. Which of the behaviors in Table 7.1 match those on your list? As you review Table 7.1, do you notice that three behaviors occur at the *beginning* of a lesson and the remaining four are implemented *during* a lesson? The beginning three behaviors set the stage for achieving lesson clarity.

1. Informing learners of the objective
2. Providing learners with an advance organizer
3. Checking for lesson-relevant prior knowledge before starting the lesson and reteaching, if necessary

Let's examine each of these behaviors teachers use to enhance the clarity of their lessons as they begin

TABLE 7.1   Indicators for Lesson Clarity

More Effective Lesson Clarity	Less Effective Lesson Clarity
1. Informs learners of the lesson objective (describes what behaviors will be tested, used orally, or required on future assignments as a result of the lesson)	Fails to relate lesson content to how and at what level of complexity the content will be used
2. Provides learners with an advance organizer (places lesson in perspective of past and/or future lessons)	Starts presenting content without first introducing the subject in a broader context
3. Checks for lesson-relevant prior knowledge at beginning of lesson (determines level of understanding of prerequisite facts or concepts and reteaches, if necessary)	Moves to new content without checking for the facts, concepts, or skills needed to acquire the new learning
4. Knows learners' current level of understanding and teaches at or slightly above it (knows students' attention spans)	Fails to ascertain whether instruction is under or over students' levels, or whether students have "tuned out"
5. Gives directions clearly (repeats directives when needed or divides them into smaller pieces)	Presents too much clerical, managerial, or technical information too quickly
6. Uses examples, illustrations, and demonstrations to explain and clarify (uses visuals to help interpret and reinforce main points)	Restricts presentation to routine verbal reproduction of text or workbook
7. Provides review or summary at end of lesson	Ends lesson abruptly without repackaging key points

instruction. Then we will practice looking for them in a classroom dialogue.

Informing Learners of Lesson Objectives

At the start of a lesson, most students don't know what will be expected of them or how they may be asked to show what they have learned. Informing students at the beginning of a lesson what they will be expected to know and how they will be asked to show it can replace unrealistic fears and uncertainty with realistic expectations. This can easily be accomplished by communicating expected lesson outcomes in terms of how they may be used—for example, by presenting an oral summary of what they have learned, participating in a class discussion representing both sides of a controversy, successfully responding in a question-and-answer session, or recording and sharing what they have learned in a cooperative group activity. Some teachers place examples of expected behaviors on the blackboard at the beginning of a unit and then place a check mark beside the ones that most apply to that day's activities. For example, a teacher introducing a unit on the environment might list the following behaviors on the board, explaining that by the end of the unit students will be expected to accomplish all four, and the first by the end of today's lesson:

- Recite a definition of global warming.
- Draw a picture of some of its possible effects on the Earth.

- Explain how it works.
- Using the map, identify which parts of the world may be affected most.

Notice that these behavioral outcomes range from memorizing a simple definition to drawing, explaining, and using information. Knowing at which of these levels they are expected to perform gives students a way of focusing their attention on the parts of the instruction that are most relevant to the desired outcome. Additionally, other outcomes listed help to organize in advance what will be expected in subsequent presentations and assignments and at the end of the unit.

Another way effective teachers inform learners of their objectives is to use verbal statements (called **verbal markers**) at the beginning of a lesson to indicate how the content will be needed in the future.

- "Remember the four definitions of power that will be presented today. Tonight, you will need to complete an assignment using these definitions." (general science)
- "Today, I want you to be able to use the possessive form to express ownership. Later I am going to ask each of you to orally express ownership in a sentence to the class." (English)
- "In the first chapter of *Charlotte's Web* we will meet a character named Fern. Later I will ask you what words you would use to describe her. (language arts)

- "At the end of class today, I will ask you to identify a mystery specimen of lower animal life using the microscope." (life science)
- "As a result of our discussion today, each of you should be able to state an opinion about our laws dealing with pollution." (social studies)

Simple statements such as these help learners organize and focus attention on the most important components of the day's lesson. If the students know that they are expected to be able to recall four definitions of power at the end of a lesson on energy, they will be more likely to focus their search, retrieval, and retention processes on the various definitions or categories of power presented during the lesson. Stating the objective enables the learner to be selective about how the lesson information should be organized and remembered and, most important, to know when the proper level of expected behavior has been attained.

It is important, too, that teachers consider cultural influences and language skills when planning learning objectives and activities. The effective teacher realizes that lesson objectives should include more than just content knowledge—students are often most motivated by objectives that recognize their feelings and include personal experiences they have encountered in life (Borich, 2004; Burnette, 1999). In other words, by considering how their students may benefit from and feel about the content to be learned and the activities to be accomplished, teachers can formulate objective statements knowing to emphasize important information, as highlighted in the following example:

- "Today we will read a story about a little girl who was called "Little Red Riding Hood" and then I will ask you one important lesson you learned from this story and whether from your experience it could be true or not." (reading circle)

As you observe teachers communicating lesson objectives, you will want to consider whether and how the personal experiences of their students are woven into the lesson as well as the content knowledge.

Observing Lesson Objectives

Instrument 7.1 provides a way for you to record whether learners have been informed of the objective, how they were informed of it, and the level of performance expected. In the first part of the record you record whether the learners were informed of the objective and, if not, why not. This is important because not every lesson will require informing learners of the objective (e.g., when the lesson is a continuation of a series of related lessons for

which the objective is already well known to learners, or when the lesson is devoted entirely to a review, in which case many different objectives may be touched on but not taught directly). After recording this information, indicate whether the objective stated is cognitive, affective, psychomotor, or some combination. Check "Affective" if the affective and personal experiences of the learner are brought into the lesson. If possible, indicate the highest level of performance expected of the learner by selecting the expected outcome that comes closest to the action verbs listed on the form. If you cannot determine the intended level of performance at the start of a lesson, you'll usually be able to infer it at or near the end of the lesson by considering the nature of the content or activities. Don't be surprised if you find yourself checking several boxes during one lesson. It is not unusual for lessons to have multiple objectives within, and even sometimes across, the cognitive, affective, and psychomotor domains for which multiple marks should be entered.

Providing Advance Organizers

Another behavior for achieving clarity involves the use of **advance organizers.** Advance organizers are concepts presented orally or in visual form (charts and diagrams), usually at the beginning of a lesson, to give an overview of the day's work as well as topics to which it will subsequently relate. An advance organizer (Ausubel, 1968; Woolfolk, 2007) gives the learner a conceptual preview of what is to come and helps prepare the learner to store, label, and package the content for retention and later use. It functions as a treelike structure with main limbs that act as pegs, or placeholders, for the branches that are to come later. Without the limbs on which to hang content, important distinctions can easily become blurred or lost. An advance organizer helps students focus their thinking in advance of the lesson by providing mental "hooks" on which to hang key ideas. This activates the learning process and focuses it in the direction that is most efficient for obtaining the expected outcome. Advance organizers have been shown to be especially helpful for students from diverse cultures and for English language learners when the organizer includes links between the instructional content and familiar concepts acquired from real-life experiences, and when sufficient time is spent building "personal knowledge bridges" that can help students understand new ideas (Burnette, 1999; Lin & Chen, 2006; Saunders & Goldenberg, 1999). The following examples demonstrate some advance organizer activities provided at the beginnings of lessons.

- Listening to examples of both vowels and consonants before teaching the vowel sounds (reading)
- Showing a picture of an event or topic to be studied and discussing what students already know about the topic (literature, science, social studies, mathematics)
- Discussing the origins of pollution before describing its effects (social studies)
- Showing a chart illustrating the skeletal evolution of humans before explaining the skeletal relationships between forms of animal life (life science)
- Drawing examples of different types of triangles and showing the similarity among them before introducing the concept of a right triangle (plane geometry)
- Explaining the origins of the periodic table of elements before introducing the elements found within it (chemistry)

Each of these examples presents a general concept as well as the specific related concept that is the subject of the day's lesson. Advance organizers are not designed to review content taught at some earlier time, but to present a concept (the alphabet, what students already know, origins of pollution, human evolution, triangular shapes, an organized system of atomic weights) into which fits not only the content to be taught that day, but also the content for all related lessons in a unit of study. Advance organizers lay the groundwork for expanding the present lesson topic, preventing every lesson from being seen as something entirely new, and integrating related concepts into larger and larger patterns that later become unit outcomes (reading words with vowel and consonant blends in complete passages, planning an anti-pollution campaign, knowing the evolution of skeletal forms, or drawing different types of triangles). An advance organizer indicates the highest level of behavior expected to result from a sequence of lessons and may illustrate graphically how the present lesson will contribute to achieving that behavior.

As in our earlier discussion of objectives, you'll discover that one of the most frequently used advance organizers is a simple verbal marker that tells students what to watch for or what behaviors will be expected of them at the end of the lesson. These verbal markers often look like, and sometimes are embedded within, a statement that informs the learner of the objective for the lesson.

Categories and Examples of Verbal Markers for Advance Organizers

1. Relating content to past learning: "Today we will apply what we learned yesterday to a real laboratory experiment involving saline solutions."

2. Verbally (and/or visually) summarizing what is to come: "The main points of today's lesson will be (a) . . . , (b) . . . , and (c) . . . ."
3. Relating content to future learning: "We will conduct a debate in which each half of the class will participate, but first I will give each side the facts they will need to win."
4. Providing clues about what to look for: "Today our topic is ways of measuring. I want you to watch carefully as I use these instruments in front of me to adjust and balance a scale for measuring weight."
5. Providing and describing a written handout at the beginning of class: "This sheet outlines what we will cover and the order in which we will cover it. Take a minute and look over each of the points identified."

More elaborate types of advance organization may be called for when the complexity of the behavioral outcome requires learners to fit many dissimilar pieces, or segments, of a lesson or unit together. Typically these more elaborate forms of organization are used to introduce units of instruction, usually with charts (e.g., the periodic table of elements), pictures (the skeletal structure of the human anatomy), or illustrations (a flow diagram summarizing the steps to be followed in conducting a debate). Advance organizers can be verbal, visual, or both and can be presented at the beginning of the lesson, during the lesson, or continually throughout the lesson, in which case the teacher returns to the advance organizer at each appropriate place in the lesson to remind students where they are in the larger unit of content.

Observing Advance Organizers

There are many varieties of advance organizers. Instrument 7.2 provides a way to catalog, or list, the advance organizers that you see being used across different content areas, grade levels, and learners. To complete this record, observe several different classes and teachers to obtain the broadest sampling of advance organizers possible. Place a check mark under beginning, middle, or end, depending on whether the organizer is introduced or used during the first, second, or last third of the lesson. A check mark under all three time periods indicates the advance organizer is woven into the lesson content and referenced repeatedly. Place a check mark in the last column each time the organizer is referenced during the lesson. You may want to keep a card file that describes the most interesting advance organizers you encounter and how they are used. Include the reference number found in the second column of the form on each card to help you remember where you saw the organizer used. Keep these cards, organized according to subject and grades, to draw from in your own teaching. You'll find them to be a valuable source of ideas as you plan your own lessons.

Checking for Lesson-Relevant Prior Knowledge and Reteaching

Researchers have found that learning is enhanced when students are able to connect new ideas to what they already know and have experienced (Chaillé, 2007; Fosnot, 2005). Most students come to school with plenty of knowledge and experiences related to almost any subject. But, without prompting, they might be unable to retrieve them or connect them to new content. Effective teachers review, summarize, restate, and stimulate into action previously acquired concepts and experiences that could be instrumental in achieving the goals of a lesson. For example, if the goal is to have learners use a microscope to differentiate an amoeba from other animals, then facts, concepts, and skills acquired previously will have to be used to achieve this new outcome. Definitions of single-celled animals, unique characteristics of an amoeba that distinguish it from other one-celled animals, and past experience with using a microscope represent just some of the prior knowledge that must be retrieved to attain the goal of the lesson. Checking for and stimulating the recall of the most relevant aspects of this knowledge at the beginning of a lesson prepares learners for the task of building new knowledge from what has already been learned. Thus, a third behavior for achieving lesson clarity is checking for and stimulating the recall of lesson-relevant prerequisite knowledge and experiences (Hunter, 1994).

A useful technique for activating prior knowledge involves the use of oral questions that bring into focus unique or memorable events that enable students to recall earlier content and experiences simply and quickly. For example, the teacher might ask the class, "Who can remember what Johnny did to see the amoeba in the microscope?" (he turned it to high magnification) "Do you remember Betty Jo's description of how fast the reproduction cycle of an amoeba is?" (she equated cell division with waking up one morning to find a new baby in the family) "How many of you recall the picture Juan drew of the cellular structure of an amoeba?" (everyone had commented on how lifelike the picture was). These questions help students retrieve prior learning not by summarizing the learning, but by tapping into a mental image created in an earlier lesson. Once the image is retrieved, students can search for details nestled

within it and bring forth still greater recall. When extensive deficiencies in lesson-relevant prior learning are apparent from oral questioning or checking of assigned work, reteaching prerequisite content will be more important than teaching the new content scheduled for the day's lesson.

Based on our discussion, you might think that beginning a lesson by activating previously learned lesson-relevant knowledge would be a common practice, especially among experienced teachers. Yet a research study by Good & Grouws (1979) found that only 50% of experienced teachers began a lesson in this fashion. This is surprising because daily checking and review at the beginning of a lesson can be accomplished in many ways:

1. Have students correct each other's assignments at the beginning of class.
2. Have students identify especially difficult concepts during a question-and-answer session.
3. Orally sample the understanding of students who are indicators of the range of knowledge possessed by the entire class.
4. Explicitly review the lesson-relevant information necessary for the day's lesson.

Some teachers may avoid reviewing at the beginning of a lesson because they know they would be wasting the time of students who already know the material. To address this concern, Dahllof and Lundgren (1970) and Rosenshine and Stevens (1986) propose that teachers check understanding with a **steering group** composed of lower-performing learners in a class to determine the extent to which review and reteaching may be needed. The steering group idea can be expanded to include a small number of lower, average, and higher performers (who change from day to day) to gain an idea of the relative understanding of class members. When high performers miss a large proportion of answers, extensive reteaching for the entire class may be necessary. If most of the high and average performers answer the questions correctly but most of the low performers do not, then individualized materials, worksheets, or a tutorial arrangement can be used to aid the low performers. Checking understanding across a steering group ensures that a large amount of class time will not be devoted to review and reteaching that may benefit only a small number of students.

Observing Lesson-Relevant Prior Knowledge and Reteaching

As you can imagine, it is important to know not only whether a teacher checks for and stimulates lesson-relevant prior knowledge, but also what prior knowledge is required for the day's lesson. For a class you are observing, make arrangements to consult the text, curriculum guide, or unit plan to determine the facts, skills, or concepts that should have been learned before the lesson and also that are expected to become lesson-relevant prior learning for subsequent lessons. These can be recorded in the following format:

1. Using the text, curriculum guide, or unit plan, list any facts, skills, or concepts that should have been attained by learners to achieve the objectives of today's lesson.
   Facts _____
   Skills _____
   Concepts _____

2. Using the text, curriculum guide, or unit plan, list any facts, skills, or concepts to be taught in future lessons that may depend on the content of today's lesson.
   Facts _____
   Skills _____
   Concepts _____

3. Cite the reason, as you see it, for teaching today's lesson at this point in the curriculum (for example, it teaches the skills that will be used to solve problems in a subsequent lesson or provides examples that illustrate the concepts taught in a previous lesson).

So far, we've discussed three teaching behaviors that can be performed at the start of a lesson to increase lesson clarity. Now let's consider four additional behaviors in Table 7.1 for achieving lesson clarity during a lesson:

4. Teaching to students' current level of understanding
5. Giving directions clearly
6. Using examples, illustrations, and demonstrations to explain and clarify text and workbook content
7. Providing a review or summary at the end of the lesson

Teaching to Students' Current Level of Understanding

Closely related to the skill of checking and stimulating the recall of lesson-relevant prior knowledge is a teacher's skill at teaching to the current level of understanding of his or her students. Because several levels of achievement are likely to be present in your classroom, it will be important to package your instructional message in the form of oral presentations, visual messages, exercises, written assignments, readings, and group interactions at or slightly above the current level of understanding of students. To accomplish this you will need to differentiate your instruction by incorporating into your lessons learning centers, computer software, reference libraries, different types of pictorial displays, and alternate texts and exercises that tap into performance levels above and below the average learner to provide a range of instructional stimuli at the level of understanding of each student. To differentiate instruction is to recognize an individual student's learning history, background, readiness to learn, interests, and acquired skill set and choose instructional strategies more tailored to small groups or to individual learners to speed their academic success, which might be slowed if only large-group instruction were available. The goal of **differentiated instruction** is to maximize each student's academic success and personal growth as a learner by meeting each student where he or she is at and providing the needed instruction and resources that lift the learner to the next step on the learning ladder.

Regardless of the level of difficulty at which a lesson begins, a lesson may be too difficult for some learners and not difficult enough for others. Unit and lesson planning in a heterogeneous classroom can be a game of averages in which the teacher attempts to provide *most* of the instruction at the current level of understanding of *most* of the learners. There are, however, some procedures that can help address the range of prior achievement and experience within a classroom through individualized and self-directed learning activities.

Tomlinson (2004) and Tomlinson and McTighe (2006) suggest that lessons can be individualized or differentiated for groups of learners across four elements: content (what the student needs to learn or how the student will access information); process (activities in which the student will engage to master the content); products (projects that ask the student to rehearse, apply, and extend his or her knowledge); and learning environment (how the classroom works and feels to promote learning). Alternatives for differentiating instruction that can adjust the classroom by providing students a degree of control over the pace of their own learning include the following methods.

Task Ability Grouping

A class can be subdivided according to particular skills required for learning specific lesson content. For example, higher-performing readers might be asked at the beginning of a lesson to read ahead and work independently on advanced exercises while remediation materials are directed to lower-performing readers. Similarly, a lesson's objectives, activities, and instructional materials as well as assessment can be divided into difficulty levels and targeted to different groups, depending on the range of previous performance and experience within the classroom.

Peer Tutoring

Some students can be assigned to help other students who have not yet acquired lesson-relevant prior knowledge. Because some students may require remediation, peer tutors can begin at a particular student's current level of understanding and bring it to the level required for a subsequent lesson.

Learning Centers

At times some students will profit more from working at learning centers or computer workstations than from exercises and workbooks above their current level of understanding. When a learning center or computer workstation contains media, supplemental resources, and exercises that present content in alternative formats (e.g., visual or auditory), it should be included as an integral part of the lesson. A learning center or computer workstation can help individualize a lesson for students who lack the prerequisite knowledge or skills required by the lesson entry level and who need to catch up before any new learning is possible.

Review and Follow-Up Materials

As noted previously, a lesson can begin with a review of lesson-relevant prior knowledge. A summary with supplementary handouts, in which the critical or most complex aspects of a previous lesson can be looked up as needed, may be sufficient to bring some students up to the required level while not boring others for whom a review might be redundant. Brief supplementary handouts or study aids can cover the prerequisite knowledge, thereby taking the minimal amount of time away from the presentation of new content and limiting an oral review for the entire class to only the essentials.

Self-Paced Software, Programmed Texts, and Audiolingual Devices

Computer software, programmed texts, and audiolingual devices break content into small segments and present the learner with immediate feedback about the correctness of a response. Although higher-performing students typically find some of these resources slow and repetitive, interactive computer software programs have been successful in helping lower-performing learners master basic facts and understandings that would not have been acquired through full-class instruction. On the other hand, classroom or library Internet connections have been especially successful in helping students at different performance levels with challenging content and assignments that can interest a wide range of students. Also, the many computerized reading and math programs that are now available provide an individualized atmosphere in which catch-up learning can take place at a high level of motivation.

Games, Simulations, and Role Playing

Games, simulations, and role playing provide still other opportunities for individualized and self-directed learning. With the large-scale availability of computers and prepackaged activities from publishers, instructional games and simulations take on added importance as instructional activities that can elicit the direct involvement of students in the learning process at their current level of understanding. These activities can become important aids to achieving clarity in heterogeneous classrooms where students are allowed time to independently pursue instructionally relevant goals using interactive activities. Role-playing opportunities can allow students to "practice" content in the guise of another character, "trying on" and testing out ideas in a safe environment.

Observing Level of Instruction

You can sense the extent to which instruction is being delivered at the students' current level of understanding by recording some of the signs of student behavior in Table 7.2. These behaviors are variously observed when instruction directed to the entire class is (a) below, (b) at or slightly above, or (c) considerably above different learners' current levels of understanding.

Circle one entry from each of the three columns in Instrument 7.3 to record the approximate percentage of learners in a class for whom the content appears below, at or slightly above, or above the learners' current level of understanding. Use the list provided in Table 7.2 as your guide. You can describe the behavioral signs that were most obvious in making your choices by filling in the blanks in Figure 7.1, selecting from and adding to the previous list of behaviors as needed. This format also can be used to identify additional behaviors related to small-group work and cooperative learning activities.

The patterns in Table 7.3 are typical of classrooms during direct or expository instruction to the entire

TABLE 7.2 Example Student Behaviors Observed at Different Levels of Instruction

Instruction below Level of Learners	Instruction at or Slightly above Level of Learners	Instruction above Level of Learners
Students talking among themselves.	Students' eyes focused on teacher.	Students off-task and inattentive.
Students don't hear questions when asked.	Students volunteer answers.	Students answer questions incorrectly.
Students working on other coursework.	Students cooperate with teacher requests.	Students don't understand questions when asked.
Students challenge teacher's authority and knowledge.	Students ask leading questions.	Students' posture and eyes not in tune with instruction.

class. For Classroom A the percentage of students for whom lesson content is below their current level of understanding suggests that the instructional materials, media, and procedures might contain previously learned content and therefore are not interesting enough to hold the attention of learners. Here, an upward adjustment in curriculum content and expected outcomes should be the target of future lessons. Percentages for Classroom B represent a fairly typical classroom in which materials, media, and procedures are generally on target but, because of the heterogeneous grouping of students, might be above or below the current level of functioning of some stu-

dents. The percentages indicate the value of integrating both remedial and alternative learning materials into the existing curriculum in an independent study, small-group, or learning center format to accommodate differences in prior knowledge and performance among students. Finally, Classroom C indicates that a downward adjustment in curriculum content and expected outcomes might be favorable to teach prerequisite skills and better match the current level of understanding of the majority of students (Smith & Ragan, 2004).

Giving Directives Clearly

One of the most frequently heard excuses from students for poor performance is that they "weren't told (or didn't understand) what to do." Students who do not understand the directions often remain silent. As a result, instructions about workbook exercises, learning center and group work, reading assignments, homework, and handouts should be communicated with the same deliberateness as lesson content.

To gain a sense of the importance of how directives should be conveyed, think about the times you were unable to retrieve someone's phone number from your voicemail because the person spoke too quickly. Or remember when someone's street directions were meaningless when trying to find your way because the person assumed you would remember everything the first time through, and you were too embarrassed to ask for a repetition.

FIGURE 7.1 Observing Behavioral Signs

1. What observable signs led you to believe that the lesson content (or group activity) was *below* the current level of understanding of _____ percent of the class (if other than 0)?

   Behavioral Signs Observed

   _____

   _____

2. What observable signs led you to believe that the lesson content (or group activity) was *at or slightly above* the current level of understanding of _____ percent of the class (if other than 0)?

   Behavioral Signs Observed

   _____

   _____

3. What observable signs led you to believe that the lesson content (or group activity) was *above* the current level of understanding of _____ percent of the class (if other than 0)?

   Behavioral Signs Observed

   _____

   _____

TABLE 7.3 Typical Patterns of Distribution (as Percentages)

	Below	At or Slightly Above	Above
Classroom A	75	25	0
Classroom B	25	50	25
Classroom C	0	25	75

An effective teacher deliberately slows the pace when conveying instructions, divides directives into steps if necessary, and then checks to see that each step is understood. Combining verbal, visual, and kinesthetic (touch) input helps support student understanding, so effective teachers also summarize instructions in writing (e.g., on an overhead, a chalkboard, or in printed copy form), in another visual form (e.g., an example of the desired end product), or physically (e.g., modeling a behavior by taking a student's hand and moving it in the desired way).

Similarly, Evertson and Emmer (1982) found differences in the way effective and ineffective teachers handled assignments, particularly homework. Giving assignments appeared almost effortless for the effective teachers; for ineffective teachers the normal classroom routine sometimes came to an abrupt halt, the noise level went up, and there was much commotion and fuss as they attempted to communicate assignments. What accounts for the differences?

The effective teachers attached assignments directly to the end of an in-class activity, avoiding awkward pauses or even the need for a transition. The assignment appeared to students as a logical extension of what was already taking place, which it should be. The practice of giving the assignment immediately after the activity to which it most closely relates, as opposed to mentioning it at the end of class or at the end of the school day, may be much like getting an injection while the physician is smiling and engaging you in a friendly conversation: If the conversation is engaging enough, you might not feel the pain. Consider how the following assignments may be received by learners.

Teacher A: I probably should assign some homework, so do problems 1 through 10 on page 61.

Teacher B: For tonight, do the problems under Exercise A and Exercise B—that should keep you busy.

Teacher C: We're out of time now, so you'll have to finish these problems on your own.

In each of these statements, there is the question of whether the homework is really needed, or whether it is being given mechanically or as some sort of punishment. Why this homework is being assigned may be a mystery to most students. The teacher requests make no mention either of the in-class activities to which the homework relates or of the future benefits that may accrue from completing the assignment. These explanations are important if anything other than a mechanical or grudging response is expected. Most students will appreciate knowing why an assignment is made before they are expected to do it.

Let's consider these same assignments again, this time with an explanation added.

Teacher A: Today we have talked a lot about the origins of the Civil War and some of the economic unrest that preceded it. But some other types of unrest were also responsible for the Civil War. These will be important for understanding the real causes behind this war. Problems 1 through 10 on page 61 will tell you about some of these other causes.

Teacher B: We have all had a chance now to try our skill at forming possessives. As most of you have found out, it's a little harder than it looks. So, let's try Exercises A and B for tonight, which should give us just the right amount of practice for forming possessives for tomorrow's lesson.

Teacher C: Well, it looks like time has run out before we could complete all the problems. The next set of problems we will study requires a lot of what we have learned today. Let's complete the rest of these for tonight to see if you've got the concept. This should make tomorrow's lesson a lot easier.

Keep in mind the strategies effective classroom teachers use when giving assignments.

- Follow closely in time the lessons or activities to which they relate.
- Provide explanations about why the assignment is, or will be, of value.
- Avoid unnecessary negative connotations (e.g., "that should keep you busy") that might make the assignment look more like a punishment than an instructional activity.

Observing Clarity of Directives

Instrument 7.4 provides a format for recording clarity of directions. Use this instrument to record each student response–teacher reaction sequence after directions have been given for any one of the several types of classroom assignments listed (e.g., homework, in-class activity, test). The purpose of this observation instrument is to help you determine how clearly a teacher's instructions are received by the students and what, if any, reaction the teacher has to a learner's difficulty in receiving them. An example of a partly completed form is provided in Figure 7.2. A description of the categories and codes to be recorded is provided in Figure 7.3. Let's look at the example.

Figure 7.2 provides data from a student response–teacher reaction sequence. The marks in the first row of Figure 7.2 indicate that some instructions about an assignment in the workbook (wb) have been given. Roberto then asks the teacher to repeat (rpt) the instructions. The teacher criticizes (crit) Roberto

FIGURE 7.2 Coding Form for Recording Student Response–Teacher Reaction during Directions

Student or Number	Assignment							Student Response				Teacher Reaction					
	wb	hw	oas	hand	test	proj	other	rpt	specif	uncert	other	crit	rpt	ans	restate	check	ignore	other
Roberto	✓							✓				✓	✓					
Alisha	✓								✓					✓		✓		

and repeats (rpt) the instructions. Next, Alisha, in response to the same instructions about the workbook, asks a specific question (specif). The teacher answers (ans) and then checks (check) to see if Alisha understands.

In this manner, student response–teacher reaction sequences are recorded to assess the clarity of the teacher's original instructions and the teacher's response to any misunderstanding by the students. Patterns across individual students and assignments might reveal, for example, more problems with directions pertaining to one type of assignment (e.g., homework) than another (a workbook), or that the teacher tends to criticize when students ask for the directions to be repeated, but not when students ask specific questions for clarification. These types of patterns are often the most revealing because they explain differences in the clarity of instructions (and sometimes the academic performance of students) across classrooms. For example, some teachers repeatedly criticize student requests for more information with expressions such as "You weren't listening," which may discourage some students from asking for clarification again. Also, it is important to check the uniformity with which the teacher responds to different students who express difficulty in understanding directions (e.g., higher and lower performers or students for whom English is their second language). These and other student characteristics can be entered beside, or instead of, a student name on the coding form, and later analyzed to reveal biases or preferences that might be unintentionally limiting the opportunity for certain groups of students to complete assignments properly.

FIGURE 7.3 Coding Symbols and Categories for Observing Clarity of Directions

Direction or Instructions Pertaining to	
wb	Workbook
hw	Homework
oas	Oral assignment
hand	Handout
test	Test
proj	Extended project or paper
other	Other type of assignment

Student Responses	
rpt	Student asks teacher to repeat directions or instructions.
specif	Student asks specific question for clarification.
uncert	Student expresses uncertainty orally (for example, "I don't understand") or physically (for example, frowns, shrugs).
other	Student uses some other measure to indicate directives or instructions were not understood.

Teacher Reactions	
crit	Teacher criticizes student for not understanding.
rpt	Teacher repeats directive or instruction.
ans	Teacher answers student question about directive.
restate	Teacher restates instructions in different words.
check	Teacher checks for understanding (for example, asks student to repeat or asks student a question).
ignore	Teacher ignores student response.
other	Teacher reacts in some other way.

Using Examples, Illustrations, and Demonstrations

The final two behaviors for achieving clarity—using examples, illustrations, and demonstrations as well as reviewing and summarizing—each have several things in common. Both behaviors occur well into the lesson, and both are intended to expand and clarify lesson content that might not be understood completely or uniformly without some reorganization and elaboration.

The content organization found within most texts, workbooks, and curriculum guides has been created for the purpose of communicating content intended to be read, not for the purpose of presenting content that must be explained orally within the time frame of a lesson. The material included under chapter titles, subheadings, or Roman numerals in curriculum outlines is often too broad to cover in a single lesson. Some teachers stick tenaciously to these formal text headings without considering the volume of content that falls within them, or the time it takes to orally explain, illustrate, and practice this content. More effective teachers realize that some texts require reorganization to better fit the needs of students and the time allocated to instruction. As a result, they learn to subdivide text material for their students, often independently of chapter headings and divisions. When effective teachers reorganize content, they often share the pattern they follow with their students. For example, they might abstract from the text for students a set of rules ("Here are some rules to follow"), steps ("We will do this, and then that"), or topics ("Here is the first of five things we will cover") that reorganize content into smaller and more memorable pieces. These teachers then provide examples, illustrations, or demonstrations as well as practice and feedback for these smaller pieces of information.

Think of a teacher who made a particular subject come alive for you. How was it accomplished? Did the teacher offer interesting oral examples? Visual illustrations? Practical demonstrations? Did she allow for plenty of group discussion and sharing of personal insights and opinions? Any of these can increase the clarity of a lesson by repackaging its content and affording students with diverse backgrounds or learning styles the opportunity to relate it to their own levels of experience and understanding. In addition, audiovisual media, worksheets, problem sets, and study aids, especially when used in the context of group activities, discussion, and question-and-answer sessions, can help make textbook content more meaningful and inclusive of diverse students' knowledge and backgrounds (Walqui, 2000a,b).

Observing Use of Examples, Illustrations, and Demonstrations

Because teachers might use examples, illustrations, and demonstrations many times during a lesson, it is important to record their frequency. Instrument 7.5 is an observation form in which you can record various types of visual and oral examples, illustrations, and demonstrations each time they occur. The purpose of this instrument is to determine the pref-erences a teacher might have for various techniques and how often they are used. Check marks are placed each time an example, illustration, or demonstration is presented visually, orally, or both. A relatively large proportion of check marks in any one row may indicate an overreliance on one form of example, illustration, or demonstration. On the other hand, few or no marks, such as in the visual categories, can indicate a lack of lesson interest or appeal, especially for learners who might favor the visual modality. Because there are many visual and oral ways of providing examples, illustrations, and demonstrations in addition to those listed, you should add other clarity-enhancing techniques to the "Other" category when you see them.

Reviewing and Summarizing

Reviews and summaries at the end of, or interspersed throughout, a lesson can have much the same effect as examples, illustrations, and demonstrations. An effective review or summary is not a simple parroting back of what was taught in an abbreviated form. Instead, an effective review or summary recasts content into a slightly different form than the original presentation, thereby elaborating on and reorganizing earlier content for efficient storage and retrieval.

One of the most effective methods of recasting is **transmediation** (Semali, 2002), which is the expression of an idea across media forms. For example, students who explore the properties of triangles in written form during a lesson might review these properties by creating a simple musical jingle. Students who read about the exploits of a particular explorer in social studies might summarize these exploits in a dramatic presentation or an artistic mural. Determining key concepts and how to best present them in another medium can add freshness to a review or summary, as well as help students better retain the information.

Planning for review and summary activities provides learners the opportunity to plug into the content at a different time and in a different manner. Content not learned or misunderstood during the lesson can be learned and clarified during summaries and reviews, if the summary and review go beyond simple repetition of content to a repackaging of the lesson and unit concepts. Another way of accomplishing this is by combining or consolidating key points into a single overall conclusion, as in the following example.

Teacher: Today we have studied the economic systems of capitalism, socialism, and communism. We have found each of these to be similar because some of the same goods and services are owned by the government. We have found them to be different, however, with respect to the degree to which various goods and services are owned by the government, with the least number of goods and services owned by a government under capitalism, and the most goods and services owned by a government under communism.

This teacher is drawing together, or highlighting, the single most important conclusion from the day's lesson. To do this, the highest level of generalization or conclusion that can be made from the lesson is expressed, without reference to any details that were necessary to arrive at it. This teacher consolidates many different bits and pieces by going to the broadest, most sweeping conclusion that could be made, thereby capturing the meaning and essence of all that has gone before.

Another procedure for summarizing and reviewing is to reiterate the most important content that has been presented. Here the teacher repeats the most important content to be sure that it is understood. Not all of the content can be repeated, so some selection is in order.

Teacher: Before we end, let's look at our two rules once again. [Writes on board as she speaks] Rule 1: Use the possessive form when an *of* phrase can be substituted for a noun. Rule 2: If the word for which we are denoting ownership is a plural ending in an s, place the apostrophe after, not before, the s.

This teacher is consolidating by summarizing, or touching on, each of the key elements of the lesson. The teacher's review is rapid and to the point, providing students with an opportunity to fill in any missing gaps about the main features of the lesson.

Still another method for reviewing and summarizing provides learners with a structure by which key facts and ideas can be remembered without a review. With this procedure, facts and ideas are reorganized into a framework for easy recall.

Teacher: Today we studied the formation and punctuation of possessives. Recall that we used two rules—one for forming possessives whenever an *of* phrase can be substituted for a noun, and another for forming possessives for plurals ending in s. From now on, let's call these rules the "*of* rule" and the "*s* rule," keeping in mind that both make use of the apostrophe.

By giving students a framework for remembering the rules (the "*of* rule" and the "*s* rule"), the teacher reorganizes the content and indicates how it should be stored and remembered. The key to this procedure is to provide students with a code or symbol system by which the contents of the lesson can be more easily stored and recalled for later use.

These examples suggest that reviewing or summarizing means more than simply calling attention to the end of a lesson. In the first instance, the highest-level generalization that could be made was restated; in the second, the content at the level at which it was taught was summarized; and in the third, students were helped in remembering each of the important categories of information with codes or symbols. Each is a valuable means of increasing lesson clarity.

Observing Review and Summary Techniques

If a lesson ends with a review or summary, you can describe the type of review or summary using the following format.

- Provides generalization to consolidate main points:
  _____
- Repeats main points: _____
- Creates framework/symbols to recall main points:
  _____
- Other (e.g., handout): _____

The purpose of this record is to observe how a summary or review can, and many times does, go beyond a simple regurgitation of the facts as they were presented, indicating how any one or a combination of the summary and review methods discussed previously were applied in a lesson. If you as an observer can identify a generalization, key point, or symbol used in conducting the summary or review, you will have gained valuable insight into the review's clarity.

CULTURAL DIVERSITY AND LESSON CLARITY

One of the most recent developments in the area of cultural diversity and lesson clarity involves the concept of **social framing**, referring to the context in which a message, such as a lesson, is received and understood (Anderson-Levitt, 2003; Ogbu, 1995a,b, 2008). A frame can be defined as a taken-for-granted context that delimits the sources from which meaning can be derived. By announcing, "Today's lesson will expect you to know how to 'borrow' when subtracting two-digit numbers," a teacher implicitly sets a frame for the lesson that conveys what the learner is expected to learn. Research has examined how best to frame a lesson so that learners can derive a common understanding from the content presented, or how to alter the frame of a lesson so that it will be more understandable to cultural or ethnic groups that might be accustomed to an alternate frame. For example, Michaels and Collins (1984) report an example of a white teacher who framed a story with linear, topic-centered patterns (e.g., "Today I will read you a series of events that happened in the lives of three characters"), while her African American students framed the task according to topic-associating patterns (e.g., "She's going to tell us the kinds of things that can happen to people"). Whereas one group primarily looked for a sequential list of events that unfolded from the beginning to the end of the story, the other group made notes about the events and the memories they evoked. Thus, frames that are ambiguous or less appropriate to one group than another can alter how content is learned and what is retained.

Ogbu (2005) makes the case for understanding the context in which different cultures expect information to be transmitted. He recommends that the teacher (1) present content from the frame most dominant to the classroom, (2) explicitly describe the frame—or context—through which learners must see the content, and (3) negotiate, when necessary, the frame with students at the start of the lesson.

There are three ways of establishing a frame at the start of a lesson that encourage students to respond in like manner (Curwin, 2003; Curwin, Mendler, & Mendler, 2008). Self-disclosure, humor, and dialogue are effective framing devices that encourage the development of warmth and respect in the classroom.

- *Self-Disclosure.* "I've been struggling to make this topic meaningful and here's what I've come up with." Being open about your feelings and emotions leading up to the lesson will encourage similar statements of self-disclosure from students, which can be used to frame the lesson.
- *Humor.* "Here's a funny thing that happened to me about what we're going to study today." Establishing a flexible, spontaneous, expressive mood at the start of a lesson from which frames can become established will encourage students to share other personal episodes that can be used to provide a context for the lesson.
- *Dialogue.* "Before we begin discussing our topic, what does it remind you of?" A back-and-forth discussion of lesson content involves random and simultaneous responding. Here every student can expect to be heard, and lesson content is expressed idiosyncratically in the words of the learners. The responses of students are then used to further structure and elaborate lesson content.

Each of these framing techniques enhances lesson clarity across cultural and ethnic groups. As you would expect, sensitive framing also encourages a warm and supportive classroom environment and encourages students to take the risks involved in learning new material and grappling with unfamiliar ideas.

PRACTICE OBSERVING LESSON CLARITY: A DIALOGUE

The following dialogue illustrates several aspects of lesson clarity presented in this chapter. To prepare for evaluating the dialogue, review the seven dimensions of lesson clarity presented in Table 7.1 and then read the dialogue, looking for the dimensions of clarity or lack thereof. Keep a record of your observations using the checklist in Instrument 7.6.

Ms. Raskin teaches computer literacy, a state-mandated requirement for all students. Her classes tend to be large (about 36 students) and heterogeneous in ability. Today she is introducing the components of a personal computer in preparation for teaching how to use the word processing software that the students will be expected to master later in the course. Today's lesson follows several introductory lessons on "What Is a Computer?" and precedes a unit entitled "How a Computer Works." We peek in on Ms. Raskin's first class of the day during the second week of school.

Ms. Raskin: [At the bell] Okay, let's settle down. No one should have their computer on. We have only a few more lessons on the basics before we will begin working with the computer, so let's be patient. Last week we introduced what a computer is and related it to our own abilities to select, remember, and process various types of information. We associated the kinds of processing a computer does with filing information, much like a manual system in a filing cabinet; subjecting information to statistical procedures, much like using a hand calculator; and creating symbols and codes, much like writing music or creating graphics. These indicate the variety of functions a computer can serve, but also that computers do essentially the same things that we humans do—only faster and more efficiently. Today we will turn our attention to those other things a computer needs to help it perform these functions. We will group these other things into two categories, *hardware* and *software*. As you can see, I've written these two categories on the board. Under hardware, I have the components [points to each word in turn with pointer]: *monitor, printer, keyboard, disk drive.* These are some of the most common components of a computer that fall under the category of hardware. At the end of today's class, I will expect you to be able to describe what each of these components does and to identify some of the differences that exist among various types of monitors, printers, keyboards, and disk drives. Now, let's see how much you remember from last week. Quann, what's missing from our list of hardware to make our computer system complete?

Quann: Remember, Ms. Raskin, I transferred in late, so I missed most of last week.

Ms. Raskin: That's right. Libby, can you help us?

Libby: I think so. It's the CPU that's missing.

Ms. Raskin: And, Alberto, what's a CPU?

Alberto: It's the central processing unit—or the heart of the whole thing.

Ms. Raskin: Keisha, you had your hand up, too.

Keisha: It's the part that does the computing.

Alberto: That's what I said!

Ms. Raskin: Alberto, remember to raise your hand. That's correct—you are both right. Can anyone remember from last week what part of our body is like the CPU? Ralph, you can give us the answer, can't you?

Ralph: It's like our brain—it's the part of the computer that does the thinking.

Ms. Raskin: Remember, we don't want to say "thinking" but . . .

Ralph: Oops, I mean processing, because humans do the thinking, and then they program the computer to do the processing.

Ms. Raskin: Yes. Does everyone remember the discussion we had last week on whether computers, or CPUs, can really think? [Most of class nods in agreement.] Keisha, do you remember how your views changed?

Keisha: Well, we all had a good laugh because I thought HAL, the computer in the movie you showed us, was actually doing his own thinking—I forgot that someone had to program him to think like a human. Also, I guess I forgot that the movie was only science fiction, and that we haven't been able to make computers come that close to thinking yet.

Ms. Raskin: Good, now let's begin today's lesson, in which we will describe and show how each of these components of hardware [Points to board again] are used by the CPU to carry out its various functions. Notice I have the word *software* written up here as another category, but I have nothing listed under it. For now, I just want you to be aware that a computer requires both hardware and software. Tomorrow when you come in, there will be some components of software written under this category, which will be the topic of our next lesson. For tonight, think about what some components of software might be, write them down, and when you come in tomorrow, see if your list is similar to mine. Pages 31 through 34 in the text will give you some hints about what to put on your list. Now, let's begin with the first component under hardware. [She points to word *computer screen*.] This one's easy because we see one every day. Debby, what is a computer screen like in our everyday lives?

Debby: Our TV at home.

Ms. Raskin: Of course. And what function does it serve?

Debby: It lets us see pictures.

Ms. Raskin: And what else? Danny.

Danny: Well, it could show us words, too, if we wanted.

Ms. Raskin: Yes, and this is particularly important for using word processing software. Oops, I just gave you one entry for your list of software tonight. Some of you may even choose to write the book report you will be doing for your English class this grading period on the computers in front of you. For that, you will need to have a screen that shows the words you write. Now, let me demonstrate various types of screens to show that not all are alike. [Teacher clicks on three computers, one after another, positioned in front of the class facing the students. Each screen displays the words "Hello, my name is HAL. What is different about me?" Some members of the class laugh as each screen lights up.]

Student: But, Ms. Raskin, I thought HAL couldn't think.

Ms. Raskin: Let's remember to raise our hands before speaking out. [Keisha raises her hand feverishly.]

Keisha: You told the CPU to show those words.

Ms. Raskin: That's right, I wrote those words and typed them to appear on the screen. Now, what about the answer to HAL's question. Anyone? David, you haven't said anything so far. What's the answer?

David: Well, in the first HAL, the letters are black and white like the old TV sets. In the second, the letters are green. And in the third, the letters are all different colors—red, green, and blue.

Ms. Raskin: That points out one of the most important differences in computer screens—a few are only black and white, some are what are called *green phosphorus*, and some are color. Today, most computers allow you to change the colors that appear on the screen. So, how many of you like the color screen the best? Raise your hands. [Most students raise their hands.] How many like the green phosphorus? [A few students raise their hands.] And how many like the black and white? [No hands are raised.] I see all of you are used to your color TVs. A color screen is most appropriate when a lot of graphics or pictures will be shown on the screen; a green phosphorus screen is sometimes preferred when a large amount of text must be read from the screen, as in airport terminals. A black-and-white screen can be the least interesting when graphics or pictures are to be displayed. Anybody notice any other differences? Trevor.

Trevor: The printing on the black-and-white screen is harder to read. It's kind of fuzzy.

Ms. Raskin: Yes. This is because the black-and-white screen is actually an old TV set; they sometimes are used as computer screens because they are inexpensive. But notice that a screen made for a TV is not as clean looking, especially in displaying fine print, as might be required in reading a book report or term paper. This aspect of a screen is called its resolution: the easier to read, the higher the resolution. Color and green phosphorus monitors can differ in resolution as well, but black-and-white TVs used as monitors have the poorest resolution. Any other differences? [No response, so teacher calls on Alberto.] Alberto.

Alberto: Well, this may be silly, but the screen on the black-and-white screen is bigger than the other two.

Ms. Raskin: That's right. And that brings up another point: The bigger the screen, the poorer the resolution, or clarity, of the picture. Since computer screens are always adjacent to a keyboard, large screens are unnecessary, so small screens, about 14 to 24 inches, are used to create high-resolution pictures. Has anyone ever seen one of those very small portable TVs? [Alberto raises his hand.] Alberto.

Alberto: My uncle in California got me one last Christmas; it's just like my iPod.

Ms. Raskin: And what's the clarity of the picture like?

Alberto: It's unbelievable! Especially compared to our large TV in the living room.

Ms. Raskin: That's my point—the smaller the screen, the higher the resolution, and the clearer the picture, unless you have high definition.

[Skipping to near the end of the lesson now, after completing similar discussions for printer, keyboard, and disk drive.]

Now it's time to look back at some of the things we have said today. [She turns on overhead projector with the columns and rows shown in Figure 7.4 predrawn on transparency.] Let's try to fill in this chart from our earlier discussion. Recall that our discussion pointed to several differences among our three HALs. One of the differences was the purpose for which each might be used, another was their cost, and a third was their resolution. Quann, if I recall correctly, we began today's lesson with you. Despite your absence last week, let's see how well you've caught on to today's lesson. Tell me what to place in the Black and White column.

Quann: Okay, I think I can. Let me start with cost, since that's the easiest. [Teacher nods.] Black-and-white screens are the least expensive, especially if they're a TV.

Ms. Raskin: Good. [Teacher writes in "least expensive" on transparency.]

Quann: Now, for resolution . . . the resolution will not be as good if it's just an ordinary TV without high definition. [Teacher writes "lowest" in the appropriate place on the transparency.] And, finally, well for uses . . . I guess it can be used for graphics and pictures as well as for reading words because it doesn't favor either one. [Teacher writes "Both text and pictures equally" on transparency.]

Ms. Raskin: That was good, Quann. Looks like you're all caught up with us. Tim, what about our next column, pertaining to our second HAL monitor?

FIGURE 7.4 Ms. Raskin's Transparency for Overhead Projector

	HAL 1 Black and White	HAL 2 Green Phosphorus	HAL 3 Color
Uses	Both text and pictures equally	Text more than pictures	Pictures more than text
Cost	Least expensive	More expensive	Most expensive
Resolution	Lowest	Higher	Highest

Tim: Well, a green phosphorus screen is sometimes preferred for reading large amounts of text. [Teacher writes each response on transparency.]

Ms. Raskin: Very good. Keisha, would you like to take our last column?

Keisha: HAL 3, that's the multicolor screen, is best suited when a lot of graphics or pictures will be displayed; it's the most expensive and has good resolution. [Teacher fills in third column with Keisha's answers.]

Ms. Raskin: This chart shows some of the most important characteristics of computer screens, so be sure to copy it into your notebooks. Let's summarize our earlier discussion about printers in the same way with this next transparency. Who'd like to begin?

TIME TO REFLECT

Take a look at your responses in Instrument 7.6. Which of the seven dimensions of lesson clarity did you observe in this dialogue? Recall that lesson clarity involves explaining concepts in a logical step-by-step order, presenting content at the students' current level of understanding, and communicating lesson content in specific, unambiguous language. Two of the most important dimensions of clarity that help ensure a lesson is understood and can be followed in a logical step-by-step order are informing the learner of the objective and providing advance organizers.

Recall that Ms. Raskin began by reviewing what had occurred in several previous lessons. This approach is sometimes called **overlapping**, where the beginning of one lesson repeats or overlaps with the end of the preceding lesson. This helps students place the content of the day's lesson in the perspective of previously learned content, emphasizing the continuity and relationships that exist among lessons within the same unit. Therefore, each new lesson is seen as an expansion or extension of content already mastered. It is in this context that Ms. Raskin informs learners of the lesson topic and the level of performance that will be expected of the students at the end of class.

Next, Ms. Raskin establishes some divisions of content that will serve as advance organizers for this and the following lesson and writes these on the board to emphasize their importance. The words *hardware* and *software* become touchstones for labeling, storing, and later retrieving discrete pieces of information that will be presented under each category—computer screen, printer, keyboard, disk drive—to which will be added a list of software in a subsequent lesson.

At this point, more overlapping occurs when Ms. Raskin asks what component is missing from those listed on the board. The teacher's goal turns from providing advance organization to checking for lesson-relevant prior knowledge and reviewing this knowledge. She asks Quann what is missing from the list to see if the topic of a previous lesson can be recalled and correctly described. Although Quann is unable to answer because he transferred into the class late, Libby responds correctly: "It's the CPU that's missing." Although we can't be sure, Ms. Raskin could have intentionally called on Libby because she was a member of a steering group, which would give the teacher an indication of how the rest of the class might have responded to this question. Recall that a steering group consists of a few students performing below average, average, and above average. Such a group can be used to estimate the level of attainment of the entire class by asking group members to recall lesson-relevant prior knowledge with a few sample questions at the start of class. In this instance, if Libby was a lower-performing learner within the steering group, chances are that most of the class had the prior knowledge needed for the day's lesson. Alberto, Keisha, and Ralph also provided knowledgeable answers to similar questions, indicating that most if not all of what had been taught in an earlier lesson had been mastered by most of the class.

Finally, to reinforce but not reteach an important previous point, Ms. Raskin asks Keisha to recount a memorable incident from a previous lesson that underscored the important distinction between processing and thinking. Keisha is asked to share with the class her mistaken notion that HAL in the movie was actually thinking rather than mimicking the words and logic programmed into it, which might conjure up for her classmates a mental image (e.g., of HAL talking to his creator) that could be used to remem-ber and better understand this distinction for a long time to come. This is one way the teacher checks for lesson-relevant prior knowledge and reinforces it before proceeding with the day's objective.

Recall that another behavior for achieving lesson clarity involves the use of examples, illustrations, and demonstrations. Are any of these evident in Ms. Raskin's lesson? Although not all lesson content can be conveniently demonstrated in the classroom using real-world examples, Ms. Raskin in this case does not fail to utilize the opportunity provided by the real-life nature of her content. Screens, printers, keyboards, and disk drives exist not only as concepts but also as devices in our everyday lives. Ms. Raskin could have chosen to discuss computer screens abstractly, simply referring to the fact that they come in different colors, shapes, and sizes. But would her lesson have had the same impact on her students? Probably not. Pictures and lifelike models used in the context of the classroom are often far more conducive to remembering key concepts than are words alone. Ms. Raskin's presentation, if composed only of words, could not possibly have related all that was being seen and recorded by her students. Thus, the demonstration of distinctions in color, size, and resolution helps increase the clarity of the lesson. This does not come, however, without some extra work on Ms. Raskin's part, as each of her three computers has to display the intended message.

An important underlying theme among teachers whose lessons routinely exhibit high levels of clarity is that they prepare examples, illustrations, or demonstrations to reinforce each key aspect of the lesson. Verbal or visual examples of lesson content, illustrations of how what is taught applies to the real world, and demonstrations of how devices and concepts work are especially effective means of reinforcing major ideas and themes and therefore of increasing lesson clarity. Ms. Raskin's online demonstration has some of each of these qualities, increasing the likelihood that her presentation will be understood and remembered.

Finally, we note that Ms. Raskin's lesson contains at least one other dimension for achieving clarity: It ends with a summary or review. This summary neatly encompasses all the relevant distinctions in a 3 × 3 table consisting of the three types of monitors classified by use, cost, and resolution. This is a succinct way of hitting the high points of the lesson without having to go back over large portions of content. Each relevant piece of information is translated into a coordinate position on the table, which is conveniently displayed on a transparency for the whole class to see. Here again, advance preparation is necessary to have a transparency ready-made for the review. By using the responses of only three students, the review is kept short and to the point.

There are, of course, some aspects of Ms. Raskin's clarity that we do not learn from this dialogue. We do not know, for example, the clarity of her instructions to the class. Few directives about how to complete an assignment are required for this lesson. Although we can presume that Ms. Raskin knows the ability level of her students and is generally teaching to it, she still could be teaching above or below the levels of at least some of her students. The use of alternative texts and assignments, as well as differentiated small-group, or self-directed learning activities, especially for those who might be more advanced or in need of lesson-relevant prior knowledge, could indicate that this dimension of clarity is being achieved. Presumably these aspects of clarity would be evident to an observer after additional observations later in the year, when differences in student skills and understanding might be more apparent.

Reactions to Ms. Raskin's lesson are summarized in the Figure 7.5 checklist. How does our checklist compare with the one you made? We believe that Ms. Raskin did an effective job of achieving most of the seven dimensions of clarity. Notice how we placed comments adjacent to each entry on the checklist to remind us of important points for later discussion, to provide useful content for review prior to a subsequent observation of the same classroom, and to focus our attention on certain unfinished areas of observation. You'll probably want to annotate your checklist when you observe in actual classrooms. For example, if we return to Ms. Raskin's class, our questions might center on whether a steering group does

FIGURE 7.5   Checklist for Observing Ms. Raskin's Classroom

Behavior	Observed	Not Observed	No Opportunity to Observe*
1. Informs learners of skills or understandings expected at end of lesson	✓ To describe and identify differences		
2. Provides learners with an advance organizer that places lesson content in perspective	✓ Overlapped present with previous content		
3. Checks for lesson-relevant prior knowledge at beginning of lesson and reteaches if necessary	✓ May have used steering group		
4. Knows learners' ability levels and uses media, materials, and procedures at or slightly above their current level of functioning			✓ Too early in year to tell
5. Gives direction clearly; checks for understanding along the way			✓ Gave only a small homework assignment
6. Uses examples, illustrations, or demonstrations to explain and clarify content in text and workbooks	✓ Demonstration effective		
7. Provides review or summary	✓ Used preorganized transparency		

*Inadequate opportunity to observe or irrelevant to the format of the lesson.

in fact exist, whether directives before an assignment are clear, and whether individualized, self-directed, or cooperative learning materials or activities are available to meet individual learning needs.

In the following chapters, we will turn our attention to several other important lenses through which to observe classrooms. These lenses—instructional variety, task orientation, student engagement in the learning process, student success, and higher thought processes—are always observed in the context of the dimensions of lesson clarity. As we turn now to our next lens, instructional variety, you'll want to keep in mind the significant impact of the dimensions of lesson clarity studied in this chapter on all the other lenses we'll discuss.

For More Information

Researchers agree that two characteristics of teaching most strongly related to student achievement are teacher clarity and teacher preparation/organization. The researchers in the following article review an extensive body of research and theory to answer the question: What do students recognize as teacher clarity? From their review they identify the classroom behaviors, characteristics, and dispositions that promote clarity in the classroom and present a practical model that captures these principles for beginning teachers. Of special interest is their instrument for observing "clear teaching behaviors" that identifies what every teacher can do in their classroom to improve instructional clarity and raise student achievement. You can access the results of their research at http://education.boisestate.edu/LROGIEN/CLEAR%20theoretical%20basis.htm.

Key Terms

advance organizer, 96
differentiated instruction, 99
overlapping, 108
social framing, 105

steering group, 98
transmediation, 104
verbal markers, 95

Activities*

1. Using the checklist shown in Instrument 7.6, observe the presentation of a lesson for signs of clarity. At the end of your observation, add a brief description to each checked box highlighting at least one specific reason why you checked it.

2. Using the 5-point scales shown in Chapter 4 as examples, convert the more effective and less effective teacher indicators in Table 7.1 into a 5-point format and then observe a lesson for signs of clarity. Consider the vertical and horizontal placement of each indicator on the page, whether words will be affixed to all or only some of the response blanks, and what verbal response alternatives will be best suited to each question. Show your scale to a classmate who has also constructed a 5-point scale. Together, create a single revised version incorporating the best features of both scales.

3. Observe a lesson using the procedure and format provided in Instrument 7.1 to determine if learners are informed of the objective.

   a. If the teacher informed learners of the objective, paraphrase the written or oral statement communicating the objective. In your opinion, was it communicated clearly and perceived accurately by the students?

   b. If the teacher did not inform learners of the objective, indicate the domain (cognitive, affective, or psychomotor) and action verb(s) that, in your opinion, best describe this lesson's objective. Using the content of the day's lesson, write a sentence or two that could be used to inform learners of the lesson objective.

4. Obtain a package of 5" × 8" index cards and a small plastic file for storing and organizing the cards. Bring several cards to each observation during the semester. During or at the completion of each observation, describe on a card any advance organizer used and when and how it was used in the context of the lesson. Number the card and place it in your file. Using the format shown in Instrument 7.2, re-

*Some of these activities may be grouped into a common activity, divided among classmates, and completed from a single observation.

cord (a) the reference number assigned with the advance organizer, (b) the grade level and subject matter for which it was used, and (c) its placement in the lesson (beginning, middle, end). Arrange to exchange your advance organizer cards with other observers to collect more organizers in areas of interest to you.

5. Using the assigned text or curriculum guide for a lesson you will be observing, list any prior facts, skills, or concepts needed to attain the lesson's objective. Explain why you believe the objective for the lesson requires this prior learning and why it might represent prior learning for a future lesson.

6. Using the categories in Figure 7.3 and the coding form in Instrument 7.4, observe and record the student response–teacher reaction sequences for clarity of directions that occur during a class period. Write a narrative description of the sequence of events occurring in this classroom with the data from each row of the coding form.

7. After observing a class period, indicate the approximate percentage of learners for whom the content appeared to be (a) below, (b) at or slightly above, and (c) above their current levels of understanding. Assign percentages to these categories so that they add up to 100%. Using the list of verbal descriptions in Table 7.2, describe the students' behavior in this classroom. Which, in your opinion, creates the greatest threat to an efficient and productive classroom: students for whom the content is below their current level of understanding or those for whom the content is above their current level?

8. Using Instrument 7.5, observe a classroom for examples, illustrations, or demonstrations that explain and clarify content. Add any additional types of examples, illustrations, and demonstrations to the instrument as they are observed. Analyze the frequency of marks you have placed for each row of the instrument. Can you detect any preferences or cultural and ethnic biases in the way the teacher likes to frame content? In your opinion, is this teacher's pattern of framing a strength or a weakness in conveying lesson content?

9. Using your observation from Activity 8, indicate whether a summary or review of lesson content was provided at or near the end of the lesson. If so, how was the lesson content repackaged? Did you find (a) a restatement of the highest generalization reached during the lesson, (b) a review of key points, or (c) the use of symbols, codes, or mnemonic devices? In your opinion, which of these or other techniques most helped learners to remember and store the content learned?

8

Verifying Instructional Variety

Daddy Fell into the Pond

Everyone grumbled. The sky was gray.

We had nothing to do and nothing to say.

We were nearing the end of a dismal day,

And there seemed to be nothing beyond,

THEN

Daddy fell into the pond!

And everyone's face grew merry and bright,

And Timothy danced for sheer delight.

"Give me the camera, quick, oh quick!

He's crawling out of the duckweed." Click!

Then the gardener suddenly slapped his knee,

And doubled up, shaking silently,

And the ducks all quacked as if they were daft

And it sounded as if the old drake laughed.

Oh, there wasn't a thing that didn't respond

WHEN

Daddy fell into the pond!

Alfred Noyes

Who among us hasn't experienced a dull lecture or a boring afternoon in class? At such times, no matter what our intention, it can be difficult to focus, and perhaps even to stay awake! The same can be true of classrooms when routines are so entrenched that *everything* is predictable and mundane. Wise teachers understand the value of instructional variety for enhancing student engagement and learning. Let's explore how variety can truly be the "spice of life" in an effective classroom.

Instructional variety refers to a teacher's variability and flexibility in delivering instructional content. It includes the planned mixing of different instructional activities, such as discussion, small-group work, cooperative learning, demonstration, explanation, questioning, and recitation within the context of a single lesson, as well as variation in physical movement and gesturing, eye contact, and voice intonation. Instructional variety also includes the use of instructional media and technology, learning materials, laboratory equipment, displays, and classroom space that encourages student involvement in problem- and project-based learning. All these components of the classroom contribute to instructional variety, which, in turn, has been found to influence both student achievement and student engagement in the learning process. Classroom research studies have reported less disruptive behavior and greater student attention in classrooms with a greater-than-average variety in classroom activities and materials (Emmer & Evertson, 2009; Evertson & Emmer, 2009); other studies have shown variety to be related to student attention.

DIMENSIONS OF INSTRUCTIONAL VARIETY

Think back to classes you have enjoyed and learned a lot from. What were some of the ways your teachers got and kept your attention? Table 8.1 summarizes teaching behaviors that contribute to instructional variety.

1. Using attention-gaining devices
2. Showing enthusiasm and animation
3. Varying instructional activities and media
4. Mixing rewards and reinforcers
5. Varying types of questions and probes
6. Using student ideas

Not all the indicators of instructional variety in Table 8.1 will be relevant to a particular lesson, depending on its purpose or content. But every lesson you observe or prepare presents the opportunity to exhibit some types of instructional variety.

PRACTICE OBSERVING INSTRUCTIONAL VARIETY: A DIALOGUE

Let's practice verifying instructional variety by visiting Mr. Marks's class and using the checklist in Instrument 8.1 to help consider six key behaviors related to instructional variety.

Today Mr. Marks is teaching a social studies lesson to his class of 33 culturally diverse students. His lesson focuses on regulatory tariffs during the time of the Civil War, in a natural transition from a previous lesson on the geography of the South. We peek in on Mr. Marks's class during the fourth month of the school year.

Mr. Marks: All desks clear. Today, I need to present some—[Interrupting himself] June, put the math book away. We're on social studies now—some information about taxes and tariffs and how they are sometimes used to control commerce—or the kind of business that goes on between states and nations. This isn't going to be as interesting as our discussion of the battles of the Civil War last week, but pay attention anyway. As I said, our topic is taxes and tariffs used to regulate commerce. Does anyone know what a tariff is? [Silence] Anyone? [Silence again] Okay. A tariff is simply a tax imposed by a government on goods imported—or brought into a country—and in some instances on goods exported—or sold outside a country. Why would a government place a tax on goods coming into its own country, and who would want such a thing? Anyone? [Silence] I can see some of you are not taking this lesson seriously. This topic will be on the test next week. [At this point, Mr. Marks sits

TABLE 8.1   Indicators for Instructional Variety

More Effective Instructional Variety	Less Effective Instructional Variety
1. Uses attention-gaining devices (e.g., begins with a challenging question, visual, or example)	Begins lessons without full attention of most learners
2. Shows enthusiasm and animation through variation in eye contact, voice, and gestures (e.g., changes pitch and volume, moves about during transitions to new activity)	Speaks in monotone, devoid of external signs of emotion; stays fixed in place for entire period or rarely moves body
3. Varies mode of presentation (e.g., presents, asks questions, and then provides for independent practice)	Rarely alters modality through which instructional stimuli are received (e.g., seeing, listening, doing)
4. Uses mix of rewards and reinforcers (extra credit, verbal praise, independent study)	Rarely reinforces student behavior; tends to use same rewards every time
5. Varies types of questions (divergent, convergent) and probes (to clarify, to solicit, or to redirect)	Always asks the same type of question (for example, What do you think about . . . ?) or overuses one type of question
6. Incorporates student ideas or participation in some aspects of the instruction (for example, uses indirect instruction or divergent questioning)	Assumes the role of sole authority and provider of information; ignores student contributions

down at his desk. Carlos, sitting in the first row directly in front of Mr. Marks, raises his hand.] Okay, Carlos is ready to work. [Points to Carlos to respond.]

Carlos: I don't understand why anybody would want to tax themselves.

Mr. Marks: Give us the answer to my question.

Carlos: Well, what I meant is, it would seem people would complain if they had to pay more for something they wanted just because someone else wanted to place a tax on it.

Mr. Marks: And actually they did complain—just before the Civil War. At that time, in 1862, the government placed taxes on domestic manufacturers and duties on imports for two reasons. Can you think of one of these reasons?

Carlos: Well, to raise money to run the government, I suppose, and maybe, like we said last week, to get ready for a war.

Mr. Marks: Okay, so a tariff on manufactured goods, whether created in this country or another, raises lots of money that could be used to run a government. What about another reason? Angel [who is sitting next to Carlos in the front row], what do you think?

Angel: It seems to me that taxes to run a government and taxes on goods coming into the country are different. If products that are made in this country are taxed, what's the point of taxing imported products, which might make TV sets and cars coming from Japan too expensive?

Mr. Marks: And then what? [Nodding to Angel to continue.]

Angel: Everyone will stop buying them because they won't be able to afford them.

Mr. Marks: And then what? [Nodding to Angel again, but now Angel looks confused.] Okay, Carlos.

Carlos: Now I get it! Sure, we'll stop buying, or at least buy fewer of these imported products, forcing us to buy ones made in the United States.

Mr. Marks: Now, this is an interesting point Carlos is raising. Who can summarize it? [Angel nods in anticipation of being called on.] Angel?

Angel: What he's saying is that, as the price of imported products goes up, we are being forced to buy similar products made in our own country. And because things like cars and TVs are taxed by our own government, money would be raised for running the government. Is that right?

Mr. Marks: Right. And who knows what we call tariffs on imported goods to encourage us to buy U.S. goods? [Silence] Okay, I'll give you a hint. What do such tariffs protect?

Carlos: U.S. businesses who are having trouble selling their products because of foreign competition.

Mr. Marks: And that's called . . . ? [Waits for Carlos to respond, and then looks at Angel, but still no response.] It's called *protectionism*. About the time of the Civil War, large tariffs were placed on goods imported from Europe—goods that were also being manufactured in the North. To increase the market for these American products in the South, and to encourage the development of a strong industrial base, located primarily in the North, taxes were placed on things like textiles, leather, paper, iron, and lead products being imported into this country. By 1864, these taxes had risen to an average of about 50% of the price of the product being imported. So what do you think the people in the South felt about these tariffs? Angel?

Angel: Well, if they had to pay more for these products, they'd be pretty mad, especially at the North, who gained from selling all these products to the South.

Mr. Marks: Well, class, do you think Carlos and Angel know what a tariff is? [Some class members respond favorably in low voices; others nod. Carlos and Angel turn around to look at the class and check on the extent of the admiration.] Okay, now I'm going to pass out this fact sheet on tariffs, which is what you'll need to know for the test. Angel, would you see that everyone gets one? [Teacher remains at desk, pushing a stack of handouts toward Angel.] As you will see from the handout, it's a bit more complicated than our discussion this morning. We're going to spend the rest of the period going over the facts on this handout. I'll ask you questions, and you look on the handout for the answers. [The handout is organized into brief explanations under different headings.]

Mr. Marks: Okay, let's begin. Ricky [who is seated behind Angel in the front row], what's a definition of *tariff*?

Ricky: [Quickly glancing over handout, and then reading directly from it.] A list or schedule of customs duties imposed by a government on imports and also, in some instances, on exports. Originally, such imports were levied for—

Mr. Marks: [Interrupting] Okay, that's sufficient. Tim, give me an example of a tariff.

Tim: Which one?

Mr. Marks: Any one. Pick one from the sheet.

Tim: Is the Tariff Act of 1862 okay?

Mr. Marks: Any one.

Tim: That was when tariffs on imported products were raised an average of 50%.

Mr. Marks: Which products? [Tim scans the paragraph nervously for clues.] What do we cover ourselves with every day?

Tim: [Hesitating] Clothes?

Mr. Marks: Of course. Under the Tariff of 1862, you'll see the word *textile*, which is yarn or cloth used in making clothes. Were any other products included under the Tariff Act of 1862? Angel, let's come back to you.

Angel: Well, I see a whole lot of products listed here . . . glass, iron, hats, leather, coffee, tea, sugar . . .

Mr. Marks: But go on. What else does it say about coffee, tea, and sugar?

Angel: They're taxed, too.

Mr. Marks: Amanda, can you add anything?

Amanda: It says the import taxes were the least, and were eventually reduced, for items such as coffee, tea, and sugar.

Mr. Marks: Why?

Amanda: Okay, now I see. Because these types of things did not really compete with U.S. products.

Mr. Marks: And that means . . . ?

Amanda: That we don't produce them in this country, so there was nothing to protect . . . there was no need for pro . . . tex . . . tionism.

Mr. Marks: Very good. Did the rest of you hear Amanda's answer? Can you summarize your answer for the class, Amanda?

Amanda: I guess I could say that tariffs work best when they apply to foreign products that compete with similar products made in the United States. Otherwise they just drive up the price of things that everyone needs and can't get anywhere else. That's why import taxes are low for some products and high for others. But there's one thing I don't understand. [Mr. Marks nods for Amanda to go on.] Wouldn't placing taxes on imported goods allow the manufacturers in this country to raise their prices unfairly?

Mr. Marks: That's a good question. Think about it for tomorrow, and then write down how you believe a tariff could work to make prices on domestic goods rise, as Amanda suggests, and how a tariff might work to lower prices on domestic goods. I'll have some of you read your answers at the beginning of class tomorrow.

◼ TIME TO REFLECT

Which of the six dimensions of instructional variety did you see in this dialogue? Obviously, not all of the dimensions of variety can be observed from this brief dialogue, but some can. Let's explore each of the six dimensions as it appeared in Mr. Marks's classroom and as it might occur in your own teaching. We'll also consider some observation instruments that can help you see instructional variety in greater detail.

Using Attention-Gaining Devices

One of the most obvious methods of instructional variety is the use of attention-gaining devices. Applied most often at the beginnings of lessons (and sometimes during) to stimulate or arouse learners' receptive modalities and cognitive processes, attention-gaining devices can take many forms, such as pictures, audiovisual media, or computer simulations, as well as live demonstrations. Less dramatic forms include posing a challenging question, presenting a dilemma or a bewildering situation, or showing a unique visual display. Dramatic or subtle, attention-gaining devices wake up the receptive modalities of sight and sound and stimulate the cognitive processes associated with them (O'Flynn, Kennedy, & Macqrath, 2004). Without this conscious change from the mood and tempo of an earlier activity or class, your learners' attention may never be fully focused on the lesson. Attention-gaining devices help create natural cycles of highs and lows that make life in classrooms more interesting and less regimented.

One of the most common attention-gaining devices is to arouse students' curiosity. This can be accomplished by asking a thought-provoking question, such as "Have you ever wondered how we got the word *horsepower?"* (from a lesson on units of measurement), "Can anyone think of a popular automobile with the name of a Greek god?" (from an introductory lesson on mythology), or "Have you ever wondered how some creatures can live both in the water and on land?" (from a lesson on amphibious animals). These questions, called **openers,** are not designed to have a single correct answer, or even to accurately reflect the fine details of what is to follow, but to amuse, stimulate, and sometimes even bewilder students so that they will be receptive to the more detailed content and questions that follow, as shown by the following list of opener types.

- *To Surprise and Astound.* "How many realize that our sun will eventually exhaust all its energy and our planet will be completely dark?" (from a science lesson)
- *To Promote Controversy.* "Some storytellers believe that the individual should always be in a struggle with the society in which one lives. Others believe the individual is meant to live in harmony with society. Which is true?" (from a reading lesson)
- *To Present a Contradiction.* "Why do you think the Greek empire collapsed when it was at its strongest?" (from a history lesson)
- *To Promote Curiosity.* "Who thinks he can see lower forms of animal life with the naked eye?" (from a biology lesson)

How did Mr. Marks begin his lesson? How did he stimulate the receptive modalities of his learners? Like many teachers, Mr. Marks relied on an opening statement that simply told the students what would be covered ("some information on taxes and tariffs and how they are sometimes used to control commerce"). This statement presented the topic of the lesson, but did little to make it exciting or to whet the appetites of students to learn more. Students who had never heard the word *tariff* might not even have understood what the lesson was about. A verbal question or statement to promote curiosity (e.g., "How many of you paid a tax on something you bought this week?"), to present a contradiction ("Do you know that the tax placed on some products helps some people at the expense of other people?"), to create controversy ("Should a group of people who think they are taxed unjustly pay their taxes?"), or to surprise or astound ("Do you know that some products imported from another country are taxed at more than 100% of their worth?") might have awakened the receptive modalities of most students and enabled them to relate the content of the day's lesson to their own experiences.

Diagrams, pictures, lifelike models, films, and interactive software and video are other aids for gaining the learners' attention. These devices are used to appeal to the students' sense of vision while the accompanying oral presentation appeals to their sense of hearing. These kinds of openers might include samples of materials to be used in the day's lesson or equipment that students can touch and feel before a lesson begins (e.g., scales, buttons, or meters). Graphics, visuals, scaled replicas or models, or equipment to be used in the context of the lesson can be particularly effective openers, especially with students who are known to be more responsive to seeing and touching than to simply hearing about a topic.

You're probably thinking that Mr. Marks could have used other, perhaps more creative attention-gaining devices in his lesson, such as a picture from an encyclopedia of a tariff that was handwritten in the nineteenth century, a cartoon from an early American newspaper making fun of tariffs, or a brief excerpt from a speech by a congressman against (or for) a tariff—all items that are readily available from general reference works. If so, Mr. Marks would have captured the attention of more of his students by putting a little more effort into his opening. Instead, the price Mr. Marks paid for his unimaginative beginning was that no one wanted to answer his questions. Most of his opening questions were met with silence, until the only alternative left was to change to a lecture format ("Okay, I'll tell you").

Observing Attention-Gaining Devices

As you begin to observe instructional variety in classrooms, you can enhance the accuracy of your observation by using the form provided in Instrument 8.2. This record can help you consider attention-gaining devices in more detail, because it divides them into four categories: verbal statements and questions, visuals, instructional media, and real or lifelike examples of the topic to be presented, also called *realia.* You will likely observe teachers using more than one of these four categories at the same time, as when a lesson begins with a question intended to promote curiosity ("How long do you think it took Columbus to reach America?") followed by a photograph of a captain's log and a scale model of a sextant used by early mariners to navigate across the ocean. In a case like this, you would place three check marks in the row corresponding to this lesson topic. You can note the repeated use of attention-gaining devices during a lesson with multiple check marks within a box. As you use this checklist to observe different teachers, your record will show the variety of attention-gaining devices used most often, those used infrequently or seldom, and those used to complement one another within the same lesson (e.g., the teacher tends to follow up verbal statements with a visual to promote curiosity). Total frequencies or percentages can be tallied in the last row. As you observe the various attention-gaining devices, you'll want to watch closely for their effect on students. These observations will help you make attention-gaining selections for your own teaching.

Showing Enthusiasm and Animation

Once a teacher has piqued the students' curiosity, interest, and excitement through successful openers in a lesson, the momentum can be maintained by learning to vary voice, eye contact, and body movement. This is the second behavior for instructional variety. Although teachers are not actors, there is a lot they can learn from the field of dramatics. Lessons, like plays, should have opening and closing acts with a main story between, and, also like plays, may have many climaxes and anticlimaxes to keep the audience's attention. How well a teacher plans the script, or lesson, will have a lot to do with its attention-getting quality. There should be natural variety in the topics and instructional activities that a lesson contains. That variety can be enhanced by a teacher's willingness to accent high points and bolster low points with changes in voice, eye movement, and body movement. Simply put, a teacher's voice inflection, eye contact, and positioning in the classroom should change often during a lesson, especially during its high points (e.g., lively group discussion) and low points (e.g., rote recitation from the workbook). These small but consistent changes are easily felt by students, who will be looking for signs that the teacher is aware of and responsive to the natural rhythm of the classroom.

What did you notice about Mr. Marks's enthusiasm and animation? Recall that he began the lesson by conveying a feeling to his students that, if not required by the curriculum, he might not even be teaching the lesson. Phrases such as "I need to present some information" and "This isn't going to be as exciting as our discussion of battles of the Civil War last week, but pay attention anyway" are not lost on perceptive students, who quickly see that the teacher is unenthusiastic about teaching the topic. The message is that students need not be enthused either.

Mr. Marks's lack of enthusiasm might be even more apparent if we could examine his eye contact and body movement. Recall that, for almost the entire length of this dialogue, Mr. Marks interacted with only two students, Carlos and Angel, both of whom were seated directly in front of his desk. Later in the lesson when Ricky (seated behind Angel) joined in,

Mr. Marks was still talking to only a small percentage of his class. Later exchanges included Tim and Amanda, but, even so, only five students were included in the discussion; three were seated in the front and center portion of the classroom closest to the teacher. This effectively excluded most others from participating and might convey the impression that the opinions of others are not valued as highly as those of Carlos, Angel, and Ricky.

Although we have no way to be certain, Mr. Marks's eye contact may have been limited to a small part of the classroom as well, because eye movement often follows the same path as verbal exchanges. Adding to this was the teacher's decision to remain seated throughout most of the lesson. Although sitting behind a desk might be appropriate when students are completing assignments in workbooks or reciting answers to problems in a drill-and-practice format, it is generally not suited to the kind of informal, spontaneous exchanges desired during question-and-answer sessions or group discussion. Staying in a single position in the classroom for long periods of time, removed spatially by the physical barrier of a desk, can detract from student interest and engagement in the lesson content.

Kounin (1970) coined the word **withitness** to refer to a teacher's ability to keep track of many different signs of student behavior simultaneously and thereby convey a sense of physical presence, or vigilance. Eye contact that scans the whole classroom is one of the most important ingredients in conveying withitness, animation, and liveliness, which can add variety to a classroom.

Teachers limit their withitness to only a portion of the classroom when they

- Talk only to the middle-front rows
- Talk with their backs to the class when writing on the chalkboard
- Talk while looking toward the windows
- Talk while some students block their view of other students

When teachers engage in these behaviors, they lose contact with the remaining parts of the classroom. One of the simplest and most effective ways for teachers to increase withitness and emphasize their presence is to remember to look around the room from time to time and to vary voice, eye contact, and body movement at intervals of rising and falling action throughout a lesson.

Kounin (1970) notes that one of the most important distinctions between effective and ineffective classroom managers is the degree to which they exhibit withitness by the variety in their voice, eye contact, and movement around the classroom. Effective classroom managers are aware of what is happening in all parts of the classroom. More important, these effective classroom managers are able to communicate this awareness to their students through variations in voice, eye contact, and body movement. How would you rate Mr. Marks's withitness in this dialogue? What suggestions might you offer him?

Observing Enthusiasm and Animation

To look more closely at a teacher's enthusiasm and animation, we can focus on four behaviors: body movement, eye contact, voice intonation, and gesturing. You can observe these four behaviors with the Likert scale in Instrument 8.3. Notice that this Likert scale is positioned horizontally with descriptive labels provided for the middle and ends of each scale, which allows you to place a check mark anywhere along the continuum, including between vertical marks, to represent the degree of the behavior you are observing. For scoring purposes, the numerical code for the scale point closest to the check mark may be used or fractional parts estimated. Also note that the middle point represents the most appropriate degree of behavior for the scale measuring body movement. To average the scores from this scale with the others that place the most desired behavior at one end, the middle point is assigned a numerical code of 5, both extreme endpoints are assigned a code of 1, and both intermediate points are assigned a code of 3.

Varying Instructional Activities and Media

Another behavior for observing instructional variety is a teacher's use of instructional activities and media. Although many general types of activities can be defined by what the *teacher* does (e.g., questioning, discussion, guided practice, and recitation), instructional activities can also be categorized by considering what is required of the *student*. According to Tomlinson (2004), Tomlinson and McTighe (2006), and Doyle (1983), an important goal of an instructional unit should be to differentiate instruction by giving students the opportunity to select different paths of increasing difficulty to show what they have learned, thereby providing all students with an opportunity for academic success. Although all students can benefit from this approach, it is particularly important for culturally, linguistically, and academically diverse learners in order to achieve adequate yearly progress toward achieving state standards mandated by the No Child Left Behind (NCLB) Act of 2001.

An instructional activity involves determining a *product* to be formulated, selecting a mental *operation* to create the product, and obtaining the *resources* needed to generate the product. Products can vary in difficulty from simple subvocal thoughts composed by students while a teacher is explaining or presenting, to an oral response in the form of an answer to a question from the teacher or text, to a written response in the form of a paragraph or essay, to a drawing or scale model of a concept. Typical mental "operations" required by the student to create these products include recognition and discrimination, application and practice, problem solving, and discovery. The "resources" consulted might include orally delivered content as well as content drawn from instructional media, such as videos and transparencies, computer files, texts, workbooks, blackboard, handouts, or the Internet. These elements are shown in the form of a differentiated activity structure checklist in Instrument 8.4 that can be applied to individual learners, groups, or the whole class. You can use this checklist to look more closely at the variety of instructional activities and media in a lesson.

Observing the Variation in Instructional Activities and Media

As you observe variations in instructional activities and media with Instrument 8.4, consider what products, operations, and resources are required by a particular task. Place a check mark in each column next to the combination of product, operation, and resource, thus breaking a more general instructional activity into three separate components. For example, if the instructional activity is to listen to new content being presented for the first time in the context of a lecture aided by the blackboard, you might place check marks alongside subvocal thought (product), recognition and discrimination (operations), and blackboard (resources). Check marks consistently repeated across different activities may represent a bias on the part of the teacher for only certain products, operations, and resources, restricting the variety or strengths of some learners in performing the instructional activity successfully. A new activity is defined as the point at which the product, operation, or resource changes, requiring the start of a new column.

Another useful categorization by which instructional activities and media can be differentiated is the sensory modality (or modalities) in which lesson content is being received by the learner. At least four different modalities can be used to engage learners in lesson content: oral, verbal (involving the written word), visual, and tactile (touch) that correspond with three "intelligences" (linguistic, spatial, and bodily-kinesthetic) proposed by Gardner (2006). In other words, lesson content can be communicated by speaking, writing, showing, touching, or any combination of these. Table 8.2 identifies some of the most common ways these modalities are used in the classroom.

Instructional variety within a classroom is increased when instructional tasks include all of these modalities or combinations of them. Effective teachers plan for activities that involve the use of different modalities in different combinations to provide task demands at the current level of understanding of individual learners and groups of similar learners. Changes across two or three modalities, or channels of communication, may be required to keep most young students attending to and engaged in the learning process. The frequency with which changes in modality in a lesson should be made will depend on the age of the student; younger learners in the early elementary grades or lower-performing learners often require a greater range of sensory stimuli and more changes across channels than higher-achieving or older students. Instrument 8.5 places these four modalities into an observation record. As you observe a lesson, place a check mark after each 5-minute interval to indicate the mix of channels through which learners are receiving lesson content and constructing their understanding of it.

If channels are used simultaneously during the interval, place multiple check marks in each row in Instrument 8.5. This might indicate, for example, that a teacher is delivering content orally while pointing to a chart or illustration. The final rows can be used to total the intervals checked within a channel and to determine the percentage of intervals in which that channel was being used. The total number of intervals should correspond to a single lesson. If instruction occurred for 50 minutes and four 5-minute intervals were checked under "visual," the percentage entered for visual would be $(4/10)100 = 40\%$, indicating that during approximately 40% (or $.40(50) = 20$ minutes) of the lesson the visual channel was being emphasized. Such percentages should be used as estimations, however, because individual check marks do not indicate that a given channel was in use during the entire interval. But the most important information involves the changes that occur from column to column, or from one interval to the next. Check marks appearing consistently in one column for large portions of a lesson might indicate a lack of instructional variety and very little differentiation of content for groups or individual learners.

With these thoughts in mind, how might a variety of instructional activities and media have changed Mr. Marks's lesson? Although Mr. Marks did not use attention-gaining devices and lacked enthusiasm at the beginning of his lesson, the tone of his lesson changed from an exclusively oral presentation to one that included both oral and written stimuli when he introduced the handout. In this sense, Mr. Marks demonstrated the value of variation in instructional activities. By altering the instructional format, Mr.

TABLE 8.2 Presentation Modalities Used to Create Variety[a]

Oral	Verbal[b]	Visual	Tactile
Teacher explaining	Teacher writing on board	Teacher using charts, graphs, illustrations	Students examining specimen
Teacher/students asking questions	Teacher writing on transparency	Students looking at diagrams, pictures in text or on board	Students using equipment
Teacher playing audiotape or record	Students reading text	Students watching film/video	Students building/constructing (pasting, gluing, cutting out, drawing)
Students reciting	Students working in small groups with text	Students seeing lifelike or scale models	Students arranging/ordering material
Students discussing in small groups	Students writing about what is discussed	Students seeing pictures of what is discussed	Students examining objects of what is discussed

[a]The olfactory modality, the sense of smell, is another channel through which the learner may receive instructional stimuli.

[b]As a *receptive* modality, this is not distinguishable from the visual. However, because it has special significance for the presentation of content, we will consider it as another channel through which learning occurs.

Marks was on the right track. But armed with a better understanding of instructional variety, Mr. Marks might have also encouraged more active engagement among his students. For example, he could have engaged his students in an activity that went beyond the fact-laden oral responses he received from their reading the handout to requiring a different product (e.g., asking them to write a make-believe tariff that could have appeared during the Civil War), a different operation (e.g., discriminating among tariffs that might and might not have led to the Civil War), and by providing the needed resources (e.g., examples of tariffs from classroom reference material). In this manner he would have changed the task demand and challenged students to compare and contrast and make judgments about information that required the integration of facts from the handout and information newly acquired from the activity.

Researchers and experienced teachers alike agree that effective teaching involves many different classroom activities. A teacher who does nothing but talk for an entire period, engages students only in prolonged seatwork, or only exposes students to attention-gaining devices will have difficulty achieving outcomes at the desired level of performance. Although some lessons will emphasize a single instructional activity, it is important that the majority of lessons require instructional tasks and media (overhead transparencies, seatwork, handouts, visuals, and, when appropriate to lesson content, computer-based software, etc.) that make different cognitive demands on the student. Effective teachers vary the products they require (e.g., oral responses, written answers, interactive computer exchanges, and Web-based searches), the operations to be used in creating the product (memorization vs. application vs. problem solving), and the resources available to produce the product (e.g., textbook, magazines, encyclopedia, electronic media). A lesson plan that includes some combination of these is preferable to one that emphasizes only a single task and a single modality of responding that may not be appropriate for all learners. We will return to the important topic of differentiated instruction in more detail in Chapter 10 to see how it can be implemented to actively engage students in a heterogeneous classroom.

Varying Rewards and Reinforcement

One of the first things you will notice when observing in classrooms is the teacher's interaction with students. Most obvious among these interchanges will be those concerning rewards and reinforcement—our fourth behavior for verifying instructional variety.

The effectiveness of rewards depends on the variety with which they are administered and the types of reinforcement with which they are associated. For example, nothing is *less* reinforcing than the phrase "That's good" or "That's correct" if it's repeated in the same tone of voice hundreds of times for different problems and learners and without further comment (Brophy, 1981; Costa & Kallick, 2004). The phrase soon becomes meaningless and loses its ability to reinforce a behavior. It is therefore important that verbal praise, like all rewards, vary in type, amount, and intensity and that it be associated with other, more durable types of reinforcers (e.g., "Would you like to tell the class how you got the right answer?"). Chapter 6 presented a list of incentives that, like verbal praise, could be used to increase the probability of a desired response, varying from a simple smile or head nod, to allowing a student to work in a group, to displaying the result of a group's discovery project for others to see. Other types of rewards that can be particularly effective in reinforcing desired behavior include using a student's answer as a model for others to follow, having a particular student retrace for the class how he obtained the correct answer, and having peers comment on the correctness of a student's answer.

Not all rewards are equally reinforcing. Some learners might dislike working in a group. Others will have no need to visit the library or a learning center. Some students like to be called on; others may be too shy to appreciate the added attention. What is a reinforcement to one student might be irrelevant to another. Finding the right reinforcer for a student is often a matter of trial and error: If a reward does not seem to increase the probability of a desired behavior, it should be changed for another until success is obtained. Knowing the interests and needs of your students can save valuable time in finding the right mix of reinforcers. For example, students who are visually oriented might enjoy time for looking at maps, charts, or models at a learning center; for others, extra time to read may be equally appealing as a reward for desirable behaviors. Students can be asked which rewards are in tune with their specific interests or can select the rewards they like best from a list you prepare at the beginning of the school year. This latter approach has the advantage of ensuring that what is chosen will be practical within the context of a given classroom (they choose from your list) and relevant to the culture and ethnicity of individual students.

Finally, it is important to note that, in a superordinate–subordinate structure such as school, there is a natural tendency for those in authority to reinforce the existing structure by imposing penalties for failing to comply with it. When this is the only form of incentive for learning and good conduct, however, it can be detrimental to the motivation of learners. Remember that learners will be far more responsive to rewards for producing acceptable behavior than to punishment for not producing it.

Let's think back to Mr. Marks's use of rewards and reinforcement. From his responses to students, it appears that Mr. Marks had not established a consistent pattern of reward and reinforcement during this lesson, although some informal types of reinforcement were evident when he asked Carlos's and Angel's peers to show admiration for their definition of a tariff in response to Amanda's thought-provoking question. We would need to observe Mr. Marks's classroom for a longer time to see any use of long-term rewards (such as extra credit, independent study projects, group work, special duties, or use of special resources such as a computer or learning center) that, when properly varied, could also contribute to instructional variety in this classroom.

Observing the Use of Rewards and Reinforcement

You can use the observation record shown in Instrument 8.6 to divide rewards and reinforcements into informal (which can be expected to occur frequently within a lesson) and formal categories (which tend to occur less frequently across lessons). The top half of the form is intended for use on a daily basis; the bottom half can be used with repeated observations over intervals of a week or longer. Some teachers will use a particular reward or reinforcement on a daily (informal) basis; others may use the same one on a less frequent (formal) basis. Although we have included common rewards and reinforcers in both categories, make changes to the list according to the situation you observe.

Although you'll probably observe fewer formal than informal rewards, the absence of check marks in this category over time or the repeated use of only a single type can indicate an inadequate variety of rewards. The repeated use of only a single informal reward, such as "gives verbal praise" or "smiles and nods," suggests a superficial reward system, which students may soon come to ignore for lack of more enduring and sincere reinforcement. Again, you'll want to consider the connections between a teacher's behaviors and student responses carefully to inform your own teaching decisions.

Varying Types of Questions and Probes

A fifth source of variety in a classroom is the teacher's use of questions and probes. The purpose of these two related techniques is to draw out a response, sometimes any response, that can then be refined and developed into a better or more complete answer. Questions and probes provide a vehicle for engaging a student in the learning process by getting the learner to think about, work with, and act on the material being presented. Questions and probes also offer the opportunity for students to share their learning processes with others and benefit from hearing different ways a question can be answered by their peers (Brualdi, 1998).

To achieve variety, questions can be convergent or divergent, followed by probes and varying according to the amount of time allowed between question and answer (Nadler & Chandon, 2004). Let's look at how these can add variety to a question-and-answer sequence.

Convergent and Divergent Questions

Convergent questions have a single or limited number of right answers that are commonly associated with the goals of direct instruction. **Direct instruction** occurs when the teacher is the major provider of information (e.g., giving a presentation as opposed to assigning a group discovery project); the teacher's role is to pass on facts, rules, or action sequences in the most direct way possible. Teachers often use convergent questions to facilitate direct instruction because they want to direct students to the correct answers as quickly and efficiently as possible. You'll likely observe many convergent questions when recitation and drill and practice occur in the form of a briskly paced question-and-answer session. Researchers note that teachers spend most of their time asking convergent questions (Dillon, 2004; Hubbard & Power, 2003).

The following examples of convergent questions have a single or limited number of right answers.

- What is 20 divided by 5?
- What is a definition of *democracy?*
- What is the chemical composition of the atmosphere on the moon?
- What are four literary devices that can make a story interesting?

Convergent questions involve the recall of facts, the summarization or paraphrasing of learned knowledge, or the application of knowledge to a context similar to that in which it was learned. Convergent questions often place heavy reliance on text or workbook content that resembles the desired response ("Look at this word and then say it." "Watch me form a possessive and then do the next one." "Read the instructions and then focus the microscope."). The task for the learner is to produce a response that resembles, as closely as possible, the form and content of a stimulus provided by the text or teacher.

Divergent questions, on the other hand, may have many right answers and are most commonly associated with the goals of **indirect instruction,** which are to help students use their own knowledge and experiences to actively construct an understanding of particular concepts and related information. A question for which there is no single best answer or for which there are many correct answers would be an indirect question because some choice in the content and form of the response resides with the students, providing learners with a degree of control over their own learning. Divergent questions usually take place in the context of inquiry, problem-solving, or discovery-type activities in which the control of the form and content of the instruction is shared between students and teacher.

The following examples of divergent questions have many right answers.

- What are some examples of things that are divisible by 5?
- Who would like to start by telling us what the word *democracy* means to them?
- What might be some ways life could be sustained on the moon?
- What types of things make a story interesting?

These questions do not require the answer to a specific problem; rather, they are asked in such a way that almost any student can search for and find an answer that would be at least partially correct. By inserting a phrase such as "means to you," "What might," or "What types of things," a teacher can encourage a response from every student.

The purpose of divergent questions is not to quiz or to teach directly, but to focus student attention on particular ideas or issues and to promote inquiry, problem solving, and discovery. By accepting many different answers, the teacher can use student responses from divergent questions to formulate subsequent questions that shape more accurate responses. The purpose of divergent questions, then, is not to arrive at a correct answer in the quickest and most efficient manner, but to begin a process of search and discovery whereby successively more acceptable answers are constructed.

The rationale given for using higher-level, divergent-type questions includes promotion of thinking, formation of concepts and abstractions, and development of decision-making and judgment skills. However, classroom researchers who have studied the effects of convergent and divergent questions on student achievement (Brualdi, 1998; Dillon, 2004; Hubbard & Power, 2003) have found that many more convergent than divergent questions occur in classrooms. Although research has not clearly substantiated that the use of higher-order questions is related to gains in student achievement, at least not as measured by tests of standardized achievement, research does indicate that higher-order questioning tends to encourage students to use more complex thought processes in composing a response. Research presented by Gall (1984) and Redfield and Rousseau (1981) indicates that teachers who ask questions requiring analysis, synthesis, and evaluation elicit these types of behaviors from their students more frequently than do teachers who use fewer higher-level questions. Therefore, the effects of higher-level questioning on the process of thinking may in themselves justify applying higher-level questions consistently at moderate rates. As you observe, you will want to pay special attention to how and when teachers utilize divergent questioning techniques in the classroom.

Probes

To help make questions more meaningful and to elicit thoughtful responses, both convergent and divergent questions can be followed up with probes that attempt to pierce the glib, superficial, or inadequate response that might be initially given. **Probes** are questions that follow questions and are carefully crafted to deepen, enrich, and extend an earlier response. Probes can be used to elicit a clarifying response to an earlier question, solicit new information related to an earlier question, or redirect the learner into a more productive area. Each of these uses can be a source of instructional variety, encouraging learners to act on and reshape their responses and, most important, their understanding.

Wait Time

Rowe (1986, 1987) and Tobin (1987) distinguish two different wait times. **Wait-time 1** refers to the amount of time a teacher gives a learner to respond when first asked a question. Classrooms with short wait-time 1s do not give learners much time to think before answering the question. In these classrooms, the teacher is repeating the question or calling on another learner to answer the same question after only a 2- or 3-second period of silence.

Wait-time 2 refers to the interval of time after a learner's first response until the teacher or other students affirm or negate the answer and the teacher then moves on. Teachers with long wait-time 2s wait at least several seconds before asking a follow-up question, correcting the answer, or otherwise commenting on what the learner said, giving that learner and other students time to rethink, extend, or modify a response. Classrooms with short wait-time 2s are characterized by little follow-up by other students, because that opportunity has been taken by the teacher.

By observing teachers who increased their wait time to 3 or more seconds, Rowe found a number of consequences directly related to the problem-solving behavior of students:

- The length of student responses increased, on average, between 300 and 700%.
- More student inferences were supported by evidence and logical argument.
- The number of questions asked by students increased.
- Student-to-student exchanges increased and teacher-centered behavior decreased.
- The number of students failing to respond decreased.
- Misbehavior decreased.
- More students volunteered to respond.

Rowe (1986) also reports that students use the teacher's wait time to determine the level of thoughtfulness they will devote to an answer: The greater the teacher's wait time, the more effort the student will make to respond in a thoughtful and logical manner.

As you consider the use of questions and probes, what are your thoughts about Mr. Marks's lesson? Let's look at the way his lesson improved over time using questions and probes that allowed student ideas to emerge. After he introduced the handout, Mr. Marks posed a convergent question to Ricky ("What's a definition of *tariff*?"). Although the correct answer could be expressed in different ways and could include different examples, the range of correct answers is limited by the nature of the question, making it convergent. The question evoked little cognitive activity on Ricky's part—he simply read the answer from the handout. So the teacher followed up with another question, this time directed to Tim ("Give me an example of a tariff"). Tim was asked to choose an example from the handout and summarize his choice. He decided to respond by choosing the Tariff Act of 1862: "That was when tariffs on imported products were raised an average of 50%." The teacher responds "Which products?" and gives the hint "What do we cover ourselves with every day?" This exchange continued, with the teacher following up each student response with a probe for further

clarification ("Can you summarize your answer for the class?"), additional information ("What else does it say about coffee, tea, and sugar?"), or redirection ("Were any other products included under the Tariff Act of 1862?"). Some of the other probes, or follow-up questions, to student responses during the last part of the dialogue included

- "Any other products included . . . ?"
- "Can you add anything?"
- "Why?"
- "And that means . . . ?"

Notice that, unlike the beginning of the lesson, Mr. Marks was now engaging his students in the learning process not with rote or mechanical questions, but with questions that force them to go beyond the words on the handout and paraphrase, summarize, and extend crude or incomplete answers. These probes and the questions that preceded them add variety to the lesson. But even more important, they were embedded in an activity structure that engaged learners in the lesson and required them to formulate a product (response to the question) and use several cognitive operations (recognition, application, and problem solving) with the aid of a resource (handout). This activity had the dual effect of maintaining student involvement and evoking responses that went beyond parroting back content in the precise form in which it was presented.

Observing Types of Questions and Probes

Instrument 8.7 can be used to observe the sequence of teacher questions, student responses, and teacher probes as they occur in the classroom. For each question asked by the teacher, determine whether the question is intended to have a single or limited number of correct answers (convergent) or many different correct answers (divergent). Next, record the student's response to the question as *accepted, partially accepted* (with qualifications or reservations), *not accepted* (wrong or irrelevant), or *no response*. Finally, record the nature of the follow-up probe, if one occurs. In recording the probes, determine whether the teacher's probe (1) asks the student to clarify or expand the answer given, (2) asks a related question to solicit additional information and lift the original answer to a more complete state, (3) redirects the student by giving hints, or (4) asks the same question of another student. The pattern of check marks across each row of the instrument indicates the sequence of questioning and responding for individual questions. An analysis of check marks down the columns will reveal the variety of questioning, responding, and probing occurring in the class, as well as how meaningful the particular series of questions and probes is. Definitions for the terms used in this observation record appear in Figure 8.1. Some of the more frequent patterns to watch for are shown in the following chart:

Another way to distinguish types of questions is to consider the degree of cognitive processing, or thinking, they require of the learner. Anderson and Krathwohl (2001); Bloom (1994); and Bloom, Englehart, Furst, Hill, and Krathwohl (1984) identify levels of

behavioral and cognitive processing that can be applied to questions. These levels are referred to in many curriculum guides and teaching materials, so you'll want to be familiar with them. Definitions for six of these levels appear in Table 8.3. You'll notice that the levels are divided into lower- and higher-order questions, depending on the relative amount of cognitive processing (thinking) they require on the part of the student. Although you might expect that teachers would rely on higher-order questions often, most research data suggest that about 70 to 80% of all questions teachers ask are lower order, with most of these at the knowledge level.

Instrument 8.8 will help you distinguish among various types of questions as you observe in classrooms. When you first observe questioning procedures, you might find that distinguishing among question types in a quickly paced lesson can be difficult. If so, you can use the middle two columns of this record, labeled *LO* (lower order) and *HO* (higher order), until you gain a sense of the teacher's questioning style. *LO* combines knowledge, comprehension, and application questions into a single category or judgment, whereas *HO* does the same for analysis,

FIGURE 8.1   Definitions for Question–Response–Probe Sequential Event System (Instrument 8.7)

Teacher Question	Convergent	Teacher asks question that has one correct answer. ("What's 6 times 6?" "Who can name each of the main characters in *Huckleberry Finn?*")
	Divergent	Teacher asks question that has more than one correct answer. ("What household products contain the element sodium?" "What did you like about *Of Mice and Men?*")
Student Response	Accepted	Teacher accepts answer as stated through verbal affirmation ("That's right," "Good," or "Okay") or expressive behavior (nods head).
	Partially Accepted	Teacher tells student that response is incomplete. ("That's not quite right," "You're on the right track.")
	Not Accepted	Teacher informs student that answer is not acceptable. ("Next," "Wrong," "No.")
	No Response	Student fails to respond. Teacher may try to get student to respond, but to no avail.
Teacher Probe	None	Teacher fails to follow up student's response. Moves to new question or other activity.
	Clarify	Teacher asks student to clarify, expand, or restate answer in other words. Teacher wants to better understand what student said.
	Solicit	Teacher tries to uplift or extend student response by getting student to supply new information.
	Redirect	Teacher attempts to change direction of student response by giving hints or clues about what direction to take.
	Asks Other	Teacher ignores student response or lack of response and asks another student the same question.

TABLE 8.3 Six Levels of Question Complexity

	Question Level	Expected Teacher Behavior	Expected Student Behavior	Instructional Process	Key Words
Lower Order	Knowledge (Remembering)	Teacher intends student to recall specific information for which there is only one correct answer.	Student remembers or recalls information and recognizes facts, terminology, and rules.	Repetition Memorization	Define Describe Identify
	Comprehension (Understanding)	Teacher intends student to translate, paraphrase, or summarize given material.	Student changes the form of a communication by translating what has been read or spoken.	Explanation Illustration	Summarize Paraphrase Rephrase
	Application (Transferring)	Teacher intends student to apply the information to a situation that is different from the situation in which it was learned.	Student applies the information learned to a context other than the one in which it was learned.	Practice Transfer	Apply Use Employ
Higher Order	Analysis (Relating)	Teacher intends student to separate, compare, or determine relationships among concepts, information, or ideas.	Student breaks a problem down into its component parts and draws relationships among the parts.	Induction Deduction	Relate Distinguish Differentiate
	Synthesis (Creating)	Teacher intends student to combine previously learned information, opinions, or concepts into an original, creative response.	Student combines parts to form a unique or novel solution to a problem.	Divergence Generalization	Formulate Compose Produce
	Evaluation (Judging)	Teacher intends student to make a choice or decision, to judge, or to select from a number of alternatives.	Student makes decisions about the value or worth of methods, ideas, people, or products according to expressed criteria.	Discrimination Inference	Appraise Decode Justify

synthesis, and evaluation questions. The last row can be used to total the number of questions in each category. A good guideline is to try to identify the first 15 questions or so only as *LO* or *HO*, before attempting to make finer distinctions.

To help you focus on wait time, use the last column to record whether the wait time allowed for a student response was less than (or more than) approximately 3 seconds. Minus or plus signs can be used to record these two alternatives, or a timepiece can be used to determine exact values. Rowe (1986) found that most teachers' wait times are about a second instead of the more appropriate 3 or more seconds. Research also suggests that teachers sometimes ask as many as four lower-order questions (knowledge, comprehension, application) for every higher-order question (analysis, synthesis, evaluation).

Using Student Ideas

The final behavior for achieving instructional variety involves the use of student ideas. Researchers have described five components of this behavior.

1. *Acknowledging.* Using the student's idea by repeating the logical connectives expressed by the student
2. *Modifying.* Using the student's idea by rephrasing it or conceptualizing it in the teacher's own words
3. *Applying.* Using the student's idea to teach an inference or predict the next step in a logical analysis of a problem
4. *Comparing.* Using the student's idea by drawing a relationship between it and ideas expressed earlier

5. *Summarizing.* Using what was said by an individual student or a group of students as a summarization of concepts

Consider a brief dialogue that incorporates some of these behaviors.

Teacher: Tom, what is the formula for the Pythagorean theorem?

Tom: $c^2 = a^2 + b^2$. [At this point the teacher could have simply said "Good!" and gone on to the next question. Instead, this teacher continues.]

Teacher: Let's show that on the board. Here is a triangle. Let's do exactly as Tom said. He said: Squaring the altitude, which is *a*, and adding it to the square of the base, which is *b*, should give us the square of the hypotenuse, which is *c*. Would someone like to come up and measure the hypotenuse of this triangle with a ruler and show us that it equals the square root of c^2?

Which, if any, of the five ways of using student ideas are present in this dialogue? First, by putting Tom's response graphically on the blackboard, this teacher *applied* Tom's answer by taking it to the next step, constructing a proof. Also, by repeating what Tom said, the teacher *acknowledged* to the entire class the value of Tom's contribution. And by having someone come to the blackboard to show the correctness of Tom's response, a *summary* of the concept was provided. All this was accomplished from Tom's simple (and only) utterance: "$c^2 = a^2 + b^2$."

There may be no greater variety than that which occurs in student responses to divergent questions. This diversity can be a problem as well as a benefit when unexpected or difficult-to-evaluate responses put the teacher on the defensive. A common response of some teachers is to create a correct answer on the spot and end the awkward pause that frequently follows an unusual and unexpected answer. This is not a proper use of divergent questioning, because two of the reasons for posing divergent questions are to incorporate student ideas and encourage participation in the lesson. The key to eliciting individual student ideas and opinions is to make the ideas and opinions useful to the goals of the lesson, thereby creating a greater understanding for all students. Rowe (1986, 1987) found that by increasing wait time after asking a question and after a student's response, teachers showed greater flexibility in responding to student comments, greater variety in number and kind of questions asked, and higher expectations for certain students.

This was accomplished, in part, by

• Encouraging students to use examples and references from their own experience.

• Asking students to seek clarification of, draw parallels to, make predictions about, and draw associations from what they already know.

• Encouraging understanding and retention of ideas by relating them to the students' own sphere of interests, concerns, and problems.

These behaviors will be further discussed in Chapter 12 to show how each can be used to promote higher thought processes. But, for now, let's consider Mr. Marks's use of student ideas.

Recall that student ideas can promote instructional variety by acknowledging, modifying, applying, comparing, or summarizing a student's contribution. We believe that Mr. Marks was somewhat effective in motivating students to use the contributions of other students, thereby according respect and status to student contributions and providing content for further discussion. For example, Mr. Marks said, "Now, this is an interesting point Carlos is raising. Who can summarize it?" "Well, class, do you think Carlos and Angel know what a tariff is?" "Very good. Did the rest of you hear Amanda's answer? Can you summarize your answer for the class?" Each of these statements acknowledged or summarized a student idea, giving these students a sense of pride in the reconstruction of lesson content. They also made varied (and often higher) demands of students in constructing their responses.

Although Mr. Marks often capitalized on his students' ideas, there were times when he chose not to acknowledge or use certain student responses, perhaps because they lacked the quality or depth needed for the discussion. Remember when he said, "Give us the answer to my question" or "Okay, that's sufficient"? In these examples, Mr. Marks failed to leave sufficient wait time to allow the student to clarify an answer that could be better or complete an answer already begun, possibly leaving these students feeling a lack of pride and sense of failure. Such curt or controlling responses, if applied consistently, can discourage students from volunteering or participating again. This may be particularly true when the teacher and student are members of different cultures or genders.

Observing the Use of Student Ideas

Instrument 8.9 can help you learn how to use student ideas to build on lesson content. Recall that five teacher behaviors are associated with the use of student ideas: *acknowledging* (repeating a student response), *modifying* (rephrasing a student response), *applying* (using a student response to take the next step), *comparing* (drawing a relationship between a student response and other responses), and *summarizing* (using a student response to draw together or synthesize what was said).

To use this observation record, place a check mark in the appropriate box under each column every time the teacher acknowledges, modifies, applies, compares, or summarizes a student's response, according to the definitions provided. To illustrate, let's return to the brief dialogue earlier between the teacher and Tom. To code this dialogue using the observation record, we would place checks in the first column after applying, acknowledging, and summarizing, indicating that these three behaviors occurred. When the action turns to another student, or the same student is provided the opportunity to respond again, the next column is coded, and so on through the lesson. Not all student responses can or should be integrated into the lesson with one or more of these behaviors. However, the infrequent use of student ideas or the consistent use of student ideas employing the same teacher behavior (e.g., acknowledging) can indicate a lack of instructional variety in a classroom.

Notice that tallies can be summarized in two ways on this record. The first, indicated by the final row of the record, shows the total number of teacher behaviors used in response to a single idea. A second total can be identified by noting, across the top, the last number checked for each specific type of teacher behavior. Each view can provide information about ways to use student ideas in the classroom.

Our reactions to Mr. Marks's lesson are summarized in Figure 8.2. All things considered, we give Mr. Marks a mixed but somewhat encouraging mark for this lesson. He exhibited some positive behaviors for three of the six dimensions of instructional variety. Comments written on the checklist identify important points for later discussion, provide content for review prior to subsequent observation, and identify unfinished areas of observation.

CULTURAL DIVERSITY AND INSTRUCTIONAL VARIETY

A number of authors have studied the effects of various forms of instructional variety on student behavior and found a connection between spatial distance and involvement in the classroom: The greater the spatial distance between teacher and students, the more some students become passive listeners and perceive the teacher's talk as a lecture. As the teacher moves closer to students, communication tends to become more interactive, with more student-to-student and student-to-teacher communication. Scollon (1985) observes that standing closer to individual students can promote involvement, because these students will be drawn into nonverbal forms of communication, such as eye contact and changes in voice and body movement, that send a message of involvement.

Neuliep (2008) and Scollon (1985) found that the use of space also can communicate a sense of power and control, which can promote involvement or uninvolvement. For example, a person who is standing expresses more power than one who is seated, and a person who speaks from a distance expresses more authority than one who is talking up close. Accordingly, teachers who stay behind their desks separated from students are expressing control and authority, which in turn can send a message that students are expected to be passive, subservient, and nonparticipatory.

Such decisions clearly affect the warmth (or lack of warmth) of the classroom learning climate. Teachers are often creative in their approaches to space and learning climate. For example, Bowers and Flinders (1991) report a case of a teacher who moved from student to student checking work while seated on a swivel chair with casters. In this manner the teacher was able to elicit more spontaneous and relaxed student responses, resulting in greater student involvement, particularly from those students who normally remained passive. Clearly, a teacher's animation and proper use of spatial variety can foster a sense of trust and sharing among students who, by virtue of their language, culture, or ethnicity, might not wish to be spotlighted in the traditional teacher-dominated manner.

In considering instructional variety, it is important to realize that interaction patterns are often related to particular cultural expectations (Martin & Nakayama, 2003). For example, students from one culture might feel threatened by the close proximity or penetrating eye contact common in another culture. Further, cultural patterns that are unfamiliar to white teachers may provide misleading signs of involvement and uninvolvement. For example, a white teacher might perceive some characteristics of minority students as inattentive and demeaning because gaze, eye contact, and body cues may not correspond with the responses of white students. Specifically, white speakers tend to look at a listener only occasionally, but when in the role of listener they look continuously at the speaker. On the other hand, African American speakers tend to look continuously at the listener, but when in the role of listener look at the speaker only intermittently.

FIGURE 8.2   Checklist for Observing Mr. Marks's Classroom

Behavior	Observed	Not Observed	No Opportunity to Observe
1. Uses attention-gaining devices		✓ Began lesson matter-of-factly	
2. Shows enthusiasm and animation through variation in eye contact, voice, and gestures		✓ Lacked liveliness especially at beginning; seemed to be talking only to a few	
3. Varies instructional activities (e.g., presenting, explaining, questioning, discussing, practicing) and media (e.g., computer software, film, workbook transparencies, the Internet)	✓ Used handout, switching from oral to verbal (written) modality		
4. Uses mix of rewards and reinforcers			✓ Insufficient time to observe, although occasional verbal praise was noted
5. Various types of questions and probes — Questions — Divergent	✓ Used both, turning more to divergent at end of lesson		
Questions — Convergent			
Probes — To clarify	✓ Followed up on student answers by asking students to continue their thought processes		
Probes — To solicit			
Probes — To redirect			
6. Uses student ideas and participation to foster lesson objectives when appropriate to goals of instruction	✓ Used student ideas to some extent, but also may have "turned off" some with curt answers		

The speech patterns of ethnic and cultural groups also must be taken into consideration when allocating the proper amount of wait time between questions and after a question. For some cultural groups, particularly those who have limited proficiency in English, Rowe (1986, 1987) suggests that a 3-second wait time may be insufficient to elicit a response and promote active participation. Although little is known about this facet of cultural diversity, wait times considerably greater than those used for the majority of students may be appropriate for some cultural groups. One finding is clear: Wait times of less than about 3 seconds seem to inhibit thoughtful responses among all students.

The results from these and other studies of cultural diversity and instructional variety suggest that

- A closer, more informal, spatial distance when asking questions and responding will be more appropriate for learners who, because of culture, language, or ethnicity, do not wish to be spotlighted in the traditional manner.
- For some cultural groups, looking at the speaker only intermittently can indicate full attention and engagement in the lesson, despite the dominant cultural pattern.
- Speech patterns of some cultural groups, especially members with limited English proficiency, may require a substantially longer wait time (greater than 3 seconds) after a question.
- A closer spatial distance tends to convey a less formal learning climate and promote more relaxed

and spontaneous responses, increasing participation among all students.

As you observe in classrooms, you'll want to become sensitive to the prevailing and accepted interaction patterns in schools and communities. This understanding will help you view verbal interactions in the social and cultural context in which they take place.

In the following chapters, we will turn our attention to several other important lenses through which to observe classrooms. These lenses—task orientation, student engagement in the learning process, student success, and higher thought processes—are always observed in the context of the dimensions of instructional variety.

For More Information

Because teaching is such a busy profession, it can be difficult for teachers to keep up with developments in technology and accompanying instructional materials. You may want to make it a regular practice to peruse monthly teaching magazines such as *Instructor* or *Teaching Pre-K–8.* Each includes regular departments introducing new technological advances, websites, and software.

A large number of websites are also dedicated to lesson planning and instructional variety. Helpful ideas for enhancing instructional variety across various academic disciplines can be found in Rekrut, M. D. (1999). Using the Internet in classroom instruction: A primer for teachers. *Journal of Adolescent & Adult Literacy, 42*(7), 546–557.

Key Terms

convergent questions, 122
direct instruction, 122
divergent questions, 123
indirect instruction, 123
openers, 117

probes, 123
wait-time 1, 123
wait-time 2, 123
withitness, 118

Activities*

1. Using the checklist provided in Instrument 8.1, observe the presentation of a lesson looking for signs of instructional variety. At the end of your observation, add a brief written description to each box highlighting at least one specific reason why you chose to place each of your check marks as you did.
2. Using the examples of 5-point scales shown in Chapter 4, convert the positively stated indicators

of instructional variety listed in Table 8.1 into a Likert scale. Consider vertical or horizontal placement of each indicator on the page, whether words will be affixed to all or only some of the response blanks, and what response alternatives will be best suited to each question. Show your scale to a classmate who has also constructed a 5-point scale. Together, create a single revised version incorporating the best features of each.

*Some of these activities may be grouped into a common activity, divided among classmates, and completed from a single observation.

3. Using the form shown in Instrument 8.2 for recording attention-gaining devices, observe several lessons in different classrooms. In each classroom, record any verbal statements/questions, visuals, media, instructional technology, and realia used to capture student attention that do not fit the predesignated categories on the record. With these other attention-gaining devices included, add the tallies in each column and enter the totals in the last row. Does your data suggest that any one category is used more frequently than the others? If so, what do you believe accounts for this result?

4. Using the Likert scales provided in Instrument 8.3 for observing a teacher's body movement, eye contact, voice intonation, and gestures, place a check mark along the point on each continuum that in your judgment best reflects the behavior of a teacher you have observed. Assign a numerical value from 1 to 5 to each check mark, and use fractional scores when your marks fall between major divisions on the scale. Be sure to note the direction of each of the scales before assigning numerical values. Overall, how would you describe this teacher's enthusiasm and animation?

5. Using Instrument 8.5, record the channels through which the content of a lesson is transmitted by observing for 40 to 50 minutes. At the end of each 5-minute interval, indicate whether the oral, verbal, visual, or tactile modalities, as described in Table 8.2, are used by the teacher to convey lesson content. Calculate the approximate number of minutes and percentage of time each of these modalities is in use. Rank the use of the four modalities in this classroom according to percentage of time. Do you believe this pattern is typical of most classrooms? What, in your judgment, would be the most desirable pattern for this lesson?

6. Using the observation record for observing informal and formal types of rewards presented in Instrument 8.6, observe several days, as close together as possible, in the same classroom. Complete a new record each day, entering a check mark each time an informal or formal teacher response or activity that serves as a reward or reinforcement occurs. Keep a list of any other rewards that do not fit the categories listed, classifying them as formal or informal. Total the number of entries within categories on each form, and then sum the totals for each category across forms (days). Which categories of formal and informal rewards were used most often? Which were used least?

7. Observe a class with a scheduled question-and-answer session or group discussion in which student questioning is likely to occur. Complete Instrument 8.7 for recording the sequence of teacher questions, student responses, and teacher probes. Continue observing until a sufficient number of both convergent and divergent questions have been recorded. Total the number of entries in each column separately for convergent and divergent, as indicated in the final two rows. Using these totals, identify the most frequent student response to a convergent question and the most frequent teacher probe to a student response following a convergent question. Do the same for a divergent question. In this class, how did student responses and teacher probes differ across types of questions?

8. Using Instrument 8.8 for observing lower-order and higher-order questions at six levels of behavioral complexity, observe another class session in which teacher–student questioning is likely to occur. For the first 15 or so teacher questions, record only whether the questions are lower or higher order. Next identify questions as knowledge, comprehension, application, analysis, synthesis, or evaluation, according to the definitions given in Table 8.3. Total the number of entries in each column. How do your results, including wait time, compare with what classroom researchers have found?

9. Observe a class discussion using Instrument 8.9 to record the teacher's use of student ideas. Complete the final row by adding the number of entries for each column. How many times did each of the five teacher behaviors for using student ideas occur in this classroom? Can you cite any unique ways in which this teacher used student ideas?

10. As teachers become familiar with innovations such as talking books on CD-ROM, they often wonder how to go beyond simply plugging students into a system to help them gain important understandings that transfer to other learning settings. Read Linda Labbo's (2000) article "12 Things Young Children Can Do with a Talking Book in a Classroom Computer Center" (found in *The Reading Teacher, 53*(7), 542–546) and list several ways her suggestions might be useful for creating instructional variety using software or computers with students (not just talking books software). Using Labbo's ideas as a springboard, identify other suggestions or cautions for teachers using software and computers in their classrooms.

9

Observing Task Orientation

Helping

Agatha Fry, she made a pie,

And Christopher John helped bake it.

Christopher John, he mowed the lawn,

And Agatha Fry helped rake it.

Zachary Zugg took out the rug,

And Jennifer Joy helped shake it.

And Jennifer Joy, she made a toy,

And Zachary Zugg helped break it.

And some kind of help

is the kind of help

That helping's all about.

And some kind of help

Is the kind of help

We all can do without.

Shel Silverstein

What kinds of tasks and what kinds of help are effective in classrooms? How do teachers formulate, introduce, and monitor learning tasks in classrooms? How do they increase the chances that a learning task will be the "kind of help that helping's all about"?

Task orientation refers to the degree to which the teacher provides students with the opportunity to learn. Patterns of this behavior include the amount of time the teacher spends covering the assigned topics and encouraging students to think about and apply the content taught, as well as the amount of intellectual or cognitive emphasis given an assigned topic by the teacher's activity structure. Most researchers agree that classrooms in which most of the interaction between students and teacher focuses on subject matter rather than administrative and clerical tasks are likely to have higher rates of achievement than those that do not. It is also probable that teachers in content-oriented classrooms are more familiar with the material likely to appear on end-of-year achievement tests, so that their instruction parallels the curriculum that guided the construction of these tests.

In short, teachers with a high degree of task orientation are goal oriented: That is, they organize instruction around their goals and stick to those goals in the midst of distracting activities that reduce students' opportunity to learn. Most important, a task-oriented teacher has high, but realistic, expectations for student performance.

DIMENSIONS OF TASK ORIENTATION

Table 9.1 summarizes five behaviors for achieving task orientation:

1. Developing unit and lesson plans that reflect the curriculum

TABLE 9.1 Indicators for Task Orientation

More Effective Task Orientation	Less Effective Task Orientation
1. Develops unit and lesson plans that reflect the most relevant features of the curriculum (each unit and lesson objective can be referenced back to curriculum guide or text)	Develops lessons almost exclusively from personal or student interests; breadth and depth of lesson content fails to distinguish between primary and secondary content in the curriculum guide and text
2. Handles administrative and clerical tasks (visitors, announcements, collection of money, dispensing of materials and supplies) efficiently by anticipating and preorganizing some tasks and deferring others to noninstructional time	Attends to every administrative and clerical task in detail during the time normally devoted to instruction
3. Prevents and corrects misbehavior with a minimum of class disruption (has preestablished academic and work rules to prevent intrusions into instructional time)	Attends to specific misbehavior at length; singles out individual students for punishment and lectures on the offense during instructional time
4. Selects the most appropriate instructional strategy for the objectives taught	Uses inefficient instruction methods for achieving lesson objectives (frequently attempts to teach facts through discussion, or concepts through drill and practice)
5. Builds toward unit outcomes with clearly definable events (weekly or monthly review, feedback, and testing sessions)	Has no systematic milestones (progress checks, reviews, individual assignments or projects) to keep the class on schedule and moving toward a clearly defined goal

2. Performing administrative and clerical tasks efficiently

3. Preventing and correcting misbehavior with a minimum of class disruption

4. Selecting the most appropriate instructional strategy for the objectives being taught

5. Establishing cycles of review, feedback, and testing

PRACTICE OBSERVING TASK ORIENTATION: A DIALOGUE

Let's practice observing these signs of task orientation by visiting Mrs. Libby's class and using the checklist in Instrument 9.1.

Today Mrs. Libby is teaching her students about reproductive systems, a topic required by the curriculum guide and covered in Chapter 3 of the adopted textbook. This lesson is intended to be a transition to a unit on the reproductive systems of higher life forms to be taught the following week. This lesson occurs during the first month of the school year.

Mrs. Libby: Okay, everyone settle down. Tricia, get to your seat. [At the bell] You, too, Mark.

Alexa: You want my homework now?

Mrs. Libby: I'll collect everyone's homework at the end of class.

Alexa: But some haven't got it, and they're just gonna do it during class.

Mrs. Libby: Alexa, let me make the decisions. You just worry about getting a good grade.

Alexa: But—

Mrs. Libby: [Notices Kyoko walking in late] And where have you been?

Kyoko: My locker got jammed and I had to get Mr. Tiller to open it for me.

Mrs. Libby: Did he give you a late pass?

Kyoko: Nope.

Mrs. Libby: You can't just walk in late without a pass. [Some murmuring is heard among the other students.]

Kyoko: I guess he forgot.

Mrs. Libby: Please get one and then come back. If I let you walk in late, everyone will do the same.

Kyoko: I'd have to interrupt his class. He's probably already teaching.

Mrs. Libby: I'm marking you absent until you come back with a pass or a note from a counselor. [Kyoko whispers something, which the teacher chooses to ignore, and then leaves the room. By this time, a few students are out of their seats visiting friends and loud talking can be heard.] Okay, that's enough. [Claps hands to restore order] Some of you may feel sorry for Kyoko, but he's got to learn that

being on time is a mark of a responsible person. Life is a series of hurdles we all have to cross, and one of them is being on time. Are we all settled down now and ready to go to work? [A few students nod; the others remain passive.] Okay, then, I can begin presenting today's lesson. It's about the reproductive cycle. [Some snickering can be heard in the back of the room.] This is serious, class, and I don't want any laughing. Who remembers from our previous discussion some of the ways lower forms of animal life reproduce? [Sudia raises his hand. The teacher nods.]

Sudia: Well, one way we studied is by dividing in half.

Mrs. Libby: Okay, this is called "reproduction by fission." That's when the parent organism splits into two or more organisms and loses its original identity. It is the way most single-celled animals reproduce. Now, this process can only be seen under a microscope. How many of you have ever used a microscope?

Milo: [Shouting out] I have one at home.

Mrs. Libby: [Ignoring Milo] Those who have used a microscope, raise your hand. [Teacher counts five hands.] Okay, well a few of you know that with a microscope things can be seen that cannot be seen by the naked eye.

Milo: [Shouting out again] Yeah, I used to put little bugs under mine and watch 'em squirm. [Class laughs.]

Mrs. Libby: [Looking at Milo] You're not supposed to call out. First of all, you spoke without raising your hand. Second, we're talking about lower forms of animal life that cannot be seen by the naked eye. So let this be a warning. Let's see now, where were we?

Kathy: [Calling out] Single-celled animals that reproduce by dividing up.

Mrs. Libby: Yes. But I wanted to say that, later, we will have an opportunity to use microscopes to see single-celled animals. These microscopes are expensive and can be damaged easily if they are not used correctly. I might as well let you know that each of you will have to pass a test before you can use our microscopes. These microscopes are new this year, and the principal is concerned about their safety. There just isn't money to replace any of them if they should be broken through carelessness. I don't know if you heard about the new rule, but students who break equipment through their own carelessness have to pay for it. So that's a warning. Can anyone think of any other means of reproduction? [Silence. Shelly looks uncertain, but captures the teacher's eye.] Shelly.

Shelly: Sometimes an egg—or something like an egg—gets fertilized.

Mrs. Libby: We're talking about lower forms of animal life. Bill. [Who is waving his hand]

Bill: Isn't there a way that new life can be created by parts of other things coming together?

Mrs. Libby: Good. You must be talking about a process called *conjugation*. This occurs when two similar organisms fuse, exchange nuclear material, and then break apart, taking two different identities. Now, can anyone think of a way higher forms of animal life reproduce?

Milo: [Calling out] You mean like dogs and cats?

Mrs. Libby: This is your second warning about calling out. One more time and I'll have to assign you extra homework. [Class snickers with delight at Milo getting in trouble] Well, now—[Catching the thought again] Many multicellular forms of animal life reproduce by having male and female reproductive cells that unite to form a single cell called a *zygote*, which then divides to form a new organism. The word that describes the union of male and female cells is *fertilization*. In this form of reproduction, half the genes in the zygote come from one parent and half from the other.

Mark: [Calling out] That's what sex is all about.

Mrs. Libby: [Pointing to Mark] That will be an extra assignment for tonight for calling out. Answer all the questions at the end of Chapter 3. Barbara, tell Mark what we are talking about.

Barbara: We're talking about zygotes!

Mrs. Libby: Yes. Now in higher animals, including humans, single species are either male or female, according to whether they produce male or female reproductive cells. Somewhere there's a picture of male and female cells in your text. Does anyone remember seeing it? [Some students nod, and others shake their heads.] Can someone find the page it's on? [Class starts thumbing through pages of book noisily, while teacher goes to her desk and looks, too.]

Bobby: I found it. It's on page 72.

Mrs. Libby: [Turning to page 72 in her book] No. That's not what I'm thinking of.

Kathy: Here it is on page 63!

Mrs. Libby: [Turning to page 63 now] No. That's not it either. Maybe I remember seeing it in one of my books. [Mrs. Libby grabs a thick book from the reference shelf behind her desk and renews the search. Class gets noisier.] Well, here's one kind of like what I was thinking of. [Holds page of book up to class] Can everyone see it? [Students in front look at picture with curiosity; students in back shout out "No." Some get up from their seats and walk to the front for a better look.] Okay, let's stay in our seats. I'll make a transparency of this tonight and we will take a better look at it tomorrow. [Closes reference book; some students moan for effect.] For those who didn't see it, the picture shows a typical male reproductive cell—called a *sperm*—and a typical female reproductive cell—called an *egg*, or—[Students start smiling and looking at each other with embarrassment. A click can be heard, indicating an announcement is about to be made over the P.A. system. Mrs. Libby goes to her desk and sits down to await the message. The noise level goes up as students talk among themselves, trying to anticipate what the rest of the lesson will be about.]

Principal: [Over the P.A. system] Teachers, I'm sorry to interrupt, but I have an important announcement. Orders for individual class pictures must be in no later than 3:00 P.M. today. Failure to place your order by that time means you will not receive pictures this year. While I have your attention, I would like to tell students to remind their parents that tonight is Parent–Teacher Night. We would like a good turnout, so be sure to remind Mom and Dad. Thank you. [Some students have gotten out of their seats to talk to others.]

Mrs. Libby: Class isn't over. Open your books to the questions at the end of Chapter 3. Let's see if you know the definitions of these words from our discussion. Some of these will be on the test next week. Damon, you take the first one. What is *fission*?

▇ TIME TO REFLECT

What examples of task orientation did you see in this dialogue? Recall that *task orientation* refers to the degree to which the teacher provides students with the maximum opportunity to learn and includes the amount of time the teacher spends covering the assigned topics and the emphasis placed on the content of the lesson, as opposed to the administration and management of the classroom. It also includes the appropriate selection of teaching strategies and student tasks to help students learn.

Preparing Unit and Lesson Plans That Reflect the Curriculum

The first behavior in Table 9.1 for maintaining task orientation pertains to unit and lesson plans that reflect the curriculum. A task-oriented lesson begins with objectives that are based on the curriculum guide and text. Without unit and lesson objectives derived from an adopted text and curriculum guide, a teacher may be tempted to translate or extend content into topics of personal interest, or those that students appear most eager to learn, regardless of the prescribed curriculum.

We learn in the introduction to Mrs. Libby's lesson that the topic to be presented, reproductive systems of lower forms of animal life, has been taken from the curriculum guide and coincides with the content in Chapter 3 of the adopted text. We also learn that this topic is required learning for a subsequent unit on the reproductive systems of higher forms of animal life. Therefore, Mrs. Libby's lesson appears to follow the prescribed curriculum for this grade and time of year.

There is, however, a more subtle aspect to task orientation: How much does the teacher revise, elaborate, or otherwise add to the curriculum to present it at students' current level of understanding? The interest, motivation, and ability level of the students in Mrs. Libby's class might have indicated that elaboration of the content and instructional resources beyond those in the text might be required. For example, given the apparent lack of student interest and participation in the topic, some elaboration of why this topic is important in this class, what significance it may have in subsequent courses or the world outside the classroom, or even some historical account of how it was first discovered and studied in the laboratory might have piqued student interest.

Although task orientation can be enhanced by elaborating and extending content, digressions irrelevant to the immediate goals of the lesson should be avoided. For example, Mrs. Libby's digression into the topic of microscopes, which included references to their expense, the principal's concern about them, and procedures for replacing them, seems irrelevant at this time. Even her reference to an exam on the use of microscopes was premature, because they would not be used for this lesson. At a different time and in another context these issues would have been relevant and deserving of coverage. But was this the time? Without the immediate event to which the comments apply, it is unlikely that many students would retain the information conveyed. This is an important part of developing unit and lesson plans, which must not only reflect the curriculum, but also must introduce content at the most relevant time.

Although curriculum guides at the department and school district levels usually are explicit about the content to be covered in a specified period of time, they may be far less explicit about the behaviors that students are expected to acquire during this time, leaving considerable judgment to the teacher. For example, one excerpt from a middle school curriculum guide for English language instruction reads:

1. Writing concepts and skills. The student shall be provided opportunities to learn

   a. The composing process
   b. Descriptive, narrative, and expository paragraphs
   c. Multiple-paragraph compositions
   d. Persuasive discourse
   e. Meanings and uses of colloquialisms, slang, idioms, and jargon

Notice how this excerpt details the content to be taught while lacking specificity concerning the level of behavioral complexity at which the content is to be learned. This is typical of many curriculum guides. Recalling the taxonomy of behavior in the cognitive domain presented in Table 8.3 in the previous chapter, the teacher might ask, "For which of these con-

tent areas will the simple *recall* of facts be sufficient? For which areas will a *comprehension* of those facts be required? For which areas will an *application* of what is comprehended be expected? For which areas will higher-level outcomes involving *analysis, synthesis,* and *decision-making* skills be desired?" These decisions involve selecting the level of behavioral complexity at which an instructional unit or lesson will be taught and the level at which student behavior will be tested. Curriculum guides seldom provide this level of specificity.

The teacher's interpretation of the curriculum guide will depend on the unique behavioral characteristics of the students, the time that can be devoted to a specific topic, and the overall behavioral outcomes desired at the unit level. A knowledge of instructional standards at the state level, the curriculum guide at the school district level, and adopted text at the subject or grade level can help ensure that the interpretations made at the classroom level result in lesson plans that are task oriented. A close relationship among expected outcomes at the state level (as expressed by state standards), goals at the school district level (as expressed by the curriculum guide), and objectives at the classroom level (as identified by the teacher and textbook) is necessary for maintaining task orientation, as illustrated in Figure 9.1.

Observing Whether Unit and Lesson Plans Reflect the Curriculum

You can use the format in Instrument 9.2 to more closely observe how a teacher relates unit and lesson plans to the curriculum guide and adopted text. Item 6 in Instrument 9.2 can provide an explanation for why some or all of the lesson content might not correspond to the curriculum guide or text. For example, it is not unusual for local priorities to supplant the established curriculum when crucial learning needs or academic deficiencies become known, or when significant current events (the election of a president, an important Supreme Court decision, a new scientific discovery, or a moral dilemma being faced by the community) provide a timely opportunity to add real-world examples and applications to the curriculum. Capitalizing on such events by seizing the instructional opportunities they present can reflect a task orientation if the topic is relevant to the grade and ability levels of the students. The results of progress tests at the district level or mandated competency tests at the state level are other examples that can reveal critical learning needs that might require immediate reteaching of task-relevant prior learning.

FIGURE 9.1 Flow of Teaching Content from the State Level to the Classroom Level

State Curriculum Framework

- Provides philosophy that guides curriculum implementation
- Discusses progression of essential content taught from grade to grade; shows movement of student through increasingly complex material
- Notes modifications of curriculum to special populations (gifted, bilingual, challenged)

↓

District Curriculum Guide

- Provides content goals keyed to state framework
- Enumerates appropriate teaching activities and strategies
- Gives outline for unit plans; lists and sequences topics
- Reflects locally appropriate ways of achieving goals in content areas

↓

Teacher's Unit and Lesson Plans

- Describes how curriculum-guide goals are implemented daily
- Refers to topics to be covered and materials and activities to be used
- Identifies evaluation procedures
- Notes adaptations to special populations

↓

Teacher's Grade Book

- Records objectives mastered
- Identifies need for reteaching and remediation
- Provides progress indicators
- Guides promotion/retention decisions

Performing Administrative and Clerical Tasks Efficiently

A second behavior for maintaining task orientation is performing administrative and clerical tasks efficiently. As noted in Chapter 6, this behavior was found to be among the most important in determining a teacher's task orientation for the entire class period. In their study on classroom management, Emmer, Evertson, and Anderson (1980) and Emmer and Evertson (2009) found that it was difficult to return to an instructional task (e.g., a group recitation) from a noninstructional activity (passing out materials or checking for supplies) without devoting

time to getting students back on task. Not only was time spent on the noninstructional activity, but just as much or more time was spent getting learners to return their attention to the instructional content. Although unexpected interruptions such as a messenger at the door or an unscheduled announcement on the public address system cannot be avoided, rules about what students will do when these events occur can be established beforehand. For example, simple procedures such as taking messages but responding to them after class, or continuing to move about the classroom silently in a businesslike fashion during unexpected announcements, can prevent off-task behavior and the loss of valuable minutes of instructional time. Less effective classroom managers often spend great amounts of time returning a class to order after interruptions because they have not planned in advance what to do when these events occur.

Effecting smooth and efficient transitions can also lessen a teacher's administrative responsibilities. From their research, Emmer and Evertson (2009) and Evertson and Emmer (2009) report that less effective classroom managers found it difficult to keep students' attention during a transition from one instructional activity to another. Switching from a presentation to seatwork, from discussion to explanation, or from seatwork to discussion is a time when some students become distracted. Moving the entire class from one activity to another in a timely and orderly manner can be a major undertaking. Problems during these transitions often occur for two reasons: a lack of readiness on the part of the learners to perform the next activity and unclear expectations about appropriate behavior during the transition.

When students are uncertain about or unaware of what is to come next, they naturally become anxious. This is when transitions get noisy. Some students will feel more comfortable with the previous activity and will not want to make the change to the next; others may not want to begin a new activity for which they feel unprepared. In this sense, transitions are as much psychological barriers as they are actual divisions in time between activities. Students must adjust their psyches for the next activity, just as they might fumble through their books and papers (or guess which ones will be needed) at the beginning of a lesson. As we saw in Chapter 6, it will help if students are taught at the start of the year or of the semester the daily routines that are expected of them. These may be second nature after a few weeks, but they deserve special mention and practice during the first days of class. Table 9.2 shows ways in which effective classroom managers respond to problems during transitions, increasing their task orientation.

TABLE 9.2 Effective Responses to Problems during Transitions

Problem	Solution
Students talked loudly at the beginning of transitions.	Teachers established a rule that no talking was allowed between transitions, acknowledging that it is difficult to allow a small amount of talking and then keep it at a small amount.
Students socialized during the transition, delaying the start of the next activity.	Teachers allowed no more time than was necessary between activities (for example, to close books, gather up materials, select new materials).
Students completed assignments before the scheduled time for an activity to end.	Teachers made assignments in terms of the time that was to be filled, not exercises to be completed, and assigned more than enough exercises to fill the allotted time.
Students continued to work on the preceding activity after a change.	Teachers gave time warnings (for example, at 5 minutes and at 2 minutes) before the end of any activity, and used verbal markers such as "Shortly we will end this work" and "Let's finish this up so that we can begin …" They also created definite beginning and end points for each activity, such as "Okay, that's the end of this activity. Now we will start …" or "Put your papers away and turn to …"
Some students lagged behind others in completing the previous activity.	Teachers didn't wait for stragglers. They began new activities on time. When a natural break occurred, they spoke privately with students still working on previous tasks to tell them that they must stop and change. They also noted the reason some students did not finish: material too hard, lack of motivation, off-task behavior).

These effective classroom managers also display prior assignments openly so that students who miss an assignment can conveniently look it up. The teacher does not have to waste valuable class time finding an assignment that might be days or even weeks old. A simple 2' × 2' sheet of art board, divided into days of the month and covered with plastic to write on, is a convenient and reusable way of communicating past assignments on a monthly basis.

What did you think of Mrs. Libby's handling of administrative and clerical tasks? We noted at least two instances in which class time was lost. The first was Mrs. Libby's unpreparedness in presenting an illustration of the male and female reproductive cells, which was relevant to the content being presented but appeared to be more of an afterthought than a planned visual aid. This led to a time-wasting game to see who could find the picture in the text. As some students searched for the illustration, others became distracted and off-task. Realizing that the momentum of the class had been broken, some students seized the opportunity to disengage themselves from the instruction. Valuable instructional time was lost searching for an illustration that should have been ready in advance. Other examples of inefficient administrative or clerical procedures, although not seen in Mrs. Libby's classroom, include stopping class to collate and staple handouts before passing them out, getting needed materials out of a file cabinet or drawer while the class is left waiting, and dispensing materials and supplies that could be placed in a central location or on students' desks in advance.

The second event that consumed class time was the P.A. announcement. Although such distractions are annoying, especially when the teacher is trying to maintain momentum, they can seldom be avoided. Plans can be made, however, to minimize their potentially disruptive effects. Visitors at the door, disturbances outside the classroom, and announcements over the P.A. all can have disorienting effects on even the most well-planned lessons if classroom rules or procedures have not been formulated and communicated in advance. Rules or procedures can simply remind students that talking and moving about are not permitted during these times. Mrs. Libby might have promoted some of the talking and disorder by retreating to her desk and shifting to a more leisurely style during the announcement, unintentionally communicating a less businesslike attitude. Continuing to circulate around the classroom and indicating a readiness to return to the instructional routine at the last word of the announcement might have communicated that this was only a momentary pause, not the end of the day's work or a transition to a new activity.

Observing Administrative and Clerical Tasks

To get a closer look at this task-oriented behavior, you can record the percentage of time the teacher is on-task, pursuing activities relevant to the objectives identified in the lesson plan. The teacher's task-oriented activities might include a formal presentation of content, review, questions and answers, group discussion, collaborative activities, recitation, guided practice, seatwork, or any other activities reflecting the content of the lesson. A simpler approach is to record the number of minutes during a class period devoted to interruptions from (a) administrative and procedural duties, (b) transitions, and (c) student conduct. A timepiece with an easy-to-read minute hand can be used to record the approximate number of minutes spent on various off-task activities in these three areas. A format for recording, with some example entries, is provided in Figure 9.2.

The minutes of off-task behavior are added, divided by the total number of minutes for the lesson, and multiplied by 100 to arrive at the percentage of the class period devoted to noninstructional events. Rounding to the minute will be sufficient for this record. For the example 50-minute observation period shown in Figure 9.2, 48% of the class was devoted to noninstructional events ($6 + 5 + 1 + 4 + 2 + 1 + 3 + 2 = 24$ minutes; $24/50 = 0.48 \times 100\% = 48\%$). This might appear to be a large amount of off-task behavior, but in fact it is not. Notice that the definition of off-task behavior includes activities that may be necessary for instruction to proceed smoothly, but are not a direct part of it. Returning papers so students can learn from their mistakes, reprimanding a student so the student then pays attention during the remainder of the class, and talking to a counselor about the special learning needs of a student all are

vital, though indirect, instructional events. Some of these indirect events are unavoidable and necessary. The effective teacher cannot eliminate these events entirely, but can minimize the time allocated to them. The percentage of time for each type of noninstructional activity can be determined in a similar manner. For our example, this teacher appears to be efficient at handling misbehavior and transitions, but somewhat less efficient at handling some administrative chores, particularly taking roll and collecting homework, to which 11 minutes, or 22% of the class time, was devoted. Instrument 9.3 can be used to record the results of your own observations.

You might also average off-task teacher behavior over several class periods and compare percentages across classes and classrooms. In making these comparisons, you can specifically choose classes and teachers that might exhibit differences in the degree of off-task teaching behavior—for example, regular classes versus advanced, first period morning versus first period after lunch, or Mondays versus Fridays. These comparisons can be made either within different periods taught by the same teacher or among different teachers.

Preventing and Correcting Misbehavior

The third behavior for maintaining task orientation involves preventing, deflecting, or stopping misbehavior

---

FIGURE 9.2 Recording Time Spent on Noninstructional Activities

Time		Noninstructional Activities		
		Administrative/Procedural	**Transitions**	**Student Conduct**
9:05	Minutes			
:05–:11	6	Takes roll		
:12–:16	5	Collects homework		
:24–24*	1			Reprimands a student
:35–:39	4		Transition to workbooks	
:40–42	2	Counselor at door		
:43–:44	1			Puts student's name on board
:49–:52	3	Passes back papers		
:53–:55	2		Class waits for bell to ring	
9:55	end			
Totals	24	16 minutes	6 minutes	2 minutes

*Counts as 1 minute.

with a minimum of class disruption. Although typically a classroom management concern, this behavior also has much to do with the task orientation of the teacher. Intrusions into teaching time due to misbehavior can be devastating to a teacher's task orientation. Not only are large amounts of instructional time lost in administering warnings, handing out reprimands, and otherwise maintaining control of a classroom, but such activities can also drain the teacher so that when the disruption is over, the teacher may lack the stamina and enthusiasm to pick up where she left off. Misconduct can be expected in every classroom, but how it is handled often makes the difference between a classroom that is task oriented and one that is not. Emmer and Evertson (2009) suggest that effective classroom managers de-emphasize the significance of misbehavior at the time it occurs and deal with it at a later noninstructional time chosen by the teacher. The classroom procedures that follow can help make this possible.

First, classroom rules, posted and delivered orally, set a tone of organization that can deter many incidents of misbehavior. Besides establishing rules, however, effective teachers tend to defuse misbehavior and absorb it into the normal flow of activities by quickly dealing with the misbehavior and moving back into the main flow of instruction. When procedures concerning misbehavior are established and communicated to students beforehand, the teacher is able to return to a task orientation almost immediately by identifying the misbehaving student and the rule pertaining to the misconduct. Effective task orientation therefore requires establishing an efficient system of rules for dealing with misbehavior so that only the rule must be cited at the time of the misbehavior; lengthier deliberations about consequences or related circumstances, if required, can be deferred to a time when the teacher's attention is undivided. The time and the arena for discussing the misbehavior can then be of the teacher's choosing.

As noted in Chapter 6, establishing rules and procedures in anticipation of misbehavior is one of the most important classroom management activities a teacher can perform. These rules and procedures reflect a commitment to providing an ounce of prevention rather than a pound of cure. Although many rules and procedures are necessary to manage a classroom effectively, they can be divided into two general categories: academic work and classroom conduct. Classroom management rules for these two areas are shown in Figure 9.3.

FIGURE 9.3
Classroom Rules for Conduct and Work

	Rules for Classroom Conduct	Rules for Academic Work
Rules Normally Communicated the First Day	• Where to sit • How seats are assigned • What to do before the bell rings • Responding, speaking out • Leaving at the bell • Drinks, food, and gum • Washroom and drinking privileges	• Materials required for class • Homework completion • Makeup work • Incomplete work • Missed quizzes and examinations • Determining grades • Violation of rules
Rules Normally Communicated the First Week	• Tardiness/absences • Coming up to teacher's desk • When a visitor comes to the door • Leaving the classroom • Consequences of rule violation	• Notebook completion • Obtaining help • Note taking • Sharing your work with others • Use of learning center and/or reference works • Communication during group work • Neatness • Lab safety

For the elementary grades, most of these rules should be presented orally, provided in the form of a handout, *and* posted for later reference by the students. In these grades, students forget oral messages quickly or choose to ignore them if there is no physical representation of the rules to serve as a reminder. In the later elementary grades and in middle school, the teacher can recite the rules while students copy them into their notebooks; for high school students, simply hearing the rules may be sufficient, as long as they are posted for later reference. Notice also that the rules in each of these categories need not be communicated to the students at the same time or in the same way. Some rules are best held until the right opportunity to reinforce the rule presents itself (e.g., when a visitor comes to the door); others should be communicated the first day of class (how to respond or speak out) or shortly thereafter (when to complete make-up work). The rule areas listed in Figure 9.3 provide examples of the types of rules that are normally needed the first day of class, shortly thereafter, or during the first week of class. Keep in mind that rules communicated orally should also be communicated in at least one other form, such as in a handout, on the bulletin board, or on an overhead projector.

Consistency is one of the most important reasons why some rules are effective and others are not. If a rule is not applied consistently, a loss of respect for the person who has created the rule is sure to follow. There are many reasons why a particular rule is not applied consistently.

- The rule is not workable or appropriate. It does not fit a particular context or is not reasonable, given the nature of the individuals to whom it applies.
- The teacher fails to monitor students closely enough, so that some individuals violating the rule are noticed but others are not.
- The teacher does not feel strongly enough about the rule to be persistent about its implementation and therefore makes exceptions to the rule.

Keep in mind that although no one likes rules and almost all students would prefer not having any, that does not mean a particular rule is not working or not necessary. A rule should be modified when it no longer achieves its original purpose or is inappropriate for a particular group of students or classroom situation. The inability to enforce the rule over a reasonable period of time is the best sign that a change is needed. Repeated misbehaviors of a similar nature also indicate the need to revise a rule or to create a new one.

What did you notice about Mrs. Libby's handling of misbehaviors? Did you notice the long discourse by Mrs. Libby after Kyoko walked in late, which used valuable class time? Because students often come in late, Mrs. Libby should have foreseen the need for a rule. Rules indicating acceptable behaviors and the consequence if they are not followed can prevent many forms of misbehavior, providing more time for instruction. Simply informing Kyoko that he was late is all that might have been required. Unfortunately, Mrs. Libby engaged Kyoko in an interrogation and then preached about the significance of his tardiness. Such extended comments provide an opportunity for misconduct to pop up elsewhere in the classroom, consuming still more instructional time. The teacher's exclusive focus on a single individual diminishes her vigilance toward other parts of the classroom: While Mrs. Libby was focusing on Kyoko, other students talked and moved about until the teacher finally had to regain the attention of the class. This might have been avoided with a shorter, more direct, preplanned response—and rule.

Observing the Prevention and Correction of Misbehavior

Because new teachers often cite classroom management as their biggest challenge, you'll want to observe how teachers minimize disruptions from misbehavior to protect the time they've allotted to instruction. As noted previously, some off-task behavior (e.g., passing back papers) is unavoidable because it indirectly serves the teaching task. The greatest portion of off-task behavior that can be controlled or minimized by the teacher, however, is the time spent responding to small misbehaviors, called "surface behaviors," and getting the class back on-task afterward. This is why the discussion of low-profile classroom management in Chapter 6 was so important to maintaining an orderly classroom and in this chapter to a teacher's task orientation. The effective teacher responds to misbehavior in the manner that is least disruptive to the momentum or flow of classroom activity. One of the simplest ways to minimize disruption and protect instructional time is to have a system of classroom rules that makes clear (a) what behaviors are unacceptable, diminishing the likelihood that misconduct will occur in these areas, and (b) the consequences for the various types of misbehavior that are likely to occur, so that these consequences do not have to be communicated during instructional time. One of the greatest benefits of a system of carefully thought-out rules is the reduction in class time devoted to classroom conduct.

To determine whether a system of rules has been communicated, compile a list of rules pertaining to academic work and classroom conduct appearing on bulletin boards or in handouts. Because rules are not always displayed openly, you may have to request a list of rules from the teacher. Record the rules in the form they have been given to students and indicate the manner in which they have been communicated. Use the format shown in Instrument 9.4. Check the appropriate boxes to record how each rule has been communicated to students. For younger students, the most important rules should be displayed, provided in a handout, or transcribed by students into their notebooks, as well as given orally.

Another method for determining the effectiveness of a system of rules is to note the number of interruptions caused by misbehavior—time spent warning, reprimanding, explaining the rule, making a new rule, or assigning punishment. Again, a timepiece with an easy-to-read second display that can be started and stopped will be helpful for recording this behavior. Figure 9.4 illustrates the recording format. Instrument 9.5 can be used to record the results of your own observations.

As soon as a misbehavior that requires a stop in the normal classroom routine occurs, the timepiece is started and kept running until the classroom is back to normal. The amount of time for this interval is placed in the last column of Figure 9.4. The misbehavior is described briefly, and the type of response is recorded by placing a check mark in a box or a combination of boxes. The amount of time can then be tallied for all misbehaviors, converted to minutes, and divided by the total number of minutes of class observation to determine the percentage of time devoted to classroom conduct during the period of observation.

How the check marks are distributed across the record indicates the way the teacher prefers to deal with misbehavior at different levels of severity. After approximately 10 or more responses to misconduct have been recorded, the observer can group off-task student behaviors by the teacher response most frequently used to deal with them. The goal is to produce a list of student behaviors requiring a nonverbal warning, a verbal warning, rule reminders, and so on. If accumulated over a variety of different classrooms, these lists can provide a general guide to what types of responses are likely to be most appropriate for student behavior in your own classroom.

Selecting the Most Appropriate Instructional Strategy for the Objectives Taught

The fourth behavior for maintaining task orientation involves using instructional time efficiently. Inefficient instructional strategies can waste as much instructional time as administrative chores and misbehavior. Unless considerable thought is explicitly given to the match between a teacher's objectives and the instructional activities used to achieve those objectives, it is easy to be misled into thinking that the desired outcomes are being achieved (Marzano, Pickering, & Pollock, 2004; Tomlinson et al., 2001).

For example, in some classrooms it is possible to observe a lesson that attempts to teach *concepts* in the context of a drill-and-practice exercise and *facts* in the context of an inquiry or problem-solving

FIGURE 9.4   Recording Time Spent on Dealing with Misbehavior

Misbehavior	Gives Look or Gestures	Verbally Warns, Scolds	Reminds/Recites Rule	Establishes New Rule	Assigns Punishment	Other	Time
1. Jumps out of seat	☑	☑	☐	☑	☐	☐	1:20
2. Talks out	☐	☐	☑	☐	☑	☐	0:10
3. Throws object	☐	☐	☐	☐	☑	☐	0:30
4.	☐	☐	☐	☐	☐	☐	
5.	☐	☐	☐	☐	☐	☐	
						Total	

discussion. Although both outcomes may eventually be achieved in either context, the teaching of concepts by rehearsing facts (memorizing vocabulary words to learn the concepts they represent, memorizing the names of the branches of government to understand what it means to live in a democracy, or memorizing a poem to learn to appreciate poetry) would be inefficient. The teaching of facts rarely allows for the generalizations and discriminations required for concepts to be acquired, and the teaching of concepts often fails to emphasize the mental processes required for the acquisition of facts. Therefore, matching the type of learning outcome to be achieved with the instructional strategy that most efficiently accomplishes that outcome is important for establishing a task orientation.

The teaching of facts, rules, and action sequences will be most efficiently achieved through a process known as the **direct-instruction model.** Direct instruction (also called *expository* or *didactic teaching*) is a strategy in which the teacher is the major provider of information. In the direct-instruction model, the teacher's role is to pass on facts, rules, or action sequences to students in the most direct way possible; this usually takes the form of explanations, examples, and opportunities for practice and feedback that recur in cycles.

Under the direct-instruction model, the behavior required of the learner is limited to:

1. Learning units of the stimulus material (such as facts, rules, or examples) in some meaningful way so that they can be remembered
2. Arranging parts of the stimulus material into a whole so that a rapid and automatic response can occur

Learning at the lower levels of the cognitive domain (knowledge, comprehension, and application) relies heavily on these two processes. Both can be put into action efficiently with stimulus material that closely resembles the desired response (e.g., "Read this word and then say it." "Watch me form a possessive and then do the next one." "Follow the instructions, and then focus the microscope."). The desired response does not need to go much beyond the directions or model provided. The learner's task is to produce a response that resembles, as closely as possible, the form and content of the stimulus given. A great deal of instruction involves behaviors at the lower levels of complexity, which require learning units of content and arranging the units into a whole so that a rapid and automatic response can occur. Thus, the direct-instruction model tends to be most efficient when the behavioral outcomes are at the knowledge, comprehension, and application levels.

But not all learning is limited to the lower levels of behavioral complexity. In fact, if all (or even most) lessons used only direct instruction, students would be unlikely to function successfully in subsequent grades or in the world outside the classroom. Most of the jobs, responsibilities, and roles performed outside of school require more authentic behaviors—analysis, synthesis, and decision making—that are only represented at higher levels of behavioral complexity (Borich & Tombari, 2004; Tombari & Borich, 1999). These behaviors are not learned in the same way as behaviors at lower levels of complexity. (In Chapter 12, we will study how to observe these higher thought processes and how to achieve them in your classroom.) Let's look at a model of instruction that can be used to efficiently promote these higher forms of behavior, and your task orientation.

When sets of stimuli are presented and learners are asked to go beyond the stimuli to form concepts and relationships, the **indirect-instruction model** is being employed. The learner acquires a behavior indirectly by transforming stimulus material (e.g., facts) into a response or behavior that differs from both

1. The stimulus used to present the learning
2. Any previous response given by the student

Because the stimulus material can be added to and rearranged by the learner during this process to make it more meaningful, the elicited response or behavior can take many different forms. Therefore, in contrast to direct instruction, there is seldom a single best answer in the indirect model of instruction. Instead, the learner is guided to an answer that goes *beyond* the problem or stimulus presented.

Indirect instruction is inefficient and even ineffective for teaching many types of facts, rules, or action sequences for which the desired response is almost identical to the learning stimulus presented. Rules for punctuation and capitalization, for example, are most efficiently taught by giving students the rules and asking them to practice applying them. Here, knowledge acquisition and application are taught with a direct-instruction strategy because the stimulus material (written rules and examples) already contains the correct answers in the form most desired. The purpose of the lesson is to apply the rules, not to discover them or to invent new ones.

Generally, a teacher's task orientation will be most efficiently maintained when the teaching functions associated with direct instruction are applied in the context of knowledge, comprehension, and application objectives and the teaching functions associated with indirect instruction are applied in the context of analysis, synthesis, and evaluation objectives that often require problem solving, inquiry, and critical thinking. Although these models may be used interchangeably within a lesson, the degree to which they are effective depends on whether the intended outcomes are primarily lower or higher order. Table 9.3 summarizes some of the teaching functions associated with the direct and indirect models of instruction. Table 9.4 provides example activities and expected outcomes for each teaching function listed in Table 9.3.

Let's consider Mrs. Libby's use of instructional strategies. Now you know that using the wrong instructional model can be as damaging to a teacher's task orientation as the presentation of irrelevant or poorly timed instructional content. Recall that our discussion

TABLE 9.3 Direct and Indirect Teaching Functions

Direct-Instruction Functions[a]	Indirect-Instruction Functions[b]

1. Reviews, checks previous day's work, and reteaches, if necessary:
   Checks homework
   Reteaches areas where there were student errors
	1. Provides a means of organizing content in advance:
	   Provides advance organizers and conceptual frameworks, which serve as "pegs" on which to hang key points that guide and channel thinking to the most productive areas.

2. Presents and structures new content:
   Provides overview
   Proceeds in small steps (if necessary), but at a rapid pace
   New skills are phased in; old skills are measured
	2. Provides conceptual development of content using inductive and deductive methods; focuses generalization to high level of abstraction by:
	   Inductive methods (selected events are used to establish concepts or patterns)
	   Deductive methods (principles or generalization are applied to specific instances)

3. Provides for guided student practice:
   High frequency of convergent questions and overt student practice (from teacher and materials)
   Prompts are provided during initial learning (when appropriate)
   All students have a chance to respond and receive feedback
   Teacher checks for understanding by evaluating student responses
   Continue practice until responses are firm
   Success rate of 80% or higher during initial learning
	3. Uses examples and nonexamples:
	   To define criterial attributes and promote accurate generalizations
	   To gradually expand set of examples to reflect the real world
	   To enrich concept with understanding of noncriterial attributes

4. Gives immediate feedback and correctives (and reteaching, if necessary):
   Feedback to students, particularly when they are correct but hesitant
   Student errors used to provide feedback to the teacher that corrections or reteaching is necessary
   Corrections by simplifying question, giving clues, explaining or reviewing steps, or reteaching last steps
   When necessary, reteaching using smaller steps
	4. Uses higher-order questions to guide the search-and-discovery process and uses questions to:
	   Raise contradictions
	   Probe for deeper level responses
	   Extend the discussion
	   Pass responsibility to the class

5. Assigns independent practice so that student responses are firm and automatic:
   Seatwork
   Practice to overlearning
   Need for procedure to ensure student encouragement during seatwork (i.e., teacher or aide monitoring)
   95% correct or higher
	5. Encourages students to use examples and references:
	   To seek clarification from their own experience and to draw parallels and associations that aid understanding and retention
	   Relates ideas to past learning and to students' own sphere of interests, concerns, and problems

6. Schedules weekly and monthly reviews:
   Reteaching, if necessary
	6. Allows students to evaluate the appropriateness of their own responses and provides guidance when necessary:
	   Provides cues, questions, or hints as needed to call attention to inappropriate responses

	7. Uses discussion: To encourage critical thinking and help students to examine alternatives, judge solutions, make predictions, and discover generalizations

[a]Entries in this column are based on Rosenshine (1983).

[b]Entries in this column are based on Borich (2010).

TABLE 9.4 Example Activities and Expected Outcomes for the Direct and Indirect Models of Instruction

Direct-Teaching Functions	Example Activities for Students	Expected Outcomes	Indirect-Teaching Functions	Example Activities for Students	Expected Outcomes
Reviews, checks	Recites answers from workbook or homework	Recall, recognition	Provides conceptual framework	Reproduces mental or graphic representation of framework	Comprehension, synthesis
Presents new content	Listens, takes notes	Comprehension	Develops content inductively and deductively	Asks questions that draw relationships to past knowledge	Analysis
Presents guided practice	Responds orally or in workbook	Application	Gives examples and nonexamples	Makes proper distinctions on handout or in workbook	Analysis, synthesis
Gives feedback	Corrects verbal or written response	Application, analysis	Asks higher-order questions	Responds orally or in writing to problem situation	Evaluation
Assigns independent practice	Completes homework or extended seatwork	Application	Encourages student ideas	Discusses own experience with class	Application, analysis
Reviews, reteaches	Asks questions, takes notes, and listens	Recall, recognition, comprehension	Allows for self-evaluation	Examines correctness of own and others' responses	Analysis, synthesis
			Guides discussion to promote critical thinking	Extends prior content to new ground	Evaluation

of instructional models encompassed the direct and indirect models of instruction. The former includes six teaching functions that are generally believed to be most efficient for teaching objectives at the knowledge, comprehension, and application levels of behavioral complexity; the latter includes seven teaching functions that are generally believed to be most efficient for teaching objectives at the analysis, synthesis, and evaluation levels of behavioral complexity. Although seldom implemented in a pure form (and sometimes used interchangeably within a lesson), these models are guides for attaining the desired outcome most efficiently. Review Tables 9.3 and 9.4 to find out which model Mrs. Libby's lesson reflected.

If you think it was the indirect model, you are right. But she also used the direct model. This brief dialogue, in a fashion typical of most classrooms, represented both models. In fact, Mrs. Libby seemed to alternate between models, perhaps indicating she did not make a conscious attempt to use either model or to combine them in any meaningful fashion. Instead, the lesson format seemed to be pulled first in one direction and then in another. Let's return to the beginning of the dialogue to examine Mrs. Libby's behavior on this dimension.

After the commotion with Kyoko has ended, Mrs. Libby begins to review and check for task-relevant prior knowledge. She asks, "Who remembers from our previous discussion some of the ways in which lower forms of animal life reproduce?" Sudia answers correctly, and his answer is rephrased by the teacher—providing a review of previous content for those who might have missed it. After her digression about microscopes, Mrs. Libby returns to the content of the lesson and asks, "Can anyone think of any other means of reproduction?" Shelly responds first, but with too broad an answer about higher forms of animal life, which is a topic to be presented later. So the teacher refocuses with the comment, "We're just talking about lower forms of animal life." Bill then responds by asking, "Isn't there a way that new life can be created by parts of other things coming together?" The teacher uses Bill's response to expand the discussion by introducing the word *conjugation*.

To determine which model of instruction these exchanges represent, we must ask what level of outcome the teacher wants to attain with this series of questions. Are these questions asked to provide guided practice with outcomes at the knowledge, comprehension, or application level (direct-instruction model), or are the questions asked to promote a search-and-discovery process with outcomes at the analysis, synthesis, or evaluation level (indirect-instruction model)?

If students are combining pieces of previously learned information (analysis) that have not been combined previously in any meaningful way (synthesis), then higher-order outcomes are being sought and the teacher would be well advised to employ the indirect model (advance organizers, induction and deduction, examples and nonexamples, student ideas). But if the students recall knowledge from an earlier lesson and parrot it in a slightly different form (comprehension) or apply it in a new context (application), then lower-order outcomes are being sought and the teacher would be well advised to employ the direct-instruction model (more correctives and feedback, guided practice, and independent seatwork). Either of these approaches might have been Mrs. Libby's goal, but until one or the other is strengthened by the addition of appropriate teaching functions (in Tables 9.3 and 9.4), neither will lead to the desired behavioral outcomes. Mrs. Libby's lesson, at least the part we saw, seemed to lack follow-through, as well as a sequence of teaching functions that converged on a common goal. It is difficult to tell what level of behavioral complexity she was asking of her students. Task orientation involves knowing where you are heading and then implementing the most efficient mix of teaching functions to get you there.

Observing the Most Appropriate Instructional Strategy for the Objectives Taught

We have observed some of the behaviors that can reduce the time a teacher devotes to instruction and thereby reduce students' opportunity to learn. But a teacher's task orientation also involves efficiently using the instructional time that *is* available. This means that there must be correspondence between intended outcomes and the teaching model (direct or indirect) used to achieve them.

As we have seen, objectives at the knowledge, comprehension, and application levels are most efficiently taught with the direct-instruction model; objectives at the analysis, synthesis, and evaluation levels are most efficiently taught with the indirect-instruction model. The learning of certain facts, rules, and action sequences must often precede the learning of concepts, patterns, and abstractions, requiring a sequence of lessons within a unit plan leading from least to most behavioral complexity. Instrument 9.6 illustrates a method of recording the relationship among different desired outcomes and the direct and indirect teaching functions that might be used to elicit them.

The behavioral outcomes listed across the top are divided into two types: lower order and higher order. The phrase "Lower Order" is used to describe knowledge, comprehension, and application outcomes; the phrase "Higher Order" is used to describe outcomes at the analysis, synthesis, and evaluation levels. The teaching functions listed on the left side of Instrument 9.6 are divided into direct- and indirect-instruction functions. Recall that in direct instruction the teacher is the primary provider of information, passing on facts, rules, and action sequences to the learner in the most direct way possible so that information can be recalled rapidly and automatically. In indirect instruction the students are active providers of content and acquire, through search and discovery, outcomes different from the stimulus material used to present the learning and any previous responses given by the student.

For the recording form in Instrument 9.6, a check mark is placed in the appropriate box *each time there is a change* in function or behavioral outcome. Multiple check marks may appear across rows for the same function (e.g., when a guided practice exercise changes from knowledge to application content) and down columns for the same behavioral outcomes (e.g., when application is taught in a presentation format and then in an inquiry-oriented group discussion). The majority of check marks may appear in the first three columns; by some estimates, as much as 80% of school instruction takes place at the knowledge, comprehension, and applications levels. With a sufficient number of observations, however, check marks should appear in the upper left quadrant (lower order/direct) as well as lower right quadrant (higher order/indirect). As other direct and indirect teaching functions are observed, they should be added to the record under "Other."

Establishing Cycles of Review, Feedback, and Testing

The final behavior for achieving task orientation involves establishing a schedule of activities built around clearly definable end products (a test, assignment, review session, or performance). These end products represent visible student goals toward which classroom activities build with increasing intensity and expectation. They also serve to create cycles of rising and falling intensity, with the high point of the cycle just before the expected event and the low point, which marks the beginning of a new cycle, immediately afterward. In the upper grades, several different cycles might occur concurrently; for example, some classroom activities prepare students to complete a paper due next week, and other classroom activities prepare students to take a test at the end of the month. Different cycles might therefore be in place for tests, assignments, and major projects, and these cycles may be staggered so that one is near its highest point when another is near its lowest. This ensures that high levels of intensity, enthusiasm, and expectation pertaining to a clearly defined end product are always present. Figure 9.5 illustrates several concurrent cycles: a book report due every month, increasingly comprehensive reviews conducted weekly, and a cycle of exams given every 6 weeks.

One of the most important activities for establishing cycles of rising and falling action in a classroom is a review. The primary purpose of periodic review is to ensure that all task-relevant information for future lessons has been taught and to identify areas for which reteaching of key objectives may be necessary. Without periodic review prior to oral or written testing, there might be no signal to the teacher that the instruction has been successful, and no signal to the

student that further study may be necessary. Thus, periodic review serves to task-orient and reorient both teacher and students.

Periodic review has long been a part of almost every instructional strategy. During direct instruction, for example, periodic review and the recycling of instruction are important because of the brisk pace at which the instruction is conducted. The teacher usually establishes the proper pace by noting the approximate percentage of errors occurring during guided practice and feedback; 60 to 80% correct responses usually indicates a satisfactory pace during didactic or expository teaching—the direct instruction model (Rosenshine & Stevens, 1986). Weekly and monthly reviews provide opportunities to determine whether the pace is appropriate and to make necessary adjustments before too much content has been covered. When student responses to questions posed in weekly and monthly review sessions are correct, quick, and firm about 95% of the time, the pace is adequate. Independent practice and homework should increase the percentage of correct responses from between 60 and 80% during guided practice and feedback to approximately 95% on weekly and monthly reviews. When results are below, and especially when they are substantially below, these levels during didactic or expository teaching, the pace has been too fast. Weekly and monthly review sessions can be used to give some learners a second chance to grasp material that was missed or only partially learned the first time through and to strengthen correct but hesitant responses of those who might not have thoroughly

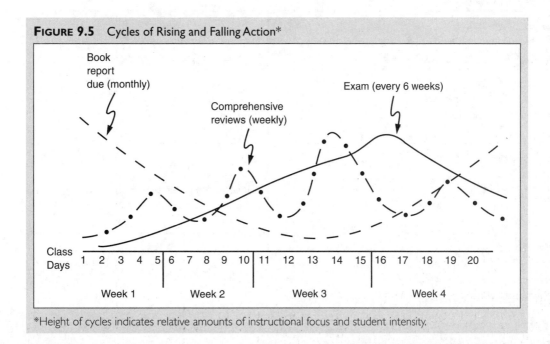

FIGURE 9.5 Cycles of Rising and Falling Action*

*Height of cycles indicates relative amounts of instructional focus and student intensity.

mastered the material the first time. Review sessions are often welcomed by students who see it as an opportunity to go over material that will be expected on unit tests or later performance activities.

What did you notice in Mrs. Libby's lesson regarding cycles of review, feedback, and testing? Did her cycles include projects, papers, major assignments, and informal but regularly scheduled question-and-answer sessions? Unfortunately, we know little about these sequences in Mrs. Libby's class, other than that a departmental test is scheduled. Cycles might have helped focus and give greater meaning to the lesson for some students. Other events would also need to be scheduled to keep students working toward a common goal with increasing expectation. Multiple milestones help establish momentum if they are planned so that expectations about one event begin as another event is completed, thereby avoiding competing student responsibilities in which the same intensity of effort is being expected. We must reserve judgment on this dimension, pending a more detailed examination of how Mrs. Libby has scheduled and sequenced cycles of review, feedback, and testing over the course of an entire grading period.

Observing Cycles of Review, Feedback, and Testing

You can observe how teachers establish a schedule of activities built around clearly identified end products such as reviews, tests, and major assignments using the format shown in Instrument 9.7. A check mark is used to indicate the end products scheduled for a given day. The absence of check marks indicates that a schedule of end products might not have been determined or that some end products are emphasized to the exclusion of others. It is important, however, that the end products checked on this record represent those that have been communicated to students ahead of time or that are part of the normal instructional routine (test every Friday; major review every other Thursday). If the opportunity arises, several students can be questioned to indicate end products for which they see themselves responsible, and their responses can be checked for agreement. This can be one indication of how clearly the end products have been communicated to the class.

Our observations about Mrs. Libby's lesson have been summarized in Figure 9.6. Notice that three

---

FIGURE 9.6   Checklist for Observing Mrs. Libby's Classroom

Behavior	Observed	Not Observed	No Opportunity to Observe
1. Develops unit and lesson plans in accordance with text and curriculum guides	✓ Lesson topic covered in text		
2. Handles administrative and clerical interruptions efficiently		✓ Lost task orientation while searching for picture in text	
3. Stops or prevents misbehavior with a minimum of disruption to the class		✓ Focused attention at length on single misbehaving student	
4. Selects the most appropriate instructional strategy for the objectives taught		✓ Instructional strategies did not converge on single approach or clearly defined outcome	
5. Builds toward unit outcomes with clearly defined events (weekly and monthly reviews, feedback, and testing)			✓ Difficult to tell; only one test was mentioned

of the five dimensions for achieving task orientation were not observed and that instructional time was lost to administrative interruptions, misconduct, and a poorly defined instructional strategy. Recall, however, that the hard-to-handle nature of this class and the sensitive subject matter would make this a particularly challenging lesson for experienced and inexperienced teachers alike.

CULTURAL DIVERSITY AND TASK ORIENTATION

Throughout much of the history of education in America, the traditional task orientation of the teacher could be characterized as teacher centered and text and workbook oriented. Today, the teacher's role in the classroom has widened considerably, and texts and workbooks have evolved to provide a variety of orientations to the teaching task, including cooperative learning, peer tutoring, self-regulation, programmed learning, thematic and interdisciplinary units and lessons, and individual computerized instruction. Recent research on the effects of individual differences and cultural and ethnic expectations on learning has helped stimulate this evolution in ways to promote a task orientation. Research has focused on the cognitive styles of learners (Gregory, 2005; Sarasin, 2006), the structure of the learning task (Doyle, 1983; Griggs & Dunn, 1996), and variations in teaching styles (Pajak, 2003).

Early studies by Castaneda and Gray (1974) found that learners could be distinguished on the basis of the cognitive processes they use to learn and whether they are presented a task in a way that allows them the opportunity to use their preferred cognitive style. Two of the cognitive styles often studied, described in Table 9.5, are **field independence** and **field dependence** (Borich & Tombari, 1997, p. 515; Riding, 2002). These authors suggest that certain cognitive styles tend to predominate among certain cultures, but that bilingual learners tend to be both field independent and field dependent (Ramirez & Castaneda, 1974).

Other researchers have related field independence and dependence to students' need for structure (Hunt, 1979; Irvine and York, 2001). These researchers suggest specific ways teachers can orient themselves to the teaching task to promote the best use of a particular cognitive style. For example, for students who require more structure, their findings suggest that the teacher should

1. Have definite and consistent rules

TABLE 9.5 Field-Independent Learners and Field-Dependent Learners

The Field-Independent Learner	The Field-Dependent Learner
Perceives content as discrete parts; easily sees details	Perceives content globally; easily sees the whole
Is attracted to abstract and analytical problem solving; likes to think in terms of cause and effect	Avoids analytical problem solving in favor of a more holistic approach; likes to think in terms of associations, relationships, and codependent actions
Is self-reliant and prefers individualistic rather than cooperative strategies of inquiry	Is sensitive and attuned to the social environment; prefers cooperative over competitive strategies of inquiry
Favors inquiry and independence; provides own structure for learning	Favors discovery and a participant approach to learning; likes to observe, reflect, and react to others
Is intrinsically motivated and less responsive to social reinforcement	Is extrinsically motivated and more responsive to social reinforcement

2. Provide specific, step-by-step guides and instructions
3. Make goals and deadlines short and definite
4. Change pace often
5. Assess problems frequently
6. Move gradually from seatwork to discussion

For students who require less structure, the teacher can

1. Provide topics to choose from
2. Make assignments longer, with self-imposed timetables
3. Encourage the use of resources outside the classroom
4. Use group work, with the teacher serving as a resource person
5. Use and encourage interest in the opinions and knowledge of others
6. Provide an opportunity for extended projects and assignments

Although our knowledge of how these aspects of a teacher's task orientation relate to specific groups of learners is still growing, research provides alternatives to the notion that the most effective task orientation for the teacher is to stand in front of the classroom lecturing or explaining to students seated in neatly arranged rows, who have few or no expectations about or experiences with the content being taught. Research findings suggest not only that some task orientations (e.g., cooperative vs. competitive) might be more appropriate for some groups than others, but that many of today's content objectives (especially multidisciplinary and interdisciplinary objectives) might require frequent variation in task orientation. Watch especially for teachers who seem to move easily from providing lots of structure to offering students a number of choices. You'll also want to discover which students appear most comfortable and productive, and in which settings. These insights will be important to you as you make instructional decisions in your own classroom.

In the following chapters, we will turn our attention to other lenses through which to observe classrooms. These lenses—student engagement in the learning process, student success, and higher thought processes—are always observed in the context of task orientation, as well as in the context of the other lenses discussed in previous chapters.

For More Information

As you have learned in this chapter, one effective teaching behavior for maintaining task orientation involves preventing, deflecting, or stopping misbehavior with a minimum of class disruption. Not only are large amounts of instructional time lost in administering warnings, handing out reprimands, and otherwise maintaining control of a classroom, but such activities can also drain the teacher so that, when the disruption is over, the teacher may lack the stamina and enthusiasm to pick up where she left off. Each month, classroom management experts Harry and Rosemary Wong publish a new collection of classroom strategies and approaches designed to help teachers—new and seasoned—master the routine matters that can consume so much of a teacher's time. Their informative monthly columns can be accessed at http://teachers.net/wong.

Key Terms

direct-instruction model, 143
field dependence, 149

field independence, 149
indirect-instruction model, 143

Activities*

1. Using the checklist in Instrument 9.1 as your guide, observe a lesson, looking for signs of task orientation. At the end of your observation, add a brief written description to each box, highlighting at least one specific reason why you chose to place each check mark where you did.

2. Using the examples of 5-point scales shown in Chapter 4, convert the positively stated indicators of task orientation listed in Table 9.1 into the form of a Likert scale. Consider the vertical or horizontal placement of each indicator on the page, whether words will be affixed to all or only some of the response blanks, and what value will be assigned to each response. Show your scale to a classmate who has also constructed a 5-point scale. Together, create a single revised version incorporating the best features of both scales.

3. Ask the teacher of a lesson you wish to observe for her objective(s). Then ask for a copy of the text or student workbook for this class and look up your school district's or state's curriculum guide on the Internet. Using Instrument 9.2, determine whether the lesson plan reflects the curriculum. If it does not, or does so only partially (some objectives correspond with content in the text and curriculum guide, but others do not), suggest reasons why. In your opinion, does the lesson content represent instructional goals that can be justified in another way (e.g., local priorities, student interests, or critical learning needs)?

4. Using the form provided in Instrument 9.3, observe a classroom for a complete lesson or class period. Record all noninstructional activities (administrative procedures, transitions, and student conduct) and the approximate number of minutes devoted

*Some of these activities may be grouped into a common activity, divided among classmates, and completed from a single observation.

to each. Total the number of minutes for each type of activity and find the percentage of time each contributes to the total amount of noninstructional time. Which consumed the most time? The least? If you were to advise this teacher on how to improve task orientation, what noninstructional activity would you bring to his attention?

5. Select one pair of observations to complete from the following list:

Higher-performing/lower-performing class
Early A.M./after lunch class
Discussion/lecture class
Social studies/math class

For the pair you have chosen, use Instrument 9.3 to determine the percentage of noninstructional time devoted to administrative procedures, transitions, and student conduct. Compare the percentages in your two classes in each of these three areas. Describe and explain any large differences. How representative do you feel the activity in each classroom was in relation to what normally might occur at these times during the school year?

6. Arrange a brief interview with a teacher whose classroom you would like to observe. Using Instrument 9.4, ask the teacher to identify the rules communicated to students with regard to academic work and classroom conduct. Enter these rules on the record, indicating the manner in which the teacher communicated them to students (on display, in a handout, orally). Note any unique or unusual means of communicating or creating rules (student handbook, group consensus). If this were your classroom, what rules would you have added or deleted?

7. Observe a class using a timepiece with a second hand that can be started and stopped while completing Instrument 9.5. Place a check mark after each misbehavior, indicating whether the teacher responded to it with a warning, a reminder, a new rule, punishment, or another response. Keep track of the approximate number of minutes of class time devoted to the misbehavior. Separate the misbehaviors you have listed into two groups: those for which response time was less than a minute and those for which response time was more than a minute. What types of teacher response characterize these two groups of misbehavior?

8. Use Instrument 9.6 to record the relationship between teaching functions and levels of behavioral outcomes over a series of observations. Write down any functions not identified on the record that indicate the teacher pursues the goals of either direct or indirect instruction. At the end of your observations, inspect the tallies in each of the four quadrants: Direct/Lower Order, Direct/Higher Order, Indirect/Lower Order, and Indirect/Higher Order. Count the total number of entries in each of the four quadrants to find a pattern. Are more tallies found in the Direct/Lower Order and Indirect/Higher Order quadrants, as would be expected, or has some other pattern emerged? If your data reflect the unexpected, explain why you believe the results turned out as they did. If your data reflect the expected, explain why lower-order outcomes tend to be associated with direct instruction and higher-order outcomes with indirect instruction.

9. Choose a classroom with which you are familiar. Using Instrument 9.7 for recording end products, place a check mark under each end product (review, test, homework, and project) according to the date on which it is to occur or was due. Complete this assignment and activity schedule over several observations. Include any other scheduled end products that are not listed and the day they occur. How might this teacher improve her task orientation by scheduling other end products or using those listed more frequently?

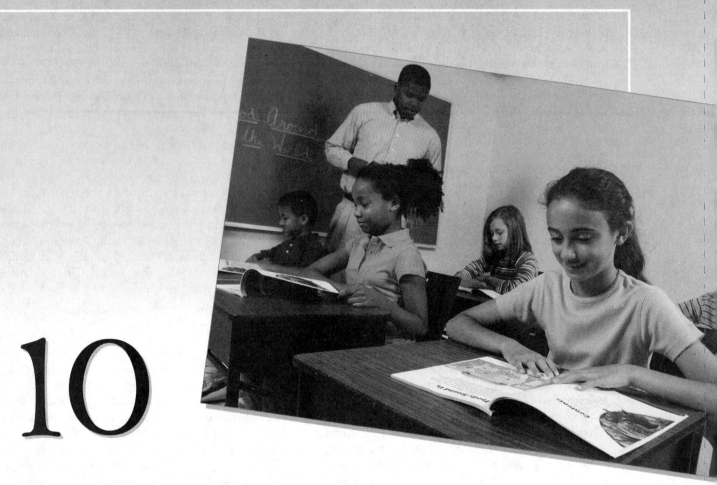

10

Examining Engagement in the Learning Process

Halfway Down

Halfway down the stairs

Is a stair

Where I sit.

There isn't any

Other stair

Quite like

It.

I'm not at the bottom,

I'm not at the top;

So this is the stair

Where

I always

Stop.

Halfway up the stairs

Isn't up,

And isn't down.

It isn't in the nursery,

It isn't in the town.

And all sorts of funny thoughts

Run round my head:

"It isn't really

Anywhere!

It's somewhere else

Instead!"

A. A. Milne

"Halfway Down" by A. A. Milne, from *When We Were Very Young* by A. A. Milne. Used by permission of Dutton Children's Books, A Division of Penguin Young Readers Group, A Member of Penguin Group (USA) Inc., 345 Hudson Street, New York, NY 10014. All rights reserved.

As you glance at the students, all eyes are on the work on their desks. Not a sound invades the engrossed silence. "Ah, the students are working," you think to yourself. Or are they? When Roberto is looking at his science book, where is his mind? Is he, like the child in the poem "somewhere else instead"? How do effective teachers engage students in their learning? And how do we know, as observers and teachers, when that engagement is occurring?

In Chapter 9, we saw that one of the ways teacher behavior influences student achievement is through the amount of instructional time devoted to a subject. This relationship can be strengthened by a teacher's task orientation. This chapter will present a related, but different, way of looking at learning time.

Separate from the teacher's task orientation is the time students are engaged in thinking about and actively learning the presented material (Abernathy & Reardon, 2001; Riggs & Gholar, 2008; Savage, 1999). This way of measuring learning time is called student engagement in the learning process and represents the amount of time during a lesson that students are thinking about, acting on, or otherwise using the presented content.

Engagement in the learning process is expressed as the percentage of time allocated to instruction that the student is on-task or engaged with the instructional materials and activities. For example, if 45 minutes is devoted to content coverage, and most of the students are engaged in the learning process (participating in discussion, completing a workbook assignment, or otherwise looking alert and attentive) for 30 minutes during this time, the engagement rate would be $(30/45)100 = 67\%$. Engagement rates tend to vary considerably from student to student and are therefore often calculated for individuals in a class; the average rate is taken as an approximate indication of the engagement rate of the entire class.

The key to understanding engagement rate is that, even though a teacher can be task oriented and provide maximum content coverage, the students might not be engaged all of this time (Kuh, Kinzie, Schuh, & Whitt, 2005; Weinstein & Mignano, 1996). This disengagement can involve an emotional or mental detachment, or both, from the lesson, which may or may not be obvious to an observer. Students who jump out of their seats, talk, read a magazine, or leave for the restroom are obviously not engaged in instruction, no matter how task oriented the teacher is. Students might also be disengaged in more subtle ways, such

as looking attentive while their thoughts are many miles away. Correcting—even observing—this type of nonengagement is a difficult task. Several studies have contributed useful information for increasing student engagement. From these studies, it was possible for Emmer and Evertson (2009), Riggs & Gholar (2008), and Rosenshine and Stevens (1986) to provide the following suggestions for increasing student engagement in the learning process:

- Teachers should have a system of rules flexible enough to allow students to attend to their personal and procedural needs (obtaining reference books, handouts, and resources) without having to obtain the teacher's permission.
- Teachers should move around the room at regularly scheduled intervals to monitor students' seatwork and to communicate an awareness of student progress.
- Teachers should avoid timing errors by using low-profile classroom management to prevent off-task behavior before it spreads to and influences other learners.
- When students work independently, teachers should ensure that the assignments are interesting and easy enough to be completed by each student working without teacher direction.
- Teachers should minimize activities such as giving directions and organizing the class for instruction by writing the daily schedule on the board. This will ensure that pupils know what activities will be expected and the order in which they will be performed.
- Teachers should make abundant use of group work, activity books, self-directed assignments, and projects that are at, or slightly above, a student's current level of understanding.
- Teachers should choose classroom activities that are compatible with ethnic and cultural expectations.

In this chapter we will take a closer look at these and other suggestions for engaging students in the learning process.

DIMENSIONS OF STUDENT ENGAGEMENT IN THE LEARNING PROCESS

Table 10.1 summarizes the behaviors related to student engagement. Effectively engaging students in the learning process involves

1. Eliciting the desired behaviors
2. Providing an opportunity for feedback in a non-critical atmosphere
3. Using individualized and self-directed learning activities to maintain interest and promote attention during the learning process
4. Using meaningful verbal praise
5. Monitoring and checking for progress

PRACTICE OBSERVING STUDENT ENGAGEMENT IN THE LEARNING PROCESS: A DIALOGUE

Let's use the checklist in Instrument 10.1 to observe a class for evidence of student engagement in the learning process. For this dialogue, we peek into the beginning of an elementary math lesson. The lesson for today is about ratios and proportions. The teacher, Mr. Swade, has noticed that math interest is not high among most members of his class. His students have been noticeably anxious about an upcoming test, and some might not have grasped all that they should have from earlier lessons.

Mr. Swade: Today we will study ratios and proportions, but we'll use more real-life problems than in previous lessons. Some of you have had trouble calculating ratios, so let's back up and review our skills in division. Who can tell me why division is so important in computing a ratio? [Marcus raises his hand.]

Marcus: It's because ratios are nothing but division problems.

Mr. Swade: Yes, that's right, in the sense that ratios can be expressed as one number over another, like this. [Writes 4/8 on board] Now let's look at some other expressions. I'll write them on the board, and you see if you can identify which ones are expressed as ratios and which ones are not. [Mr. Swade writes the following: 8, 1/2, 6 × 6, 5/10.] Okay, which ones are expressed as ratios? Remember what Marcus just said. Think about the first one. Is it a ratio, yes or no? Class?

Class: [With most members responding] No.

Mr. Swade: And why not, Marcus?

Marcus: It doesn't show division.

Mr. Swade: Okay, let's take the next one.

Class: [Again with most members responding] Yes.

Mr. Swade: Right again. Notice how easy it is to spot a ratio; it's because of the division. Ratios are the result of one number being divided by another. Today we will study a special type of ratio called a *proportion*, in which one number is always divided by a bigger number. But before we get to these problems, let's finish our last two. [Mr. Swade points to 6 × 6 on board.]

Class: No.

TABLE 10.1   Indicators for Engaging Students in the Learning Process

More Effective Student Engagement	Less Effective Student Engagement
1. Elicits the desired behavior after presentation of instructional stimuli (provides exercise or workbook problems with which the desired behavior can be practiced)	Fails to ask learners to attempt the desired behavior
2. Provides opportunities for feedback in a noncritical atmosphere (asks students to respond as a group or subvocally the first time through)	Evaluates initial student responses in ways that could be threatening or embarrassing
3. Uses individual and self-directed activities (performance contracts, programmed texts, games and simulations, learning centers, and reciprocal learning) as instructional strategies	Fails to use alternative instructional methods to accommodate the learning needs of special students (less able or remedial learners)
4. Uses meaningful verbal praise to get and keep students actively participating in the learning process	Fails to provide praise that is timely and meaningful to the student (never says why something is correct)
5. Monitors seatwork and frequently checks progress during independent practice	Does not evenly monitor students' progress during seatwork (spends too much time with some students and fails to observe work of others)

Mr. Swade: And— [Mr. Swade points to the last one, 5/10.]

Class: [In almost perfect unison] Yes.

Mr. Swade: Good. Now you see that ratios are often expressed as one number over another, like this. [Points to 4/8 on the board] Now let's look at this cereal box. Calley, take the box in your hands and tell me how full it is.

Calley: Well, I don't exactly know. It feels pretty heavy—I mean . . . it's kind of full.

Mr. Swade: What if I asked you to tell me how much "kind of full" is?

Calley: I'd say kind of full means almost full—well, maybe a little less than almost full. [A few members of the class laugh.]

Mr. Swade: I think some of the class may have thought your answer was funny because they would like to know what "a little less than almost full" means. Now, because this is a typical problem—the kind people face every day at home and at work—it would be nice to express some things more accurately without the use of words, which can be imprecise when describing amounts of things. How might we be more precise, Tomás?

Tomás: Maybe we could express it as a ratio.

Mr. Swade: Okay. But how do we go about forming a ratio to describe the amount of cereal in this box? Can you tell us some more?

Tomás: Well, we need to know how much the box holds.

Mr. Swade: That's right. You've got the first step. Now, Tim, what's the next step?

Tim: I don't know.

Mr. Swade: Maria? [Silence for 10 seconds] Britta? [Silence; addressing the class] I know you can do it. Think about our earlier examples and Marcus's answer.

Britta: [Catching the hint] I think we should divide by comparing how much it has in it with how much the box holds.

Mr. Swade: So, our second step, Britta, is . . . ?

Britta: To measure how much is in the box.

Mr. Swade: That's right. You have just given us the form of a proportion without actually saying it. The form is [Writes on board]

$$\frac{\text{what is}}{\text{what could be}} = \frac{\text{a little less than almost full}}{\text{full}}$$

Now comes the hard part. How will we find numbers to put in the top and bottom of this division problem? Any suggestions? [Danny waves his hand.]

Danny: I have an idea. Let's see how many glasses of water the box holds and then see how many glasses of water it takes to fill the box to where the cereal is.

Mr. Swade: That's a pretty clever idea, but it may have a problem. Bobby, you look like you want to say something— what about Danny's idea?

Bobby: The box isn't going to hold water long enough to do the counting.

Mr. Swade: Right. And what if the box doesn't fill up exactly at a full glass? Let's look on the box and read how this food company measured what's inside. [Hands box to Terri]

Terri: It says, "Six 8 ounce servings measured by volume."

Mr. Swade: So, how many ounces does the whole box contain? Let's review. You supply the answers as I go down the list. [Writes $1 \times 8 =$]

Class: 8.

Mr. Swade: [Continuing to write]

$$2 \times 8 = 16$$
$$3 \times 8 = 24$$
$$4 \times 8 = 32$$
$$5 \times 8 = 40$$
$$6 \times 8 = 48$$

So, 48 ounces is our total. Now, let's go back to Danny's original idea about the water, but let's measure the contents of the box using ounces instead. I happen to have an 8-ounce measuring cup. Marcus, you pour while the rest of us count.

Class: One. [As the cup is filling]

Marcus: Where do I empty it?

Mr. Swade: Let's put it in this empty box.

Class: [As the remaining contents are poured out] Two . . . three . . . four . . . five . . .

Marcus: The sixth one's not full.

Mr. Swade: Okay. Read on the side of the cup how full it is.

Marcus: It's right at "2" on the cup.

Mr. Swade: That means 2 ounces. Let's do a little arithmetic. What's our total? Who wants to do this problem? [Maria raises her hand.]

Maria: Well, we had five full cups, so that's 8 plus 8 equals . . . 16, plus 8 equals . . . 24, plus 8 equals . . . 32.

Class: One more.

Maria: Yeah, I guess that's only four, so 32 plus 8 equals . . . 40, and then the 2 at the end makes . . . . 42.

Mr. Swade: Okay, now we have all that we need to form a proportion that can tell us exactly how full the box was. What does the form of this proportion look like, class?

Class: [With most responding] 42 divided by 48.

Mr. Swade: [Writes on board]

$$\frac{48}{42} = \frac{\text{what is}}{\text{what could be}}$$

Now let's practice what we've learned. Britta and Tom, would you pass these sheets around? [Gives stack to Britta and Tom, who are on opposite sides of the room] On the sheet, you'll find 10 word problems similar to our cereal example. Each problem gives you all the information you will need to form a proportion that represents "what is" over "what could be." [Points to words on the board] Work on these for the next 15 minutes by yourselves, and I'll come around to check your work. Be sure to read the problems carefully. Form a ratio just as we did with the cereal example, and then do the division. Show your work in the space provided and place your answer on the blank at the right. Your answer will be in the form of a proportion that will require the use of a decimal. If you're having trouble, raise your hand. I'll come to those having difficulty first. [After a few minutes Alex raises his hand, and Mr. Swade moves over to help him.]

Alex: [Quietly to Mr. Swade] This first one confuses me. [Mr. Swade draws a circle around the words representing "what is" and "what could be" in the word problem and draws arrows to the top and bottom of a line to the right, indicating division. Mr. Swade then moves to the back of the room to check Niko's paper. He finds Niko's second answer is incorrect and places an X beside it.]

Niko: What did I do wrong?

Mr. Swade: What always goes on the bottom?

Niko: What could be.

Mr. Swade: How large is the can of fruit?

Niko: Oh. I get it. [Mr. Swade moves to front of class, spot-checking answers from Marcus, Britta, and Calley. Mr. Swade scans Marcus's paper and nods approvingly; he then says "Good" to Britta after reviewing her first three answers, but finds two errors among Calley's responses.]

Mr. Swade: [To Calley] Problems 2 and 4 are wrong. Think some more about these after you've finished the rest. I'll be back to check on these. [Mr. Swade goes back to his desk to grade papers until the class finishes. As students finish, noise picks up. A few students start to laugh and giggle at a note passed around by Alex, who has finished in about half the allotted time.]

TIME TO REFLECT

What dimensions of student engagement did you see in this dialogue? Recall that student engagement involves the amount of time in which students are thinking about, acting on, or otherwise using the content presented. Although student engagement in the learning process might not always be obvious to an observer, our description of student engagement in this chapter will focus on teacher activities that encourage students to think about, act on, and use the content presented.

Eliciting the Desired Behavior

The first dimension for promoting student engagement involves eliciting the desired behavior after the presentation of new content. Did you see any examples of this in the dialogue? If you said yes, you are correct. In fact, Mr. Swade did a pretty good job of ar-

ranging his lesson so that students could practice the behaviors as they are taught. This was accomplished with the use of prepared examples and exercises. Notice how Mr. Swade was able to catch his students' attention and focus them on the content by inserting a question, problem, or exercise at regular intervals throughout the lesson.

The first example of this comes at the outset of the lesson, when Mr. Swade asked the class if the expressions placed on the board are examples of ratios. Four expressions were written on the board, only two of which are ratios. Mr. Swade guided his class through the initial problem by saying, "Remember what Marcus just said." In this brief series of problems, Mr. Swade's purpose appeared to be getting his students to make their first crude association between the process of division and ratios. For each of the four problems presented, students were asked to determine its correctness in their own minds. Critical judgments of any one student's response, which might dampen a student's willingness to respond to the next problem and remain engaged in the lesson, were avoided. Although Mr. Swade's goal was simple, he accomplished it not by telling or showing students ratios involving division, but by having his students think about the distinction and identify examples placed on the board.

Next, notice how Mr. Swade actively involved the class in the lesson after Terri reads from the cereal box. Instead of simply providing the answer—that $6 \times 8 = 48$ ounces—or calling on a student to provide the answer for the entire class, the teacher had the class calculate the total themselves by reviewing multiplication by 8. Here, Mr. Swade composed, probably on the spur of the moment, six multiplication problems ($1 \times 8 =$, $2 \times 8 =$, and so on) and required the class to provide the correct answers. This also helped focus class attention, which might have begun to drift by this time. Inserting these small exercises that require the immediate response of students at the end of important segments of the lesson is particularly effective for engaging learners, especially young learners, in the learning process and keeping them engaged throughout the lesson.

Finally, Mr. Swade assigned a practice exercise so that he could evaluate the responses of individual students by checking their answers to the problems on the handout. Recall that one of the purposes of guided practice is to motivate students to make a crude first response, sometimes any response, and then to refine it gradually by trial and error. The earlier guided practice activities motivated some students to begin thinking about and formulating a response; this last activity added an evaluative component to help revise and refine earlier responses. It provided still more opportunity for practice that required all students to respond overtly and thereby makes evaluation possible.

As we have seen, engagement in the learning process begins when the learner is given the opportunity to practice using the content that is taught. Without immediate practice to engage the student in the learning process, learning rarely occurs. Some teachers, however, teach as they themselves were taught in the college classroom, without realizing the vast differences that separate the adult from the elementary or secondary school learner. At the college level, where considerable independence and motivation are expected, the instructor can appropriately assume that engagement in the learning process will take place at the convenience of and on the initiative of the individual student working through the lecture material in the privacy of the study room or library.

At the elementary and secondary school levels, however, content presentation and practice go hand in hand, separated by minutes, not days. Engagement in the learning process must be an integral part of the instruction itself, because the learner at this age is not likely to know how to make the leap from content presentation to practice without the active and direct guidance of the teacher. In Chapter 12 we will study eliciting activities that promote student engagement by challenging learners to go beyond the content presented to develop higher thought processes. In this chapter, we will study eliciting activities that encourage students to make a first response from which higher thought processes can develop.

Oral questions, workbook exercises, problem sets, activity handouts, and discussion, under the guidance of the teacher, are some of the ways students are encouraged to think about, act on, or otherwise practice content. This practice should be provided as soon as possible after the instruction to which it relates and, for complex material, should be interspersed at intervals throughout the lesson, creating cycles of presentation and practice.

The primary ways of accomplishing this integration of instruction and practice include the use of workbooks, handouts, textbook study questions, verbal and written exercises, and computer-assisted practice aids in which students are asked to immediately apply what was learned, including rehearsing content in the privacy of their own minds. The idea is to position a classroom activity as close in time as possible to the presentation of new material to en-

courage an immediate response. It is important that the eliciting activity be noncritical to encourage a response unhampered by anxiety and a fear of failure, which can occur in a test-taking situation. The goal of the eliciting activity is to encourage the learner to organize a first response that strives for, but may not attain, the intended behavior. Sometimes these activities can be inserted at the end of each unit of information or throughout the lesson, which adds variety. In either case, the eliciting activity that brings forth the response is brief, noncritical, and focused on posing a condition (such as a question, problem, or exercise) for which the learner must organize and produce a response. The response may be written, oral, or subvocal (e.g., when the teacher poses a question and the students answer silently to themselves).

Abernathy and Reardon (2001) and Rosenshine and Stevens (1986) have suggested several different types of eliciting activities:

- Preparing a large number of oral questions beforehand
- Asking many brief questions on the main points, supplementary points, and the process that is being taught
- Asking students to summarize a rule or process in their own words
- Having all students write their answers (on paper or the chalkboard) while the teacher circulates through the room
- Having all students write their answers and check them with a neighbor (frequently used with older students)
- Writing the main points on the chalkboard at the end of a presentation/discussion and then having the class work cooperatively in groups to summarize them (especially helpful for older students)

Observing Eliciting Activities

Eliciting the desired behavior involves guided practice. The goal of guided practice is to elicit from the learner a first response and then to keep the learner responding in trial-and-error fashion until initial responses are gradually refined into correct, quick, and firm responses. As we have seen, typical methods for eliciting learner responses include oral questions, exercises in the text or workbook, problems presented in handouts, and problems or questions written on the board or on an overhead. These and other eliciting activities can be recorded with the format shown in Instrument 10.2.

For this record, a check mark is placed in the appropriate box each time an eliciting activity occurs during a lesson. Notice that the proximity of the practice activity to the presentation of lesson content is recorded simultaneously. Guided practice is most effective when it is interspersed throughout, or immediately follows, the presentation of content. Also notice that five different alternatives (from *Interspersed* throughout the lesson to *Indefinite* or at the student's discretion) are provided to record when the eliciting activity recurs. The more immediate the eliciting activity is to the presentation of content, the greater the chance that feedback and correctives will improve the learner's initial response and keep the learner responding until responses are correct, quick, and firm. The longer the time between the presentation of content and the questions, problems, or exercises of the eliciting activity, the less effective the activity becomes.

Providing Feedback and Correctives in a Noncritical Atmosphere

A second behavior for engaging students in the learning process is providing feedback about the correctness of the elicited response. At this point in the learning process, it is important that feedback be supportive to encourage a response, both among mainstream learners and among English language learners and other culturally diverse students (Burnette, 1999). At this stage of student engagement crude and often inadequate initial responses are refined, through repetition, into slightly less crude and more adequate responses, which in turn provide the basis for finely tuned responses at a high level of accuracy.

The feedback provided must unambiguously inform the learner about the adequacy of any response and must be given in a manner that will not embarrass or humiliate the learner or lower the learner's own expectations. Because initial responses to a guided practice exercise might be crude, sometimes illogical, and occasionally funny (in others' eyes), the potential for emotional harm is greatest during this phase of learning. The teacher's job is not to pass judgment, but to provide nonjudgmental feedback so that the learner can judge his own work. This can be accomplished by having students respond in unison, showing answers on a transparency after each problem is completed individually, or simply supplying the correct answers at the end of a designated work time. It might also include requesting that students write out their responses or orally respond so that the teacher can be certain that individual students are engaged in the problem solution and do not simply wait for the answer to be given by others.

Opportunities for feedback should always be closely connected in time and substance to the eliciting activity, which will promote learning if the learner can determine the correctness of the attempted response, whether oral, written, or subvocal, immediately after the response has been given. Although the response itself must be an individual's attempt to recall, summarize, paraphrase, apply, or solve a problem, the feedback that follows can be directed to the entire class to create immediacy for everyone. For example, the teacher may either reveal his answer to a problem or question, or choose a student's answer. A wrong response by a student, however, should be responded to with encouragement to maintain the supportive flavor of the learning activity. Responses such as "That's a good try," "That's not quite what I'm looking for," or "Keep thinking; you'll get it" can switch the focus to more supportive responses without penalizing the student for attempting and producing a crude initial response. Several other ways of confirming correct responses are also possible.

- Reading aloud the correct answers from the workbook
- Providing a handout with the correct answers
- Showing the answers one by one on a transparency after students complete each question
- Nodding or smiling to indicate the correctness of an individual performance or to encourage the revision of a wrong response

These and other ways of providing feedback to individuals, small groups, and the full class are summarized in Table 10.2.

What did you notice about how Mr. Swade provided correctives? Did you notice that Mr. Swade's practice opportunities at the start of the lesson were oriented toward the entire class, avoiding any potential embarrassment to individual students whose initial responses might have been crude, funny, or illogical? In the first two guided practice activities, students responded in choral fashion, completely avoiding an evaluation of individual responses at this early stage of learning. The teacher provided the correct response with which students could evaluate their own answers. When students have difficulty grasping a concept and large numbers of initial responses are likely to be incorrect, choral responses or responses made privately can minimize potentially embarrassing answers and possible humiliation to individual students that can diminish a student's willingness to try again. Mr. Swade might have known that some of

TABLE 10.2 Methods of Providing Feedback

Individual Students	Small Groups	Class
Nod while walking past	Sit with group and discuss answers	Place answers on a transparency
Point to correct answer in workbook or text	Have one group critique another group's answers	Provide answers on a handout
Show student the answer key	Give each group the answer key when finished	Read answers aloud
Place X beside incorrect answers		Place answers on the board
Have students grade each other's papers, using the text or assigned reference as a guide	Assign one group member the task of checking the answers of other group members	Have selected students read their answers aloud
		Have students grade each other's papers as you give answers orally

his students did not learn all that they should have from earlier lessons, and this could be the reason he decided to start his lesson with class-corrected rather than individually corrected exercises. Class-corrected exercises and choral responses are no guarantee, however, that all students will participate. More formal feedback also will be necessary to check the accuracy of earlier choral and private responses.

Mr. Swade's final exercise provided the individual student evaluation that the earlier practice activities lack. Notice that even though this last activity was evaluative, it too was nonjudgmental. The teacher responded to students individually, not in the presence of other students. Notice also that, for the most part, Mr. Swade's feedback was immediate, with the shortest possible time between the generation of a response and information about its correctness. This tends to strengthen a correct response, reinforcing its value for the learner and making it more likely that the response will be remembered.

Because oral questions are an important eliciting activity, Mr. Swade's responses to these kinds of questions deserve examination as well. Let's look at just a few of these exchanges to see how he engaged his students in the learning process with feedback and correctives.

Mr. Swade's first question was typical of his questioning strategy throughout the dialogue. He asked, "Who can tell me why division is so important in computing a ratio?" Marcus replied, "It's because ratios are nothing but division problems." The teacher responded, "Yes, that's right, in the sense that ratios can be expressed as one number over another, like this (writes 4/8 on board)." Notice that the teacher first affirmed that the student response is correct—or partially correct. Then the teacher rephrased or elaborated on the question for both the student and the rest of the class. In other words, this teacher's response took the student's answer and rephrased it in a manner useful for moving to the next part of the lesson. For example, the teacher extended Marcus's response "nothing but division problems" to "one number over another" to provide a transition. Indeed, we find the idea of "one number over another" played a key role throughout the lesson as the teacher developed the model "what is/what could be" to communicate the notion of a proportion and to respond to problems on the handout. Thus, the feedback provided to Marcus's answer not only evaluated his response but also lifted his answer to a new level.

This question–answer–feedback strategy appeared throughout the dialogue in several different forms. For example, at another point Mr. Swade asked, "How do we go about forming a ratio to describe the amount of cereal in this box?" Tomás replied, "Well, we need to know how much the box holds." The teacher responded, "That's right. You've got the first step. Now, Tim, what's the next step?" Here, the teacher affirmed the correctness or partial correctness of the response, and then went on to use the answer as a springboard for additional content. Each student response laid the groundwork for additional content added by the teacher or provided in the form of a new question to another student. This type of feedback uses student responses as transitions to new content. It is characterized by more praise and affirmation than negation and criticism because most student responses are interpreted as partially correct, with some usable content for a transition to the next idea. As discussed later, meaningful verbal praise is a significant component of teacher feedback and an important aspect of engaging students and keeping them engaged in the eliciting activity.

Observing Feedback and Correctives

Although the recording format in Instrument 10.2 indicates the nature of the guided practice activity, it does not indicate whether any correctives are being provided to individual students. When practice activities are interspersed throughout the presentation of content, provided immediately afterward, or saved until the end of the lesson, correctives may or may not be provided. Even oral questions interspersed in the presentation of content might not be corrective. The teacher might pose a question and then immediately answer it without giving students time to respond or just not pause for any response. The teacher might also indicate that a response is wrong but give no indication why.

After getting familiar with eliciting activities using the recording format in Instrument 10.2, you will want to observe student responses and teacher reactions to those responses to obtain a more detailed account of the specific interactive sequences during an eliciting activity. Chapter 11 will introduce an observation record (Instrument 11.2) for documenting these sequences from the research of Good and Brophy (2007). For now, notice how often a teacher provides a reason why an answer is correct or why it is wrong after a student response and what, if any, corrective is given with it. These informal observations will afford you the opportunity to see the teacher's use of both correctives and meaningful verbal praise. For example, a teacher may praise a right answer but not provide feedback about why the answer was correct, thereby preventing the response from being used as a model for others to follow. On the other hand, a teacher who frequently finds opportunities to meaningfully praise by providing reasons why an answer is correct and who uses a variety of correctives (e.g., explains an answer, repeats or rephrases a question, or gives a clue) in response to partly right or wrong answers is providing effective feedback.

Using Differentiated and Self-Regulated Learning Activities

Chapter 8 introduced differentiated instruction for increasing instructional variety. In this chapter we will see its role in engaging students in the learning process. Recall that to differentiate instruction is to recognize an individual student's learning history, background, readiness to learn, interests, and acquired skill set and choose instructional activities tailored to small groups and individuals that speed their academic success, which might be slowed if only large-group instructional activities were avail-

able. The goal of differentiated instruction, therefore, is to maximize each student's academic success and personal growth as a learner by meeting each student where they are at and providing the needed instruction and resources that lift the learner to the next step of the learning ladder.

Tomlinson (2004) and Tomlinson and McTighe (2006) identify three elements of the curriculum, consisting of content, process, and products that can be differentiated to make instruction more responsive to the individual needs of learners.

As we saw in Chapter 8 with regard to content, differentiation can take the form of varying the modalities in which students gain access to important learning, for example, by (a) listening, reading, and doing; (b) presenting content in incremental steps, like rungs in a ladder, resulting in a continuum of skill-building tasks; and (c) offering learners a choice in the complexity of content with which they will begin a learning task that matches their current level of understanding so that every learner can experience academic success.

With regard to process, differentiation takes the form of grouping flexibly, for example, by (a) varying from whole class, to collaborative groups, to small groups, to individuals and (b) providing incentives to learn based on a student's individual interests and current level of understanding.

With regard to products, Tomlinson suggests varying assessment methods, by (a) providing teachers a menu of choices that might include oral responses, interviews, demonstrations and reenactments, and portfolios as well as formal tests, (b) keeping each learner challenged at his or her level of understanding with content at or slightly above the learner's current level of functioning, and (c) allowing students to have some choice in the means by which they express what they know—for example, writing a story, drawing pictures, or telling about a real-life experience that involves what is being taught.

But most important, differentiated instruction provides an opportunity for the teacher to take into consideration multiple characteristics of a learner *simultaneously* in choosing an instructional strategy for the particular learner and learning objective. Therefore, differentiated instruction is ideally suited for engaging learners in the heterogeneous classroom in which learning histories and learner styles and interests and skills, as well as disabilities representing special populations, may impair learning. Overall, the goal of differentiated instruction is to give learners alternate paths by which to learn. Students working below grade level can be given resources that retrace major objectives that have already been taught while learners above grade level can be asked to produce work that requires more complex and advanced thinking than the average student. By varying teaching strategies the teacher makes sure that each student has the opportunity to learn in a manner compatible with his or her own learning strengths and preferences. The curriculum is no longer defined in terms of what a teacher will teach but rather in terms of what a student will be able to demonstrate.

The use of differentiated and self-directed activities, therefore, is the third behavior for engaging students in the learning process. For some students, guided practice and noncritical feedback will not be sufficient. These learners need additional incentives to become sufficiently energized or excited about learning to attempt an initial response to practice opportunities. Differentiated instruction and self-directed learning give students a degree of control over their own learning and can be useful in getting these students, who might represent a sizable portion of a class, engaged in the learning process. Techniques for accomplishing this include

- Focusing on concepts, understanding, and sense-making, not just retention and regurgitation of fragmented facts
- Using ongoing assessments of readiness and interests to find students needing more support and those who can leap forward by tackling different tasks that don't assume all students learn in the same way
- Making grouping flexible by letting students work alone sometimes and also in groups based on readiness, interests, or learning styles, using whole-group instruction for introducing ideas, planning, or sharing results.
- Seeing yourself as a guide, helping students set goals based on readiness, interests, and their learning profile and assessing based on individual growth and goal attainment.

Teaching to different groups (and even individual learners) in addition to the regular class is not a matter of choice in many of today's heterogeneous and mainstreamed classrooms. A collection of appropriate individualized materials (including performance contracts, interactive computer software, instructional games and simulations, talking books, and learning centers) for challenged, at-risk, and special learners can allow different learning needs to be met in the midst of a heterogeneous class of learners, engaging those who might otherwise be left behind.

Lower-performing learners are often disengaged from the learning process. Many have difficulty learning at an average rate from the instructional resources, texts, workbooks, and learning materials that have been designated for the majority of students in the classroom. These learners will benefit from special instructional pacing, frequent feedback, remedial instruction, or modified materials, all administered under conditions flexible enough to engage them in the learning process. These learners may also require more than the usual amount of variation in method of presentation (direct or indirect), instructional materials (DVDs, workbooks, games, and simulations), and learning activities (oral questioning, group discussion, and tutoring). Also, some will respond favorably to the frequent reinforcement of small segments of learning typically found in interactive media and computer software, whereas others may learn more efficiently by seeing and hearing than by reading. Incorporating video and audio into the learning process can help accommodate instruction to the learning modalities that are strongest among these learners (Baum, Viens, & Slatin, 2005).

In addition to these formal approaches to differentiating instruction, some group tasks can be presented in a form that gives learners the opportunity to self-regulate the pace and complexity of their responses. For example, cooperative group activities and tasks can employ self-directed learning activities (e.g., demonstration of a concept or principle, problem-solving reports, oral presentations on current events or debates) to gradually transfer control over the learning process to students, thereby increasing each student's responsibility for his own learning. Using self-directed learning activities in the context of cooperative groups can be particularly helpful when the variety of student abilities, interests, and motivation in a classroom is so great that it precludes the use of any prepackaged set of materials intended for a homogeneous subgroup.

What did you observe about Mr. Swade's use of differentiated and self-regulating activities to promote engagement in the learning process? This dialogue might have been too brief to provide sufficient information. But subsequent observations could focus on what Mr. Swade does with those students who cannot grasp the concepts on his guided practice handout, perhaps as evidenced by a large proportion of incorrect responses after two or three cycles of monitoring and checking. Our observations could focus on how Mr. Swade handles Alex, who finished early, and students like him, who seem more advanced than the rest of the class. To keep these special types of students engaged, differentiated activities in the form of self-regulated tasks, interactive computer programs, instructional games and simulations, peer tutoring, cooperative group work, teams, and independent projects may well be in order.

Observing Differentiated and Self-Regulated Learning Activities

As we have seen, some students learn best by reading and seeing, whereas others prefer a learning modality, such as listening and telling, that might not correspond to the needs of the majority of the class. At other times, the teacher might want learners to assume some of the responsibility for their own learning. Many activities and materials are available that transfer a degree of control of the pace and complexity of learning to the student. The use of some of these activities and materials in a classroom can be recorded by identifying them under the categories shown in Instrument 10.3.

Because the use of individual and self-regulated activities will need to be recorded over time, Instrument 10.3 is intended for use in a classroom in which you will make multiple observations, such as your cooperating teacher's classroom. The category "Other" can be used to describe any additional activities (such as flexible homework assignments or practice activities) that provide students with a degree of control over the pace or complexity of instructional activity.

Using Meaningful Verbal Praise

The fourth behavior for engaging students in the learning process is the use of *meaningful* verbal praise. Recall that in Chapter 6 praise was mentioned as a tool of the effective classroom manager, particularly when used as an incentive for good conduct that others can see and emulate. And in Chapter 8, the concept of praise was mentioned as one of many ways of bringing variety to a classroom, particularly regarding the variety with which a learner can be rewarded. Here, we return to this powerful tool of the effective teacher, this time with regard to its important role in heightening a student's willingness and motivation to become actively engaged in the learning process.

Verbal praise provided frequently in the absence of genuine accomplishment may be seen by students as mechanical and devoid of reinforcing value. Between glib responses such as "Correct," "Okay," or "Yep" and overly emotional responses such as "That's wonderful," "Fantastic," or "Awesome" lies a range of verbal praise that neither passes by nor embarrasses a student in the eyes of others. Meaningful verbal praise links a student's response to the level of accomplishment attained while pushing the learner forward to higher levels of achievement. For example, instead of simply being informed that the response is correct, the learner can be told that the response is correct because the directions were followed carefully, the correct sequence of events was chosen, or care was taken to consult the text. In addition to stating that a response is correct, the teacher has the opportunity to explain to the whole class the higher-level thought processes that might have been used to produce the response (e.g., the answer shows the ability to find relationships between information in different chapters). In each of these instances, the desire to keep engaged in the learning process is enhanced because verbal praise is provided in the context of a successfully accomplished operation. In other words, **meaningful verbal praise** should be

- Specific to the particular behavior being reinforced
- Applied immediately after the behavior occurs
- Varied according to the situation and the student being reinforced

Meaningful verbal praise is especially important in the case of partially correct or correct-but-hesitant responses. Here, praise must be tempered with a sign that a better or less hesitant response is desired. To ignore the inadequacy or hesitation in favor of a simple "OK" may give an indication to others that they, too, can provide a less than satisfactory response. In this case, the praise must be proportional to the adequacy of the response, such as "That's partly correct, but now let's see if you can put it all together" or "Good try. Now change one thing and you'll have it." Comments such as these point out the subtle differences between a partially correct answer and a wrong answer, which is often a matter of judgment. The effective teacher chooses to see an answer as partially correct where possible and give praise with qualification. Table 10.3, based on a review by Brophy (1981, 2002), provides some guidelines for using praise effectively to increase the level of student engagement in a classroom.

Praise occupies surprisingly little class time for most teachers, and only a small percentage of a teacher's day is devoted to any kind of praise. Yet there is little doubt among behavioral psychologists that a reward contingent on an appropriate behavior increases the frequency of that behavior. A positive verbal response tells the student that the reward is contingent on appropriate performance, pushing the learner forward. More important, it tells learners that by producing a correct response, *they* can control the flow of accomplishment and reward.

When meaningful praise is consistently applied, the link between the performance and the praise is

TABLE 10.3 Guidelines for Effective Praise

Effective Praise	Ineffective Praise
1. Is delivered contingently	1. Is delivered randomly or unsystematically
2. Specifies the particulars of the accomplishment	2. Is restricted to global positive reactions
3. Shows spontaneity, variety, and other signs of credibility; suggests clear attention to the student's accomplishment	3. Shows a bland uniformity, which suggests a conditioned response made with minimal attention
4. Rewards attainment of specified performance criteria (can include effort criteria)	4. Rewards mere participation, without consideration of performance processes or outcomes
5. Provides information to students about their competence or the value of their accomplishments	5. Provides no information at all, or gives students little information about their status
6. Orients students toward better appreciation of their own task-related behavior and problem solving	6. Orients students toward comparing themselves with others and competition
7. Uses students' own prior accomplishments as the context for describing present accomplishments	7. Uses the accomplishments of peers as the context for describing students' present accomplishments
8. Is given in recognition of noteworthy effort or success at particularly difficult tasks	8. Is given without regard to the effort expended or the meaning of the accomplishment
9. Attributes success to effort and ability, implying that similar successes can be expected in the future	9. Attributes success to ability alone, or external factors such as luck or ease
10. Fosters endogenous attributions (students believe that they expend effort on the task because they enjoy the task and/or want to develop task-relevant skills)	10. Fosters exogenous attributions (students believe that they expend effort on the task for external reasons—to please the teacher or win a competition or reward)
11. Focuses students' attention on their own task-relevant behavior	11. Focuses students' attention on the teacher as an external authority figure who is manipulating them
12. Fosters appreciation and desirable attributions about task-relevant behavior after the process is completed	12. Intrudes into the ongoing process, distracting attention from task-relevant behavior

Source: Adapted from Brophy, J. (1981). Teacher praise: A functional analysis. *Review of Educational Research, 51,* 5–32.

strong enough to promote student engagement in the learning process and a need to achieve. This link becomes internalized by the learner and directs her to anticipate the next reward. Praise is a strategy that is always available to the teacher. As such, it is one of the most effective means of engaging students in the learning process when it is specific, applied immediately, and varied according to the situation and student being reinforced.

Finally, it should be noted that verbally punishing students for responding thoughtlessly or carelessly (e.g., "I'm ashamed of you," "That's a dumb mistake," "I thought you were brighter than that") rarely teaches them to avoid the mistake in the future and can often promote disengagement. Reminders to study harder, pay more attention, think some more, or go over mistakes are often far more effective stimulants to learning and should not be confused with phrases that ridicule, demean, or draw the class's attention to someone's abilities. The latter rarely, if ever, lead a learner to change the behavior that led to the careless response.

What did you think of Mr. Swade's feedback to his students? You might have noticed that Mr. Swade's style of feedback closely matches our definition of meaningful verbal praise—responses that are specific, applied immediately, and varied according to the student being reinforced for the purpose of maintaining or heightening the student's engagement in the learning process. That is, the teacher's response is tailored to fit the specific answer given by the student and the characteristics of the student giving the answer. Meaningful praise often explains the value of a learner's response and extends or picks up on the response for further discussion by the teacher and other students.

How often did Mr. Swade's responses do this? Notice that Mr. Swade's responses to correct or partially correct answers did not stop at neutral affirmation, such as "OK" or "That's right," but went on either to explain the value of the response to the class or use the response to move the discussion to a new or different level.

- "Yes, that's right, in the sense that . . . "
- "Right again. Notice how easy it is to spot . . . "
- "Good. Now you see that . . . "
- "Okay. But how do we go about . . . "
- "That's right. You've got the first step. Now . . . "

In each of these expressions, Mr. Swade does not stop at a simple expression of praise. He goes on to provide a response that is tailored to the level of correctness of the answer given, making the praise meaningful to the student. Mr. Swade uses each response as an opportunity to move deeper into the topic. He tends to look on the bright side of every response, to see that the glass is half full rather than half empty. Responses like this blend student answers into a discussion that other students can join rather than letting them become dead ends. Mr. Swade has combined probing with meaningful praise. Each of his responses leaves the student feeling good about his response but also thinking more about it. This is how meaningful praise engages students in the learning process at the same time as it rewards, reinforces, and helps manage the classroom.

Observing Meaningful Verbal Praise

Recall that, to be effective, praise must be contingent on the performance of the specific behavior to be reinforced, clearly identified with that behavior (given immediately following the behavior), and adjusted to the characteristics of the student being praised (e.g., shy and retiring, easily embarrassed, or outgoing and gregarious). These three ingredients separate ineffective praise with little or no influence on student engagement from praise that is likely to reinforce behavior and increase the probability that the desired behavior will recur. As we have seen, this latter type of praise is called *meaningful praise.*

The recording form in Instrument 10.4 divides praise into two categories. The first category lists the ways in which praise can be delivered to the student: orally, through body language (such as a nod of the head or a pat on the back), or written (such as a smiley face or note at the top of a paper or exercise). The second category divides praise that is delivered orally into four types, described in Figure 10.1.

These categories attempt to separate praise into more and less meaningful types: the first two ("Gives Neutral Affirmation" and "Expresses Surprise, Delight, or Excitement") are generally less meaningful than the latter ("Explains Value" and "Uses, Extends, Picks Up On"). The latter two tend to be more meaningful because the praise is specific to the context in which the response was given and more tailored to the unique product of the student. Note that the teacher's responses to the first two categories could serve any correct response provided in any context by any student, which is not true for the latter two categories.

Finally, notice that the first column provides an opportunity to record the time in which an incident of praise was observed. Using check marks the "delivery

---

FIGURE 10.1   Four Types of Oral Praise

Gives Neutral Affirmation
Teacher uses expressions such as "Okay," "Good," and "Yep" to indicate response is accepted, but goes no further.

Expresses Surprise, Delight, or Excitement
Teacher shows some emotion, such as "Great," "That shows real talent," or "You're doing remarkably well."

Explains Value
Teacher explains to class why the answer is correct and points out qualities used to arrive at the answer, implying superior performance.

Uses, Extends, Picks Up On
Teacher takes student response to next level, or uses it to arrive at a subsequent step in a process.

---

mode" and "type of praise" can be recorded for each incident across the row. For comparisons across classes or classrooms in which different amounts of time might have been devoted to observation, it may be convenient to convert praise rates to a common measure using the following formula to express rate of praise per unit of class time:

$$\frac{\text{Number of incidents of praise}}{\text{Number of minutes of observation}} \times 60 =$$

Praise rate/Hour

For example, if 4 incidents of praise were recorded after 60 minutes of observation during which there was an opportunity for praise, the rate of praising would be 4 praises per hour of instructional time ($4/60 \times 60 = 4$). Using the same formula for a classroom in which there were 9 incidents of praise during only 30 minutes of observation for which there was an opportunity for praise, the rate would be 18 praises per hour of instructional time ($9/30 \times 60 = 18$). In this manner classrooms in which there are different amounts of time devoted to observation of praise can be compared.

Praise rates can be calculated separately for each of the four "Types of Praise" and entered in the last row of the record, labeled "Rate." A type of praise should be recorded separately each time it occurs. For example, when a teacher expresses surprise, but then goes on to explain why the response was correct, it should be recorded as two different incidents of praise. Because incidents of praise do not occur frequently, several class periods may be necessary to determine the rate of each type of praise representative of a classroom. For smaller blocks of total observation time, say, an hour or less, a single rate combining all the types of praise can be used. Praise rates for academic work and conduct-related behaviors reported in six research studies reviewed by Brophy (1981) were 4.52 and 0.12 incidents of praise per hour, respectively, showing that surprisingly little praise occurs in most classrooms.

Monitoring and Checking

The final behavior for engaging students in the learning process involves monitoring and checking. Monitoring is the process of observing, mentally recording, and, when necessary, redirecting or correcting student behavior. The teacher looks for active, alert eyes during discussion sessions; eyes down and directed at the book or assignment during seatwork; raised hands during a question-and-answer period; and general signs that indicate the learner is participating in the classwork. These signs of engagement (or their absence) can indicate when changes should be made in the pace with which the content is being delivered, the difficulty of the material, or even the activity itself.

An important aspect of monitoring to promote engagement in the learning process is observing more than one activity at a time. This requires what we characterized in Chapter 8 as *withitness,* or the ability to observe all or at least many aspects of a classroom simultaneously (Kounin, 1970). Although few teachers are blessed with eyes in the backs of their heads, there are several simple ways of increasing withitness. One is changing the purpose of attention as eye contact is focused on different parts of the room. For example, progress on assigned seatwork might be the focus of a teacher's observations when scanning students in the front of the class, but potential disciplinary problems might be the focus of observation when scanning the back of the class; then the sequence is reversed. Therefore, the teacher switches back and forth from conduct-related observations to work-related observations with a change in eye contact. One of the greatest impediments to making this switch, however, is a tendency to focus exclusively on one student who is having either conduct- or work-related problems. Once students become aware that the teacher is preoccupied with a single student, other problems can arise.

An equally important aspect of monitoring is checking for student understanding and, when necessary, providing prompts that help convert wrong answers to correct responses. Prompting is an important way of engaging learners in the learning process because encouraging them to use aspects of the answer that

have already been given builds their confidence in working toward the correct response.

Checking for understanding and prompting can be accomplished by asking students to respond privately in writing and encouraging those having problems to request individual help. Another approach is to call on students whether or not their hands are raised, thereby seeking out opportunities to prompt and correct wrong answers (Sternberg, 1994). A version of this approach is referred to as *ordered turns,* in which the teacher systematically goes through the class and expects students to respond when their turn comes. This approach has been found to be more effective than randomly calling on students in producing gains in student achievement when groups are small (Anderson, Evertson, & Brophy, 1979; Brophy & Evertson, 1976), but less effective than randomly selecting students to respond during full-class instruction, because a student's turn will become predictable and the student can safely become unengaged for longer periods of time (Anderson, Evertson, & Brophy, 1982). Another approach is to have students write out answers to be checked and, if need be, corrected by a classmate. Finally, the teacher can prepare a number of questions beforehand to test for the most frequently occurring errors. Students are then asked to provide responses, which the teacher checks for accuracy and then probes when necessary. This approach has the advantage of assuming that not everyone understands or has the correct answer when no responses are heard following a call for questions. These methods for checking for understanding and probing can be summarized as follows:

1. Ordered turns (best with small groups)
2. Calling on students randomly (best with full class)
3. Having students write out answers that are then checked by classmate
4. Asking questions (ordered or random) to check for the most frequently occurring errors

During instructional activities such as guided practice and independent seatwork, monitoring should be done within a systematic routine of checking. Rather than simply scanning the classroom, the teacher circulates among students and checks their responses in workbooks or exercises. It is important, however, that this circulating behavior not be seen by learners as punitive, but rather as a helpful response to their work. A casual glance at papers is more constructive than long interactions with individual students, whose self-esteem and engagement may be stifled by a long stay at their desk because others might see this as a sign of poor performance. Interactions with individual students should be limited to brief exchanges, most lasting about 30 seconds, and to responses that are focused on a student's particular problem. This cycle may be repeated if the teacher wants to look for other types of student errors on subsequent rounds. Monitoring and checking for progress, especially during guided and independent practice, are important tools for effectively engaging students in the learning process.

What did you notice about Mr. Swade's use of monitoring and checking behaviors? Did he have a systematic routine of monitoring and checking to accomplish his goals? We see that, for the most part, he did. Recall that an effective routine for monitoring and checking involves evaluating the work of as many students as possible by limiting individual student contact to brief exchanges of less than a minute. Therefore, circulating throughout the classroom and giving approximately equal time to all zones of the room is important. Checking the work of individual students can be accomplished orally, in writing, or simply through body language to indicate that a particular response is correct. Some examples of each appeared in the dialogue.

For example, the teacher's response to Alex's request for help was simply to draw circles and arrows leading him to the correct response without any verbal exchange. The teacher gave Niko a verbal hint to correct a wrong answer with the words "What always goes on the bottom?" For Marcus, a simple nod of the head conveyed the message that all was correct. What do these various types of exchanges have in common? Although they employ three different channels of communication—written, oral, and visual—they are all brief and to the point. Brevity—the ability to make an evaluation quickly and then disengage to make another—is one of the most important characteristics of effective monitoring and checking. Our everyday communications tend not to be brief exchanges, and therefore it is often difficult to utilize such an approach in the classroom without being rude or incomplete. Yet the ability to avoid extended discussion with individual students, even when it is content related, is necessary during monitoring and checking. Simple body language or checks, pluses, or smiley faces written silently on papers are often effective, especially with a student who is prone to drawing the teacher into an extended discussion.

Although we have given Mr. Swade some compliments on his monitoring and checking behavior, he seemed to give it only a halfhearted effort. He was off to a good start, but we learn at the end of the dialogue that his monitoring and checking activity lasted for less than half of the 15 minutes allotted to the guided practice activity. Mr. Swade then returned to his desk to grade papers and the class was left to finish the exercise without the benefit of feedback, Mr. Swade missed an opportunity to discover students who might not have been sufficiently prepared to even begin the activity. This is not uncommon. Some students will look engaged to disguise their embarrassment at not being able to begin the exercise, and teachers readily get distracted by their own uncompleted work. Because some students will disengage from practice activity at the first sign of difficulty or when the teacher appears preoccupied or unavailable to help, the effectiveness of monitoring and checking depends on the active participation of the teacher throughout the entire practice exercise.

The practice exercise that ended the lesson was a handout containing 10 word problems. This eliciting activity differed from the preceding activities because it provided the opportunity for the teacher to evaluate the correctness of individual student responses. Yet the teacher's evaluation of these individually written responses was nonthreatening because students were asked to respond privately at their desks. Crude, funny, or illogical responses did not become a source of embarrassment or humiliation, as they might have if individuals were called on to report their answers to the class. The success of this final eliciting activity depends on a systematic routine of (1) monitoring to encourage the students to apply themselves to the exercise and (2) checking to ensure that students are improving the accuracy of their responses, refining them until they are increasingly correct, quick, and firm.

Observing Monitoring and Checking

As we have seen, the teacher can promote student engagement by monitoring and checking activities during assigned seatwork. At this time it is important that the teacher have frequent contact with students and that the teacher's contact be spread evenly among students throughout the classroom. Several approaches can be used to observe these teacher behaviors.

The number of students whose work is checked and the duration of each student contact represent a pattern of behavior that is typical of classroom monitoring. Six different combinations or levels of these dimensions are illustrated in Table 10.4. Unless special circumstances prevail, the most effective strategy is to check the work of most students briefly. This allows the teacher to cover more ground with fewer classroom management problems than the other alternatives, which might engage the teacher in protracted

TABLE 10.4 Sample Guidelines for Student–Teacher Contacts

Intensity of Contact	Number of Students Contacted		
	Few	**Some**	**Most**
Brief	Checks work of 1–3 students for a minute or less each	Checks work of 4–8 students for a minute or less each	Checks work of more than 8 students for a minute or less each
Extensive	Checks work of 1–3 students for more than a minute	Checks work of 4–8 students for more than a minute	Checks work of more than 8 students for more than a minute

conversations with individual students, perhaps causing her to miss academic work- or conduct-related problems occurring elsewhere in the classroom. The lengthier the contact, the more unlikely it is that the work of most students can be monitored. Monitoring the work of most students intensely would be desirable only if time permitted and classroom management problems could be avoided. Generally less than a minute of student contact, and typically 30 seconds or less, is optimal unless the class is small.

The movement of the teacher throughout the classroom can be another important sign that monitoring and checking are taking place. However, students closest to the teacher and engaged in the lesson might represent only a small portion of the classroom. Therefore, a picture or map of the teacher's circulating activity may be important for discovering implicit biases that can, over the course of time, leave some members of the class without any individual teacher contact, promoting disengagement.

The visual classroom map in Figure 10.2 indicates how the circulating activity of the teacher can be recorded. Connecting lines indicate the pattern of rotation. Notice how this teacher seems to favor the center of the classroom, excluding those seated along the sides and back. Also, only about one-quarter (26%) of the 27 students in this classroom have their progress checked by the teacher or have an opportunity to pose a question about the work. Although a single observation period might not reveal the typical monitoring and checking behaviors of a teacher, visual maps such as these can reveal why some students are or are not engaged in the learning process, especially if completed over more than a single observation period.

A third approach to observing monitoring and checking is to combine several signs into a single format. In Instrument 10.5 the manner in which feedback is provided to the student, the time devoted to feedback, and the location of the student in the classroom are all recorded simultaneously. Figure 10.3 provides a description of each of the columns

on this form. Notice that Instrument 10.5 allows you to record the mode in which feedback is provided to the learner, including the use of body language, which is often the predominant form of feedback for brief contacts. In addition, you can record three levels of duration, which correspond, respectively, to three principal reasons for initiating student contact: to encourage, praise, or correct with no opportunity for student response; to encourage, praise, or correct with opportunity for student response; and to reteach or diagnose specific weaknesses with opportunity for student response.

FIGURE 10.2 Visual Map of a Teacher's Circulating Activity

FIGURE 10.3 Description of Indicators for Observing, Monitoring, and Checking

Mode of Feedback		
Oral	Teacher comments orally.
Written	Teacher places mark on paper ("OK," check after wrong answer, smiley face, or star), writes in correct answer, or corrects one already written.
Body Language	Teacher nods yes or shakes head no without speaking.

Duration		
A Few Seconds	Teacher stops at desk only long enough to say a word or two. Student is not expected or given time to respond.
Longer Than a Few Seconds, but Less Than a Minute	Teacher engages in conversation with student but reaches closure rapidly. Student is given time to ask question or respond to teacher's comment.
More Than One Minute	Teacher allows two, three, or more exchanges to occur. Teacher may reteach needed content, work through one or more problems with student, or give student additional problems to identify specific weaknesses. Teacher may allow noninstructional conversation to occur, which increases contact time.

Zone		
1—Front		
2—Left Front	Zone 1	Desk
3—Right Front	Zone 2	Zone 3
4—Left Rear	Zone 4	Zone 5
5—Right Rear		

Finally, the physical movement of the teacher is recorded by checking zones rather than by recording movement among individual seats. Although this method is less accurate than a seat map, it can be used to detect general zone biases. Zone 1 represents the case when students are expected to come to the teacher to have their work checked. Divisions among the other zones can be determined arbitrarily by assigning an equal number of desks to each.

To conclude our discussion of engaging students in the learning process, Figure 10.4 summarizes our re-

actions to Mr. Swade's lesson. How does our checklist compare with yours? We saw signs of three out of five behaviors for engaging students in the learning process in Mr. Swade's classroom. Although incomplete, Mr. Swade's monitoring and checking behaviors are also commendable. All things considered, Mr. Swade deserves good marks for this lesson.

CULTURAL DIVERSITY AND STUDENT ENGAGEMENT

We have seen that a teacher's task orientation and student engagement must go hand in hand in order to be effective. A task-oriented teacher who maximizes content coverage and gives students the greatest opportunity to learn will have little effect on learning if students are not involved, acting on, and otherwise thinking about the material being presented. Likewise, students who are actively engaged, but in ways that are irrelevant to the goals of the lesson, will fail to learn. The key to bringing these two important dimensions of effective teaching together rests with how the teacher interacts with students to invoke a willingness to respond and apply what they have been learning—to practice what has been presented with exercises, classroom activities, homework assignments, and projects. In classrooms where individual, cultural, and special learners are prominent, student engagement in the learning process can be a major challenge to achieving performance outcomes.

One facet of research dealing with cultural diversity and special learners has focused on differences in fluency and oral expression among learners. For example, Lustig and Koester (2006) studied how student fluency or quickness to respond can be influenced by nurturing and expressive qualities of the teacher. The implication of these findings is that for some cultural groups, student hesitancy in responding and becoming engaged in the learning process might be more a function of the attitude and cultural style of the teacher than of student ability.

Chen and Starosta (1997) have shown that student engagement is, in part, an expression of the interactive process between student and teacher. Specifically, their research found that body posture, language, and eye contact form a pattern of metacommunication that is recognized by the learner and acted on according to the message being conveyed, intentionally or not. For example, a formal body posture and questions posed in an expressionless voice, without eye contact, may not invoke a commitment

FIGURE 10.4   Checklist for Observing Mr. Swade's Classroom

Behavior	Observed	Not Observed	No Opportunity to Observe
1. Provides for guided practice	✓ Uses two oral (choral response) and one written (individual response) exercises		
2. Provides feedback to guided practice	✓ Extends, lifts student responses, and uses as transitions		
3. Uses individualized or self-directed materials and activities to promote learning, when appropriate			✓ Not enough information; check with respect to Alex on next observation
4. Uses meaningful verbal praise	✓ Affirms partially right answers		
5. Monitors seatwork by circulating and frequently checking progress		✓ Begins monitoring seatwork but stops halfway through to return to desk	

to respond. In other words, teachers must convey a sense of caring about the learner before engagement can take place. Engagement techniques alone (eliciting the desired behavior, providing feedback, individualizing instruction, praising, and monitoring) will not be sufficient to actively engage students in the learning process unless they are accompanied by the appropriate expressions of nurturance and caring (Noddings, 1992), such as the following:

- Use culturally appropriate examples to clarify concepts and model performance. "Let me give you an example that will help you see the relationship."
- Accept the student's way of understanding new concepts. "That's an interesting answer. Would you like to tell us how you arrived at it?"
- Reduce feelings of competitiveness. "Today, those who wish to can work with a partner on the practice exercise."
- Increase opportunities for social reinforcement. "If you like, you can ask someone sitting nearby how they worked the problem."
- Facilitate group achievement. "When you're finished with your work, you can join another group to help them solve the problem."

- Praise and support students regardless of who they are or how they perform. "Those of you who have finished the first part, keep working. I'll be helping the others."
- Use and expect culturally appropriate eye contact with students. "Amanda, I'm going to sit down next to you and watch you work the first problem."
- Recognize longer pauses and slower tempo. "Take your time. I'll wait for you to think of an answer."
- Respond to unique or different questions during a response. "You're asking about something else. Let me give you that answer, and then we'll go back to the first question."
- Balance compliments and reinforcement equally. "Let's not forget, both Angel and Damon got the right answer, but in different ways."

Although much is still unknown about culturally diverse and special populations, one thing is clear: Students of any culture and background are more likely to engage in the learning process in an atmosphere that

1. Emphasizes the importance of unique learner responses

2. Reduces feelings of individual competitiveness
3. Teaches social reinforcement and peer interaction
4. Conveys a sense of nurturance and caring

In the remaining chapters, we will turn our attention to two equally important lenses through which to observe classrooms. These lenses are student success and higher thought processes. As we turn now to our next lens, student success, keep in mind the significant impact of the dimensions of student engagement studied in this chapter.

For More Information

The body of educational research that has come to be known as effective school research identifies the practice of monitoring student learning as an essential component of high-quality education. Careful monitoring of student progress is shown in the literature to be one of the major factors differentiating effective schools and teachers from ineffective ones. Indeed, analyses that have sought to determine the relative effectiveness of different instructional practices have identified monitoring student progress as a strong predictor of student achievement. School improvement research conducted by the Northwest Regional Educational Laboratory identifies the key activities pursued by teachers to keep track of the progress of learners for purposes of making instructional decisions and providing student feedback. You can learn about the results of this innovative study online at www.nwrel.org/scpd/sirs/2/cu4.html.

Key Term

meaningful verbal praise, 162

Activities*

1. Using the checklist provided in Instrument 10.1 as your guide, observe a lesson for signs of student engagement. At the end of your observation, add a brief written description to each box, highlighting at least one reason why you chose to place each of your check marks as you did.
2. Using the examples of 5-point scales shown in Chapter 4, convert the positively stated indicators of student engagement listed in Table 10.1 into the form of a Likert scale. Consider the vertical and horizontal placement of each indicator on the page, whether words will be affixed to all or only some of the response blanks, and what response alternatives will be best suited to each question. Show your scale to a classmate who has also constructed a 5-point scale. Together, create a single revised version, incorporating the best features of both scales.
3. Using the form provided in Instrument 10.2 for recording eliciting activities and their proximity in time to the presentation of content, observe a classroom for an entire lesson. Total the number of entries you have made in each column and in each row of the form. List any other eliciting activities that you observed during the lesson and include them in your totals. What was the preferred communication channel for presenting eliciting activities in this classroom (oral, written, or visual)? How close were the eliciting activities to the presentation of content in this classroom?
4. Using the categories of differentiated and self-regulating learning activities provided in Instrument 10.3 and any others that you believe are relevant, identify one example from a classroom you have observed. List your example on an index card, with the grade and subject matter (if applicable) to which the activity pertains. Place your card with those of your classmates in a central location, so that everyone can read and copy these cards for the grades and subject matter most relevant to their teaching specialization.
5. Using the record in Instrument 10.4, observe for at least one period the praise provided by two different teachers teaching similar content at approximately the same level. Total the number of entries of praise for each of the three delivery modes, the first two types of praise combined, and the third and fourth

*Some of these activities may be grouped into a common activity, divided among classmates, and completed from a single observation.

types of praise combined. Recall that the last combined category represents instances of meaningful praise. Using the formula

$$\frac{\text{Number of incidents of praise}}{\text{Number of minutes of observation}} \times 60 =$$

Praise rate/Hour

calculate the praise rate for each of the three modes of delivery and then for each of the two (combined) types of praise. In each of the two classrooms, what is the ratio of the number of incidents of the first two types of praise to the number of incidents of the last two types of praise? Did you find more instances of meaningful praise in one classroom than in the others? How would you account for the differences in terms of the teacher's personality, student ability, and lesson content?

6. Observe part of a lesson involving seatwork (e.g., students completing exercises in a workbook, on a handout, or in a text), during which the teacher is monitoring and checking student progress. Draw a visual map of the classroom and indicate the placement of each occupied seat. During the seatwork, determine (and record) whether the student occupying each seat on the map appears engaged or disengaged by scanning each student consecutively. Enter codes, such as + for engaged and – for disengaged. Use 0 for any student whose engagement cannot be determined. Afterward draw a series of connected lines indicating the path taken by the teacher to monitor the work of individual students. Do you see any relationship between the path taken by the teacher and your codes for engaged and disengaged students?

7. Using Instrument 10.5, which combines mode of feedback, duration of contact, and teacher movement, observe a classroom in which students are responding to an eliciting activity. What mode of feedback is preferred by this teacher? What is the average duration for each of the three modes of feedback? Were all zones covered?

11

Measuring Student Success

The Little Elf

I met a little Elf-man once,

Down where the lilies blow.

I asked him why he was so small

And why he didn't grow.

He slightly frowned and with his eye

He looked me through and through.

"I'm quite as big for me," said he,

"As you are big for you."

J. K. Bangs

"The Little Elf" by John Kendrick Bangs from *The Posy Ring: A Book of Verse for Children* (1903), chosen and classified by Kate Douglas Wiggins and Nora Archibald Smith.

One of the great challenges of teaching is creating an environment in which your students can succeed and yet be challenged enough to grow. Add to this the need to evaluate student growth and progress—to decide "how big" a student is—and you have what some educators view as an insurmountable task. How do effective teachers encourage student success? And how do they know when it occurs? The answers to these questions are critical for understanding effective teaching.

As we saw from the previous chapter, an important focus of research on student engagement has been the level of difficulty at which content is presented. One way of determining level of difficulty is to measure the rate at which students understand and correctly complete exercises based on the material taught. Three measures of success have been used to gauge level of difficulty: high success, in which the student understands the task and makes only occasional errors; moderate success, in which the student has partial understanding but makes substantive errors; and low success, in which the student does not understand the task at all and makes many errors. Findings indicate that as the teacher becomes more task oriented and student engagement goes up, the learner can master more difficult content with higher rates of success.

For the direct instruction model, where knowledge, comprehension, and application outcomes are desired, a moderate to high rate of success on practice problems, workbook assignments, and oral exercises usually corresponds with higher levels of task orientation and student engagement in the learning process, higher levels of student self-esteem, and more positive attitudes toward the subject taught (Bennett, Desforges, Cockburn, & Wilkinson, 1981; Marzano, Pickering, & Pollock, 2004; Zemelman, Daniels, & Hyde, 2005).

The average student in a typical classroom spends about half of his time working on tasks that provide the opportunity for high success. Researchers have discovered that students who spend more than the average time in high-success activities during expository or didactic teaching have higher achievement scores, better retention, and more positive attitudes toward school. These findings suggest that, during direct instruction, students should spend from 60 to 80% of their time on tasks that allow an opportunity for moderate to high levels of success and that students should make only occasional careless errors the first time through the material (Rosenshine, 1983).

During indirect instruction, where the analysis, synthesis, and evaluation levels of student outcomes are emphasized, the success rate attained may be less important than the conditions under which it occurs. Here the goal is to achieve moderate success, but also to emphasize **functional errors** (Watson & Steege, 2003), which occur when a wrong or partially correct response prompts additional cues (e.g., probes from teacher, responses of other students) that can modify the task ("Can you think of an example of your own?") or situation ("Could you write it on the board?") to help the learner attain success on repeated trials.

This chapter uses the phrase "moderate to high rates of success" to represent both the functional errors important to attaining higher behavioral outcomes (e.g., analysis, synthesis, and evaluation) and the correct, quick, and firm responses important to attaining outcomes at lower levels of complexity (e.g., knowledge, comprehension, and application). A moderate to high success rate helps produce mastery of the lesson content, but even more important, it provides an opportunity for the student to use learned knowledge in practical ways, such as asking questions, making decisions, and solving problems. Tasks providing moderate to high success rates allow the pieces that are learned to fall into place, a crucial final step in the learning process. Some classrooms do not devote enough time to this stage of learning. Organizing and planning instruction that yields moderate to high success rates without being boring or repetitive is a key behavior for effective teaching. In this chapter, you will learn how to observe some of the instructional activities and tasks that influence student success—and how to improve your students' chances for success.

DIMENSIONS OF STUDENT SUCCESS

Table 11.1 summarizes behaviors that promote student engagement in the learning process at moderate to high rates of success.

TABLE 11.1 Indicators for Rates of Student Success

More Effective Rates of Student Success	Less Effective Rates of Student Success
1. Established unit and lesson content that reflects prior learning (for example, planning lesson sequences that consider lesson-relevant prior information)	Fails to sequence learning in advance to ensure that all task-relevant prior knowledge has been taught before moving to next lesson
2. Provides mediated feedback to extend and enhance student learning	Leaves students on their own to practice and learn immediately after presenting new content; waits until next day to show correct responses
3. Plans units and lessons at, or slightly above, learners' current level of understanding (for example, establishes bite-sized lessons that can be easily digested by learners at their current level of functioning)	Packages instruction in chunks that are too large or too small (for example, teaches a lesson that is too complex too early in an instructional sequence)
4. Plans transitions to new material in easy-to-grasp steps (for example, changes instructional stimuli according to a preestablished thematic pattern so that each new lesson is seen as an extension of previous lessons)	Changes instructional topics or perspectives abruptly from one lesson to another without themes and interconnections
5. Varies the pace at which stimuli are presented and continually builds toward a climax or key event	Maintains same pace continuously, leading to a monotonous and static level of intensity and expectation

1. Establishing unit and lesson content that reflects prior learning
2. Providing mediated feedback to extend and enhance student learning
3. Planning units and lessons at, or slightly above, the learners' current level of understanding
4. Making transitions to new content in small, easy-to-grasp steps
5. Establishing momentum that keeps students engaged in the learning process

PRACTICE OBSERVING STUDENT SUCCESS: A DIALOGUE

The following dialogue illustrates several dimensions of student success. Review the dimensions in Table 11.1 and then read the dialogue using the checklist in Instrument 11.1 to look for signs of student success.

In this dialogue we look into Ms. Chau's classroom, where she is teaching her students the rules of writing. The curriculum guide specifies a unit on forming and punctuating possessives, but it is vague about how to teach this topic. Ms. Chau has decided to organize her lesson into rules for using possessives. Today's lesson, which will be used as a point of departure for introducing possessives, follows several previous lessons on the parts of speech.

Ms. Chau: Today we will learn how to avoid embarrassing errors such as this [Points to and circles an incorrectly punctuated possessive in a newspaper headline] when forming and punctuating possessives. At the end of the period, I will give each of you several examples of errors taken from my collection of mistakes found in newspapers and magazines. You will make the proper corrections and report them to the class. Who knows what a possessive is? [Bobby waves his hand.]

Bobby: It means you own something.

Ms. Chau: Yes, a possessive is a way to indicate ownership. It comes from the word *possession,* which means "something owned" or "something possessed." Forming possessives and punctuating them correctly can be difficult, as this newspaper example shows [Points to error in headline again], but I will give you two simple rules that will help you form possessives correctly. Before we can form possessives, however, we must know who or what is doing the possessing. Mary, can you recall the parts of speech from last week's lesson? [Mary hesitates and then nods.] What part of speech is most likely to own or possess something?

Mary: Well, umm . . . I think . . . I think a noun can own something.

Ms. Chau: Yes. A noun can own something. What is an example of a noun that owns something? Tommy.

Tommy: I don't know.

Ms. Chau: Debbie.

Debbie: Not sure.

Ms. Chau: Ricky.

Ricky: A student can own a pencil. The word *student* is a noun.

Ms. Chau: Good. Who can remember our definition for a noun? [Pointing to Jim]

Jim: It's a person, place, or thing.

Ms. Chau: Good. Our first rule will be: Use the possessive form whenever an "*of* phrase" can be substituted for a noun. [Ms. Chau points to this rule, which has been written on the board.] Let's look at some phrases on the board to see when to apply this rule. Darnell, what does the first one say?

Darnell: The daughter of the policeman.

Ms. Chau: How else could we express the same idea of ownership?

Mary: We could say "the policeman's daughter."

Ms. Chau: And we could say "the policeman's daughter" because I can substitute a phrase starting with *of* and ending with *policeman* for the noun, *policeman*. Notice how easily I could switch the placement of *policeman* and *daughter* by using the connective word *of*. Whenever this can be done, you can form a possessive by adding an apostrophe and an *s* to the noun following *of*. Now we have the phrase [Writes on board] "policeman's daughter" [points to the apostrophe]. Keisha, what about our next example, "holiday of three days"?

Keisha: We could say "three day's holiday."

Ms. Chau: Come up and write that on the board just the way it should be printed in the school paper. [Keisha writes "three day's holiday."] Would anyone want to change anything? [Susan raises her hand, and Ms. Chau nods.]

Susan: I'm not sure, but I think I would put the apostrophe after the *s* in *days*.

Ms. Chau: You're right, which leads to our second rule: If the word for which we are denoting ownership already ends in an *s*, place the apostrophe after, not before, the *s*. This is an important rule to remember because it accounts for many of the mistakes that are made in forming possessives. As I write this rule on the board, copy these two rules into your notebooks for use later. [Ms. Chau finishes writing the second rule on the board.] Now let's take a moment to convert each of the phrases on the overhead to the possessive form. Write down your answer to the first one. When I see all heads up, I will write the correct answer. [All heads are up.] Good. Now watch how I change this first one to the possessive form. Pay particular attention to where I place the apostrophe, and then check your answer with mine. [Ms. Chau converts "delay of a month" to "month's delay."] Any problems? [Ms. Chau pauses for any response.] Okay, do the next one. [After all heads are up, Ms. Chau converts "den of lions" to "lions' den."] Any problems? [Darnell looks distressed.] Darnell, what did you write?

Darnell: [Pronouncing each letter] L-I-O-N-apostrophe-S.

Ms. Chau: What is the noun?

Darnell: [Still sounding uncertain] *Lions.*

Ms. Chau: Look at what you wrote for the second rule. What does it say?

Darnell: Add the apostrophe after the *s* when the word already ends in an *s*. Oh, I get it. The noun already has the *s*, so it would be *s* apostrophe. That's the mistake you showed us in the headline, isn't it?

Ms. Chau: Now you've got it. Let's continue. [Ms. Chau proceeds with the following phrases in the same manner: "speech of the president" to "president's speech," the "television set of Mr. Eggar" to "Mr. Eggar's television set," and "pastimes of boys" to "boys' pastimes."] Now open your workbooks to the exercise on page 87. Starting with the first row, let's go around the room and hear your possessives for each of the sentences listed. Spell the word indicating ownership aloud so we can tell if you've placed the apostrophe in the right place. Debbie.

Debbie: [Looking at "wings of geese"] "Geeses wings'"—spelled W-I-N-G-S-apostrophe.

Ms. Chau: That's not correct. What word is doing the possessing?

Debbie: The geese, so it must be G-E-E-S-E-apostrophe-S.

Ms. Chau: Good. Next.

Alan: "The author's work" . . . spelled A-U-T-H-O-R-apostrophe-S.

Ms. Chau: Okay, next.

TIME TO REFLECT

Which of the five dimensions of student success did you see in the dialogue? Recall that students should experience a moderate to high success rate that helps produce mastery of the lesson content and provides an opportunity for them to use learned knowledge in practical ways, such as answering questions or solving problems. Tasks providing moderate to high success rates allow the pieces that are learned to fall into place, a crucial final step in the learning process. Organizing and planning instruction that yields moderate to high success rates without being boring or repetitive—or wasting time—is a key behavior for effective teaching.

Planning Unit and Lesson Content That Reflects Prior Learning

As you can guess, obtaining a moderate to high success rate begins with unit planning: Unit outcomes should be identified, and a logical sequence of lessons should be developed to achieve those outcomes. Surprisingly, teachers sometimes plan units with little or no consideration given to lesson sequence. Although certain unit outcomes may be achieved by giving learners content in any order, the cost in instructional time can be considerable. The result of this type of planning is often heard in expressions such as "I've run out of time," "We couldn't get to topic X," or "We've had too many interruptions to finish the unit."

Effective unit planning involves arranging lessons in a sequence that works for, not against, you. Recall from Chapter 7 on lesson clarity that **lesson-relevant prior knowledge** is knowledge preceding a lesson that helps students connect new ideas with what they already know and have experienced. Some teachers might not realize that making each new lesson relate to a previous lesson can result in great savings in instructional time. Lesson-relevant prior knowledge that is reviewed or stimulated immediately preceding or as close as possible to the lesson or lessons in which it will be needed can result in time savings from not having to reteach important skills and concepts required for the day's lesson or not having to reteach an entire lesson after it is discovered that the necessary information has not been learned. Effective unit planning results in a sequence of instruction that gradually builds to unit outcomes in a logical, systematic order. Without unit plans, content might just be randomly thrown at learners, some of whom could be struggling to make the transition from earlier lessons.

Lesson plans result in higher rates of success and increased achievement when

1. *Unit* outcomes are identified at higher levels of behavioral complexity than *lesson* outcomes.
2. Lesson content is planned so that outcomes of previously taught lessons are instrumental in building toward and achieving the outcomes of subsequent lessons.

3. Lesson content derives from unit outcomes in small pieces suitable for presentation in one or two instructional periods.
4. Lesson content is added to or rearranged when necessary to provide the lesson-relevant prior knowledge required for subsequent learning.

When lessons are planned without any thought to a higher-level unit outcome, attention falls exclusively on each individual lesson without considering the relationships among the lessons. The result of such an assembly of isolated lesson outcomes could be confusion, anxiety, and resentment on the part of the students, regardless of how meticulously each lesson is delivered or how effective it is in accomplishing its stated, but isolated, outcome.

Let's gain some insight into this dimension by looking at how Ms. Chau's lesson fits into a sequence of instruction on the parts of speech. A graphic plan of the content in the lesson and in the previous lesson might appear as shown in Figure 11.1.

Notice from this plan that knowledge of the parts of speech was needed for Ms. Chau's lesson. This content had to precede the lesson for students to be able to recognize the nouns used in forming and punctuating possessives. Also notice the progression of outcomes from the knowledge level to the application level. This series of topics began with teaching the definition of a noun and ended with applying this knowledge in combination with Rules 1 and 2 to form and punctuate possessives. Thus, this series of topics ended at a higher behavioral outcome than it began and proceeded in a least-complex (knowledge) to most-complex (application) order.

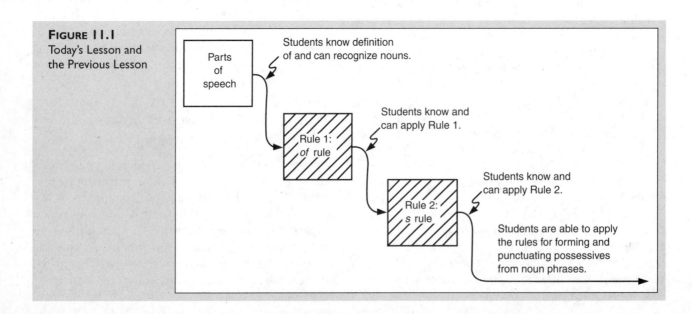

FIGURE 11.1
Today's Lesson and the Previous Lesson

Ms. Chau relied on an understanding of lesson-relevant prior knowledge to begin her lesson when she asked, "Who can remember our definition for a noun?" Fortunately Jim remembered, and this provided Ms. Chau the opportunity to present her first rule, which presupposed a knowledge of nouns. Ms. Chau's lesson might presuppose other lesson-relevant knowledge as well. Some of this knowledge could be familiar to students from other contexts—for example, recognition of an apostrophe and a prepositional phrase. By examining the success rate in Ms. Chau's classroom and the types of correctives used to remediate incorrect or partially correct responses, we gain an impression of how well her lesson-relevant prior knowledge has been taught. To determine the success rate of students in this classroom, let's examine the question–answer–feedback sequences used by Ms. Chau to evaluate and correct her students' responses.

In Figure 11.2 all the key question–response sequences in the dialogue are coded using a format suggested by Good and Brophy (2007) and recorded with Instruments 11.2a and 11.2b. Notice that the data are recorded according to three categories of information: correctness of student answer (right, partially right, wrong response, no response), teacher response to student answer (praise, affirm, no reaction, negate, criticize), and teacher feedback to student (gives answer, explains, asks other, etc.). To determine the success rate (columns 1 and 2) of this sequence of 15 questions, we would divide the total number of correct (+) or correct plus partially correct (+/−) responses by the total number of student responses: $(9/15)100 = 60\%$. Because there were no partially correct responses, our final percentage will be based solely on the completely correct answers provided in column 1. Question 7, directed to Darnell, received no student response tally because it

FIGURE 11.2 Coding Form and Example Data for Observing Success Rate

Columns after Student: *Student Response* = (+, +/−, −, 0); *Teacher Response* = (++, +, 0, −, −−); *Teacher Feedback* = (Gives Answer, Explains, Asks Other, Other Calls, Repeats, Clue, New Question)

Number	Student	+	+/−	−	0	++	+	0	−	−−	Gives Answer	Explains	Asks Other	Other Calls	Repeats	Clue	New Question
1	Bobby	✓					✓					✓					
2	Mary	✓					✓										
3	Tommy			✓				✓						✓			
4	Debbie			✓				✓						✓			
5	Ricky	✓				✓											
6	Jim	✓				✓											
7	Darnell							✓									✓
8	Mary	✓					✓					✓					
9	Keisha			✓				✓									✓
10	Susan	✓					✓					✓					
11	Darnell				✓			✓								✓	
12	Darnell	✓					✓										
13	Debbie				✓				✓							✓	
14	Debbie	✓				✓											
15	Alan	✓						✓									
Totals		9	0	3	2	3	5	6	1	0	0	3	2	0	0	2	2

*See Instrument 11.2b for an explanation of the symbols and codes used.

was nonsubstantive, asking only that Darnell read what was written on the board. It did not require that he apply any of the content of the lesson. Thus, the number of correct student responses to the total number of substantive questions asked by Ms. Chau was actually 9/14, not 9/15, revising the success rate upward to about 64%.

As noted previously, research suggests that for direct instruction, a success rate of 60 to 80% the first time through the material is optimal for achievement, retention, and a positive attitude toward the subject matter. This success rate helps produce mastery of the lesson content and correct, quick, and firm response patterns, while ensuring that the material is not so easy that it becomes boring and disengages students from the learning process. It also ensures that new content is covered, affording students an opportunity to learn. We saw that Ms. Chau's classroom met and might have slightly exceeded this mark. It is not possible to know what Ms. Chau's final success rate for this lesson will be or how heterogeneous her class is, which could require adjustments of the flow and difficulty of her presentation later in the lesson. But from the trend established thus far, we would expect a high success rate by the end of the lesson as students are confronted with more practice opportunities and have a greater opportunity to learn from the mistakes of others. A 60% success rate at the beginning of a practice activity changing to an 80% or better success rate by the end is a good target to shoot for.

Observing Unit and Lesson Content That Reflects Prior Learning

As we have seen, lessons should be sequenced so that all information required for a lesson has been taught in preceding lessons. The sequence of lessons within a unit can be arranged by describing the unit goal and the objectives for each individual lesson, as shown previously in Figure 11.1. This graphic format can be used for any number of lessons, with the sequence shown by connecting arrows. The key to observing this dimension is noting the relationships among lessons. For each lesson objective, two questions should be asked: Has all lesson-relevant information needed to attain the objective been taught earlier in the sequence? And when prerequisite skills are required for a lesson, have they been taught (or scheduled to be reviewed) close in time to the lesson in which they are needed? To answer these questions and complete a graphic plan of the unit, the following information will be needed from the classroom teacher who will be observed.

Unit title: _____

Unit goal or objective that expresses the highest level of behavior to be attained (knowledge, comprehension, application, etc.):

_____

_____

Number of lessons in the unit: _____

Objective of first lesson: _____

Highest level of behavior to be attained (e.g., knowledge):

_____

_____

Objective of second lesson: _____

Highest level of behavior to be attained (e.g., comprehension):

_____

_____

This recording format should be continued for each lesson in the unit. The level of behavioral outcome can be determined from lesson plans, text, workbook, handouts, and exercises and then expressed as outcomes in the cognitive, affective, and psychomotor domains. Table 11.2 provides a guide for selecting behaviors in the cognitive, affective, and psychomotor domains.

From the information already recorded, a diagram like the one in Figure 11.1 can be completed. Connecting arrows can show the sequence of lessons planned for the unit, if sequence is relevant, and the boxes can show the objective for each lesson and for the entire unit. As behavioral complexity increases (e.g., from knowledge outcomes in early lessons to comprehension or application outcomes in later lessons), the objectives of previous lessons should reflect the required prerequisite behavior for the subsequent lessons. If this is not the case, or if you believe the intended lesson sequence can be improved in some way, redraw your graphic unit plan to indicate a lesson sequence in which all required lesson-relevant knowledge is taught prior to each lesson.

Providing Mediated Feedback to Extend and Enhance Learning

A second behavior for achieving moderate to high rates of student success is the provision of feedback that can extend and enhance an initially crude or incomplete response. During guided practice, when the desired behavior is elicited for the first time, correctives should be given immediately after the learner's initial response. In the case of language learning, it is especially helpful for English language learners if

TABLE 11.2 A Guide to Selecting Behaviors in the Cognitive, Affective, and Psychomotor Domains

Cognitive	Affective	Psychomotor
1. *Knowledge*. Learner can recognize and recall facts (define terms, recall names/dates, identify words)	1. *Receive*. Learner is aware of listening to or passively attending to certain stimuli.	1. *Imitation*. Learner, when exposed to a visual model, can repeat the model.
2. *Comprehension*. Learner can interpret, translate, summarize, or paraphrase material.	2. *Respond*. Learner complies with expectations by participating or obeying.	2. *Manipulation*. Learner can follow written directions independent of a visual model to complete an action.
3. *Application*. Learner can use material in a situation that is different from that in which it was originally learned.	3. *Value*. Learner displays behavior consistent with a belief or attitude in situations with which she is not forced to comply.	3. *Precision*. Learner attains skill in performing an action independent of either a visual or verbal model, attaining accuracy and control.
4. *Analysis*. Learner can separate a complex topic into its parts, drawing comparisons and establishing relationships among the elements.	4. *Organization*. Learner is committed to a set of values and displays, provides rationale for, or communicates the values.	4. *Articulation*. Learner can coordinate a series of acts by establishing appropriate sequence and accomplishing harmony or internal consistency among different acts.
5. *Synthesis*. Learner can combine pieces, parts, or elements and arrange them into a new, original form.	5. *Characterization*. Learner's total behavior is consistent with values (internalizes them).	5. *Naturalization*. Learner can routinely perform an action; attains spontaneity, automaticity, and smoothness.
6. *Evaluation*. Learner can make decisions, judge, or select based on a set of criteria.		

teachers are explicit in making comparisons between students' native language and English (Cheng, 1996). Lockwood and Secada (1999) also point out that the use of visuals helps many diverse learners better understand the correction.

As noted in Chapter 10 on student engagement, the amount of time between practice and feedback is one of the most important elements of learning. The longer feedback is delayed, the less likely it is to influence the learner's performance on subsequent attempts to produce the behavior because the learner must maintain a mental image of the first response for the feedback to be effective. Unfortunately, mental images fade quickly, especially in young learners, so the effectiveness of the feedback deteriorates rapidly with any delay. For the learner to link feedback to his response, the corrective must follow immediately—for example, by calling out the right answer after each practice item has been completed or by having a student write on the board how a partially correct answer was attained. Also, to promote spontaneity and risk-taking behavior, which are necessary for revising and refining what might be an initially crude response, feedback should be administered in a noncritical atmosphere.

Researchers have identified four categories of student response and strategies for handling these responses to extend and enhance an initially incorrect or incomplete response. The first category, which most teachers hope to inspire, is *correct, quick, and firm* student responses. Although such responses most frequently occur during the later stages of a direct instruction lesson, they can occur at almost any time and in the context of other types of instructional goals. A moderate to high percentage of correct, quick, and firm responses is important if students are to stay actively engaged in the learning process. The best teacher response to a correct, quick, and firm student response is to affirm the correct response by indicating the reason it is correct (e.g., "You followed all the steps," "The picture you drew is lifelike," "You followed the directions carefully"). This increases the potential for feedback to accomplish its intended results. If time does not permit, quickly move on to another student with a similar question. The teacher should keep the lesson moving at a brisk pace, involving as many students in the practice exercise and covering as many problems as possible. Attaining a moderate to high rate of correct answers will establish a rhythm and momentum that will heighten student attention and engagement and provide for a high level of task orientation. Also, a brisk pace of right answers, especially during direct instruction, will help ensure that irrelevant student responses and classroom distractions are kept to a minimum.

The second category of student response is *correct but hesitant* responses, which frequently occur in a practice or question-and-answer session. It is important to provide positive feedback to the student who supplies a correct but hesitant response. The first feedback provided should be a positive, reinforcing statement, such as "Good" or "That's correct," because the correct but hesitant response is likely to be remembered more easily when it has been linked to a warm and acknowledging reply. Then, to firm up the student's confidence, ask him or her another similar question. This helps to make the student's subsequent responses to the same type of question correct, quick, and firm.

Affirmative replies are rarely sufficient in themselves to effect significant changes in subsequent responses of the same type unless the reasons behind the hesitation are addressed. Although discovering the precise reason for a student's hesitant response is desirable, a quick restatement of the facts, rules, or steps needed to obtain the right answer often accomplishes the same end more efficiently. This restatement will aid the student giving the correct but hesitant response and reduce subsequent wrong or hesitant responses from other students who hear the restatement and incorporate it into their own responses.

The third category of student response includes *careless incorrect* responses. Sometimes as many as 20% of student responses fall into this category, depending on the time of day and the students' level of inattentiveness. The temptation is to scold, admonish, or even verbally punish students for responding thoughtlessly when they know the correct response. Researchers and experienced teachers agree that attempting to deal emotionally with this type of problem (e.g., with statements such as "I'm ashamed of you," "That's a dumb mistake," or "I thought you were brighter than that") often does more harm than good.

Verbal punishment rarely teaches a learner to avoid careless mistakes. Experience has shown that the rhythm and momentum built and maintained through a brisk and lively pace can easily be broken by off-task attention to an individual student. Emotional reaction rarely has a positive effect; the best procedure is to acknowledge that the answer is wrong and then move immediately to the next student for the correct response. The point will be made to the careless student when the opportunity to respond and receive recognition is immediately passed to the next student.

The final category includes responses that are *incorrect because of a lack of knowledge*. These errors typically occur, sometimes in large numbers, during the initial stages of a lesson or unit and throughout indirect instruction. Providing hints, using probes, or changing the question or task demand to a simpler one that engages the student in finding the correct response is more desirable than merely giving the student the correct response. The goal is not to get the correct answer from the student in any way possible, but to engage the learner in a process to find the right answer ("Let's go through the steps again," "Think about the question some and then try again," "Can someone in the class help?"). Any time an instructional task can channel a student's thoughts to result in the right answer without the teacher giving that answer, a framework has been provided for producing a correct response in all subsequent problems of a similar nature.

Some common strategies for mediating feedback when student answers are incorrect but careless or incorrect because of lack of knowledge include:

- Reviewing key facts or rules needed for a correct response
- Explaining the steps used to reach a correct response
- Asking the learner to take time to think before moving on to the next learner
- Prompting with clues or hints (adjusting the situation or context)
- Taking a different path with a similar problem and guiding the student to the correct solution (changing the task)

The use of these strategies to make on-the-spot adjustments in content difficulty and pacing to accommodate individual learning needs is called **teacher mediation** (Duffy & Roehler, 1989). The teacher's role during mediation is to adjust the instructional dialogue to help students construct their own meanings and restructure their responses, moving them closer to the intended outcome.

Teacher mediation is accomplished by adjusting the pace and level of content (through brief reviews, questions, prompts, and wait time) to provide cognitive stimulation at the proper time to help the learner acquire the intended outcome through her own reasoning. This on-the-spot adjustment in the difficulty and pacing of lesson content should be targeted to the level of content difficulty and behavioral complexity from which the student can most benefit at that moment.

This level of content difficulty and behavioral outcome, called the learner's **zone of maximum response opportunity** (Borich, 2010; Vygotsky, 1978), is the zone of behavior that, if stimulated by the teacher, will bring a learner's response to the next level of refinement. Therefore a teacher's response directed at the zone of maximum response opportunity must be at or near the learner's current level of understanding, but also designed to lift the learner's response to the next, higher level. The teacher's response directed to the zone of maximum response opportunity need not elicit the correct answer because the learner at that precise moment may be incapable of benefiting from it. It should, however, encourage the learner to refine an initially incomplete response. The concept of a *zone* affords the teacher latitude within which to construct and create meanings and understandings that consider the unique learning needs of the student. Because this type of corrective feedback is delivered orally within the naturally occurring dialogue of the classroom, its effects can benefit the entire class.

Typically, success rates for the entire class are lower during indirect instruction than rates during direct instruction, sometimes as low as 40 to 60% compared with 60 to 80%. Because time and breadth of content do not allow sampling the behavior of large numbers of students during indirect instruction, a few students who reflect the general composition of the class can be chosen to check whether the concept, pattern, or relationship being taught has been learned by most of the class. If not, teacher mediation and the learners' zones of maximum response opportunity can play a critical role in promoting a gentle interplay between learner and teacher, pulling and pushing each participant in a student-response–teacher-reaction dialogue that helps each learner climb to the next rung of the learning ladder.

In what ways could students learn from their mistakes in Ms. Chau's classroom? Ms. Chau tended to praise or affirm correct answers and only occasionally reacted neutrally to or negated a wrong answer. This suggests that Ms. Chau places more emphasis on motivating students to risk making a response—any response—than on passing judgment on the responses given. Presumably her goal at this stage of the lesson was to get and keep students responding by making them feel comfortable enough so that their risk-taking behavior will not embarrass or humiliate them if it produces a wrong, illogical, or even funny response. Thus, Ms. Chau tended to ignore nonresponses and sometimes even wrong responses, quickly moving to another student.

Finally, Ms. Chau tended to provide feedback to her students, either by explaining a correct response further or, in the case of a wrong response, by providing clues useful in finding the correct response. An example of explaining occurred after Ms. Chau asked her first question: "Who knows what a possessive is?" Bobby replied, "It means you own something." Ms. Chau responded, "Yes, a possessive is a way of indicating ownership. It comes from the word *possession*, which means 'something owned' or 'something possessed.'" Here the teacher not only affirmed the response, but used it as an opportunity to explain more fully the meaning of Bobby's response. An example of probing occurred when Darnell looked distressed about giving a wrong response ("L-I-O-N-apostrophe-S") to "home of lions." The teacher responded, "What is the noun?" thereby focusing Darnell on the content of Rule 2. Still, Darnell seemed not to understand, so the teacher focused him still more with the probe, "Look at what you wrote for the second rule." These examples indicate how student responses, whether correct, partially correct, or incorrect, can be followed up with explanations and probes that further enhance the original response and provide new content. A moderate to high success rate will depend on the teacher's liberal use of feedback that can correct and expand wrong or partially wrong student responses in ways that benefit the entire class.

Observing Mediated Feedback to Extend and Enhance Learning

Our second behavior for achieving a moderate to high success rate can be recorded using the student-response–teacher-reaction instrument shown in Instrument 11.2a. Recall that a student's response (Right, Part right, Wrong, No answer) is recorded, followed by the teacher's reaction to the response (Praise, Affirm, No reaction, Negate, Criticize), followed by the type of feedback given by the teacher (Gives answer, Explains, Asks other, etc.). This instrument is suitable for not only for observing and recording student success rate pertaining to oral questions but also for understanding student success, because both the teacher's reaction to a student response and the nature of the feedback given are recorded in sequence. Also, by tallying the number of correct oral responses given by students during a practice exercise, the observer can determine the percentage of correct responses. Figure 11.3 provides some example data and Instrument 11.2b provides definitions of the coding categories. Some coding categories may be combined (e.g., Right with Part right and Praise with Affirm), reducing the number of coding categories for your initial observations.

In the example data for Dave and Mark provided in Figure 11.3, the first question–answer–feedback sequence indicates that Dave responds correctly, after which the teacher praises him and then explains why the answer is correct. In the second exchange, Mark responds to a question with a partially correct answer; the teacher affirms the answer, but then gives the complete answer followed by an explanation of why it is correct. After a sufficient number of exchanges, the success rate for all students can be determined by adding the total number of correct (or correct plus partially correct) student responses, dividing by the total completed rows, and multiplying the result by 100. The final result is an estimate of the success rate of all students expressed as a percentage—60 to 80% is desirable the first time through the material if the lesson is didactic or expository. If problem solving, inquiry, or discovery learning is the goal of the lesson, a success rate of approximately 40 to 60% (from a steering group) may be more appropriate (40% representing about the minimum percentage of correct or partially correct responses needed to establish a degree of classroom momentum).

An observer can examine why a success rate below, equal to, or above this mark was achieved by looking for patterns of teacher feedback. In the Dave and Mark example, the teacher might achieve a moderate to high success rate by always praising or affirming a response when it is correct or even partially correct, and then explaining to the student (with all the class listening) why the response is correct. Patterns in other classrooms might indicate that praise, affirmative explanation, and clues tend to correspond with a high degree of teacher mediation in which correct responses are built around the students' own interpretations and meanings of content shared in the context of a classroom dialogue.

When student success is the primary focus of the observation, Instrument 11.3 with its abbreviated format can be used to simplify the observation and recording process. Complete this record for a lesson in which oral responses are required—for example, in the form of oral questions to the class, recitation of workbook content, or responses to items on a written activity sheet. Try to observe several lessons that vary in the complexity of the student outcome(s) expected (e.g., knowledge vs. application) and then compare success rates. Initial success rates generally are higher for knowledge outcomes than for higher-order outcomes.

A 60 to 80% success rate should be attained the first time through the material if task-relevant prior skills have been taught and the instructional content is clearly presented. A 60% success rate is not uncommon when only the percentage of right answers is considered, but close to an 80% success rate should be attained when the number of entries in both the right and partially right columns are combined, especially if the lesson is targeted to student outcomes at the knowledge or comprehension levels.

Another way of calculating student success rate is averaging the number of correct student responses on a class, workbook, or homework assignment and determining the percentage of students who attain a score of, say, 80% correct. For example, assume 10 students achieved the following scores after an assignment worth 30 points: 24, 16, 24, 25, 30, 26, 29, 24, 21, 28. Eight of the 10 students, or 80% of this class, achieved 80% or more correct responses. The average score among all students is 24.7, which is slightly above the 80% mark ($30 \times .80 = 24$) and indicates a moderate to high rate of success when going through the material for the first time.

An approach to determining success rate in a heterogeneous classroom is to record expected as well as actual scores of each student on a class, workbook, or homework assignment. For example, assume the following scores on a 30-point assignment were obtained from a heterogeneous group of 10 students: 18, 28, 16, 15, 22, 29, 18, 22, 24, 26. Ask the teacher before grading the assignment to indicate what score might be expected from each student on this assign-

FIGURE 11.3 Example Data for Dave and Mark

Number	Student	Student Response* +	Student Response* + −	Student Response* −	Student Response* 0	Teacher Response + +	Teacher Response +	Teacher Response 0	Teacher Response −	Teacher Response − −	Teacher Feedback Gives Answer	Teacher Feedback Explains	Teacher Feedback Asks Other	Teacher Feedback Other Calls	Teacher Feedback Repeats	Teacher Feedback Clue	Teacher Feedback New Question
	Dave	✓				✓						✓					
	Mark		✓			✓					✓	✓					

* + right, ± partially right, − wrong, 0 no response, + + praise, + affirm, 0 no response, − negate, − − criticize

TABLE 11.3 Expected versus Actual Scores for 10 Students

Student	Expected	Actual	Difference
1	14	18	+4
2	26	28	+2
3	16	16	0
4	12	15	+3
5	20	22	+2
6	24	29	+5
7	18	18	0
8	24	22	−2
9	20	24	+4
10	28	26	−2

Mean Actual Score = 21.8

ment, given his or her learning history with the subject matter being taught, with each expected score chosen to reflect a realistic degree of progress, given the student's prior performance. Now let's assume the expected scores have been recorded for each of the 10 students and placed next to their actual scores, as indicated in Table 11.3.

Using this method for determining success rate, we find that only four students, or 40% of this class, are expected to equal or exceed a score of 24, or 80% correct. The average of actual scores for this class is 21.8, indicating that the performance of the class on this assignment is below the 80% mark. Notice, however, that 8 of the 10 students met or exceeded expectations; only 2 did not. Therefore, in terms of student expectations, this heterogeneous class did fairly well. When classes are heterogeneous or include English language and special learners, absolute standards can be unrealistic indicators of success rate. In these cases, the percentage of students meeting or exceeding expectations, when formulated with a knowledge of the unique learning history of each learner, will be more indicative of the true success rate within a classroom.

Planning Units and Lessons at, or Slightly above, Students' Current Level of Understanding

The third behavior for achieving a moderate to high success rate is matching unit and lesson plans to the learners' current level of understanding. Experience has shown that units should cover less content than might be originally desired simply because the depth and breadth of content that is comprehensible to the teacher seldom is comprehensible at the same depth and breadth to learners. Units that ramble through many historical periods, physical laws, mathematical operations, social issues, or elements of reading may prevent learners from attaining the larger concepts, organizing principles, and relationships for which the unit was intended. Recent trends toward thematic teaching can help teachers avoid these pitfalls, but only if the themes that organize the unit are chosen carefully and in ways that help students understand content connections and relationships to their own lives (Roberts & Kellough, 2006).

Perhaps most perplexing to new teachers is deciding at which level of behavioral complexity a lesson should begin. Does a lesson always begin by teaching facts (to instill knowledge), or can a lesson begin with activities at the application, or even synthesis and decision-making, levels? All of these alternatives are possible, but each makes different assumptions about the behavioral characteristics of the students and the sequence of lessons that has gone before. Beginning a lesson or a sequence of lessons at the knowledge level (to list, recall, recite, etc.) assumes that the topic of the lesson is mostly new material. Such lessons usually occur at the beginning of a sequence of lessons that use this knowledge to build toward more complex behaviors, perhaps ending at the application, synthesis, or evaluation level. When no lesson-relevant prior knowledge is required, the starting point for the lesson is often at the knowledge or comprehension level. Lessons that begin at higher levels of behavioral complexity will require lesson-relevant prior knowledge.

The proper level of behavioral complexity with which to start the lesson, therefore, depends on where the lesson falls in the sequence of lessons. Typically, a unit plan should attempt to instill a range of behaviors and to end at a higher level of behavioral complexity than it began. Some units might begin at the application level and end at a higher one, provided a previous unit has taught the knowledge and understandings required. It is also possible in some content areas to move from one behavioral level to another within a single lesson. Although this becomes increasingly difficult when lessons start at the higher levels of behavioral complexity (e.g., analysis or synthesis) because of the instructional time required to achieve these more complex outcomes, it is possible and often desirable to move from knowledge to comprehension and even to application activities within a single lesson.

Finally, individual lesson content must be at the learner's current level of understanding if moderate

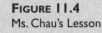

FIGURE 11.4
Ms. Chau's Lesson

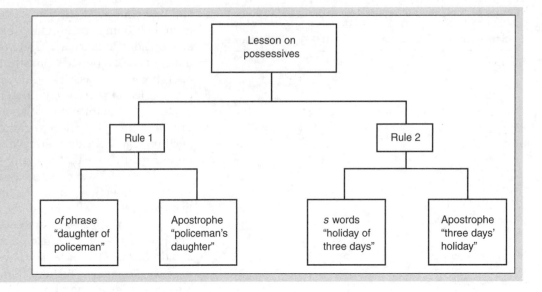

to high success rates are to be achieved. When lengthy guided practice or group discussion sessions do not provide moderate to high rates of success, lesson content may be too broad or too complex for learners. This is a sign that the content taught might not be bite-sized and that the material should have been divided into smaller segments. Keep in mind also that some unfinished lessons should be continued in other lessons, especially when the unfinished content represents important learning for subsequent lessons.

Do you think Ms. Chau's division of content was understandable to her students within the context of the single lesson we observed? Without knowing more about the current level of understanding of her students, the answer must be tentative. Sufficient signs exist, however, to suggest that Ms. Chau's selection of content for this lesson was understandable to most of her students. Two signs in particular point to the fact that Ms. Chau organized her content around her students' current level of understanding: She was able to achieve a 60 to 80% success rate within only a brief instructional period, and her division of content within the lesson was easily recognized by her students. Figure 11.4 shows how easy it is to identify the parts of her lesson and portray their relationship.

Each part is defined within the context of the lesson and labeled appropriately ("Rule 1," "Rule 2"). Definitions and examples are provided to aid the retention of each part ("daughter of policeman," "holiday of three days"). Also, the presentation is organized into stages, or events that prepare her learners to receive, understand, and practice what is presented: Her content is made more understandable by a lesson format that lets the content evolve gradually in small, distinctive steps. Table 11.4 reviews instructional events

and key phrases from the dialogue that suggest a particular model of lesson planning had been used. Ms. Chau's organization of content and its presentation in

TABLE 11.4 Instructional Events in Ms. Chau's Lesson

Instructional Event	Key Phrase
1. Gaining attention	"Today we will learn how to avoid embarrassing errors such as this (circles an incorrectly punctuated possessive in a newspaper headline)."
2. Informing learners of objective	"At the end of the period, I will give each of you several additional examples of errors taken from my collection of mistakes . . . and you will make the proper corrections and report them to the class."
3. Stimulating recall of lesson-relevant prior knowledge	"Mary, can you recall the parts of speech from last week's lesson? What part of speech is most likely to own or possess something?"
4. Presenting new content	"Our first rule will be . . . ." "You're right, which leads to our second rule . . ."
5. Eliciting the desired behavior	"Let's take a moment to convert each of the phrases on the overhead to the possessive form."
6. Providing feedback	"When I see all heads up, I will write the correct answer."
7. Assessing the behavior	

gradual steps helped students achieve a moderate to high success rate.

Observing Instruction at, or Slightly above, Students' Current Level of Understanding

How a teacher achieves a moderate to high success rate can be determined from a graphic unit plan (Figure 11.1) and from a tabulation of the success rates of learners (from tests, question-and-answer sessions, and activity sheets) across lessons. If the relationship between the unit goal and the objectives of individual lessons is not immediately apparent from the graphic unit plan and the average success rate for individual lessons is low, chances are that individual lessons cover more content or teach at a higher level of complexity than can be readily digested by learners. Lesson topics should fit neatly into the organizational divisions of an adopted text or curriculum guide. If a basis for lesson content cannot be found in these sources, the content might be either too broad or irrelevant to the unit goal. Both of these conditions can reduce student success rate.

Another reason for a low success rate can be the manner in which content is organized and presented within a lesson. Although there are many different ways of organizing a lesson (e.g., Gagné & Briggs, 2005; Hunter, 1994), most lessons (or units) should include the following instructional events:

1. Gaining the learners' attention (focusing; establishing an anticipatory learning set)
2. Informing the learner of the objective (stating the purpose and level of behavior expected)
3. Stimulating recall of prerequisite learning (reviewing lesson-relevant prior learning)
4. Presenting the stimulus material (input and modeling)
5. Eliciting the desired behavior (providing guided practice)
6. Providing feedback and correctives (checking for understanding; closure)
7. Assessing the behavior (providing independent practice and testing)

Although not all lessons will (or should) have all of these components, each component should be discernible across a unit.

Failing to stimulate the recall of prerequisite learning (e.g., by reviewing at the beginning of a lesson), elicit the desired behavior (through hands-on activities or practice exercises), or provide feedback and correctives (by providing model answers or correcting workbooks) will make the content of subsequent lessons more difficult for most students to learn. Instrument 11.4 can be used to record how often these instructional events occur within a unit. For this record, six observations are spread across the beginning, middle, and end of a unit. Some of these observations can be completed at the same time Instrument 11.3 is used to record the percentage of correct and partially correct student responses.

For the observation record in Instrument 11.4, a check mark is used to indicate the presence of any of the instructional events. The absence of check marks for an instructional event could indicate a bias to avoid that event frequently enough to make the unit difficult for learners at their current level of understanding. The instructional events listed in Instrument 11.4 may be rephrased to follow the specific model of lesson planning being taught at your institution.

Making Transitions between Lesson Content

The fourth behavior for establishing moderate to high success rates involves transitions between lessons. Although planning lesson content in bite-sized pieces helps learners make transitions between old and new content, this may not be sufficient to ensure a moderate to high success rate in question-and-answer sessions, workbook exercises, hands-on activities, tests, and practice assignments. In addition, the teacher needs to organize lesson content to establish overall themes that "stick with" learners from lesson to lesson and that connect different parts of a unit together. The goal is to help learners see what is being taught at the moment as part of a bigger picture. In this manner, the learner is able to build an understanding of the topic gradually and in measured steps, as opposed to receiving the big picture only at review and test times. Increasing one's understanding in a stairstep fashion, lesson by lesson, is possible only when there is a preplanned direction and continuity among lessons; without these elements students quickly lose the underlying theme and learning is reduced to memorization of pieces. Unless the relationship among lessons is recognized from the start, it is unlikely to be understood by learners later. The following are some ways of organizing content across (and within) lessons to create meaningful transitions in easy-to-grasp steps.

- *Simple to complex.* Arranging unit content in a simple to complex progression so that students see each lesson as part of a hierarchy leading to more detail, greater depth, or more real-world application
- *Concrete to abstract.* Arranging unit content in a concrete to abstract order (or vice versa) so that students see each succeeding lesson as a *funneling*

(widening or narrowing) of facts, concepts, or principles

- *Step by step.* Arranging unit content in a sequential order so that students see each succeeding lesson as a step toward a final destination or goal
- *Whole to part.* Arranging unit content so that a topic is introduced in its most general form and then divided into easy-to-distinguish subdivisions in succeeding lessons
- *Problem centered.* Arranging unit content as a series of problems to be solved so that students see each succeeding lesson as a problem to be solved before the next topic (lesson) can be encountered
- *Decision centered.* Arranging unit content into a set of key decisions to be made so students see each succeeding lesson as a step in the decision-making process

Because some transitions across units, especially interdisciplinary units, emphasize knowledge across subjects, called **lateral knowledge,** their graphic portrayal is different than disciplinary units, which emphasize knowledge within a subject, called **vertical knowledge** (as represented by Ms. Chau's unit plan in Figure 11.1).

The graphic technique you use to express lateral knowledge must allow for content from different topic areas or disciplines to be woven in and out of lessons as the opportunity arises. Hence a more free-form, web-type visual format may be needed to capture a lesson or unit theme. This type of format shows how content is *nestled* within other content, how different subject areas share a common theme, how a single theme is *threaded* through different content areas, or how one field of study is *immersed* in another. All important themes and issues in an interdisciplinary unit plan are therefore shown simultaneously in association with one another.

The following rules can help you in creating these types of graphic outlines or webs for a unit:

1. Identify the most essential theme or idea.
2. Place this theme or idea in the center of your web.
3. Use arrows or lines going outward from the main idea to show relationships with other, subordinate issues, topics, or content, which can become the topics of individual lessons.
4. Label the arrows and all key concepts with code words or phrases to describe the relationships you have expressed.

Figure 11.5 provides an example of the use of a thematic web to express the interrelationships of ideas among lessons. This approach, which can be shared with your students, will help you and the students visualize connections that go beyond those expressed in separate classes or subjects. The principal aim of interdisciplinary instruction, either within a lesson or across an entire unit, is to present learners with an opportunity to discover relationships and patterns that often extend beyond a specific discipline, systematically binding different aspects of our world together. Interdisciplinary units, for example, often represent themes that relate to several different disciplines or subject matter areas at the same time—for example, to English, reading, science, social studies, and the expressive arts. Effective interdisciplinary units also often require learners to go beyond the instruction provided—to conduct research that requires the cooperation of other learners, the independent use of materials, and classroom dialogue in which learners are expected to reason critically, ask questions, make predictions, and, with the aid of the teacher, evaluate the appropriateness of their responses.

How do you think Ms. Chau did with respect to her transitions between lesson content stages? It might be difficult to tell without seeing her unit plan; however, a number of possibilities are apparent. Recall that Ms. Chau began the lesson by showing a punctuation mistake in the headline of a newspaper. Her approach to this sequence of lessons might have been to recognize and correct grammatical errors as they appear in real contexts (e.g., newspapers and magazines). Every lesson could begin with examples of errors related to different lesson topics that have been published in one form or another (to arouse interest) and end with exercises that ask students to find and correct those types of errors (to apply the rules learned). Ms. Chau's goal was to teach her students to recognize when various rules are applicable and to decide which rule to use in what order. Ms. Chau chose a step-by-step approach, emphasizing how rules are used in sequence, and a decision-centered approach, emphasizing when and where to apply the rules. With each of these approaches, she establishes a theme at the beginning of a unit (e.g., "errors in punctuation and grammar") and carries it through each lesson using a simple-to-complex, step-by-step, decision-centered, problem-solving, or other approach, providing continuity and transitions to new content in familiar, easy-to-grasp steps.

Observing Transitions between Lesson Content

Transitions at the beginnings and ends of lessons help interconnect the concepts that will be required later

FIGURE 11.5 Visual Representation of the Interdisciplinary Unit Theme "What Makes Things Tick"

Source: S. J. Kovalik (1994). *The Model.* Kent, WA: Books for Educators. Copyright © 1994 by S. Kovalik. Reprinted with Permission. See also *Exceeding Expectations: A User's Guide to Implementing Brain Research in the Classroom.* Susan J. Kovalik and Karen D. Olsen.

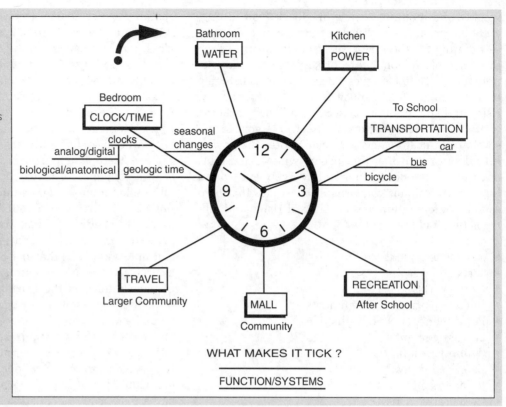

to achieve unit outcomes. One way of establishing an interconnection between lessons is to use advance organizers (Ausubel, 1968; Woolfolk, 2009). Recall from Chapter 7 that an advance organizer at the end of one lesson or at the beginning of the next provides learners with a conceptual preview that helps prepare the learner to store, label, and package lesson content for retention and later use. Advance organizers, presented orally or in the form of charts or web-type diagrams, provide an overview of the day's work and the topics to which it will subsequently relate. Many advance organizers are creative inventions of the teacher that help students see the underlying thread that binds lessons together within a unit. Burnette (1999) recommends concluding lessons or units with the same advance organizer that introduced them to help diverse students better envision where instruction began and ended.

For this observation, you will need to use the knowledge you acquired from studying a unit plan and completing some of the previous observation records. Following the general form for recording advance organizers in Instrument 7.2, p. 232, observe two lessons in sequence, indicating whether a simple-to-complex, concrete-to-abstract (or reverse), step-by-step, whole–part, problem-centered, or decision-centered rela-

tionship can be noted across the lessons. Use your knowledge of the teacher's unit plan, if available, to help you. Note any organizers that bind these lessons together in some logical way but do not fit any of these standard designations. These creative organizers are often the most effective methods because they are tailor-made for a particular unit of content and for a classroom of learners who might have specialized skills, experiences, and backgrounds.

Establishing Momentum That Engages Learners in the Learning Process

The final behavior for establishing moderate to high success rates is related to several other teaching behaviors that have already been discussed. This last dimension, which adds a subtle but important feature to the establishment of the weekly and monthly review and testing cycles discussed in Chapter 9, involves the forward movement, expectancy, and sense of accomplishment that exists within a classroom—in other words, its **momentum.**

Momentum is established by varying the pace at which tasks are presented during the process of reaching a climax or key event. In teaching, this can be accomplished by first establishing cycles of weekly and monthly review, feedback, and testing, and then gradually increasing the pace and intensity as the time for the major event draws near. Playing the same instructional note, or keeping the same monotonous pace too long, can be as boring as listening to a drab and lifeless musical score. Consequently, rising and falling action must be established to set the instruction moving toward a discernible goal for all students. Educators have especially noted the powerful effect on learning that occurs when classrooms of diverse students are marked by lively and varied types of milestones. Classroom milestones that help establish momentum and a tempo of rising and falling action include

- Review and feedback
- Tests and quizzes
- Homework
- In-class workbook assignments
- Performance or skill evaluations
- Lab assignments
- Oral presentations
- Extended essays
- Independent projects
- Cooperative activities

For example, momentum can be the result of gradually increasing the coverage and depth of weekly reviews until the time for a comprehensive monthly review arrives. The objective would be to create a review cycle that rises and falls in 1-month cycles. The low point of the cycle would occur at the start of a unit, when only 1 week's material is reviewed. The reviews would then become increasingly comprehensive until a major monthly review restates and checks for understanding all of the previous month's learning. Momentum is built by targeting greater and greater amounts of instruction for review, but in gradual stages so that students are not overwhelmed by the review content and always know what will be covered. Both teacher and students continually work toward a product that is seen as a meaningful intermediate step to achieve the desired behavioral outcome at the end of the unit. Most important, this creates a sense of forward movement, expectancy, and accomplishment that instills in the learner a desire to achieve at moderate to high rates of success.

What did you think of Ms. Chau's momentum—the sense of forward movement, expectation, and accomplishment in her lesson? Momentum is established by the intensity with which a lesson builds toward clearly established milestones. Recall that homework, seatwork, feedback sessions, class quiz-

zes, and cooperative projects are some of the vehicles with which momentum can be established within a classroom. A moderate to high success rate often depends on an organized unfolding of events such as those listed earlier to give learners opportunities for accomplishment and to keep them alert and looking forward to each new opportunity and expected activity. Momentum can be established across lessons with weekly or monthly schedules of assignments, review, testing, and feedback and within lessons with a sequence of instructional events that gradually builds intensity and student expectation. We do not have information about Ms. Chau's weekly or monthly schedule, which would indicate the major goals toward which her students are working. We can note, however, that the brisk instructional pace established within her lesson appears to engage most of her students in the learning process, through an orderly progression of instructional events that included a variety of presentation modes (visual, oral, and written) and classroom activities (questions and answers, examples on overheads, and recitation using problems in the workbook). All of these elements contributed to a high level of student involvement and a moderate to high success rate.

Observing Momentum

Momentum regulates the intensity with which lesson content builds toward major milestones. Homework, seatwork, prepared handouts, feedback sessions, and class quizzes leading to a major event such as a test, term paper, research project, oral report, or group performance can create momentum within a classroom. A moderate to high success rate depends on an organized succession of events that gives learners opportunities both to practice and respond and to look forward to new and challenging activities. Without this organization and the momentum it creates, life in classrooms can become static and dull, eventually disengaging students from the learning process and from actively practicing the concepts and skills taught.

Instrument 11.5 can be used to observe major events that can create momentum through cycles of rising and falling action. Using the symbols in Figure 11.6, note the activities that occur in a classroom over time corresponding roughly to a grading period. Make your entries at the end of each observation so that the record represents the activities that actually occurred, not those that were planned. Up to four codes may be recorded for any given day.

A moderate to high success rate is promoted by the use of these and similar activities throughout a grad-

FIGURE 11.6 Codes for Instrument 11.5

T	Test, quiz, or departmental exam
H	Homework exercise
F	Feedback given on test or major assignment
R	Review of content (before a test or at regularly scheduled intervals)
A	In-class assignment due (workbook exercises, essay)
I	Independent study time (e.g., for catching up)
O	Oral presentation, performance, or report
L	Lab assignment/activity
R	Research project/paper due
P	Performance evaluation (assessment of how to pronounce the vowels, adjust a microscope, swing a bat, etc.)
Ot	Other

ing period, rather than concentrated at one time (e.g., tests only at the beginning and end). A variety of activities systematically placed over the entire grading period establish a rhythm of rising and falling intensity and a sense of forward movement, expectation, and accomplishment.

Our reactions to Ms. Chau's lesson are summarized in Figure 11.7, which gives Ms. Chau high marks on this lesson because we observed at least some evidence of all of the dimensions for achieving a moderate to high success rate. If time permitted, however, we might return to Ms. Chau's classroom during a problem-solving, inquiry, or discovery lesson to see if her success can be repeated for these higher-order outcomes.

CULTURAL DIVERSITY AND STUDENT SUCCESS

One of the most recent advances in the study of cultural diversity has focused on the influence of teacher mediation and feedback on learner success. Based on work pioneered by Bowers and Flinders (1991) and Palincsar and Brown (1989), it underscores the importance of the diverse patterns teachers must use in responding to student questions and answers in a heterogeneous classroom.

There are two important dimensions of the teacher's role in controlling and modifying classroom dialogue to foster the goals of instruction. One of these dimensions is teacher mediation—on-the-spot adjustments made by the teacher to extend or refocus a student response to move the learner onto the next rung of the learning ladder. The second dimension focuses on mental modeling, a topic addressed in the next chapter.

As we have seen in this chapter, teacher-mediated learning comprises on-the-spot adjustments in the level of content and pacing during a lesson in which the learner is an active participant. In teacher-mediated learning, more learners are encouraged to participate in the question-and-answer dialogue of the classroom because the content and pacing are continually adjusted to each participant's current level of understanding. Typically, researchers have found that student success rate (frequency of correct responses) during teacher-mediated dialogues increases compared to traditional lessons in which the teacher conveys content exclusively through explaining and lecturing (Floden, 1991).

The explanation for these findings derives from the research on meaningful verbal learning (Fosnot, 2005), in which learners who were given the opportunity to construct their own interpretations and meanings from content were able to retain content longer and more easily generalize it to new contexts. The role of the teacher in these learning contexts is to take the acquired interpretations, experiences, and meanings expressed by learners to the next level of refinement through the use of follow-up questions, probes, and the responses of other learners. Thus, the teacher's response to a correct answer, a correct but hesitant answer, an incorrect or partially correct answer, or a careless answer can be chosen on the basis of the needs of the learner (Tomlinson & McTighe, 2006).

These results have been applied to culturally diverse classrooms through various forms of social interaction that encourage students to construct their own meanings and interpretations and to revise and extend them under the guidance of the teacher. Of the many techniques for promoting the concept of teacher mediation, among the most popular are **reciprocal teaching** (Oczkus, 2003; Palincsar & Brown, 1989) and **problem-based learning** (Baden & Major, 2004; Lambros, 2002; Ronis, 2007). Both involve the teacher eliciting student responses at the student's current level of understanding based on personal experiences with, assumptions about, and predictions

FIGURE 11.7 Checklist for Observing Ms. Chau's Classroom

Behavior	Observed	Not Observed	No Opportunity to Observe
1. Unit and lesson organization reflects lesson-relevant prior learning	✓ Lesson in sequence with parts of speech		
2. Provides mediated feedback to extend and enhance student learning	✓ Tends to praise and affirm right and partially right answers; treats wrong answers and nonresponses neutrally		
3. Plans lessons at, or slightly above, learners' level of understanding	✓ Divides lesson into small, easy-to-grasp rules		
4. Plans transitions to new content in small, easy-to-grasp steps			✓ Opportunity for several interconnecting themes, but no chance to observe related lessons to see if any are operating
5. Established momentum, for example, pacing and intensity gradually build toward major milestones			✓ Momentum evident within lesson as a result of changing activities; no evidence available about momentum across lessons

from the content to be taught. This is followed by classroom dialogue in which the teacher and learners participate in revising and refining earlier responses, accomplished by the following steps:

- *Predicting*. Discussion begins by generating predictions about the content to be learned from the text, based on
  a. its title or subheading in the text
  b. the group's prior knowledge or information pertaining to the topic
  c. experience with similar kinds of information

  Following the group's predictions about what they expect to learn from the text, the group reads or listens to a portion of it.

- *Questioning*. One individual is chosen to lead a discussion of each portion of the text that is read. Afterward, the discussion leader asks questions about the information. Students respond to the questions and raise additional questions.

- *Summarizing*. The discussion leader summarizes the text, and other students are invited to comment or elaborate on the summary.
- *Clarifying*. If points in the text are unclear (e.g., concepts or vocabulary), they are discussed until clarity is achieved. In this case, more predictions may be made and portions of the text may be re-read for greater clarity.

Notice how with these steps the teacher is able to support the participation of all students in the classroom dialogue. The teacher's aim is to engage as many students as possible in the learning process by providing reactions to student responses that are in their zones of maximum response opportunity. The teacher thus mediates the instruction by adjusting the flow and complexity of content to accommodate individual learning needs. This is accomplished by (1) offering ample opportunity for students to participate in the dialogue from their perspective and (2) elaborating on student responses with prompts, wait time, and questions that guide subsequent responses. These are important elements of instruction to look for when observing student success.

In the final chapter, we turn our attention to observing higher thought processes and performance outcomes. As we turn to this lens through which to observe classrooms, keep in mind the significant impact of the dimensions of student success studied in this chapter.

For More Information

The Laboratory for Student Success, located at Temple University, is one of 10 Regional Educational Laboratories funded by the Institute of Education Sciences (IES) of the U.S. Department of Education. Its mission is to revitalize and reform educational practices to improve student success and to bring about lasting improvements in the achievement of diverse student populations. As a result of their extensive research and development efforts they continually produce reports, books, and articles that can help teachers and schools increase their students' achievement and transform low-performing schools into high-performing schools. Their resources for teachers and administrators can be accessed at www.temple.edu/lss.

Key Terms

functional errors, 173
lateral knowledge, 186
lesson-relevant prior knowledge, 176
momentum, 187
problem-based learning, 189

reciprocal teaching, 189
teacher mediation, 180
vertical knowledge, 186
zone of maximum response opportunity, 181

Activities*

1. Using the checklist in Instrument 11.1 as your guide, observe a lesson for signs of student success. At the end of your observation, add a brief written description to each box, highlighting at least one specific reason why you chose to place each of your check marks as you did.

2. Using the examples of 5-point scales in Chapter 4, convert the positively stated indicators of student success listed in Table 11.1 into the form of a Likert scale. Consider the vertical or horizontal placement of each indicator on the page, whether words will be affixed to all or only some of the response blanks, and what response alternatives will be best suited to each question. Show your scale to a classmate who has also constructed a 5-point scale. Together, create a single, revised version incorporating the best features of each.

3. Using a teacher's lesson plan, textbook, and/or curriculum guide, identify a unit goal and the lesson objectives that relate to it. From this information and following the examples in this chapter, construct a graphic plan of the content taught in this unit, using either the vertical box format shown in Figure 11.1 or the lateral web format shown in Figure 11.5. Be sure to label all concepts and indicate where lesson sequence is important to achieving lesson-relevant prior knowledge.

4. (Instrument 11.2 may be used for Activities 4, 5, and 6.) Using the Good and Brophy question–answer–feedback instrument presented in Instrument 11.2, observe and code a practice or recitation session lasting 15 minutes or longer. Try to select a time when students are expected to respond orally to questions or problems in a workbook, on a handout, on the chalkboard, or on an overhead. At the end of the session, determine student success by adding the total number of correct student responses, dividing the number by the total number of questions or problems coded, and multiplying by 100. Create a second index of student success by combining correct responses with any partially correct responses that have been coded. What is the percentage difference between these two values? If the content was presented for the first time, which index of student

*Some of these activities may be grouped into a common activity, divided among classmates, and completed from a single observation.

success might be more sensitive to the instruction that took place?

5. Turn to the Teacher Feedback section of the Good and Brophy coding form used in Activity 4. Look for a predominant pattern of teacher reaction and feedback to the student responses coded (a) correct, (b) partially correct, and (c) incorrect. Do you see any differences in the teacher's reaction and feedback to student responses in these three categories? Do these differences explain why this teacher achieved the success rates identified in Activity 4?

6. Using the Good and Brophy question–answer–feedback instrument, observe and code an inquiry, problem-solving, or discovery lesson. Try to select a lesson in which there will be student discussion and questions and answers. Use the question and answers to determine the rate of student success and compare the rate with that obtained in Activity 5. Did you observe any teacher mediation during this lesson?

7. Prior to a scheduled test or graded assignment, ask the teacher to indicate expected scores that would indicate a reasonable amount of progress had been made by each student, given their ability and learning history. Using the scores achieved by each student on the test or assignment, calculate the success rate for the class by determining (a) the percentage of students who achieved 80% correct (if a test) or 60% correct (if an assignment involving new content) and (b) the percentage of students who met or exceeded expectations. How do these two values differ? Which would you accept as the most accurate index of success in this particular classroom?

8. Observe at least one lesson using the form provided in Instrument 11.4 for recording instructional events. Be sure to place each check mark in the appropriate column indicating placement in the unit (beginning, middle, or end). Analyze the record to determine (a) which instructional events were most frequently observed, (b) which were least frequently observed, and, if apparent, (c) which instructional events were more frequently observed at the beginning of a unit than at the end.

9. Choose a classroom with which you can have extended contact. Using Instrument 11.5, record any major activities (tests, reviews, assignments) that establish a sense of forward movement, expectancy, and accomplishment. Add any other major events you learn about in conversation with the teacher. In your opinion, does this class have a sense of forward movement, expectancy, and accomplishment? How might its momentum be improved?

12

Looking for Higher Thought Processes and Performance Outcomes

Be Like the Bird

Be like the bird, who

Halting in his flight

On limb too slight

Feels it give way beneath him,

Yet sings,

Knowing he hath wings.

Victor Hugo

Victor Hugo, "Be Like the Bird."

To give our students wings is the noble goal of education! But how do we help them find their way into the heights of higher thought processes and performance outcomes? In this chapter, we'll explore ways teachers can help their students push beyond the simple regurgitation of facts to be able to make decisions, to solve problems, and to think critically in a real-world performance environment.

In this chapter we will observe teaching and learning activities that promote higher thought processes and performance outcomes, such as critical thinking, decision making, and problem solving, that cannot be measured by paper-and-pencil tests of achievement alone. Your students, for example, might be able to recite all the rules of grammar without hesitation, but be unable to write about a simple event that they have experienced. They could recite the reasons behind world tensions, but be unable to solve problems cooperatively. They might know a law of science, but be unable to demonstrate how that law works in real life. They could know the cellular structure of plant life, but be unable to use a microscope to see what they know. They might be enthusiastic about communicating their thoughts to close friends, but be afraid to make an oral presentation to the class.

These performance behaviors require application, analysis, synthesis, and decision-making objectives and outcomes that are believed to be stimulated more by interaction with others (peers and adults) and by an awareness of one's own learning (**metacognition**) than by books and lectures (Anderson & Krathwohl, 2001). Many of these behaviors require interaction with others to unleash the motivation and imaginative and intuitive capacities required for complex thought and performance in the real world.

Teaching students to think critically, make decisions, and solve problems requires several unique teaching functions:

- Demonstrating mental models and strategies for learning
- Illustrating how these strategies are used to think through solutions to real-world problems
- Encouraging learners to become actively involved in the subject matter by going beyond the information given, restructuring it according to their own way of thinking and prior understanding
- Gradually shifting the responsibility for learning to students through practice exercises, question-and-answer dialogues, or discussions that engage them in increasingly complex patterns of thought

- Monitoring, correcting, and evaluating student responses as needed

In this chapter, we will see how each of these teaching functions can be observed and achieved.

DIMENSIONS OF HIGHER THOUGHT PROCESSES AND PERFORMANCE OUTCOMES

Table 12.1 summarizes the behaviors that promote higher thought processes and performance.

1. Using collaborative and group activities
2. Demonstrating mental models and strategies
3. Arranging for student projects and demonstrations
4. Engaging students in oral performance
5. Providing opportunities for students to learn from their mistakes
6. Using portfolios and performance assessments

PRACTICE OBSERVING HIGHER THOUGHT PROCESSES AND PERFORMANCE OUTCOMES: A DIALOGUE

Let's look at some of the ways higher thought processes and performance outcomes can be observed in the classroom using the six behaviors presented in Table 12.1. Use the checklist in Instrument 12.1 to record your observations of the following class.

For this dialogue, we look into Ms. Brokaw's literature class. Today's lesson begins a poetry unit. The class has just finished a unit on American literature in which they read excerpts from Jack London and Mark Twain. Some students are noticeably anxious about the change to this new and seemingly less interesting topic.

TABLE 12.1   Indicators of Higher Thought Processes and Performance Outcomes

More Effectively Promotes Performance Outcomes and Higher Thought Processes	Less Effectively Promotes Performance Outcomes and Higher Thought Processes
1. Uses collaborative and group activities (cooperative learning, small groups, teamwork, panel discussion, peer tutoring)	Fails to encourage shared work and group problem solving
2. Demonstrates mental models and strategies for learning (for example, how learners are to think systematically about solving a certain problem)	Fails to demonstrate how to think critically, reason, and solve problems
3. Arranges for students to apply what they've learned through student projects and demonstrations	Fails to allow students the opportunity to use what they've learned
4. Engages students in oral performance and expression (for example, encouraging the understanding of content and its organization through communication)	Fails to require students to speak out, justify their answers, and express themselves
5. Provides opportunities for independent practice that allow students to learn from their mistakes in understanding	Fails to provide supplemental material (exercises, problem sets, activity sheets) that challenge students
6. Uses performance assessment of learning	Fails to assess the integration of learning in authentic contexts

Ms. Brokaw: [A poem is written on the board; Ms. Brokaw reads it to the class.]

> Man is but a mortal fool
> When it's hot, he wants it cool
> When it's cool, he wants it hot
> He's always wanting what is not.

Today I want to illustrate some ways to understand a poem like the one I've just read. This may seem like a simple poem, but its author put a lot of care and meaning into each word. Now, let me give you an approach to study poems like these and to gain from them the meaning intended by their authors. First, let's try to identify the key words in this poem. Bobby, what do you think are some of the most important words?

Bobby: Well, I'd say the word *man* because it's the first.

Ms. Brokaw: [Still looking at Bobby] Any others?

Bobby: Not that I can see.

Ms. Brokaw: Anissa?

Anissa: The words *hot* and *cool* have to be important because they appear twice and they rhyme with the last words of the first and last lines.

Ms. Brokaw: Any other key words? Ricardo?

Ricardo: Well, I think "a mortal fool" is supposed to be telling us something, but I don't know what.

Ms. Brokaw: Good. So, now we've identified some words we think are especially important for understanding this poem—that's a first step. Why don't we look up the meanings of any of these words we don't know or are unsure of in the dictionary? That will be our second step. Ted, look up the word *mortal* for us while we begin work on our next step. That step will be to paraphrase what you think this author is saying. Hee-Won, can you paraphrase what he is saying?

Hee-Won: I think he's saying we're always changing our minds and that's why we look so stupid sometimes.

Ms. Brokaw: We are all human, so we certainly change our minds a lot, don't we? Rhonda looks like she wants to say something. Rhonda?

Rhonda: Well, I'd say it's not because we're stupid that we change our minds, but that it's just part of who we are—we can't help wanting what we can't have.

Ms. Brokaw: So you've added a little something to Hee-Won's interpretation. What do you think, Hee-Won? Do you agree?

Hee-Won: Yeah, we're not stupid, we're just mortals.

Ms. Brokaw: Chris, do you want to add anything?

Chris: I'd say that we're not stupid at all; that to really enjoy something, we must have experienced its opposite—otherwise, we wouldn't know how good it is.

Ms. Brokaw: Now that brings us to our fourth and last step. Let's try to relate what Chris just said to our own experience. Anyone ready? Bobby?

Bobby: I agree with Chris because I remember thinking how much I welcomed winter because of how hot it was last summer.

Ms. Brokaw: [Marcia is waving her hand.] Marcia, what do you have to say about this?

Marcia: But now that it's winter, I can't wait for the cold weather to end so I can go swimming again. [Class nods in agreement.]

Ms. Brokaw: It looks as though Chris was right. We sometimes have to see both sides of something—hot/cold, good/bad, light/dark—to fully appreciate it. Now, Ted, what did you find for *mortal* in the dictionary?

Ted: It says "having caused or being about to cause death," "subject to death," and "marked by vulnerability."

Ms. Brokaw: Which of those do you think best fits the use of *mortal fool* in our poem?

Ted: Well, hmm, . . . the last one, because it kind of goes with what we have been saying about how we choose one thing and then another . . . like when we get too cold we dream of summer, and then when summer comes we think it's too hot.

Ms. Brokaw: I agree. It fits with what we all have experienced in our lives. In other words, it touches us in some way—and that means we are on the right track to the interpretation the author intended. Now, let's go one step further. Putting all of our ideas together, what is this poet saying? [Nodding to Meijean]

Meijean: Well, I'd say life's a kind of circle. We keep going around and around, back to where we've come from, and then trying to escape to where we've been. Maybe that's one kind of vulnerability, like it said in the dictionary.

Ms. Brokaw: That's good thinking, Meijean. Bobby, we began with you, so I'll let you have the final word.

Bobby: I think Meijean got it because now I understand why the author thinks we're all fools: We're like a dog going in circles, chasing its tail, always wanting what we don't have. That explains the first and the last line, doesn't it? Because we are human, we are vulnerable to always "wanting what is not." Yes, so we're "mortal fools." I get it.

Ms. Brokaw: Very good. Now let's break into our assigned groups to study the next set of poems. I will give each group leader a copy of a different poem, which they will read slowly and carefully to their group. Then each group will discuss among themselves the meaning of the poem using the four steps we just went through to understand "Man is but a mortal fool." I will write the four steps on the board while the group leaders are reading the poem to their groups. These steps will be your guide to interpreting the meaning of your poem. Assistant group leaders, please see that your group has a dictionary from the resource shelf. After about 20 minutes, I will ask each of the groups to read their poem to the class and give the group's interpretation, so each group will need to select a reader and presenter. I will be around to visit each group to help with questions or problems.

▓ TIME TO REFLECT

Which of the six dimensions of higher thought processes and performance outcomes did you see in this dialogue? Recall that these behaviors require analysis, synthesis, and decision making that are believed to be stimulated more by interaction with others and by an awareness of one's own learning than by being "told" by books and lectures. They involve encouraging learners to become actively involved in the subject matter by going beyond the information given,

restructuring it according to their own way of thinking and prior understanding. Then the teacher gradually shifts the responsibility for learning to students through practice exercises, question-and-answer dialogues, or discussions that engage them in increasingly complex patterns of thought.

Using Collaborative and Group Activities

The first behavior for promoting higher thought processes involves collaborative and group activities (Jacobs, Power, & Loh, 2002; Johnson & Johnson, 2005). Students must not only learn to get along in a turbulent, ever-changing society, they must also be prepared to contribute to it. When carefully planned, collaborative and group activities help build the skills learners will need to think critically, reason, and solve problems in an adult world, and help them acquire the social skills that can make their reasoning and problem solving effective.

In planning a cooperative learning activity, the teacher must decide

- The type of interactions to have with students
- The type of interactions students will have with one another
- The tasks and materials that will be used
- The roles and responsibilities that will be assigned to students

The first goal in planning a cooperative learning activity is to promote teacher–student interaction that encourages independent thinking. Exchanges between learners and the teacher in a cooperative classroom focus on getting learners to think for themselves, independently of the text. To accomplish this goal, the teacher models, intervenes, and collaborates with learners in a question-and-answer format.

The way teacher–student interaction is developed during cooperative learning is different from group discussion, which the interaction is usually one on one, with verbal messages directed to individuals one at a time and adjusted to their current levels of understanding. In cooperative learning, the interaction occurs in groups of four to six members who share a common purpose and task, so the teacher's task is to tailor her responses to the level of understanding common to the group. The goal is not only to bring individuals to a greater understanding and awareness of their own thinking, but also to help the group become more self-reflective and aware of its own performance. "Think about that some more," "Why not check the reference book at the learning center," and "Be sure you've followed the guidelines" are expressions frequently addressed to a group of learners assigned a specific task. The teacher's role is to intervene at critical junctures and then to retreat, allowing the group to independently grapple with and go beyond the information given. In this manner, the teacher monitors and collaborates with the group during brief but focused interventions, keeping them on course and following a productive line of reasoning. Teacher–student interactions are well-timed, brief intrusions into the group's thinking that stimulate new ideas.

A second goal in planning a cooperative learning activity is to promote student-to-student interaction that facilitates the performance of other group members. Interaction among students in cooperative learning groups should be intense and prolonged. Unlike group discussion, in which the learner is expected to take much of the responsibility for his own learning, students in cooperative learning groups gradually take responsibility for each other's learning. During cooperative learning, feedback, reinforcement, and support come from peers in the group rather than from the teacher. Interactions among students constitute the majority of activity during cooperative learning, unlike the modest amount of direct student-to-student interaction that occurs during large-group discussion. Groups of four to six students working together in the physical closeness promoted by a common task encourage collaboration, support, and feedback from the closest, most immediate source—one's peers. An essential ingredient of cooperative learning is the desire of each learner to facilitate the performance of fellow group members.

A third goal in planning a cooperative learning activity is to choose a task that encourages group sharing and decision making. Cooperative learning tasks are preplanned activities; they are timed, completed in stages, and placed within the context of the work of others (e.g., the tasks of other groups). The choice of task and supporting materials is important to meaningful student–student interaction. A specific well-defined task and the sharing of materials with which to complete the task (e.g., reference books, maps, calculators, videos, DVDs, computers) distinguish cooperative learning from group discussion.

Finally, the assignment of roles is important to the success of a cooperative learning activity. In addition to the group's assigned tasks, individuals often are given specialized roles to perform within their groups to facilitate the group's work and promote communication and shared decision making among the members.

1. *Summarizer*. Paraphrases and plays back to the group major conclusions to see whether the group agrees and to prepare for the group's presentation before the whole class

2. *Checker*. Checks controversial or debatable statements and conclusions for authenticity against the text, workbook, or other references and ensures that the group will not be using unsubstantiated facts or be challenged by more accurate representations of other groups

3. *Researcher*. Reads reference documents and acquires background information when more data are needed (e.g., might conduct an interview or seek a resource from the Internet); differs from a checker in that the researcher provides critical information for the group to complete its task, whereas the checker verifies the accuracy of the work while it is in progress or after it has been completed

4. *Runner*. Acquires anything needed to complete the task: materials, equipment, references; requires creativity, shrewdness, and cunning to find the necessary resources, which other groups might also be diligently searching for

5. *Recorder*. Commits to writing the major product of the group; when individuals are required to write their own conclusions, she collates, synthesizes, and renders in coherent form the work of individual group members

6. *Supporter*. Chosen for his upbeat, positive outlook; praises members when their individual assignments are completed and encourages them in times of disappointment (e.g., if proper references can't be found); keeps the group moving forward by encouraging less vocal group members to contribute and by recording major milestones achieved on a chart for the whole class to see

7. *Observer/Troubleshooter*. Takes notes and records information about group progress that might be useful during whole-class discussion; reports to a class leader or to the teacher when problems appear insurmountable for the group or individual members

The success of a cooperative learning activity depends on communicating role responsibilities and modeling them when necessary. This is why cooperative learning bears little resemblance to loosely formed discussion groups—not only must tasks be divided among learners, but roles must be delegated to foster the orderly completion of a task. Research on the effectiveness of various cooperative learning techniques (Marzano, Pickering, & Pollock, 2004; Slavin, 2001) found that improved decision making, problem solving, communication, and self-esteem among students result when

1. Rewards are provided for successful performance of the group as a whole.
2. Individual accountability is maintained by selecting group tasks that require the participation of every group member for successful completion.
3. Equal opportunities for success are made available to each student by measuring individual success in terms of improvement over past performance.

What did you notice about Ms. Brokaw's use of collaborative and group learning? We noticed that she began setting the stage for a collaborative activity early in her lesson by informing her students of a strategy, a plan of action, by which they could interpret the meaning of a poem. She then illustrated, one by one, each step of the strategy:

1. Identify key words important for understanding the poem
2. Look up in a dictionary the meanings of key words they are unsure of
3. Paraphrase what they think the author is saying
4. Relate what the author has said to their own experience

Notice how Ms. Brokaw provided this strategy to her learners. First, she presented four easy-to-follow steps that were sufficiently familiar and practical to be followed by almost any student, regardless of ability or experience. Not just divisions of the task, these actual mental steps encouraged learners to go beyond the content presented to find their own meaning based on personal experience and individual thinking. In other words, there were no wrong answers with this strategy—only answers that could be improved to raise the learner to the next rung of the learning ladder.

Second, the strategy provided wasn't just routinely given to the learners by listing its steps on the board; instead the steps were illustrated in the context of a real problem, just as the students would be expected to do in a later cooperative activity. The application was a real-world task and typical of others to which they would be asked to apply the strategy.

Third, the learners were invited to become participants in the learning, not just passive listeners waiting to be told what to do. Because the teacher used a question-and-answer dialogue to provide a structure for the learners' opinions and experiences, students became an active part of the process of generating new knowledge and learning how to engage in personal inquiry (Tower, 2000). They were in a sense their own teachers, without knowing it. This was made possible through the format of an unscripted discussion, which removed any fear of producing a wrong response that might have prevented some learners from participating.

Fourth, as the lesson evolved, more and more of the most important conclusions were provided by the students, not the teacher. The highest level of interpretation, which ended the lesson, came almost entirely from the summarizing remarks of students. By the end of the lesson, the teacher's role was that of a monitor and codiscussant rather than an information provider, that role having been assumed by the students themselves as they were assigned to apply each of the steps given earlier in the lesson with their cooperative groups.

Students working collaboratively in small groups also contributed to the higher thought processes and performance outcomes in Ms. Brokaw's classroom. Notice that the teacher's goal with this format was to promote application of the model and independent thinking. But for small-group work to be effective, it needs teacher–student interaction, student–student interaction, specification of the task and materials, and the assignment of roles. Notice that each of these elements was provided by the teacher at the end of the classroom dialogue. A particular task was assigned to each group, which required the original interpretation of a poem using the model provided. Role assignments made the execution of the task efficient and effective. There were group leaders and assistants, readers, and presenters to help provide structure and direction to the group work. A time limit was imposed that, together with group-by-group visits by the teacher, would help keep the class on task. Thus, all four elements of a collaborative activity—teacher–student interaction, student–student interaction, task specification, and materials and roles—were present in Ms. Brokaw's organization of group work, supported and reinforced by the learning strategy presented earlier in the lesson.

Observing Collaborative and Group Activities

Collaborative and group activities require teacher–student interaction, interaction among students, a specified task and materials, and the assignment of roles. The presence of these four components can determine the effectiveness of a collaborative learning activity. Instrument 12.2 provides a format to observe and record these four components. Complete this form for Ms. Brokaw's collaborative activity, indicating your judgment as to the extent to which all or some of these components were present.

Demonstrating Mental Models and Strategies for Learning

The second behavior for promoting higher thought processes and performance outcomes involves demonstrating mental models and strategies for learning. Although most teaching takes place in large- and small-group formats, a considerable portion of teaching time (as much as 40% in some grades and subjects) is taken up with seatwork and one-on-one dialogue, in which teacher responses must be tailored to the achievement, interest, and ability levels of individual students. This tailored interaction might occur in the context of discussion involving the whole class or during monitoring of seatwork. In either setting, the teacher's role is to assist the individual in internalizing, understanding, and applying the content being learned. These goals can be achieved most efficiently by modeling for the learner the mental processes needed to understand and apply the content to be learned. Modeling involves three steps (Methe & Hintze, 2003):

1. Demonstrating to students the reasoning processes needed
2. Making students aware of this reasoning process
3. Helping students apply the reasoning process

These steps usually are carried out through verbal statements that help learners through the process of attaining a correct solution. They might begin with verbal markers such as

- "Now I will show you how to solve this problem by talking out loud as I go through it, identifying exactly what is going on in my mind."
- "Think about each decision I make, where I stop to think, and what alternatives I choose—as though you are making the same decision in your own mind."
- "Listen to me as I think out loud, completing each of the steps you will need to answer this question."

Notice that the teacher is not giving the learner the mechanics of getting a right answer—"Do step A, step B, and then step C"—but, more important, is providing an actual demonstration of the mental procedures that lie behind the completion of a problem.

These mental procedures help students internalize, recall, and then generalize problem solutions to different content at a later time. The teacher does not just convey information, but demonstrates the decision-making process as it occurs. By contrast, the mechanical memorization of steps rarely helps learners solve similar problems in other contexts or

allows content to be recalled when the present topic has lost its immediate importance (no exam in sight or no homework due).

Mental modeling is particularly important when we ask students to engage in complex tasks—such as Internet searches, which require higher-order thinking skills to revise a search strategy, evaluate its results, discard inapplicable items, and synthesize the findings. Each of these areas poses a number of challenges for learners, challenges that can be addressed through modeling ways for students to organize their thinking. As you observe in classrooms, you will want to watch for instances of mental modeling and note particularly effective approaches you see.

Consider the following dialogue, based on Mr. Swade's lesson in Chapter 10, in which he provided a mental model for acquiring the concept of a proportion.

Mr. Swade: When you see a proportion, such as 4/5 [Writes it on board], think of the number on top as "what is" and the number on the bottom as "what could be." Think about that box of cereal you made your breakfast from this morning. If I wrote the proportion of cereal in the box as 3/4 [Writes it on board], I would say to myself, the full box is equal to the number 4—that's the "could be" part—but this morning, after I poured myself breakfast, it's only the number 3—that's the "what is" part. I can tell the box is still pretty full because the number for "what is" is close to the number for "what could be." Juan, explain to me what it means when it says on a label that the vitamin C in one 4-ounce glass of orange juice is 1/2 the minimum daily requirement.

Juan: I'm not sure.

Mr. Swade: Okay; what words can we use to describe the number on top?

Juan: You said, "what is."

Mr. Swade: What does that mean?

Juan: I guess it's how much vitamin C is really in the glass.

Mr. Swade: And now for the bottom.

Juan: You said the bottom is "what could be." Does that mean that it's all you need?

Mr. Swade: Yes, it does—good. Now, think of another example—one of your own—in which something was less than it could have been.

Juan: Well, I finished Ms. Enro's social studies test before the end of the period.

Mr. Swade: And how long was the period?

Juan: Umm, about 40 minutes, I guess.

Mr. Swade: Using our words, what would you call that part of the problem?

Juan: "What could be." OK, I get it. Then, the time I actually took is what really happened? Yeah, I finished the test in about 20 minutes.

Mr. Swade: So how would you express that proportion in numbers?

Juan: It would be 20, for "what is," over 40, for "what could be." The top is half of the bottom, so I guess one glass of orange juice gives you half the vitamin C you need in one day.

Mr. Swade: Good.

Now, imagine that Juan relives this episode in another classroom with a different teacher. After the same introductory remarks, Juan is asked an identical question.

Teacher: Now, Juan, explain to me what it means when it says on a label that the vitamin C in one 4-ounce glass of orange juice is 1/2 the minimum daily requirement. [After a pause] Look, if the number 1 is on the top and the number 2 is on the bottom, it must mean the top is less than the bottom. Right?

Juan: Right.

Teacher: So, if the top number represents what is and the bottom number what could be, "what is" is one-half of "what could be." And that can only mean the glass contains half of the minimum daily requirement of vitamin C. Got it?

Juan: Yep.

Maybe Juan does, and maybe he doesn't. Notice that in the first example Mr. Swade provided mental steps for Juan to follow that moved the dialogue closer to the intended goal of the lesson. The dialogue provided a step by which Juan lifted himself onto the next rung of the learning ladder.

The second teacher simply provided the right answer. This gave Juan no opportunity to construct his own response and thereby derive a process to use for arriving at other right answers in similar circumstances. The first teacher focused on developing for the learner a process of reasoning that would give the content its own individual meaning and be consistent with the intended goal of the lesson.

Through classroom dialogues such as these, the teacher can encourage learners to construct their own meanings and interpretations: for example, to substitute their own unique constructions for "what is" and "what could be" and to share them with others through discussion and classroom dialogue. Such modeling activates a learning dialogue. By calling forth unique histories, specialized abilities, and personal experiences, mental modeling encourages higher thought processes.

Observing Mental Models and Strategies for Learning

Mental models and strategies require demonstrating the reasoning involved in obtaining a correct solution, making students conscious of the steps used, and helping them apply these steps to independently arrive at other right answers in similar circumstances. These steps often are accomplished with verbal markers, such as "Now I will show you the next step," "Think about the steps I'm going through ," or "Listen to how I think through this."

Phrases such as these are intended to alert students to the line of reasoning to use in obtaining the correct solution for themselves and enable them to construct their own meanings and interpretations that can be applied time and again to similar problems. Instrument 12.3 provides a format for recording how these three components of mental modeling are applied in the classroom. Using the dialogue in this chapter as your guide, see if you can find verbal phrases used by Ms. Brokaw during the course of the lesson that represent any or all of the steps in mental modeling.

Arranging for Student Projects and Demonstrations

The third behavior for promoting higher thought processes and performance outcomes is arranging for student projects and demonstrations. Most teachers encourage students to explore and demonstrate the concepts and principles they have been taught. Students enjoy seeing what otherwise might be considered dull schoolwork come alive by applying what they've learned. Practical applications to the real world can take the form of reports, projects, experiments, videos, drawings, scale models, dramatizations, or other tasks that students can choose from to apply the concepts and principles they have been taught. Because projects and demonstrations are often of the student's own choosing, they pose a special opportunity to encourage higher thought processes in heterogeneously grouped classrooms.

For student projects and demonstrations to be effective in promoting higher thought processes, however, students should be given guidelines to the level of thinking and production that will be expected and should also participate in their development (Curtis, 2002). And care should be taken to help students select intellectually rigorous topics that are worth their time and have the potential to extend beyond current study (Katz & Chard, 1998). Project guidelines should be specific enough to ensure that the projects conform to the assignment, fit within space limitations, and are safe, while also communicating the level of inquiry, creativity, and individuality expected. Planning these guidelines in advance and illustrating them to students are crucial steps in promoting higher thought processes. The following examples demonstrate guidelines that can be developed from both student and teacher input:

- *Guideline 1.* Communicate the real-world complexity of your topic. Example: "We've all heard that the brain is like a computer. Now, can you show me how the brain works like a computer?"
- *Guideline 2.* Avoid being vague or overly abstract. Example: "When you hear the word *horsepower,* what specific examples come to mind?"
- *Guideline 3.* Use the professional vocabulary that is appropriate to your topic. Example: "How do the earth's crust, core, and tectonic plates create geologic activity?"
- *Guideline 4.* Use appropriate examples to communicate your topic. Example: "In what ways do you see the rapid pace of technology, such as the development of the microchip, influencing our everyday lives?"
- *Guideline 5.* Connect your topic to your own personal experience. Example: "Tell us some of the ways your neighborhood has taught you to appreciate that people are different."

To make guidelines clearer, sample projects or demonstrations in several categories can be exhibited to show various degrees of performance (e.g., "superior," "advanced," or "meets expectations"). In this manner students get to see and contribute to the quality of performance and thought that is expected. Selected students can be asked to donate their completed project as an example for other classes, or a photograph or video of their work can be taken. For teachers teaching multiple classes of the same subject, staggering the time the assignment is given among classes will allow projects from one class to serve as examples for other classes.

An important addition to student projects and demonstrations, peer review promotes higher levels of thinking and performance, sometimes far exceeding the results that can be obtained through teacher review. The need to show off and receive recognition is part of human nature, and having a product or demonstration scrutinized by peers ensures that a captive audience of those we respect will be there to witness us at our best. Assembling a collection, gathering specimens, building scale models, and showing examples all provide opportunities to be creative and imaginative. The energy exerted by students in a peer review often results in a more thorough and competent performance.

Did you notice anything about Ms. Brokaw's use of student projects and demonstrations? Unfortunately, a single observation is insufficient to determine the extent of her planning in this area. Think, however, about what student projects and demonstrations pertaining to the content of this lesson Ms. Brokaw might have provided to her students. For example, she could have asked her students to try writing a poem, interpreting a favorite poem, or drawing a picture that expresses their interpretation of a poem—each of these activities could stimulate higher thought processes. Use your own creativity and higher thought processes to propose a project or demonstration that Ms. Brokaw could use with the content of this lesson at another time.

Observing Student Projects and Demonstrations

Recall that the purpose of student projects and demonstrations is to get students to apply what they have learned under real-world conditions. Projects and demonstrations—exhibits, experiments, Internet searches, scale models, videos, graphic representations, and the like—encourage students to make judgments and decisions on their own and to use their individual backgrounds, abilities, and learning histories in creative ways. Instrument 12.4 asks you to list examples of projects and demonstrations on display in the classroom that reflect the independent thought and judgment of individual students. This instrument also suggests the types of projects and demonstrations to look for and provides an opportunity to add others that might be specific to a particular subject, grade, or classroom.

Engaging Students in Oral Performance

A fourth behavior for promoting higher thought processes and performance outcomes is engaging students in oral performance. Oral competence—the ability to express oneself through speech and recitation—is important in every subject area. Although oral performance may not be the primary objective for most subjects, few objectives in any subject will be met if the results of instruction cannot be observed and evaluated orally. Reading, social studies, science, and even math require some type of oral performance. The type of oral performance required of students can vary considerably from subject to subject, but most often it will take the form of reports to the class, reading in front of the class, stating an opinion, justifying a response, giving a speech, or performing in a skit, a play, or a demonstration. All of these require higher thought processes and forms of expression. Oral performance is one way students can share what they have learned.

Oral performances test students' knowledge and organization of a topic as well as their delivery of it. For example, recitation of an original poem involves both knowledge of the structure of poetry and the ability to deliver it orally in ways that communicate and emphasize its meaning. The ability to represent a character in a skit or play involves knowing how the character might dress and act, remembering the lines the character is to speak, and being able to convey this characterization orally to others to create a feeling of empathy. Giving a report to the class involves both having something to say and saying it in a way that promotes acceptance and understanding of a particular point of view. In other words, content and process each must be given proper emphasis.

Proper emphasis on content and process can be accomplished by observing two facets of oral performance: (1) delivery and (2) content and organization.

Characteristics of Delivery
- Enunciation (speaking clearly)
- Pronunciation (using correct word sounds)
- Rate of speech
- Word choice
- Use of gestures

Characteristics of Content and Organization
- Quality and accuracy of ideas
- Logical development of ideas
- Organization of ideas
- Style and individuality
- Wording and phrasing

More importance may be given to some categories than to others; for example, because a great deal of care and time might have been taken in introducing students to the library, the quality and accuracy of ideas could be considered twice as important as other dimensions of content and organization.

Oral performances in one subject might be quite different from those in another subject. In an English class, for example, word usage may take on a greater importance than it would in the social studies class. Generally, the mechanical aspects of speaking occupy less attention in the higher grades because these skills presumably have already been attained, and the focus of the instruction at this level is on the development of ideas, organization, style, wording, and phrasing. Thus, the oral dimensions to be observed should be flexible, varying with both subject matter and grade level.

Notice that Ms. Brokaw made several efforts to encourage oral performance among class members. First, she engaged her students orally during the lesson, preventing them from becoming passive learners. This teacher's dialogue with her students required not just student responses, but responses that encouraged students to reason out and justify their answers to the class, thereby promoting higher thought processes. Her small-group activity, by virtue of assigned roles, required a degree of oral performance from every student in the group. Group leaders would read the poem to their group, group members would discuss its meaning using the model provided, and a presenter would read the poem to the class. In this manner, oral performance was encouraged from as many members of the class as possible, in as many ways as possible. Students who didn't contribute to the class discussion could contribute to a more informal discussion within their groups.

Observing Students in Oral Performance

Oral performances include a wide range of behavior, from simply answering a teacher's question to giving a speech or report or performing in a classroom skit or play. In any of its varied forms, oral performance is important because of its capacity to translate content learned in one way (e.g., from lecture or text) into a new and more complete form (e.g., oral report to the class). For example, most oral performances require the learner to translate, summarize, or paraphrase what has been learned through books or a presentation into a more integrated whole, thereby raising the learner's thought process to a higher level, such as from knowledge of facts to the comprehension and application of these facts in an adult-like task. Because oral performance can be less time consuming than projects and demonstrations, it can be used more often and in more varied ways.

There is little doubt that, in every classroom, students should be accustomed to expressing their knowledge as well as their ideas and opinions orally. Therefore, almost every lesson should include some attention to teacher–student or student–student interaction. However, besides these simple oral performances, there are other, more formal types of oral expression that should occur over a unit or sequence of related lessons. These include assigned reports to the class, reading from one's own work, discussing an extended idea or theme, justifying a response in one's own words, critically analyzing the response of another student, and delivering a formal presentation. Instrument 12.5 provides a format for observing the degree to which any or all of these examples of oral expression occur over a unit or sequence of lessons. Because some forms of oral expression are more likely than others on any given day, observations for this behavior should take place over multiple observations. Instrument 12.5 can be used to accumulate your observations.

Providing Opportunities for Students to Learn from Their Mistakes

The fifth behavior for eliciting higher thought processes and performance outcomes involves independent practice to allow students the opportunity to discover and learn from their mistakes (Stipek, 2002). This approach allows the learner to discover the results of his efforts to learn. It requires of the teacher the ability to anticipate student errors and to develop (or select from workbooks, texts, and resources) handouts and exercises that provide the opportunity to make these mistakes for the purpose of learning from them. It is by this process that the learner can expand, clarify, or revise a response. Learning from mistakes takes the form of exercises, handouts, problem sets, and activity sheets tailored to the whole class or subgroups of learners that push students toward higher levels of understanding and can reveal errors that can inhibit later learning.

As we saw in Chapter 11, student errors play an important role in moving learners to the next rung of the learning ladder. If an assigned problem, question, or exercise promotes an inaccurate and meaningless response, little has been achieved for the learner. But if an assigned problem, question, or exercise creates (or even intentionally promotes) a student response that is inaccurate but instructive, the learner gains a chance to repeat the performance with better understanding. Recall that these kinds of student errors were called *functional errors*. Whether these errors are unexpected or are anticipated by the teacher, they can be used to enhance the learner's understanding of the content. This chapter presents functional errors that can stimulate new higher-order thought processes and performance outcomes. Consider the following exercise designed to challenge a student's understanding of the Civil War.

Fill in the blanks with the correct answers.

Abraham Lincoln was president at the time of the Civil War.

His government represented the Northern region of our country, called the Confederacy.

This student responded to the third blank incorrectly, but because of the relationship among the questions it was easy for the teacher to detect the nature of the error. Notice that this set of questions encouraged the learner to extend his knowledge to the point that, if understanding was incomplete or the proper relationship had not been acquired, it would become apparent in a response to a later question. But what if this teacher had raised a less thoughtful, lower-order sequence of questions? Imagine the following exercise completed by this same student.

Underline the letter representing the correct answer.

President of the United States at the time of the Civil War:

(a) Douglas, (b) Lincoln, (c) Davis, (d) Franklin

Regions of our country fighting were

(a) North vs. West (b) South vs. East
(c) North vs. South (d) East vs. West

Name of one of the sides fighting:

(a) The Constitutionalists (b) The Confederacy
(c) The Pilgrims (d) The Americans

Despite getting all the answers correct, this student could still erroneously associate the Confederacy with Lincoln and the North. Here it is impossible to assess the student's higher thought processes involving important relationships, because only a regurgitation of facts was required. Because the questions did not test for functional errors useful for lifting this student to the next rung of the learning ladder, the teacher has no easy way to determine if there is a problem.

Tailoring seatwork to reflect functional errors requires anticipating the kinds of errors that are most likely to occur and providing an opportunity for them to occur in the context of a learning experience. This means that exercises, problem sets, and activities, as well as a teacher's oral responses, need to challenge a learner's current level of understanding. They must promote a response—correct or incorrect—that is *functional* for moving the learner to the next rung of the learning ladder. This is why scripted approaches to instruction (e.g., publishers' workbooks), drills, and practice exercises are not, by themselves, sufficient to promote higher thought processes. These sources might provide practice, but often do not provide sufficient opportunity for higher thought processes to occur. Frequently, these resources need to be supplemented by teacher-prepared or teacher-selected seatwork directed at, or slightly above, the learners' current level of understanding, so that student errors useful for providing redirection and remediation can be brought to the surface.

What learning activities could Ms. Brokaw use with this lesson? A specially prepared worksheet that asks students to write an interpretation of a poem

FIGURE 12.1 Form for Practicing the Model Used to Interpret a Poem

Poem 1 _____

_____

_____

_____

Step 1: List the key words in this poem.

_____

_____

_____

_____

Step 2: Find the dictionary meaning of at least one key word whose meaning you are unsure of.

Word: _____ Meaning: _____

_____

Step 3: Paraphrase what you think the author is saying.

_____

_____

_____

Step 4: Describe an experience in your own life that relates to what this poet is saying.

_____

_____

_____

using the four steps presented in the lesson could provide an opportunity for functional errors, as opposed to regurgitating the four steps to interpreting a poem. This worksheet might take the form shown in Figure 12.1. Can you think of any other exercise that Ms. Brokaw could use that would inform the learner of what higher-level thought processes had or had not been learned from this lesson? What might a form for recording student responses to your exercise look like?

Observing Activities for Students to Learn from Their Mistakes

Activities that allow students to learn from their mistakes often involve independent practice, which should challenge the learner enough so that the most critical and pervasive errors are brought to the surface. Workbook problems and end-of-chapter exercises can provide opportunities for this type of learning when they are sufficiently challenging. But when published exercises provide monotonous drill either below or above students' current level of understanding, alternative materials will be needed.

Instrument 12.6 provides a format for recording independent practice opportunities that may be used to provide students with a knowledge of their mistakes involving higher-level thought processes. Check for these over the course of one or more observations.

Using Portfolios and Performance Assessments of Learning

Our final behavior for promoting higher thought processes and performance outcomes involves the assessment of what has been learned. Classroom assessment, particularly beyond the early elementary grades, is sometimes almost exclusively based on paper-and-pencil tests that indicate, rather than directly measure, what students have learned. For example, we could measure an understanding of the scientific method not by having learners plan, conduct, and evaluate an experiment (a direct measure), but by asking them to list the steps of the scientific method, write about the difference between a hypothesis and a theory, or choose the correct definition of a control group from a list of choices (all indirect assessment). Or, we might measure children's understanding of money not by observing them buying food, paying for it, and getting the correct change (direct assessment), but by asking them to recall how many pennies there are in a dollar, or to write down how much change they would get back from a $10 bill if they paid $6.75 for a T-shirt (indirect assessment).

There are obvious advantages to indirect assessment of achievement and learning. Directly measuring all learning that goes on in a classroom would be very time-consuming. But indirect assessment raises a problem: How do you know that the assessment is measuring what you say it is? In other words, how authentic is your assessment? **Authentic assessments** (Borich & Tombari, 2004; Tombari & Borich, 1999) measure directly what teachers really care about. For example, if learners are presented a demonstration of how to focus a microscope and then coached while practicing it themselves, an authentic test would ask them to correctly focus a microscope to identify a mystery specimen—not to label the parts of the microscope on a diagram.

Performance assessment of learning authentically measures higher thought processes that are often measured only as isolated bits of behavior on multiple-choice, true–false, or structured-essay tests. Many teachers assert that the performance assessment of learning can best be measured by oral reports, extended essays, projects, portfolios of student work, scientific investigations, creative scores and scripts, physical models, and similar overt signs that demonstrate "bits" of behavior being successfully converted into an "integrated performance" in a context different from that in which they were learned. Performance assessments typically take place over a period of hours or days in which students work at their own pace and, with the aid of guidelines provided by the teacher, select the tasks and projects with which to demonstrate their competence against a set of known criteria.

The goal of performance assessment is to reduce the importance of artificial knowledge, which may be unintentionally promoted by exclusive or heavy reliance on true–false, multiple-choice, matching, and fill-in-the-blanks tests and to increase the importance of verbal explanations and justifications, critical thinking, and problem solving related to authentic professional and social responsibilities. A secondary goal is to diminish the weight generally accorded to traditional test-taking skills in student evaluation, especially students for whom such skills might be weak.

Important Characteristics of Performance Assessments

- Demonstrating understandings and intellectual skills that were modeled, coached, and practiced in class
- Using learned knowledge in an authentic, real-world context
- Integrating and simultaneously using higher thought processes rather than simply recalling information
- Producing outcomes for which the routine use of previously learned information is not sufficient
- Setting standards by showing what it means to perform competently in the real world
- Illustrating some of the end products of schooling
- Representing real-life challenges rather than bookwork, which might be artificial or fragmented and could have been selected for ease in grading

Performance assessments, therefore, are designed to measure intellectual skills in a problem-solving, decision-making context that should exhibit three important characteristics: (1) a hands-on exercise or problem to solve, which produces (2) an observable real-world outcome or product (a typed business letter, a map, a graph, a piece of clothing, an oral presentation, or a poem) such that the teacher can (3) observe the solution process. The teacher observes and assesses not only the product, but also the behaviors used to get there—for example, relating, composing, justifying, differentiating, and diagnosing.

Types of performance assessments can include individual projects, such as portfolios, investigations and experiments, oral presentations, demonstrations, and exhibits, as well as classroom activities, such as assignments, journals, essays, reports, reading logs, and discussion groups. Examples include the following:

- Learners assemble a portfolio of the best examples of their writing, using poetry, essay, short story, or autobiographical contributions.
- Learners prepare a visual story on a crucial problem affecting their community.
- Learners select and use laboratory equipment appropriately to test a hypothesis.
- Learners program calculators to solve an equation with two unknowns.
- Learners challenge the ideas of their peers in a class discussion using three known principles of logic.
- Learners develop their own math problem and show at least two alternative ways to solve it.

Guidelines for completing and evaluating a project or performance can be developed from technical criteria, which might include key observable features of the project or performance to be judged (such as technical quality, accuracy, or usability) and process criteria, which might include how the learner goes about completing the product or performance (such as use of resources, extent of group sharing, neatness, or overall effort). Student input and reflection on these criteria is an important part of a successful portfolio or performance assessment project, even for very young students (Lightfoot, 2006). Also, performance assessments should be aligned with local, state, and national curriculum standards when possible (Reynolds & Rich, 2006). Writing performance assessment rubrics from these standards helps teachers and students judge how well they are meeting the standards, but can also serve to complement (and sometimes challenge) other assessment results. Sample guidelines were presented on page 201.

Observing Portfolios and Performance Assessments

Performance assessments are authentic assessments in which students are asked to integrate bits of knowledge that might have been learned in isolated contexts into a single, unified product with a real-world character such as might be found outside the classroom. The product should allow the student a degree of flexibility regarding the form in which it is expressed and the resources consulted in producing it. The requirements for grading a portfolio or performance assessment should include both product and process criteria. The work of Arter and McTighe (2000) emphasizes the importance of placing these criteria into a rating plan, called a **rubric,** that carefully describes the degrees or levels of performance that can be expected and rated.

Product criteria include key observable features of the product or performance, such as

- Technical quality
- Accuracy
- Practicality or usability
- Organization
- Application of materials and resources

Process criteria include how the learner went about solving the problem or creating the product and can include attributes such as

- Creativity
- Neatness
- Sharing
- Articulation
- Use of references and resources

Process criteria are often difficult to grade on an all-or-nothing basis, so they often have several degrees of effort assigned to them: for example, 3 = high effort, 2 = average effort, and 1 = low effort.

Performance assessments need not take place at the same time for the whole class. Learners can be assessed at different times, individually or in small groups. For example, learners can rotate through classroom learning centers and be assessed when the teacher feels they are acquiring mastery. Or performance assessments can take place within ongoing classroom activities, rather than consuming extra time during the day.

Instrument 12.7 provides a format for observing a performance assessment. Your observation, and the portfolio or performance assessment, will be more reliable if (1) the performance to be judged (process and product) is clearly specified, (2) the ratings or criteria in making the judgments are determined beforehand, and (3) two or more raters independently grade the performance.

Although Ms. Brokaw's lesson did not afford us the opportunity to observe all six dimensions of higher-order processes and performance outcomes directly, we can infer or imagine how they may be incorporated in future lessons. For example, efforts at writing a poem, interpreting a favorite poem, or drawing a picture that expresses some aspect of a poem could stimulate higher thought processes.

Specially prepared worksheets that ask students to follow the model for a poem could provide an opportunity for both functional errors and performance assessment. For example, an activity handout that would afford learners the opportunity to practice the model independent of their teacher and group could be provided, as was shown in Figure 12.1.

Responses from different students could be anonymously shared with the class to provide feedback as to how well the model was followed. If product and process criteria were applied to each student's response, a performance assessment could be undertaken to see how well the learners were able to integrate different pieces of information in a more realistic and expanded context. Student portfolios consisting of projects and demonstrations from past lessons (e.g., on bulletin boards, shelves, and cabinets and at learning centers) could provide evidence that higher thought processes and performance assessments were occurring.

Figure 12.2 summarizes an observer's reaction to Ms. Brokaw's lesson. How does it compare with your thoughts? Generally, Ms. Brokaw was given good marks for her attempts to promote higher thought processes and performance outcomes. The lesson provided strong indications of collaboration and group work, mental modeling, and oral performance. However, the observer was unable to view student projects or demonstrations, how learners might learn from their mistakes, or performance assessment. This will be typical of many lessons that, because of lesson objectives and time, do not allow for more than a few activities that promote higher thought processes and performance outcomes.

CULTURAL DIVERSITY AND PERFORMANCE OUTCOMES

Traditionally, teachers from elementary school to college have perceived making tests and assigning grades to be two of the more bothersome aspects of teaching. Many have come to view these as chores that have to be done to please administrators and parents, rather than as a pattern of practice integral to the teaching process itself. In other words, some forms of testing and evaluation have become (or have been used as) ends unto themselves instead of the teaching tools they were originally intended to be. The performance assessment of learning is an attempt to redress the gap between assessments that grade and assessments that teach by

- Reactivating previously learned skills and knowledge

FIGURE 12.2 Checklist for Observing Ms. Brokaw's Classroom

Behavior	Observed	Not Observed	No Opportunity to Observe
1. Uses collaborative and group activities	✓ Used grouping effectively		
2. Demonstrates mental models and strategies for learning	✓ Modeled correct procedure		
3. Arranges for students to apply what they've learned through products and demonstrations			✓ May relate to subsequent lessons
4. Engages students in oral performance	✓ Asked students to participate orally		
5. Provides opportunities for independent practice that challenge student understanding			✓ Plenty of opportunities, which may be followed up in subsequent lessons
6. Uses performance assessments			None required for this lesson

- Providing opportunities to practice and consolidate new information
- Motivating learners to higher degrees of effort
- Establishing for learners a realistic picture of their own ability
- Communicating performance and progress accurately to parents, future teachers, and employers
- Making allowances for differences in gender, culture, and abilities

The relevance of performance assessment for culture- and gender-fair testing is one of its most important strengths. In heterogeneously grouped classrooms, student interests, experiences, skills, and abilities vary considerably, making some traditional test-taking formats fairer for some learners than for others. For example, paper-and-pencil tests that assume a common reading speed and vocabulary will be less appropriate for a classroom with bilingual students or English language learners than performance-based projects in which learners are given some latitude in the time required to complete the activity, as well as in the focus of their efforts. Likewise, performance-based assessments provide the opportunity for learners to utilize their own unique abilities, interests, and learning styles to complete projects within specified guidelines that may be devised with their input (Borich & Tombari,

2004; Tannenbaum, 1996). Some learners, because of their learning history, culture, or ethnicity, might excel in test-taking skills and others may not, making performance assessment a more accurate indication of learning than pencil-and-paper tests. Performance assessments have been shown to have a substantial impact on culturally and ethnically diverse learners by increasing their motivation to complete a project, influencing their choice of study patterns and learning strategies, and accessing their preferred modes of responding. For these reasons, it is important that a range of evaluation activities be used, including performance assessment.

In this chapter we studied six dimensions of the classroom that underscore the important role of performance outcomes and higher thought processes: collaborative grouping, mental modeling, projects and demonstrations, oral performance, learning from mistakes, and portfolio and performance assessment. As you begin observing these dimensions, keep in mind their significant impact on all the other effective teaching behaviors we have studied—learning climate, classroom management, lesson clarity, instructional variety, task orientation, student engagement in the learning process, and student success.

For More Information

When performance assessments really "work," they often involve the creation of something new or novel, as well as something that can be enjoyed or used by others. Read the listed article (either on your own or with a class colleague). Think about the concept of "envisionments" as discussed in the article, as well as how some of these envisionments transform existing technologies and approaches to achieve a performance assessment goal.

Karchmer, R. A., & Leu, D. D. (1999). The Miss Rumphius Effect: Envisionments for literacy and learning that transform the Internet. In D. J. Leu, Jr. (Ed.), "Exploring literacy on the Internet." *The Reading Teacher, 52*(6), 636–642.

Key Terms

authentic assessments, 204
metacognition, 194

performance assessments, 205
rubric, 206

Activities*

1. Using the checklist in Instrument 12.1, observe a lesson, looking for signs of performance outcomes and higher thought processes. At the end of your observation, add a brief description to each box, highlighting at least one specific reason why you placed each of your check marks as you did.

2. Convert the positively stated indicators listed in Table 12.1 into a 5-point Likert scale. Consider the vertical or horizontal placement of each indicator on the page, whether words will be affixed to all or only some of the response blanks, and what verbal response alternatives will be best suited to each question. Show your scale to a classmate who also has constructed a 5-point scale. Together, create a single revised version incorporating the best features of each.

3. Using the format provided in Instrument 12.2, observe a collaborative or group activity for (a) teacher–student interaction, (b) student–student interaction, (c) task specification and materials, and (d) role assignment. Overall, how successful do you feel this particular activity was in getting students to think critically, reason, or problem solve?

4. Using the format provided in Instrument 12.3, look for a mental strategy or model students can use to learn the content presented during a lesson. Note the steps or procedures to be followed by the students and write a brief description of them.

5. Using the format provided in Instrument 12.4 for observing student projects and demonstrations, record any physical signs in and around the classroom that indicate students have applied what they have learned. If no signs are observable, ask the teacher what opportunities students have to put into practice what they have learned.

6. With the aid of the format provided in Instrument 12.5, record the types of oral performances that occur during a lesson. Make a list of any additional types of oral responses that you believe would promote higher thought processes.

7. Using the format provided in Instrument 12.6, observe a lesson, looking for opportunities for independent practice that might help students learn from their mistakes. Identify any supplemental handouts and whether they were teacher-made, assembled from different published sources, or selected from existing texts, workbooks, and other resources.

8. Using the format provided in Instrument 12.7, observe a classroom in which learners have recently completed a product or performance. In your opinion, did this product or performance provide an alternative format to accurately assess higher thought processes for culturally and ethnically diverse learners? What were its strengths and weaknesses?

*Some of these activities may be grouped into a common activity, divided among classmates, and completed from a single observation.

Appendix A

HOW TO DETERMINE PERCENTAGE OF OBSERVER AGREEMENT FOR A COUNTING OBSERVATION SYSTEM

Assume that two people have observed the same teacher for 30 minutes. During this time, one observer counts 36 instances of *asking questions;* the other counts 30 instances. The agreement between observers can be estimated from a formula suggested by Emmer and Millett (1970):

$$\text{Percentage agreement} = 100\left(1 - \frac{A - B}{A + B}\right)$$

A and *B* are the frequency counts of each of two observers for the behavior *asking questions.* The smaller frequency (*B*) is always subtracted from the larger frequency (*A*). Thus, the percentage of agreement between these two observers for the frequency with which the teacher asked questions during this period of observation was

$$100\left(1 - \frac{36 - 30}{36 + 30}\right) = 100\left(1 - \frac{6}{66}\right) = 91\%$$

The percentage of agreement for each behavior on the instrument is similarly determined. Behaviors for which less than 75% agreement is obtained are examined for their clarity and understanding among observers. Generally, after an initial practice session, 30 minutes of observation should provide enough data to determine a percentage of observer agreement. If a behavior fails to occur or occurs infrequently during this period, the period may have to be extended to allow for more observation.

Appendix B

INSTRUMENTS

212

Instructions: For each lens, place a check mark on the blank closest to the word that best describes the classroom you are observing.

Learning Climate

Teacher Centered __ __ __ __ __ __ __ Student Centered

Classroom Management

Orderly __ __ __ __ __ __ __ Disorderly

Lesson Clarity

Clear __ __ __ __ __ __ __ Unclear

Instructional Variety

Varied __ __ __ __ __ __ __ Static

Teacher's Task Orientation

Focused __ __ __ __ __ __ __ Unfocused

Students' Engagement in the Learning Process

Students
Involved __ __ __ __ __ __ __ Students
Uninvolved

Students' Success in Basic Academic Skills

High __ __ __ __ __ __ __ Low

Higher Thought Processes and Performance Outcomes

Many __ __ __ __ __ __ __ Few

Instructions: For each lens, place a check mark on the blank closest to the word that best describes the classroom you are observing.

Learning Climate

Teacher Centered __ __ __ __ __ __ __ Student Centered

Classroom Management

Orderly __ __ __ __ __ __ __ Disorderly

Lesson Clarity

Clear __ __ __ __ __ __ __ Unclear

Instructional Variety

Varied __ __ __ __ __ __ __ Static

Teacher's Task Orientation

Focused __ __ __ __ __ __ __ Unfocused

Students' Engagement in the Learning Process

Students Involved __ __ __ __ __ __ __ Students Uninvolved

Students' Success in Basic Academic Skills

High __ __ __ __ __ __ __ Low

Higher Thought Processes and Performance Outcomes

Many __ __ __ __ __ __ __ Few

INSTRUMENT 3.2   Recording Subjects and Grade Levels to Be Observed

Major Teaching or Interest Area	Minor (Secondary) Teaching or Interest Area	Other Special Areas of Interest
❏ _____	❏ _____	❏ _____
Grade	Grade	Grade
Subject	Subject	Subject
❏ _____	❏ _____	❏ _____
Grade	Grade	Grade
Subject	Subject	Subject
❏ _____	❏ _____	❏ _____
Grade	Grade	Grade
Subject	Subject	Subject
❏ _____	❏ _____	❏ _____
Grade	Grade	Grade
Subject	Subject	Subject
❏ _____	❏ _____	❏ _____
Grade	Grade	Grade
Subject	Subject	Subject
❏ _____	❏ _____	❏ _____
Grade	Grade	Grade
Subject	Subject	Subject
❏ _____	❏ _____	❏ _____
Grade	Grade	Grade
Subject	Subject	Subject
❏ _____	❏ _____	❏ _____
Grade	Grade	Grade
Subject	Subject	Subject
❏ _____	❏ _____	❏ _____
Grade	Grade	Grade
Subject	Subject	Subject

INSTRUMENT 4.1   Studying Classroom Management

Type	Controlling Behaviors	5-Minute Intervals									Number of Intervals Observed
Verbal Control	1. Acknowledges, agrees, complies										
	2. Praises										
	3. Asks for status										
	4. Suggests, guides										
	5. Feedback, cites reason										
	6. Corrects with criticism										
	7. Questions for control										
	8. Questions, states behavior rule										
	9. Directs with reason										
	10. Directs without reason										
	11. Uses time pressure										
	12. Reminds, prods										
	13. Interrupts, cuts off										
	14. Supervises closely, immobilizes										
	15. Criticizes, warns										
	16. Orders, commands										
	17. Scolds, punishes										
Physical Control	18. Nods, smiles, facial feedback										
	19. Uses "body English," waits										
	20. Gestures										
	21. Touches, pats										
	22. Shakes head, eye contact										
	23. Takes equipment, book										
	24. Signals										
	25. Glares, frowns										
	26. Holds, pushes, speaks										
	27. Ignores, abandons										

Use the scale below to indicate your level of concern

1. Not concerned
2. A little concerned
3. Moderately concerned
4. Very concerned
5. Totally preoccupied

When I think about teaching, how concerned am I about this?

1. ❑ Having insufficient clerical help
2. ❑ Gaining students' respect
3. ❑ Coping with too many extra duties and responsibilities
4. ❑ Doing well when I'm observed
5. ❑ Helping students to value learning
6. ❑ Having insufficient time for rest and class preparation
7. ❑ Getting too little assistance from specialized teachers
8. ❑ Managing my time efficiently
9. ❑ Losing the respect of my peers
10. ❑ Having too little time for grading and testing
11. ❑ Coping with the inflexibility of the curriculum
12. ❑ Having too many standards and regulations set for teachers
13. ❑ Worrying about my ability to prepare adequate lesson plans
14. ❑ Having my inadequacies become known to other teachers
15. ❑ Increasing students' feelings of accomplishment
16. ❑ Dealing with the rigid instructional routine
17. ❑ Diagnosing students' learning problems
18. ❑ Wondering whether the principal thinks there's too much noise in my classroom
19. ❑ Helping students reach their potential
20. ❑ Obtaining a favorable evaluation of my teaching
21. ❑ Having too many students in my class
22. ❑ Recognizing the social and emotional needs of students
23. ❑ Challenging unmotivated students
24. ❑ Losing the respect of my students
25. ❑ Getting more financial support for my school
26. ❑ Trying to maintain control of the class
27. ❑ Having insufficient time to plan
28. ❑ Getting students to behave
29. ❑ Understanding why certain students make slow progress
30. ❑ Having an embarrassing incident occur in my classroom for which I might be judged responsible
31. ❑ Being unable to cope with troublemakers
32. ❑ Worrying that my peers may think I'm not doing an adequate job
33. ❑ Being able to manage and work with disruptive students
34. ❑ Finding ways to meet students' health and nutrition needs

(continued)

35. ❑ Appearing competent to parents
36. ❑ Meeting the needs of different kinds of students
37. ❑ Seeking alternative ways to ensure that students learn the subject matter
38. ❑ Understanding cultural differences that can affect students' behavior
39. ❑ Adapting myself to the needs of different students
40. ❑ Coping with the large number of administrative interruptions
41. ❑ Guiding students to intellectual and emotional growth
42. ❑ Working with too many students each day
43. ❑ Getting students to apply what they learn
44. ❑ Teaching effectively when another teacher is present
45. ❑ Motivating students to learn

Student Spontaneity

| High | 1 | 2 | 3 | 4 | 5 | 6 | 7 | Low |

Amount of Teacher Talk

| High | 7 | 6 | 5 | 4 | 3 | 2 | 1 | Low |

Student Risk-Taking Behavior

| High | 1 | 2 | 3 | 4 | 5 | 6 | 7 | Low |

Task Orientation

| High | 7 | 6 | 5 | 4 | 3 | 2 | 1 | Low |

Student-Initiated Responding

| High | 1 | 2 | 3 | 4 | 5 | 6 | 7 | Low |

Teacher Authority

| High | 7 | 6 | 5 | 4 | 3 | 2 | 1 | Low |

Use of Praise and Rewards

| High | 7 | 6 | 5 | 4 | 3 | 2 | 1 | Low |

Amount of Criticism, Scolding, and Reprimanding

| High | 1 | 2 | 3 | 4 | 5 | 6 | 7 | Low |

Use of Student Ideas

| High | 7 | 6 | 5 | 4 | 3 | 2 | 1 | Low |

Reference to Formal Rules and Procedures

| High | 1 | 2 | 3 | 4 | 5 | 6 | 7 | Low |

Responsiveness to Student Requests

| High | 7 | 6 | 5 | 4 | 3 | 2 | 1 | Low |

Use of Punishment

| High | 1 | 2 | 3 | 4 | 5 | 6 | 7 | Low |

INSTRUMENT 5.4 Plotting Data from Instruments 5.2 and 5.3

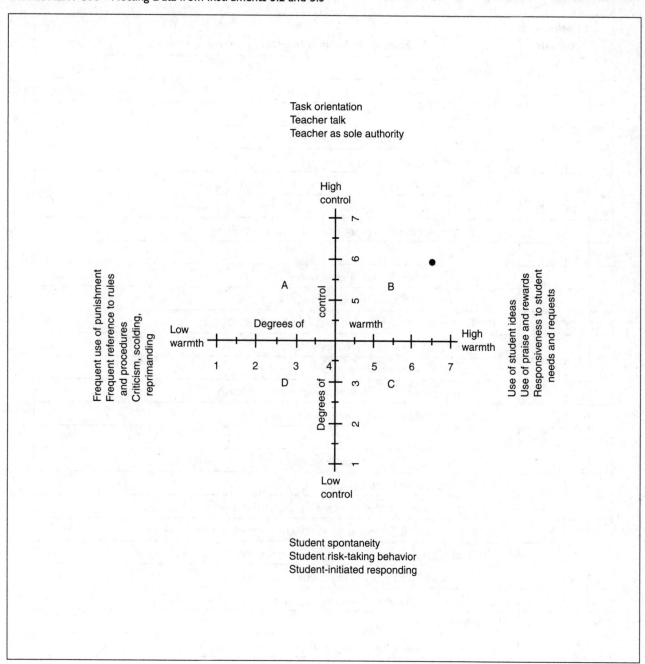

INSTRUMENT 5.5   Observing Dimensions of Classroom Warmth and Control

15-Minute Intervals				Teacher Behaviors Indicating Learning Climate
1	2	3	4	A. High Warmth
				1. Teacher praises or rewards student's behavior.
				2. Teacher uses student's ideas in presenting lesson.
				3. Teacher responds to student's expression of need.
				4. Teacher nods or gestures approvingly.
				5. Teacher provides clue or hint to student to find right answer.
				6. Teacher gives encouragement to student after wrong answer.
				7. Teacher agrees with student or accepts student's feelings.
1	2	3	4	B. Low Warmth
				8. Teacher criticizes, scolds, or admonishes.
				9. Teacher cuts off or interrupts student.
				10. Teacher calls class's attention to student's deficiencies.
				11. Teacher ignores student's request to speak.
				12. Teacher glares or frowns at student.
				13. Teacher orders or commands student to do something.
				14. Teacher criticizes wrong answer without giving reason.
1	2	3	4	C. High Control
				15. Teacher accepts only one answer as correct.
				16. Teacher occupies center of attention.
				17. Teacher expects student to come up with answer teacher has in mind.
				18. Teacher expects student to know rather than guess answer.
				19. Teacher asks question that student can answer only by studying the lesson.
				20. Teacher evaluates work of student by set standard.
				21. Teacher accepts only answers or suggestions closely related to topic.
1	2	3	4	D. Low Control
				22. Teacher organizes learning around student's own problem or question.
				23. Teacher has student make own selection and analysis of subject matter.
				24. Teacher has student work independently on what concerns student.
				25. Teacher makes a wide range of information available.
				26. Teacher makes doing something center of student's attention.
				27. Teacher encourages student to put ideas to a test.
				28. Teacher has student participate actively.

Source: Parts A and B from the author. Parts C and D based on *Experimental Mind in Education,* by B. Burton Brown. Copyright © 1968 by B. Burton Brown. Reprinted by permission of Harper & Row, Publishers, Inc.

INSTRUMENT 5.6 Observing Social Environment in the Classroom

	Strongly Disagree	Disagree	Agree	Strongly Agree	No Information
1. A student in this class has the chance to get to know all other students (cohesiveness).	1	2	3	4	N/I
2. The class has students with many different interests (diversity).	1	2	3	4	N/I
3. There is a set of rules for the students to follow (formality).	1	2	3	4	N/I
4. Most of the class has difficulty keeping up with the assigned work (speed).	1	2	3	4	N/I
5. The books and equipment students need or want are easily available in the classroom (environment).	1	2	3	4	N/I
6. There are tensions among certain students that tend to interfere with class activities (friction).	1	2	3	4	N/I
7. Most students have little idea of what the class is attempting to accomplish (goal direction).	4	3	2	1	N/I
8. The better students' questions are answered more sympathetically than those of the average students (favoritism).	1	2	3	4	N/I
9. Some students refuse to mix with the rest of the class (cliquishness).	1	2	3	4	N/I
10. The students seem to enjoy their classwork (satisfaction).	1	2	3	4	N/I
11. There are long periods during which the class does nothing (disorganization).	1	2	3	4	N/I
12. Some students in the class consider the work difficult (difficulty).	1	2	3	4	N/I
13. Most students seem to have a concern for the progress of the class (apathy).	4	3	2	1	N/I
14. When group discussions occur, all students tend to contribute (democracy).	1	2	3	4	N/I
15. Most students cooperate rather than compete with one another in this class (competitiveness).	4	3	2	1	N/I
16. Students in this class are not in close enough contact to develop likes and dislikes (competitiveness).	4	3	2	1	N/I
17. The class is working toward many different goals.	1	2	3	4	N/I
18. Students who break the rules are penalized.	1	2	3	4	N/I
19. The class has plenty of time to cover the prescribed amount of work.	4	3	2	1	N/I
20. A comprehensive collection of reference material is available in the classroom for the students to use.	1	2	3	4	N/I
21. Certain students seem to have no respect for other students.	1	2	3	4	N/I
22. The objectives of the class are not clearly recognized.	4	3	2	1	N/I
23. Every member of the class is given the same privileges.	4	3	2	1	N/I
24. Certain students work only with their close friends.	1	2	3	4	N/I
25. There is considerable student dissatisfaction with the classwork.	4	3	2	1	N/I
26. Classwork is frequently interrupted by some students with nothing to do.	4	3	2	1	N/I
27. Most students in this class are constantly challenged.	1	2	3	4	N/I
28. Some members of the class don't care what the class does.	1	2	3	4	N/I
29. Certain students have more influence on the class than others.	4	3	2	1	N/I
30. Most students in the class want their work to be better than their friends' work.	1	2	3	4	N/I

(continued)

	Strongly Disagree	Disagree	Agree	Strongly Agree	No Information
31. This class is made up of individuals who do not know each other well.	4	3	2	1	N/I
32. Different students are interested in different aspects of the class.	4	3	2	1	N/I
33. There is a right and a wrong way of going about class activities.	4	3	2	1	N/I
34. There is little time in this class for daydreaming.	4	3	2	1	N/I
35. There are bulletin board displays and pictures around the room.	4	3	2	1	N/I
36. Certain students in this class are uncooperative.	1	2	3	4	N/I
37. Most of the class realizes exactly how much work is required.	1	2	3	4	N/I
38. Certain students in the class are favored over others.	1	2	3	4	N/I
39. Most students cooperate equally well with all class members.	4	3	2	1	N/I
40. After an assignment, most students have a sense of satisfaction.	1	2	3	4	N/I
41. The class is well organized and efficient.	4	3	2	1	N/I
42. Most students consider the subject matter easy.	4	3	2	1	N/I
43. Students show a common concern for the success of the class.	4	3	2	1	N/I
44. Each member of the class has as much influence as any other member.	4	3	2	1	N/I
45. Students compete to see who can do the best work.	4	3	2	1	N/I

INSTRUMENT 6.1 Observing Dimensions of Classroom Management

Behavior	Observed	Not Observed	No Opportunity to Observe
1. Arranges classroom to match instructional goals			
2. Has preestablished classroom rules in place			
3. Exhibits use of instructional routines for most frequently performed activities			
4. Institutes incentives and consequences to promote appropriate behavior and discourage inappropriate behavior			
5. Uses low-profile classroom management to maintain instructional momentum			

Placement of items to consider:
- Teacher's desk
- Student desks/tables
- Blackboard
- Media (for example, overhead projector)
- Reference books/shelves
- Learning center
- Worktable(s)
- Rugs and visual texture
- Space dividers

The social and organizational context of this classroom is best suited for (check all that apply):

❑ group projects

❑ independent work

❑ lecture and discussion

❑ other _____

1. Getting out of seat:

2. Responding, speaking out:

3. Communicating during group work/discussion:

4. Make-up work:

5. Violating due dates:

6. Assignment completion:

7. Rule violation:

8. Other:

	How Well Students Learned Routine		
	1	2	3

Beginning of class routine

Steps:

Handing in assignments routine

Steps:

Transition to next activity routine

Steps:

Violation of rule routine (disciplinary)

Steps:

Other _____

Steps:

1. Using praise and encouragement:

2. Providing explanations:

3. Offering to help:

4. Accepting diversity:

5. Providing reinforcement or reward:

INSTRUMENT 6.6 Observing Low-Profile Classroom Management

	Times Observed					
	1	2	3	4	5	6
Anticipation						
back-and-forth scanning	❑	❑	❑	❑	❑	❑
faster pace	❑	❑	❑	❑	❑	❑
louder voice/high pitch	❑	❑	❑	❑	❑	❑
greater movement	❑	❑	❑	❑	❑	❑
change to other activity	❑	❑	❑	❑	❑	❑
other _____	❑	❑	❑	❑	❑	❑
Deflection (Nonverbal)						
moving closer to student	❑	❑	❑	❑	❑	❑
personal eye contact	❑	❑	❑	❑	❑	❑
facial expression	❑	❑	❑	❑	❑	❑
other _____	❑	❑	❑	❑	❑	❑
Deflection (Verbal)						
rule reminder (prompting)	❑	❑	❑	❑	❑	❑
name dropping	❑	❑	❑	❑	❑	❑
peer recognition	❑	❑	❑	❑	❑	❑
other _____	❑	❑	❑	❑	❑	❑
Reaction						
warning	❑	❑	❑	❑	❑	❑
incentive	❑	❑	❑	❑	❑	❑
loss of privilege	❑	❑	❑	❑	❑	❑
punishment (detention)	❑	❑	❑	❑	❑	❑
other _____	❑	❑	❑	❑	❑	❑

Place a check in the appropriate boxes.

Teacher *did* inform learners of objective. If so, how?

❑ verbally   ❑ on board or overhead   ❑ with handout

Teacher *did not* inform learners of objective. If not, why?

❑ Learners knew objective from previous lesson (lesson continuation)

❑ Not relevant to goals and purposes of lesson (review)

❑ Other (identify) _____

❑ No reason apparent

    ❑ *Cognitive*

       ❑ Recall, name, or identify

       ❑ Explain, summarize, paraphrase

       ❑ Use, solve, demonstrate

       ❑ Relate, differentiate, distinguish

       ❑ Create, design, compose

       ❑ Judge, justify, defend

    ❑ *Affective*

       ❑ Listen, attend, notice

       ❑ Comply, obey, participate

       ❑ Prefer, convince, value

       ❑ Formulate, systematize, theorize

       ❑ Display, internalize, exhibit

    ❑ *Psychomotor*

       ❑ Repeat, follow from visual

       ❑ Repeat, follow from verbal directions

       ❑ Perform accurately, proficiently

       ❑ Perform with speed, timing

       ❑ Perform effortlessly, automatically

INSTRUMENT 7.2 Cataloging Advance Organizers

Type	Reference Number	Advance Organizer		Time in Lesson Used			Number of References
		Grade	Subject	Beginning	Middle	End	
Verbal	1			☐	☐	☐	
	2			☐	☐	☐	
	3			☐	☐	☐	
	4			☐	☐	☐	
	5			☐	☐	☐	
	6			☐	☐	☐	
Visual	7			☐	☐	☐	
	8			☐	☐	☐	
	9			☐	☐	☐	
	10			☐	☐	☐	

INSTRUMENT 7.3   Recording Approximate Percentage of Learners at Each Level of Instruction

Observation 1 (Percentages)

Content Appears below Students' Level	Content Appears at or Slightly above Students' Level	Content Appears above Students' Level
0	0	0
25	25	25
50	50	50
75	75	75
100	100	100

Observation 2

Content Appears below Students' Level	Content Appears at or Slightly above Students' Level	Content Appears above Students' Level
0	0	0
25	25	25
50	50	50
75	75	75
100	100	100

Observation 3

Content Appears below Students' Level	Content Appears at or Slightly above Students' Level	Content Appears above Students' Level
0	0	0
25	25	25
50	50	50
75	75	75
100	100	100

Student	Assignment							Student Response				Teacher Reaction						
or Number	wb	hw	oas	hand	test	proj	other	rpt	specif	uncert	other	crit	rpt	ans	restate	check	ignore	other

Direction or Instructions Pertaining to

wb   Workbook

hw   Homework

oas   Oral assignment

hand   Handout

test   Test

proj   Extended project or paper

other   Other type of assignment

Student Responses

rpt   Student asks teacher to repeat directions or instructions.

specif   Student asks specific question for clarification.

uncert   Student expresses uncertainty orally (e.g., "I don't understand") or physically (e.g., frowns, shrugs).

other   Student uses some other measure to indicate directives or instructions were not understood.

Teacher Reactions

crit   Teacher criticizes student for not understanding.

rpt   Teacher repeats directive or instruction.

ans   Teacher answers student question about directive.

restate   Teacher restates instructions in different words.

check   Teacher checks for understanding (e.g., asks student to repeat or asks student a question).

ignore   Teacher ignores student response.

other   Teacher reacts in some other way.

INSTRUMENT 7.5 Recording the Use of Examples, Illustrations, and Demonstrations to Explain and Clarify Content

	Indicator	Occurrences									
		1	2	3	4	5	6	7	8	9	10
Visual	Writes on board										
	Uses overhead										
	Points to or holds up visual										
	Shows slides or film										
	Demonstrates with model or equipment										
	Other										
Oral	Provides or asks for example										
	Tells illustrative story										
	Recalls personal experience										
	Relates to past learning										
	Poses problem										
	Compares and contrasts										
	Other										

235

INSTRUMENT 7.6 Observing Lesson Clarity

Behavior	Observed	Not Observed	No Opportunity to Observe
1. Informs learners of skills or understandings expected at end of lesson.			
2. Provides learners with an advance organizer that places lesson content in perspective.			
3. Checks for lesson-relevant prior knowledge at beginning of lesson and reteaches if necessary.			
4. Knows learners' ability levels and uses media, materials, and procedures at or slightly above their current level of functioning.			
5. Gives directions clearly. Checks for understanding along the way.			
6. Uses examples, illustrations, or demonstrations to explain and clarify content in text and workbooks.			
7. Provides review or summary.			

INSTRUMENT 8.1   Observing Instructional Variety

Behavior		Observed	Not Observed	No Opportunity to Observe
1. Uses attention-gaining devices				
2. Shows enthusiasm and animation through variation in eye contact, voice, and gestures				
3. Varies instructional activities (e.g., presenting, explaining, questioning, discussing, practicing) and media (e.g., computer software, film, workbook transparencies, the Internet)				
4. Uses mix of rewards and reinforcers				
5. Various types of questions and probes	Questions — Convergent			
	Questions — Divergent			
	Probes — To clarify			
	Probes — To solicit			
	Probes — To redirect			
6. Uses student ideas and participation to foster lesson objectives when appropriate to goals of instruction				

INSTRUMENT 8.2   Recording Use of Attention-Gaining Devices

Date	Lesson Topic	Verbal Statements and Questions					Visual				Media			Realia			
		To Promote Curiosity	To Present a Contradiction	To Create Controversy	To Surprise/Astound	Other	Diagrams/Charts	Blackboard	Photographs/Pictures	Other	Audio	Film/TV/Video	Computer	Living Things	Scale Models	Technical/Laboratory Equipment	Other
Totals																	

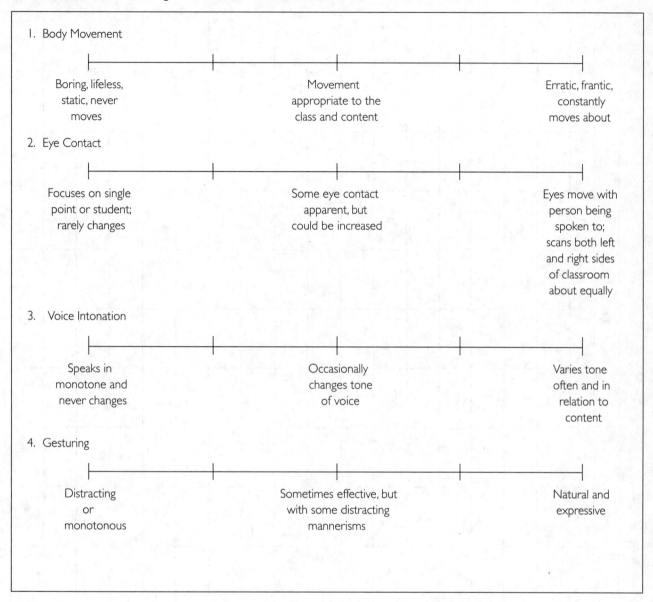

1. Body Movement

| Boring, lifeless, static, never moves | Movement appropriate to the class and content | Erratic, frantic, constantly moves about |

2. Eye Contact

| Focuses on single point or student; rarely changes | Some eye contact apparent, but could be increased | Eyes move with person being spoken to; scans both left and right sides of classroom about equally |

3. Voice Intonation

| Speaks in monotone and never changes | Occasionally changes tone of voice | Varies tone often and in relation to content |

4. Gesturing

| Distracting or monotonous | Sometimes effective, but with some distracting mannerisms | Natural and expressive |

INSTRUMENT 8.4 Observing Differentiated Activity Structures

			Tasks								
Task Components	1	2	3	4	5	6	7	8	9	10
Task Products	Subvocal thought										
	Oral response										
	Written response										
	Picture/drawings										
	Other										
Task Operations	Recognition and discrimination										
	Application and practice										
	Problem solving										
	Invention, discovery										
	Other										
Task Resources	Computer/Internet										
	Text/workbook										
	Blackboard										
	Handout										
	Transparencies										
	Learning center/library										
	Other										

INSTRUMENT 8.5 Observing the Four Modalities

Five-Minute Intervals	Oral (Speaking, Hearing/ Listening)	Verbal (Written)	Visual (Showing, Viewing)	Tactile (Touching)
1				
2				
3				
4				
5				
6				
7				
8				
9				
10				
Total				
Percent				
Minutes (approx.)				

INSTRUMENT 8.6   Recording Informal and Formal Types of Rewards

	Teacher Response/Activity	Times of Occurrence									
		1	2	3	4	5	6	7	8	9	10
Informal (Daily)	Gives verbal praise only ("good"), smiles, nods head only										
	Gives verbal praise with reason why response is correct										
	Uses student answer as model (puts on board)										
	Has student help/tell others how to do it										
	Asks peers to show admiration ("Isn't it good?")										
	Allows work in groups										
	Allows use of the learning center										
	Allows independent study time										
	Other										
Formal (Weekly, Monthly, etc.)	Gives extra credit, writes on assignment										
	Allows use of games, simulations, or special materials										
	Allows work in groups										
	Selects student for special duty										
	Gives recognition certificate										
	Allows use of learning center, library, or reference desk										
	Allows independent study time										
	Posts assignment/exam										
	Writes message to parents										
	Other										

INSTRUMENT 8.7   Recording Student–Teacher Interaction

Question Number	Teacher Question		Student Response				Teacher Probe				
	Convergent	Divergent	Accepted	Partially Accepted	Not Accepted	Don't Know/No Response	No Probe	Asks to Clarify	Solicits More Information	Redirects (Hints)	Asks Another Student Same Question
1											
2											
3											
4											
5											
6											
7											
8											
9											
10											
11											
12											
13											
14											
15											
Totals	Convergent										
	Divergent										

INSTRUMENT 8.8 Distinguishing among Six Types of Questions

Number	Question Level							Wait Time
	Knowledge	Comprehension	Application	LO	HO	Analysis	Synthesis	Evaluation	
1									
2									
3									
4									
5									
6									
7									
8									
9									
10									
11									
12									
13									
14									
15									
Totals									

INSTRUMENT 8.9 Observing Use of Student Ideas

Teacher Behavior	Times Student Ideas Are Used														
	1	2	3	4	5	6	7	8	9	10	11	12	13	14	15
1. Acknowledging															
2. Modifying															
3. Applying															
4. Comparing															
5. Summarizing															
Totals															

Behavior	Observed	Not Observed	No Opportunity to Observe
1. Develops unit and lesson plans in accordance with text and curriculum guides			
2. Handles administrative and clerical interruptions efficiently			
3. Stops or prevents misbehavior with a minimum of disruption to the class			
4. Selects the most appropriate instructional strategy for the objectives taught			
5. Builds toward unit outcomes with clearly defined events (weekly and monthly reviews, feedback, and testing)			

INSTRUMENT 9.2 Studying Relationships between Unit/Lesson Plans and Curriculum Guide/Text

1. Subject and grade: _____

   _____

2. Topic or main objective of lesson to be observed: _____

   _____

3. Title of adopted text and, if applicable, accompanying workbook: _____

   _____

4. Chapter and/or workbook subheadings and pages pertaining to the objective(s):

   Text: _____   pages: _____

   _____   _____

   _____   _____

   Workbook: _____   pages: _____

   _____   _____

   _____   _____

5. Lesson activities observed:

   ❑ Media:

   ❑ Manipulative:

   ❑ Student collaboration:

   ❑ Teacher lecture/demonstration:

   ❑ Group discussion:

   ❑ Other tasks or assignments:

6. If a correspondence between lesson activities and text and/or workbook is not apparent, suggest the reason why, if evident (e.g., teacher is off-task, compensatory remedial materials are being used, critical local priorities are being addressed instead, students are unable to grasp textbook content):

   _____

   _____

   _____

   _____

   _____

INSTRUMENT 9.3 Recording Time Spent on Noninstructional Activities (see Figure 9.2 for example entries)

Time	Noninstructional Activities		
	Administrative/Procedural	Transitions	Student Conduct
Minutes			
Totals	_____ minutes	_____ minutes	_____ minutes

	On Display	Handout	Given Orally
Rules about Academic Work			
1. _____	❑	❑	❑
2. _____	❑	❑	❑
3. _____	❑	❑	❑
4. _____	❑	❑	❑
5. _____	❑	❑	❑
6. _____	❑	❑	❑
7. _____	❑	❑	❑
8. _____	❑	❑	❑
9. _____	❑	❑	❑
10. _____	❑	❑	❑
11. _____	❑	❑	❑
12. _____	❑	❑	❑
Rules about Classroom Conduct			
1. _____	❑	❑	❑
2. _____	❑	❑	❑
3. _____	❑	❑	❑
4. _____	❑	❑	❑
5. _____	❑	❑	❑
6. _____	❑	❑	❑
7. _____	❑	❑	❑
8. _____	❑	❑	❑
9. _____	❑	❑	❑
10. _____	❑	❑	❑
11. _____	❑	❑	❑
12. _____	❑	❑	❑

	Teacher Response						
Misbehavior	**Gives Look or Gestures**	**Verbally Warns, Scolds**	**Reminds/ Recites Rule**	**Establishes New Rule**	**Assigns Punishment**	**Other**	**Time**
1. _____	❑	❑	❑	❑	❑	❑	_____
2. _____	❑	❑	❑	❑	❑	❑	_____
3. _____	❑	❑	❑	❑	❑	❑	_____
4. _____	❑	❑	❑	❑	❑	❑	_____
5. _____	❑	❑	❑	❑	❑	❑	_____
6. _____	❑	❑	❑	❑	❑	❑	_____
7. _____	❑	❑	❑	❑	❑	❑	_____
8. _____	❑	❑	❑	❑	❑	❑	_____
9. _____	❑	❑	❑	❑	❑	❑	_____
10. _____	❑	❑	❑	❑	❑	❑	_____
11. _____	❑	❑	❑	❑	❑	❑	_____
12. _____	❑	❑	❑	❑	❑	❑	_____
13. _____	❑	❑	❑	❑	❑	❑	_____
14. _____	❑	❑	❑	❑	❑	❑	_____
15. _____	❑	❑	❑	❑	❑	❑	_____
16. _____	❑	❑	❑	❑	❑	❑	_____
17. _____	❑	❑	❑	❑	❑	❑	_____
18. _____	❑	❑	❑	❑	❑	❑	_____
19. _____	❑	❑	❑	❑	❑	❑	_____
20. _____	❑	❑	❑	❑	❑	❑	_____
						Total	_____

INSTRUMENT 9.6   Recording the Relationship between Levels of Behavioral Complexity and Teaching Functions

Teaching Functions		Lower Order			Higher Order		
		Knowledge	Comprehension	Application	Analysis	Synthesis	Evaluation
Direct Functions	Reviews, checks previous day's work						
	Presents new content, lectures						
	Provides guided practice, drill and practice						
	Asks convergent, closed questions having a single right answer						
	Assigns independent practice, workbook						
	Reviews previously learned content						
	Other						
Indirect Functions	Organizes content in advance and provides advance organizers						
	Uses induction and deduction to arrive at desired outcomes						
	Presents examples and nonexamples to identify critical attributes						
	Asks divergent, open questions having more than a single right answer						
	Provides for group discussion						
	Allows students to respond from their own experience or point of view						
	Other						

Week	Day	Review, Limited	Review, Cumulative	Test, Limited	Test, Cumulative	Major Assignment (Book Review, Paper, Problem Set, Notebook)	Other (Feedback on Test, Question-and-Answer Session)
1	Mon.						
	Tues.						
	Wed.						
	Thurs.						
	Fri.						
2	Mon.						
	Tues.						
	Wed.						
	Thurs.						
	Fri.						
3	Mon.						
	Tues.						
	Wed.						
	Thurs.						
	Fri.						
4	Mon.						
	Tues.						
	Wed.						
	Thurs.						
	Fri.						

INSTRUMENT 10.1 Observing Student Engagement in the Learning Process

Behavior	Observed	Not Observed	No Opportunity to Observe
1. Provides for guided practice			
2. Provides feedback to guided practice			
3. Uses differentiated and self-regulated learning activities to promote learning, when appropriate			
4. Uses meaningful verbal praise			
5. Monitors seatwork by circulating and frequently checking progress			

Date: _____   Lesson Content: _____

Eliciting Activity	Proximity of Eliciting Activity to Content Presentation				
	Interspersed (throughout Content Presentation)	Immediate (at End of Content Presentation)	Interrupted (at End of Class, Separated by Other Activities)	Delayed (for Homework)	Indefinite (at Student's Discretion)
Oral Questions					
Exercises in Text or Workbook					
Problems Presented in Handout					
Activities Written on Board or Overhead					
Other					

Differentiated/Self-Regulating Materials

❑ Remedial/alternative learning material:

_____

_____

_____

❑ Programmed learning materials:

_____

_____

_____

❑ Game and stimulation materials:

_____

_____

_____

❑ Audiovisual media:

_____

_____

_____

❑ Computer/software:

_____

_____

_____

❑ Resource/reference/library:

_____

_____

_____

❑ Other:

_____

_____

_____

❑ Performance contracting:

_____

_____

_____

❑ Learning centers:

_____

_____

_____

❑ Peer tutoring:

_____

_____

_____

❑ Group discussion:

_____

_____

_____

❑ Teams, pairs:

_____

_____

_____

❑ Independent projects:

_____

_____

_____

❑ Other:

_____

_____

_____

INSTRUMENT 10.4 Recording Praise Contingent on a Specific Performance

Time	Number	Delivery Mode			Types of Praise				
		Oral	Body Language	Written	Gives Neutral Affirmation	Expresses Surprise, Delight, or Excitement	Explains Value	Uses, Extends, Picks Up On	Other
	1								
	2								
	3								
	4								
	5								
	6								
	7								
	8								
	9								
	10								
	11								
	12								
	13								
	14								
	15								
	16								
	17								
	18								
	19								
	20								
	21								
	22								
	23								
	24								
	25								
Rate									

INSTRUMENT 10.5 Observing the Relationship among Different Monitoring and Checking Behaviors

Contact*	Mode of Feedback			Duration			Zone				
	Oral	Written	Body Language	A Few Seconds	More Than a Few Seconds But Less Than One Minute	More Than One Minute	1	2	3	4	5
1. _____	❑	❑	❑	❑	❑	❑	❑	❑	❑	❑	❑
2. _____	❑	❑	❑	❑	❑	❑	❑	❑	❑	❑	❑
3. _____	❑	❑	❑	❑	❑	❑	❑	❑	❑	❑	❑
4. _____	❑	❑	❑	❑	❑	❑	❑	❑	❑	❑	❑
5. _____	❑	❑	❑	❑	❑	❑	❑	❑	❑	❑	❑
6. _____	❑	❑	❑	❑	❑	❑	❑	❑	❑	❑	❑
7. _____	❑	❑	❑	❑	❑	❑	❑	❑	❑	❑	❑
8. _____	❑	❑	❑	❑	❑	❑	❑	❑	❑	❑	❑
9. _____	❑	❑	❑	❑	❑	❑	❑	❑	❑	❑	❑
10. _____	❑	❑	❑	❑	❑	❑	❑	❑	❑	❑	❑
11. _____	❑	❑	❑	❑	❑	❑	❑	❑	❑	❑	❑
12. _____	❑	❑	❑	❑	❑	❑	❑	❑	❑	❑	❑
13. _____	❑	❑	❑	❑	❑	❑	❑	❑	❑	❑	❑
14. _____	❑	❑	❑	❑	❑	❑	❑	❑	❑	❑	❑
15. _____	❑	❑	❑	❑	❑	❑	❑	❑	❑	❑	❑
16. _____	❑	❑	❑	❑	❑	❑	❑	❑	❑	❑	❑
17. _____	❑	❑	❑	❑	❑	❑	❑	❑	❑	❑	❑
18. _____	❑	❑	❑	❑	❑	❑	❑	❑	❑	❑	❑
19. _____	❑	❑	❑	❑	❑	❑	❑	❑	❑	❑	❑
20. _____	❑	❑	❑	❑	❑	❑	❑	❑	❑	❑	❑

*These blanks can be used to record an individual's ability level (less able, LA; average, AV; more able, MA), gender (M, F), ethnicity, or other characteristic for which bias might occur.

INSTRUMENT 11.1 Observing Success Rate

Behavior	Observed	Not Observed	No Opportunity to Observe
1. Unit and lesson organization reflects lesson-relevant prior learning			
2. Provides mediated feedback to extend and enhance student learning			
3. Plans lessons at, or slightly above students' current level of understanding			
4. Plans transitions to new content in small, easy-to-grasp steps			
5. Establishes momentum (for example, pacing and intensity gradually build toward major milestones)			

INSTRUMENT 11.2A Coding Form, Example Data, and Definitions for Observing Success Rate

(See Instrument 11.2B for an explanation of the codes used.)

Number	Student	Student Response*				Teacher Response					Teacher Feedback Reaction							
		+	+/−	−	0	+/+	+	0	−	−	Gives Answer	Explains	Asks Other	Other Calls	Repeats	Clue	New Question

Student Response

+	Right		The teacher accepts the student's response as correct or satisfactory.
±	Part right		The teacher considers the student's response to be only partially correct, or correct but incomplete.
–	Wrong		The teacher considers the student's response to be incorrect.
0	No answer		The student makes no response or says he or she doesn't know (code student's answer here if teacher gives a feedback reaction before he or she is able to respond).

Teacher Response

++	Praise		Teacher praises student either in words ("Fine," "Good," "Wonderful," "Good thinking") or by expressing verbal affirmation in a notably warm, joyous, or excited manner.
+	Affirm		Teacher simply affirms that the student's response is correct (nods, repeats answer, says "Yes," "Okay," etc.).
0	No reaction		Teacher makes no response whatever to student's response—he or she simply goes on to something else.
–	Negate		Teacher simply indicates that the student's response is incorrect (shakes head, says "No," "That's not right," "Hm-mm," etc.).
– –	Criticize		Teacher criticizes student, either in words ("You should know better than that," "That doesn't make any sense—you better pay close attention," etc.) or by expressing verbal negation in a frustrated, angry, or disgusted manner.

Teacher Feedback

Gives Answer	Teacher gives answer	Teacher provides the correct answer for the student.
Explains	Teacher explains after answer	Teacher explains or gives reason why an answer is correct or incorrect.
Asks Another	Teacher asks another student	Teacher redirects the question, asking a different student to try to answer it.
Other Calls	Another student calls out answer	Another student calls out the correct answer, and the teacher acknowledges that it is correct.
Repeats	Repeats question	Teacher repeats the original question, either in its entirety or with a prompt ("Well?" "Do you know?" "What's the answer?").
Clue	Rephrase or clue	Teacher makes original question easier for student to answer by rephrasing it or by giving a clue.
New Question	New question	Teacher asks a new question (for example, a question that calls for a different answer than the original question called for).

Note: The teacher feedback category "Explains" has been added to the original instrument.

Source: Good and Brophy (1990).

Lesson Number _____

Student Response	Right	Partially Right	Wrong	No Answer
1. _____ _____	☐	☐	☐	☐
2. _____ _____	☐	☐	☐	☐
3. _____ _____	☐	☐	☐	☐
4. _____ _____	☐	☐	☐	☐
5. _____ _____	☐	☐	☐	☐
6. _____ _____	☐	☐	☐	☐
7. _____ _____	☐	☐	☐	☐
8. _____ _____	☐	☐	☐	☐
9. _____ _____	☐	☐	☐	☐
10. _____ _____	☐	☐	☐	☐
11. _____ _____	☐	☐	☐	☐
12. _____ _____	☐	☐	☐	☐
13. _____ _____	☐	☐	☐	☐
14. _____ _____	☐	☐	☐	☐
15. _____ _____	☐	☐	☐	☐
Totals	_____	_____	_____	_____
Percentages (totals ÷ number of responses × 100)	_____	_____	_____	_____

INSTRUMENT 11.4 Recording the Frequency of Seven Instructional Events within a Unit

Instructional Events	Lessons					
	Beginning of Unit		Middle of Unit		End of Unit	
	1	2	3	4	5	6
Gaining attention						
Informing learner of objective						
Stimulating recall of prerequisite learning						
Presenting the stimulus material						
Eliciting the desired behavior						
Providing feedback and correctives						
Assessing the behavior						

	Mon.	Tues.	Wed.	Thur.	Fri.
Week 1					
Week 2					
Week 3					
Week 4					
Week 5					
Week 6					

Note: See Figure 11.6 for codes for Instrument 11.5.

INSTRUMENT 12.1 Observing Higher Thought Processes and Performance Outcomes

Behavior	Observed	Not Observed	No Opportunity to Observe
1. Uses collaborative and group activities			
2. Demonstrates mental models and strategies for learning			
3. Arranges for students to apply what they've learned through products and contributions			
4. Engages students in oral performance			
5. Provides opportunities for independent practice that allow students to learn from their mistakes			
6. Uses performance assessments			

1. Teacher–student interaction

   ❑ Did not occur   ❑ Seldom occurred   ❑ Occasionally occurred   ❑ Frequently occurred

   When the teacher interacted with students during the collaborative learning activity, was it directed toward

   Individuals: Small groups: Full class:

   ❑ Not at all   ❑ Not at all   ❑ Not at all

   ❑ Seldom   ❑ Seldom   ❑ Seldom

   ❑ Occasionally   ❑ Occasionally   ❑ Occasionally

   ❑ Frequently   ❑ Frequently   ❑ Frequently

2. Student–student interaction

   Approximately what percent of time during the activity was devoted to student–student interaction?

   ❑ Less than 25%   ❑ 26–49%   ❑ 50–75%   ❑ More than 75%

   Most of the student interaction was

   ❑ One student talking to another student

   ❑ Students talking among themselves in groups

   ❑ Students in one group talking to students in another group

   ❑ Other _____

3. Task and material specification

   Identify the task toward which this collaborative activity was directed and the supporting materials (if any) with which it was to be conducted.

   Task: _____

   _____

   _____

   _____

   Supporting materials (references, sourcebooks, handouts, etc.): _____

   _____

   _____

   _____

4. Role assignment

   Identify any roles assigned to individual students carrying out this collaborative activity (leader, recorder, summarizer, etc.).

   _____

   _____

   _____

   _____

1. Demonstrating to students the reasoning involved

What concept or principle was being demonstrated and how was it being demonstrated (orally, visually, or by physical demonstration)?

_____

_____

_____

_____

_____

_____

2. Making students aware of the reasoning involved

What verbal markers did the teacher use to alert students to the reasoning required? For example, "Now watch me . . ." or "Notice as I do . . ."

_____

_____

_____

_____

_____

_____

3. Helping students apply the reasoning involved

How did the teacher involve students in actually applying the reasoning required? For example, "How would you do this problem?" or "Let's think of another example."

_____

_____

_____

_____

_____

_____

Identify observable signs of any of the following and describe briefly their nature.

❏ Journals, writing assignments, letters, and reports

_____

_____

_____

❏ Physical science experiments/investigations

_____

_____

_____

❏ Drawings and graphics

_____

_____

_____

❏ Lifelike renderings (for example, sculpture or clay figures)

_____

_____

_____

❏ Video/audio

_____

_____

_____

❏ Scale models (physical replicas)

_____

_____

_____

❏ Aquatic and plant life

_____

_____

_____

❏ Other

_____

_____

_____

Times Observed

	1	2	3	4	5	6
Oral performance	☐	☐	☐	☐	☐	☐
Students respond to questions orally	☐	☐	☐	☐	☐	☐
Students read or present assignments informally	☐	☐	☐	☐	☐	☐
Students discuss idea or theme	☐	☐	☐	☐	☐	☐
Students critique or analyze responses of other students	☐	☐	☐	☐	☐	☐
Students read from text or own material	☐	☐	☐	☐	☐	☐
Students give formal speech or report	☐	☐	☐	☐	☐	☐
Other _____	☐	☐	☐	☐	☐	☐

INSTRUMENT 12.6 Recording Activities for Students to Learn from Their Mistakes

	Times Observed					
Practice Opportunities	1	2	3	4	5	6
End-of-Chapter Exercises						
In class	☐	☐	☐	☐	☐	☐
Homework	☐	☐	☐	☐	☐	☐
Workbook Problems						
In class	☐	☐	☐	☐	☐	☐
Homework	☐	☐	☐	☐	☐	☐
Supplemental Handouts						
In class	☐	☐	☐	☐	☐	☐
Homework	☐	☐	☐	☐	☐	☐
Problems on Board/Transparency						
In class	☐	☐	☐	☐	☐	☐
Homework	☐	☐	☐	☐	☐	☐
Other ____	☐	☐	☐	☐	☐	☐

Identify signs of any of the following and briefly describe their nature.

❑ Product criteria (technical quality, accuracy, usability, etc.)

_____

_____

_____

_____

❑ Process criteria (creativity, neatness, use of resources, etc.)

_____

_____

_____

_____

❑ Rating scale or point system for product and/or process criteria

_____

_____

_____

_____

Did the product or performance require of learners any of the following?

❑ Incorporate what was learned from classroom instruction in a more realistic and expanded context

❑ Integrate isolated bits of knowledge rather than the recall of information

❑ Producing outcomes for which the routine use of previously learned information was not sufficient

❑ Apply standards by which one performs competently in the real world?

❑ Represent real-life challenges, not bookwork that is easy to grade?

Glossary

Activity structure   How lesson content is organized (e.g., for recitation, drill and practice, discussion) and how student responses are to be provided (e.g., cooperatively, individually).

Advance organizer   Concepts presented orally or visually, usually at the beginning of a lesson, that give an overview of the day's work and content to which it will be subsequently related, helping the learner to store, label, and package the content for retention and later use.

Anecdotal report   A brief narrative description of a critical or unusual incident that occurs in a classroom, which may be related to an event of larger consequence.

Authentic assessment   A performance assessment that requires the student to produce a real-world (hence, authentic) outcome or product.

Checklist   A scale in which a behavior that would be difficult to evaluate in degree is measured either as present or absent.

Classroom coding systems   Observation systems that record the frequency with which various teacher and student behaviors occur.

Classroom management   How teachers organize the classroom and anticipate and respond to student behavior to provide an environment for efficient learning.

Classroom routine   An expected sequence of events that is repeated daily or weekly to accomplish a given student activity in the quickest and most efficient manner possible.

Concerns theory   According to Fuller (1969), the natural stages of a beginning teacher's development, progressing from concerns about oneself to concerns about the teaching task to concerns about one's impact on student learning.

Convergent questions   Questions, usually with a single right answer, that involve the recall of facts, the summarization or paraphrasing of learned knowledge, or the application of knowledge to a context similar to that in which it was learned.

Counting system   A system that tallies which behavior on an instrument occurs during certain time intervals (e.g., every 30 seconds).

Culturally responsive teaching   Knowing the values, socialization practices, interests, and concerns of learners and incorporating this knowledge into what and how content is taught.

Differentiated instruction   Maximizing each student's growth by providing alternate paths to learning and the needed individualized instruction and resources to lift the learner onto the next rung of the learning ladder.

Direct instruction   A form of instruction in which the teacher is the major provider of information and primarily passes on facts, rules, or action sequences in a lecture, drill, or recitation format.

Divergent questions   Questions with many right answers designed to stimulate students to use their own past knowledge and experiences to actively construct new knowledge and understanding.

Engaged learning time   The amount of time during a lesson learners spend thinking about, acting on, or working with a learning task.

Ethnographic record   A method of observing and recording in narrative form that reports events sequentially, as they occur, without selecting a specific focus or incident.

Field dependence   A cognitive style that influences learners to perceive complex stimuli in terms of larger patterns and relationships.

Field independence   A cognitive style that influences learners to perceive complex stimuli in terms of the discrete, individual elements that constitute it.

Flanders Classroom Interaction Analysis System   A popular counting system that measures the extent to which direct versus indirect teaching occurs, measured in 3-second intervals.

Functional errors   When a wrong or partially correct student response prompts additional cues (e.g., probes from teacher, responses of other students) that can modify the task to help the learner attain success on repeated trials.

Higher thought processes   Critical thinking, reasoning, and problem-solving behaviors that alone cannot be measured by tests of cognitive achievement.

Indirect instruction   A form of instruction in which the teacher encourages students to use their own knowledge and experiences to actively construct knowledge and understanding, providing learners a degree of control over their own learning.

Instructional routine   A set of rules or expected sequence of events organized around a particular time (beginning of day), concept (group work), or place (library, learning center, playground) that helps students accomplish a given task in the quickest and most efficient manner possible.

Instructional variety The teacher's use of different modes of learning (visual, oral, and tactile) to maintain interest and attention and promote learning.

Intercultural competence The ability to interact smoothly and effectively with members of other cultures.

Interstate New Teacher Assessment and Support Consortium (INTASC) NBPTS board-compatible standards reviewed by professional organizations and state agencies as a basis for licensing beginning teachers.

Lateral knowledge Knowledge acquired across, as opposed to within, subject matter disciplines, as in interdisciplinary units of instruction.

Learning climate The physical and emotional environment of the classroom indicating its degree of warmth, cohesion, interaction, and cooperation.

Lesson clarity The teacher's ability to speak clearly and directly to the class and to organize and structure content at the students' current level of understanding.

Lesson-relevant prior knowledge Knowledge that precedes a lesson that helps students connect new ideas with what they already know and have experienced.

Low-profile classroom management A set of classroom management techniques that require anticipation by the teacher to prevent problems before they occur, deflection in order to redirect disruptive behavior that is about to occur, and reaction to unobtrusively stop disruptions immediately after they occur.

Meaningful verbal praise When a teacher's response is tailored to fit the specific answer, applied immediately after the answer is given, and varied according to the student being reinforced.

Metacognition Mental devices used to think through a problem for oneself, such as self-interrogation, self-checking, self-monitoring, mentally scanning alternative strategies, use of memory aids (mnemonics), and classifying information for better comprehension.

Microethnography The study of the interaction of language, culture, and action in classrooms by which student and teacher communicate and interpret meaning.

Momentum Regulating the forward movement, expectancy, and sense of accomplishment that exists within a classroom with which lessons build toward major milestones (e.g., review, test, oral presentation, project).

National Board for Professional Teaching Standards (NBPTS) A set of standards prepared mostly by and for teachers indicating what teachers should be able to do along with a voluntary system to certify teachers who meet these standards.

Open-ended report A narrative report that gives the observer considerable flexibility in what events to record and the depth to which they are recorded.

Openers Questions that do not have a single correct answer, intended to amuse, stimulate, and sometimes even bewilder students so that they will be receptive to the lesson that follows.

Overlapping An instructional technique in which the beginning of one lesson repeats or overlaps with the end of the preceding lesson to help students place the content of the day's lesson in the perspective of previously learned content.

Performance assessment Assessment in the form of a hands-on exercise or problem that produces an observable outcome or product (e.g., a typed business letter, a map, an oral presentation, a poem) such that the teacher can observe the mental processes used by the student to achieve the product.

Probes Questions that follow questions, carefully crafted to deepen, enrich, and extend an earlier response.

Problem-based learning Promoting intrinsic interest and inquiry skills by organizing instruction around problems that can be solved within the time span and content of one or more lessons.

Professional frame An objective viewpoint from which to evaluate and act on events critical to becoming an expert.

Proximity control A classroom management procedure by which the teacher physically moves closer to a student to promote compliance with classroom rules.

Rating scale A structured instrument that not only records the behaviors observed but the degree to which they occurred, usually in a 5- or 7-point format.

Reciprocal distancing The use of language to include or exclude various individuals from the group.

Reciprocal teaching A technique for eliciting student responses at the student's current level of understanding based on personal experiences with, assumptions about, and predictions from the content to be taught (Palincsar & Brown, 1989).

Reflective teaching Consciously considering your own teaching behavior and embracing a commitment to a program of professional growth as a teacher.

Rubric A rating scale that expresses specific criteria for assessing a student's report, essay, or portfolio content.

Selective perception Seeing what we want to see, or allowing our perceptions to be unduly influenced by things outside the immediate context of the observation.

Sign system A type of classroom coding system in which a behavior is recorded only once no matter how many times it occurs during a designated time interval.

Social framing The taken-for-granted context in which a message, such as a lesson, is received and understood.

Steering group A small group of lower-, average-, and higher-performing learners in a class who may be questioned to determine the extent to which reteaching may be needed before the start of a lesson.

Student engagement The amount of time out of the total lesson time in which the student is actively thinking about, working with, or applying the content being taught.

Student success The rate of which a student understands and correctly completes exercises and assignments. A high success rate is achieved when the student understands the subject matter taught and makes only occasional careless errors.

Summated ratings A type of scale in which the observer compares what is observed with what is on the scale and chooses the degree that best matches the observation, then sums and takes the average of all the comparisons made—for example, as in 5-point scales.

Surface behaviors The majority of disruptive behaviors that occur in classrooms, which include laughing, talking out of turn, passing notes, daydreaming, not following directions, combing hair, doodling, humming, and tapping.

Tacit knowledge Knowledge that teachers have from experience, but rarely articulate.

Task orientation The teacher's use of practices that help maintain an instructional focus by managing classroom activities efficiently, handling misbehavior with a minimum disruption to the class, and reducing instructional time devoted to clerical duties to provide students the maximum opportunity to learn.

Teacher mediation The on-the-spot adjustments in content difficulty and pacing from which the student can most benefit at that moment to move to the next rung of the learning ladder.

Thematic notes A form of narrative reporting in which facts are recorded in traditional outline form according to predesignated categories of observation, much like a detective at the scene of a crime who jots down facts about suspects, motives, times, and places.

Transmediation The expression of an idea across media forms—for example, exploits of a particular explorer read about in social studies are summarized in a dramatic presentation or artistic mural.

Verbal markers Oral phrases that tells students what to watch for or what behaviors will be expected of them at the end of a lesson.

Vertical knowledge Knowledge acquired within, as opposed to across, subject matter disciplines.

Visual map A picture or drawing that portrays the spatial relationships among physical objects that may be important to fully understand a narrative report.

Wait time Time allowed for a student response after a teacher question, with typical wait times for convergent questions being 1 second or less and optimum wait times being 3 or more seconds (Rowe, 1986).

Withitness The ability of a teacher to keep track of many different signs of student behavior simultaneously and thereby convey a sense of physical presence or vigilance (Kounin, 1970).

Zone of maximum response opportunity That zone of behavior that, if stimulated by the teacher, will bring a learner's response to the next level of refinement.

References

Abernathy, R., & Reardon, M. (2001). *Hottips for teachers: 30 steps to student engagement.* Thousand Oaks, CA: Corwin Press.

Alberto, P., & Troutman, A. (2002). *Applied behavior analysis for teachers: Influencing student performance* (6th ed.). Upper Saddle River, NJ: Prentice Hall.

Alberto, P., & Troutman, A. (2006). *Applied behavior analysis for teachers* (7th ed.). Upper Saddle River, NJ: Merrill/Prentice Hall.

Anderman, E. M., & Maehr, M. L. (1994). Motivation and schooling in the middle grades. *Review of Educational Research, 64*(20), 287–309.

Anderson, G. (1973). *The assessment of learning environments: A manual for the Learning Environment Inventory and the My Class Inventory.* Halifax, Nova Scotia: Atlantic Institute of Education.

Anderson, K. (1996). *Changing woman: A history of racial ethnic women in modern America.* New York: Oxford University Press.

Anderson, L., & Krathwohl, D. (Eds.). (2001). *Taxonomy for learning, teaching, and assessing: A revision of Bloom's taxonomy of educational objectives.* New York: Longman.

Anderson, L., Evertson, C., & Brophy, J. (1979). An experimental study of effective teaching in first-grade reading groups. *Elementary School Journal, 79,* 193–223.

Anderson, L., Evertson, C., & Brophy, J. (1982). *Principles of small group instruction in elementary reading.* East Lansing, MI: Institute for Research on Teaching.

Anderson-Levitt, K. (Ed.). (2003). *Local meanings, global schooling: Anthropology and world culture theory.* New York: Palgrave Macmillan.

Antón-Oldenburg, M. (2000, September). Celebrate diversity! *Scholastic Instructor,* 46–48.

Arter, J., & McTighe, J. (2000). *Scoring rubrics in the classroom: Using performance criteria for assessing and improving student performance.* Thousand Oaks, CA: Corwin Press.

Ausubel, D. (1968). *Educational psychology: A cognitive view.* New York: Holt, Rinehart & Winston.

Baden, M., & Major, C. (2004). *Foundations of problem based learning.* Berkshire, UK: Open University Press.

Bamburg, J. (1994). *Raising expectations to improve student learning.* Oak Brook, IL: North Central Regional Laboratory. (ERIC Document Reproduction Service No. ED378290)

Banks, J. A. (1997). *Teaching strategies for ethnic studies* (6th ed.). Boston: Allyn & Bacon.

Banks, J., & Banks, C. (Eds.). (2001). *Handbook of research on multicultural education.* San Francisco: Jossey-Bass.

Banks, J., & Banks, C. (2006). *Multicultural education: Issues and perspectives.* Hoboken, NJ: Wiley.

Baum, S., Viens, J., & Slatin, B. (2005). *Multiple intelligences in the elementary classroom: A teacher's toolkit.* New York: Teachers College Press.

Benard, B. (2004). *Resiliency: What we have learned: Turning it around for all youth.* San Francisco: WestEd.

Bennett, C. (1990). *Comprehensive multicultural education: Theory and practice* (2nd ed.). Boston: Allyn & Bacon.

Bennett, N., Desforges, C., Cockburn, A., & Wilkinson, B. (1981). *The quality of pupil learning experiences: Interim report.* Lancaster, UK: University of Lancaster Centre for Educational Research and Development.

Bloom, B. (1994). *Bloom's taxonomy: A forty year retrospective.* Chicago: NSSE, University of Chicago Press.

Bloom, B., Englehart, M., Furst, E., Hill, W., & Krathwohl, D. (1984). *Taxonomy of educational goals. Handbook I: Cognitive domain.* New York: Longman.

Bluestein, J. (2004). *21st century discipline.* Lebanon, IN: Pearson Learning Group.

Blythe, T., & Associates (1997). *The teaching for understanding guide* (Jossey-Bass Education Series). San Francisco: Jossey-Bass.

Borich, G. (1993). *Clearly outstanding: Making each day count in your classroom.* Boston: Allyn & Bacon.

Borich, G. (2004). *Vital impressions: The KPM approach to children.* Austin, TX: KPM Institute.

Borich, G. (2008). Characteristics of effective teaching. In N. Salkind (Ed.), *Encyclopedia of educational psychology.* Thousand Oaks, CA: Sage Publications.

Borich, G. (2010). *Effective teaching methods* (7th ed.). Boston: Allyn & Bacon.

Borich, G., & Tombari, M. (1997). *Educational psychology: A contemporary approach* (2nd ed.). New York: Addison-Wesley/Longman.

Borich, G., & Tombari, M. (2004). *Educational assessment for the elementary and middle school classroom.* Upper Saddle River, NJ: Merrill/Prentice Hall.

Bowers, C., & Flinders, D. (1991). *Culturally responsive teaching and supervision: A handbook for staff development.* New York: Teachers College Press.

Brophy, J. (1981). Teacher praise: A functional analysis. *Review of Educational Research, 51,* 5–32.

Brophy, J. (1983). Classroom organization and management. *Elementary School Journal, 83,* 265–285.

Brophy, J. (Ed.). (1989). *Advances in research on teaching.* Greenwich, CT: JAI Press.

Brophy, J. (2002). *Teaching: Educational Practices* Series No. 1. United Nations Educational, Social, and Cultural

Organization (UNESCO). Geneva, Switzerland: International Bureau of Education.

Brophy, J., & Evertson, C. (1976). *Learning from teaching: A developmental perspective.* Boston: Allyn & Bacon.

Brown, B. (1968). *The experimental mind in education.* New York: Harper & Row.

Brualdi, A. C. (1998). Classroom questions. *ERIC Digest.* College Park, MD: ERIC Clearinghouse on Assessment and Evaluation. (ERIC Reproduction Service No. ED422407)

Burbules, N., & Bruce, B. (2001). Theory and research on teaching as dialogue. In V. Richardson (Ed.), *Handbook of research on teaching* (4th ed.). Washington, DC: American Educational Research Association.

Burke, D. L. (1997). Looping: Adding time, strengthening relationships. *ERIC Digest.* Washington, DC: Office of Educational Research and Improvement & U.S. Department of Education. (ERIC Document Reproduction Service No. ED414098)

Burnette, J. (1999). Critical behaviors and strategies for teaching culturally diverse students. *ERIC/OSEP Digest* E 584. Reston, VA: ERIC Clearinghouse on Disabilities and Gifted Education. (ERIC Document Reproduction Service No. ED435147)

Cambourne, B. (2000). Conditions for literacy learning: Observing literacy learning in elementary classrooms: Nine years of classroom anthropology. *The Reading Teacher, 53*(6), 512–515.

Canter, L. (2001). *Assertive discipline: Positive behavior management for today's classroom* (3rd ed.). Los Angeles: Canter & Associates.

Cantrell, S. C. (1998/1999). Effective teaching and literacy learning: A look inside primary classrooms. *Reading Teacher, 52*(4), 370–378.

Castaneda, A., & Gray, T. (1974). Bicognitive processes in multicultural education. *Educational Leadership, 32*(3), 203–207.

Cazden, C. (1988). *Classroom discourse.* Portsmouth, NH: Heinemann.

Chaille, C. (2007). *Constructivism across the curriculum in early childhood classrooms.* Boston: Allyn & Bacon.

Charles, C., & Senter, G. (2007). *Building classroom discipline* (8th ed.). Boston: Allyn & Bacon.

Chen, G.-M., & Starosta, W. (1997). *Foundations of intercultural communication.* Boston: Allyn & Bacon.

Cheng, L. (1996, October). Enhancing communication: Toward optimal language learning for limited English proficient students. *Language, Speech and Hearing Services in Schools, 28*(2), 347–354.

Cheng, L. (1998). Enhancing the communication skills of newly-arrived Asian American students. *ERIC/CUE Digest,* 136. New York: ERIC Clearinghouse on Urban Education. (ERIC Document Reproduction Service No. ED420726)

Cheng, L., Chen, T., Tsubo, T., Sekandari, N., & Alfafara-Killacky, S. (1997). Challenges of diversity: An Asian Pacific perspective. *Multicultures, 3,* 114–145.

Clark, C., & Peterson, P. (1986). Teacher's thought processes. In M. C. Wittrock (Ed.), *Handbook of research on teaching* (3rd ed., pp. 255–296). New York: Macmillan.

Clark, J. V. (1999). Minorities in science and math. *ERIC Digest.* Columbus, OH: ERIC Clearinghouse for Science, Mathematics, and Environmental Education.

Compton-Lilly, C. (2000). "Staying on Children": Challenging stereotypes about urban parents. *Language Arts, 77*(5), 420–427.

Costa, A., & Kallick, B. (Eds.). (2004). *Activating and engaging habits of mind.* Cheltenham, Australia: Hawker Brownlow Education.

Cotton, K. (1996). *Schoolwide and classroom discipline.* Close-Up #9. Portland, OR: Northwest Regional Educational Laboratory. Retrieved October 24, 2006, from www.nwrel.org/scpd/sirs/5/cu9.html

Curtis, D. (2002). The power of projects. *Educational Leadership, 60,* 50–53.

Curwin, R. L. (2003). *Making good choices: Developing responsibility, respect and self-discipline in grades 4–9.* Thousand Oaks, CA: Corwin Press.

Curwin, R. L., Mendler, A., & Mendler, B. (2008). *Discipline with dignity: New challenges, new solutions.* Alexandria, VA: ASCD.

Dahllof, U., & Lundgren, U. P. (1970). *Macro and micro approaches combined for curriculum process analysis: A Swedish educational field project.* Goteborg, Sweden: University of Goteborg, Institute of Education.

Delgado-Gaitan, C. (2006). *Building culturally responsive classrooms: A guide for K–6 teachers.* Thousand Oaks, CA: Corwin Press.

Delpit, L. (1995). *Other people's children: Cultural conflict in the classroom.* New York: New Press.

Delpit, L., & Dowdy, J. (2008). *The skin that we speak: Thoughts on language and culture in the classroom.* New York: New Press.

Delpit, L., Boyd, F., Brock, C., & Rozendal, M. (2003). *Multicultural and multilingual literacy and language: Contexts and practices (Solving problems in teaching of literacy).* New York: Guilford Press.

Diller, D. (1999). Opening the dialogue: Using culture as a tool in teaching young African American children. *Reading Teacher, 52*(8), 820–828.

Dillon, D. (1989). Showing them that I want them to learn and that I care about who they are: A microethnography of the social organization of a secondary low-track English reading classroom. *American Educational Research Journal, 26,* 227–259.

Dillon, J. T. (2004). *Questioning and teaching: A manual of practice.* San Jose, CA: Resource Publications.

Dilworth, M., & Brown, C. (2001). In V. Richardson (Ed.), *Constructivist teacher education: Building new understandings* (pp. 643–667). Washington, DC: Falmer Press.

Doyle, W. (1983). Academic work. *Review of Educational Research, 53,* 159–200.

Doyle, W. (1986). Classroom organization and management. In M. Wittrock (Ed.), *Handbook of research on teaching* (3rd ed., pp. 392–431). New York: Macmillan.

Duffy, G., & Roehler, L. (1989). The tension between information-giving and mediation: Perspectives on instructional explanation and teacher change. In J. Brophy (Ed.), *Advances in research on teaching: Vol. 1* (pp. 1–33). Greenwich, CT: JAI Press.

Dunn, L., & Kontos, S. (1997). Research in review: What have we learned about developmentally appropriate practice? *Young Children, 52*(5), 4–13.

Dunn, R., Griggs, S., & Price, G. (1993). Learning styles of Mexican-American and Anglo-American elementary-school students. *Journal of Multicultural Counseling and Development, 21*(4), 237–247.

Edwards, S., & Kuhlman, W. (2007). Culturally responsive teaching: Do we walk our talk? *Multicultural Education, 14*(4), pp. 45–62.

Emmer, E., & Evertson, C. (2009). *Classroom management for middle and high school teachers* (7th ed.). Boston: Allyn & Bacon.

Emmer, E., & Gerwels, M. (2006). Classroom management in middle and high school classrooms. In C. Evertson & C. Weinstein (Eds.), *Handbook of classroom management*. Mahwah, NJ: Lawrence Erlbaum.

Emmer, E., & Millett, G. (1970). *Improving teaching through experimentation: A laboratory approach.* Upper Saddle River, NJ: Prentice Hall.

Emmer, E., Evertson, C., & Anderson, L. (1980). Effective classroom management at the beginning of the school year. *Elementary School Journal, 80*(5), 219–231.

Evertson, C., & Emmer, E. (1982). Effective management at the beginning of the second year in junior high classes. *Journal of Educational Psychology, 74,* 485–498.

Evertson, C., & Emmer, E. (2009). *Classroom management for elementary teachers* (7th ed.). Boston: Allyn & Bacon.

Flanders, N. (1970). *Analyzing teacher behavior.* Reading, MA: Addison-Wesley.

Floden, R. (1991). What teachers need to know about learning. In M. Kennedy (Ed.), *Teaching academic subjects to diverse learners* (pp. 189–216). New York: Teachers College Press.

Forton, M. (2003). *Rules in school (Strategies for teachers, 4).* Turner Falls, MA: Northeast Foundation for Children.

Fosnot, C. (Ed.). (2005). *Constructivism: Theory, perspectives and practice.* New York: Teachers College Press.

Fraser, B. (1981). Australian research on classroom environment: State of the art. *Australian Journal of Education, 25,* 238–268.

Fraser, B., & Walberg, H. (Eds.). (1991). *Educational environments: Evaluation, antecedents and consequences.* New York: Pergamon.

Fraser, B., Anderson, G., & Walberg, H. (1982). *Assessment of learning environments: Manual for the Learning Environment Inventory (LEI) and My Class Inventory (MCI)* (3rd ed.). Perth: Western Australian Institute of Technology.

Fuller, F. (1969). Concerns of teachers: A developmental conceptualization. *American Educational Research Journal, 6,* 207–226.

Gage, N., & Berliner, D. (1998). *Educational psychology* (6th ed.). Boston: Houghton Mifflin.

Gagné, M., & Deci, E. L. (2005). Self-determination theory and work motivation. *Journal of Organizational Behavior, 26,* 331–362.

Gagné, R. M., & Briggs, L. (2005). *Principles of instructional design.* New York: Holt, Rinehart & Winston.

Gall, M. (1984). Synthesis of research on questioning. *Educational Leadership, 42,* 40–47.

Gallego, M., Cole, M., & The Laboratory of Comparative Human Cognition (2001). Classroom cultures and cultures in the classroom. In V. Richardson (Ed.), *Handbook of research on teaching.* Washington, DC: American Educational Research Association.

Gardner, H. (2006). *Multiple intelligences: New horizons in theory and practice.* New York: Basic Books.

Gay, G. (2000). *Culturally responsive teaching: Theory, research, and practice.* New York: Teachers College Press.

Gerald, D. E., & Hussar, W. J. (2003). *Projections of education statistics to 2013 (NCES 2004–013).* U.S. Department of Education, National Center for Education Statistics. Washington, DC: U.S. Government Printing Office.

Gill, J. (2000). *The tacit mode: Michael Polunya's postmodern philosophy.* Albany: SUNY Press.

Ginott, H., Ginott, A., & Goddard, W. (2003). *Between parent and child.* New York: Three Rivers Press.

Glasgow, N., McNary, S., & Hicks, C. (2006). *What successful teachers in diverse classrooms: 71 research-based classroom strategies for new and veteran teachers.* Thousand Oaks, CA: Corwin Press.

Glasser, W. (1998a). *Choice theory in the classroom* (rev. ed.). New York: HarperPerennial.

Glasser, W. (1998b). *The quality school: Managing students without coercion* (rev. ed.). New York: HarperPerennial.

Glasser, W. (1998c). *The quality school teacher: Specific suggestions for teachers who are trying to implement the lead-management ideas of the quality school in their classrooms* (rev. ed.). New York: HarperPerennial.

Good, T., & Brophy, J. (2007). *Looking in classrooms* (10th ed.). Boston: Allyn & Bacon.

Good, T., & Grouws, D. (1979). Teaching effects: A process–product study in fourth grade mathematics classrooms. *Journal of Teacher Education, 28,* 49–54.

Gootman, M. (2008). *The caring teacher's guide to discipline: Helping students learn self-control, responsibility, and respect, K–6.* Thousand Oaks, CA: Corwin Press.

Gregory, G. (2005). *Differentiating instruction with style: Aligning teacher and learner intelligences for maximum achievement.* Thousand Oaks, CA: Corwin Press.

Griggs, S., & Dunn, R. (1995). Hispanic-American students and learning style. *Emergency Librarian, 23*(2), 11–16.

Griggs, S., & Dunn, R. (1996). Hispanic-American students and learning style. *ERIC Digest.* Washington, DC: Office of Educational Research and Improvement & U.S. Department of Education. (ERIC Document Reproduction Service No. ED393607)

Hargreaves, A. (2000). Mixed emotions: Teachers' perceptions of their interactions with students. *Teaching and Teacher Education, 16,* 811–826.

Henderson, N., & Milstein, M. (2002). *Resiliency in schools: Making it happen for students and educators.* Thousand Oaks, CA: Corwin Press.

Hensley, M., Powell, W., Lamke, S., & Hartman, S. (2007). *The well-managed classroom: Strategies to create a productive and cooperative social climate in your learning community.* Boys Town, NE: Boys Town Press.

Hopkins, D. (2002). *A teacher's guide to classroom research* (3rd ed.). Maidenhead, Berkshire, UK: McGraw-Hill Education Open University Press.

Hubbard, R., & Power, B. (2003). *The art of classroom inquiry: A handbook for teacher-researchers.* Portsmouth, NH: Heinemann.

Hunt, D. (1979). Learning style and student needs: An introduction to conceptual level. In *Student learning styles: Diagnosing and prescribing programs.* Reston, VA: National Association of Secondary School Principals.

Hunter, M. (1994). *Enhancing teaching.* Upper Saddle River, NJ: Merrill/Prentice Hall.

Irvine, J., & York, D. (2001). Learning styles and culturally diverse students: A literature review. In J. Banks & C. Banks (Eds.), *Handbook of research on multicultural education* (pp. 484–497). San Francisco: Jossey-Bass.

Irvine, J., Armento, B., Causey, V., Jones, J., Frasher, R., & Weinburgh, M. (2001). *Culturally responsive teaching: Lesson planning for elementary and middle grades.* Boston: McGraw-Hill.

Jackson, R. (1968). *Life in classrooms.* New York: Holt, Rinehart & Winston.

Jacobs, G., Power, M., & Loh, W. (2002). *Teacher sourcebook for cooperative learning.* Thousand Oaks, CA: Corwin Press.

Johnson, D., & Johnson, R. (2005). Learning groups. In S. Weelan (Ed.), *The handbook of group research and practice* (pp. 441–461). Thousand Oaks, CA: Sage.

Jolliffe, W. (2007). *Cooperative learning in the classroom: Putting it into practice.* Thousand Oaks, CA: Sage.

Jones, J., & Jones, L. (2007). *Comprehensive classroom management: Creating communities of support and solving problems.* Boston: Allyn & Bacon.

Katz, L. G., & Chard, S. C. (1998). Issues in selecting topics for projects. *ERIC Digest.* Washington, DC: Office of Educational Research and Improvement & U.S. Department of Education. (ERIC Document Reproduction Service No. ED424031)

Kea, C. D. (1996, Fall). Focus on ethnic and minority concern. *Council for Children with Behavioral Disorders Newsletter, 10*(3), 3.

Kounin, J. (1970). *Discipline and group management in the classroom.* New York: Holt, Rinehart & Winston.

Krogh, G., Ichijo, K., & Nonaka, I. (2000). *Enabling knowledge creation: How to unlock the mystery of tacit knowledge and release the power of innovation.* Oxford, UK: Oxford University Press.

Kuh, G., Kinzie, J., Schuh, J., & Whitt, E. (2005). *Assessing conditions to enhance educational effectiveness: The inventory for student engagement and success.* San Francisco: Jossey-Bass.

Lambros, A. (2002). *Problem-based learning in K–8 classrooms: A teacher's guide to implementation.* Thousand Oaks, CA: Corwin Press.

Land, M. (1987). In M. Duncan (Ed.), *The international encyclopedia of teaching and teacher education* (pp. 392–397). New York: Pergamon.

Landrum, T., & Kauffman, J. (2006). Behavioral approaches to classroom management. In C. Evertson & C. Weinstein (Eds.), *Handbook of classroom management.* Mahwah, NJ: Lawrence Erlbaum.

Larson, J., & Irvine, P. D. (1999). "We call him Dr. King": Reciprocal distancing in urban classrooms. *Language Arts, 75*(5), 393–400.

Levin, J., & Nolan, J. F. (2006). *Principles of classroom management: Professional decision-making model.* Boston: Allyn & Bacon.

Lightfoot, P. (2006), *Student portfolios: A learning tool.* Bloomington, IN: BookSurge Publishing.

Lin, H., & Chen, T. (2006). *Decreasing cognitive load for novice EFL learners: Effects of question and descriptive advance organizers in facilitating EFL learners' comprehension.* New York: Elsevier.

Llagas, C. (2003). *Status and trends in the education of Hispanics* (NCES 2003–008). U.S. Department of Education, National Center for Education Statistics. Washington, DC: U.S. Government Printing Office.

Lockwood, A. T., & Secada, W. G. (1999, January). *Transforming education for Hispanic youth: Exemplary practices, programs, and schools. NCBE Resource Collection Series, No. 12.* Washington, DC: National Clearinghouse for Bilingual Education. (ERIC Document Reproduction Service No. ED434788)

Lustig, M., & Koester, J. (2006). *Intercultural competence: Interpersonal communication across cultures* (5th ed.). Boston: Addison-Wesley.

Manson, T. (Ed.). (2005). *How to teach children at risk of educational failure.* Lewiston, NY: Edwin Mellen.

Martin, J., & Nakayama, T. (2003). *Intercultural communication in contexts.* New York: McGraw-Hill.

Marzano, R., Pickering, D., & Pollock, J. (2004). *Classroom instruction that works: Research-based strategies for increasing student achievement.* Alexandria, VA: Association for Supervision and Curriculum Development.

Mercado, C. (2001). The learner: "Race," "ethnicity," and linguistic difference. In V. Richardson (Ed.), *Handbook of research on teaching* (pp. 668–694). Washington, DC: American Educational Research Association.

Merten, D. E. (1997). The meaning of meanness: Popularity, competition, and conflict among junior high girls. *Sociology of Education, 70*(3), 175–191.

Methe, S., & Hintze, J. (2003). Evaluating teacher modeling as a strategy to increase student reading. *School Psychology Review, 32*(4), 617.

Michaels, S., & Collins, J. (1984). Oral discourse styles: Classroom interaction and the acquisition of literacy. In D. Tamen (Ed.), *Coherence in spoken and written discourse.* Norwood, NJ: Ablex.

Miller, H. M. (2000). Teaching and learning about cultural diversity: All of us together have a story to tell. *Reading Teacher, 53*(6), 666–667.

Miller, M. J. (1992). *Model standards for beginning teacher licensing and development: A resource for state dialogue.* Retrieved October 24, 2006, from www.ccsso.org

Minami, M., & Ovando, C. (2001). Language issues in multicultural contexts. In J. Banks & C. Banks (Eds.), *Handbook of research on multicultural education* (pp. 427–444). San Francisco: Jossey-Bass.

Moran, C., & Hakuta, K. (2001). Bilingual education: Broadening research perspectives. In J. Banks & C. Banks (Eds.), *Handbook of research on multicultural education* (pp. 445–462). San Francisco: Jossey-Bass.

Murphy, N. (1996). Multicultural mathematics and science: Effective K–12 practices for equity. *ERIC Digest.* Columbus, OH: ERIC Clearinghouse for Science, Mathematics, and Environmental Education. (ERIC Reproduction Service No. ED402146)

Nadler, G., & Chandon, W. (2004). *Smart questions: Learn to ask the right questions for powerful results.* San Francisco: Jossey-Bass.

National Board for Professional Teaching Standards. (2001). *Five core propositions.* Retrieved October 24, 2006, from www.nbpts.org

National Science Foundation. (2000). *Women, minorities, and persons with disabilities in science and engineering.* Washington, DC: Author.

Neuliep, J. (2008). *Intercultural communication: A contextual approach.* Thousand Oaks, CA: Sage.

Newton, D. (2007). *Teaching for understanding.* Boca Raton, FL: Taylor & Francis.

Ngeow, K. Y. (1998). Motivation and transfer in language learning. *ERIC Digest.* Bloomington, IN: ERIC Clearinghouse on Reading. (ERIC Document Reproduction Service ED427318)

Noddings, N. (1992). *The challenge to care in schools.* New York: Teachers College Press.

Oczkus, L. (2003). *Reciprocal teaching at work: Strategies for improving reading comprehension.* Washington, DC: International Reading Association.

O'Flynn, S., Kennedy, H., & Macqrath, M. (2004). *Getting their attention!: How to gain pupils' respect and thrive as a teacher.* London: David Fulton.

Ogbu, J. (1995a). Cultural problems in minority education: Their interpretations and consequences—Part one: Theoretical background. *Urban Review, 27*(3), 189–205.

Ogbu, J. (1995b). Cultural problems in minority education: Their interpretations and consequences—Part two: Case studies. *Urban Review, 27*(4), 271–297.

Ogbu, J. (2008). *Minority status, oppositional culture and schooling.* New York: Routledge.

Olneck, M. (2001). Immigrants and education. In J. Banks and C. Banks (Eds.), *Handbook of research on multicultural education* (pp. 310–330). San Francisco: Jossey-Bass.

Pajak, E. (2003). *Honoring diverse teaching styles: A guide for supervisors.* Arlington, VA: Association for Supervision & Curriculum Development.

Palincsar, A., & Brown, A. (1989). Classroom dialogues to promote self-regulated comprehension (Vol. 1). In J. Brophy (Ed.), *Advances in research on teaching* (pp. 35–71). Greenwich, CT: JAI Press.

Parsons, T. (1959). The school class as a social system: Some of its functions in American society. *Harvard Educational Review, 9,* 298–318.

Parsons, T., & Shills, E. (Eds.). (1951). *Toward a general theory of action.* Cambridge, MA: Harvard University Press.

Peretz, M., Eilam, E., & Yankelevich, E. (2006). Classroom management in multicultural classes in an immigrant country: A case of Israel. In C. Evertson & C. Weinstein (Eds.), *Handbook of classroom management.* Mahwah, NJ: Lawrence Erlbaum.

Pianta, R. (1999). *Enhancing relationships between children and teachers.* Washington, DC: American Psychological Association.

Pianta, R. (2005). Teacher–child relationships and children's success in the first years of school. *School Psychology Review, 33*(3), 444–454.

Polanyi, F. (1958). *Personal knowledge.* Chicago: University of Chicago Press.

Public Agenda. (1997). *Getting by: What American teenagers really think about their schools.* Bloomington, IN: ERIC Clearinghouse on Reading. (ERIC Document Reproduction Service ED404756)

Ramirez, M., & Castaneda, A. (1974). *Cultural democracy, bicognitive development, and education.* New York: Academic Press.

Redfield, D., & Rousseau, E. (1981). A meta-analysis of experimental research on teacher questioning behavior. *Review of Educational Research, 51,* 237–245.

Reeve, J. (2006). Extrinsic rewards and inner motivation. In C. Evertson & C. Weinstein (Eds.), *Handbook of classroom management.* Mahwah, NJ: Lawrence Erlbaum.

Reeve, J. (2008). *Understanding motivation and emotion.* Hoboken, NJ: Wiley.

Reynolds, N., & Rich, R. (2006). *Portfolio keeping: A guide for students.* New York: Bedford/St. Martin's Press.

Richardson, V. (Ed.). (2001). *Handbook of research on teaching.* Washington, DC: American Educational Research Association.

Riding, R. (2002). *School learning and cognitive styles.* New York: Routledge.

Riggs, E., & Gholar, C. (2008). *Strategies that promote student engagement: Unleashing the desire to learn.* Thousand Oaks, CA: Corwin Press.

Rinne, C. (1984). *Attention: The fundamentals of classroom control.* Columbus, OH: Merrill.

Rist, R. (1970). Student social class and teaching expectations: The self-fulfilling prophecy in ghetto education. *Harvard Educational Review, 40,* 411–451.

Roberts, P., & Kellough, R. (2006). *A guide for developing interdisciplinary thematic units* (4th ed.). Upper Saddle River, NJ: Prentice Hall.

Rogan, R., Borich, G., & Taylor, H. (1992). Validation of the stages of concern questionnaire. *Action in Teacher Education, 14*(2), 43–49.

Ronis, D. (2007). *Problem-based learning for science and math: Integrating inquiry and the Internet.* Thousand Oaks, CA: Corwin Press.

Rosenshine, B. (1971). *Teaching behaviors and student achievement.* London: National Foundation for Educational Research in England and Wales.

Rosenshine, B. (1983). Teaching functions in instructional programs. *Elementary School Journal, 83,* 335–351.

Rosenshine, B., & Stevens, R. (1986). Teaching functions. In M. C. Wittrock (Ed.), *Handbook of research on teaching* (3rd ed., pp. 376–391). New York: Macmillan.

Rowe, M. B. (1986). Wait time: Slowing down may be a way of speeding up. *Journal of Teacher Education, 23,* 43–49.

Rowe, M. B. (1987). Wait time: Slowing down may be a way of speeding up. *American Educator, 11*(1), 38–43, 47.

Sable, J., & Hoffman, L. (2008). *Characteristics of 100 largest public elementary school districts in the United States: 2005–2006.* Washington, DC: National Center for Educational Statistics.

Saito, L. T. (1999). Sociocultural factors in the educational achievement of Vietnamese American students. (Doctoral dissertation, University of California, Irvine, 1999). *Dissertation Abstracts International, 60*(08), 2802A.

Sanford, A. J., & Garrod, S. C. (1981). *Understanding written language.* New York: Wiley.

Santos, R. M., & Reese, D. (1999). Selecting culturally and linguistically appropriate materials: Suggestions for service providers. *ERIC Digest.* Washington, DC: Office of Educational Research and Improvement & U.S. Department of Education. (ERIC Document Reproduction Service No. ED431546)

Sarasin, L. (2006). *Learning style perspectives: Impact in the classroom.* Bel Air, CA: Atwood Publications.

Saunders, W., & Goldenberg, C. (1999). *The effects of instructional conversations and literature logs on the story comprehension and thematic understanding of English proficient and limited English proficient students.* Washington, DC: Center for Research on Education, Diversity and Excellence.

Savage, T. (1999). *Teaching self-control through management and control.* Boston: Allyn & Bacon.

Schmuck, R., & Schmuck, P. (2001). *Group processes in the classroom* (6th ed.). New York: McGraw-Hill.

Schwartz, W. (2000). New trends in language education for Hispanic students. *ERIC/CUE Digest,* Number 155. New York: ERIC Clearinghouse on Urban Education. (ERIC Document Reproduction Service No. ED442913)

Scollon, R. (1985). The machine stops: Silence in the metaphor of malfunction. In D. Tannen & M. Saville-Troike (Eds.), *Perspectives on silence.* Norwood, NJ: Ablex.

Semali, L. (Ed.). (2002). *Transmediation in the classroom.* New York: Peter Lang.

Shalaway, L. (1989). *Learning to teach.* Cleveland, OH: Edgell Communications.

Slavin, R. (1991). *Educational psychology: Theory into practice.* Upper Saddle River, NJ: Prentice Hall.

Slavin, R. (2001). Cooperative learning and intergroup relations. In J. Banks & C. Banks (Eds.), *Handbook of research on multicultural education.* San Francisco: Jossey-Bass.

Smith, P., & Ragan, T. (2004). *Instructional design.* Hoboken, NJ: Wiley.

Soar, R. (1968). Optimum teacher-pupil interaction for pupil growth. *Educational Leadership Research Supplement, 1,* 275–280.

Soar, R., & Soar, R. (1983). Context effects in the learning process. In D. C. Smith (Ed.), *Essential knowledge for beginning educators* (pp. 156–192). Washington, DC: American Association of Colleges of Teacher Education.

Sternberg, R. (1994). Answering questions and questioning answers: Guiding children to intellectual excellence. *Phi Delta Kappan, 76*(2), pp. 136–143.

Sternberg, R. (2007). *Wisdom, intelligence, and creativity synthesized.* Cambridge, UK: Cambridge University Press.

Stipek, D. (1996). Motivation and instruction. In D. C. Berliner & R. C. Calfee (Eds.), *Handbook of educational psychology* (pp. 85–113). New York: Simon & Schuster/Macmillan.

Stipek, D. (2002). *Motivation to learn: Integrating theory and practice* (4th ed.). Boston: Allyn & Bacon.

Sutton, R., & Wheatley, K. (2003). Teachers' emotions and teaching: A review of the literature and directions for future research. *Educational Psychology Review, 15*(4), 327–358.

Szymanski, C., & Haas, M. (2007). *Social studies for elementary and middle grades: A constructivist approach* (3rd ed.). Boston: Allyn & Bacon.

Tannenbaum, J. (1996). Practical ideas on alternative assessment for ESL students. *ERIC Digest.* Washington, DC: Office of Educational Research and Improvement & U.S. Department of Education. (ERIC Document Reproduction Service No. ED395500)

Tauber, R. T. (1997). *Self-fulfilling prophecy: A practical guide to its use in education.* Westport, CT: Praeger.

Tauber, R. T. (1998). *Good or bad, what teachers expect from students they generally get!* Washington, DC: Office of Educational Research and Improvement & U.S. Department of Education. (ERIC Document Reproduction Service No. ED378290)

Taylor, B. M., Pearson, P. D., Clark, K. F., & Walpole, S. (1999). Effective schools/accomplished teachers. *Reading Teacher, 53*(2), 156–159.

Tharp, R., & Gallimore, R. (1989). *Rousing minds to life: Teaching, learning, and schooling in social context.* New York: Cambridge University Press.

Tobin, K. (1987). The role of wait-time in higher cognitive level learning. *Review of Education and Research, 57,* 69–95.

Tombari, M., & Borich, G. (1999). *Authentic assessment in the classroom: Classroom applications and practice.* Upper Saddle River, NJ: Merrill/Prentice Hall.

Tomlinson, C. (2004). *How to differentiate instruction in mixed ability classrooms* (2nd ed.). Alexandria, VA: Association for Supervision and Curriculum Development.

Tomlinson, C., & McTighe, J. (2006). *Integrating differentiated instruction and understanding by design.* Alexandria, VA: Association for Supervision and Curriculum Development.

Tomlinson, C., Kaplan, S., Renzulli, J., Purcell, J., Leppien, J., & Burns, D. (2001). *The parallel curriculum.* Thousand Oaks, CA: Corwin Press.

Tower, C. (2000). Questions that matter: Preparing elementary students for the inquiry process. *Reading Teacher, 53*(7), 550–557.

Verloop, N. (1989). *Interactive cognitions of student teachers.* Arnhem, Netherlands: National Institute for Educational Measurement.

Vygotsky, L. (1978). In M. Cole (Ed.), *Mind in society: The development of higher psychological processes.* Cambridge, MA: Harvard University Press.

Walberg, H. (1966). *Classroom climate questionnaires.* Cambridge, MA: Harvard University Press.

Walberg, H., & Anderson, G. (1968). Classroom climate and individual learning. *Journal of Educational Psychology, 59,* 414–419.

Walqui, A. (2000a). Access and engagement: Program design and instructional approaches for immigrant students in secondary school. In *Topics in Immigrant Education 4, Language in Education: Theory and Practice* (p. 94). Washington, DC: Center for Applied Linguistics.

Walqui, A. (2000b). Strategies for success: Engaging immigrant students in secondary schools. *ERIC Digest.*

Washington, DC: Office of Educational Research and Improvement & U.S. Department of Education. (ERIC Document Reproduction Service No. ED442300)

Wasserman, B. (1987). Teaching for thinking: Louis E. Rath revisited. *Phi Delta Kappan, 68*(6), 400–406.

Watson, T., & Steege, M. (2003). *Conducting school-based functional behavioral assessments: A practitioner's guide.* New York: Guilford.

Weinstein, C., & Mignano, A. (1996). *Elementary classroom management: Lessons from research and practice* (2nd ed.). New York: McGraw-Hill.

Wells, R. (2005). *Yoko's world of kindness: Golden rules for a happy classroom.* New York: Hyperion.

Werner, E., & Smith, R. (1992). *Overcoming the odds: High-risk children from birth to adulthood.* New York: Cornell University Press.

Williams, R. (2003). *Higher order thinking skills: Challenging all students to achieve.* Thousand Oaks, CA: Corwin Press.

Wittrock, M. (Ed.). (1986). *Handbook of research on teaching* (3rd ed.). New York: Macmillan.

Woolfolk, A. (2007). *Educational psychology* (10th ed.). Upper Saddle River, NJ: Pearson.

Woolfolk, A. (2009). *Educational psychology* (11th ed.). Upper Saddle River, NJ: Merrill/Prentice Hall.

Zemelman, S., Daniels, H., & Hyde, A. (2005). *Best practice: Today's standards for teaching and learning in America's schools* (3rd ed.). Portsmouth, NH: Heinemann.

Name Index

Subject Index